The
WARREN
COURT
and the
DEMOCRATIC
CONSTITUTION

MORTON J. HORWITZ

Afterword by Erwin Chemerinsky

GEORGETOWN UNIVERSITY PRESS / WASHINGTON, DC

The publisher is not responsible for third-party websites or their content. URL links were active at time of publication.

Library of Congress Cataloging-in-Publication Data

Names: Horwitz, Morton J., 1938– author.
Title: The Warren Court and the democratic Constitution / Morton J. Horwitz.
Description: Washington, DC : Georgetown University Press, 2024. | Includes
    bibliographical references and index.
Identifiers: LCCN 2023045717 | ISBN 9781647124755 (hardcover) |
    ISBN 9781647124762 (ebook)
Subjects: LCSH: United States. Supreme Court—History. | Civil rights—United
    States—History. | Political questions and judicial power—United States—History. |
    Constitutional law—United States. | Segregation in education—Law and
    legislation—United States—History. | School integration—Law and legislation—
    United States—History. | Warren, Earl, 1891–1974. | Judges—United States—
    Biography. | United States. Supreme Court—Officials and employees—History.
Classification: LCC KF8748 .H67 2024 | DDC 347.73/2609045—dc23/eng/20231005

LC record available at https://lccn.loc.gov/2023045717♾ This paper meets the requirements of ANSI/NISO Z39.48-1992 (Permanence of Paper).

25 24   9 8 7 6 5 4 3 2   First printing

Printed in the United States of America

Cover design by Jason Alejandro
Interior design by BookComp, Inc.

For Joan Kelly-Gadol
(1928–1982)
Mentor and Inspiration

CONTENTS

PREFACE

The Warren Court and the Democratic Constitution seeks to portray the work of the US Supreme Court during the sixteen years (1953–1969) that Earl Warren served as its chief justice. I previously published *The Warren Court and the Pursuit of Justice* (1998), which served as a preliminary sketch of the Warren era. In writing *The Warren Court and the Democratic Constitution*, I have borrowed from my earlier work.

Now, more than half a century after the Warren Court came to a close, it has become ever clearer that it represented a unique and revolutionary chapter in American constitutional history.

When Earl Warren became chief justice in 1953, few would have predicted that when he retired sixteen years later the Warren Court would be remembered for initiating a progressive constitutional revolution that changed the entire landscape of American law and life. At the time, few believed that the Supreme Court was institutionally capable of achieving fundamental constitutional change. For most of American history, in fact, the court had thrown the weight of its authority behind the owners of property, whether of the enslaved, corporate, or landed property. After the American Civil War the court, for complex reasons, systematically interpreted the Civil War amendments—the Thirteenth through Fifteenth Amendments—to deprive the newly freed and their descendants of virtually all the protections that the authors of those amendments hoped had been put in place.

The Warren Court was thus the first to attempt to redeem the promises of the Civil War amendments for Black citizens. Coming right at the beginning of the Warren era, the historic decision in *Brown v. Board of Education* was a nuclear event that generated multiple tidal waves of reaction that engulfed the court. These ranged from southern white "massive resistance" against desegregation to an inspired civil rights movement whose protests triggered novel questions about constitutional protections of social protest movements.

The range of the Warren Court's influence was enormous. The court initiated a revolution in race relations, expanded the constitutional guarantee of "equal protection of the laws," dramatically expanded the protections of

freedom of speech and the press, overturned unequally apportioned legislative districts, accorded defendants in criminal cases massively expanded constitutional protections, and recognized for the first time a constitutional right
to privacy.

My approach to this history calls for some comment. Ordinarily, I am
inclined to render historical narratives from an "external" perspective. An
example is chapter 7, the discussion of the Warren Court revolution in criminal justice. There I seek to show how the discovery of the widespread use of
the "third degree" by police to extract confessions from criminal suspects influenced the justices as they confronted criminal appeals.

However, different from my usual tendency, in this book I spend a great
deal of time discussing and analyzing the internal deliberation of the justices.
The availability of two new sources led to this result. The first, *The Supreme
Court in Conference* by Dell Dixon, contains unofficial notes of conference discussions compiled by one or more justices. The second is a collection of essays
by Justice William Brennan's clerks ("The Histories") discussing, sometimes in
great detail, the cases in which Justice Brennan was involved during their terms.
Together these sources have allowed me to present many unspoken factors that
influenced a decision.

An important thesis of this book is that there are multiple sources that
combined in varying ways to produce the Warren Court. The first and probably
most important influence in shaping the Warren Court is the school desegregation case, *Brown v. Board of Education. Brown* was decided at almost the very
beginning of the Warren era. It not only helped to revive the long-dormant
Equal Protection Clause of the Fourteenth Amendment but also made the
clause a central component of its jurisprudence.

But *Brown* had a still more far-reaching effect. There is virtually no area of
the constitutional jurisprudence of the Warren Court that was uninfluenced by
Brown. The cases dealing with reform of the criminal justice system and with
the reapportionment of legislative districts expressed a new recognition of the
significance of race. The free speech provisions of the First Amendment were
drawn into adjudicating the various struggles for racial justice, most notably
in the sit-in cases.

After *Brown,* a second important determinant of the character of the
Warren Court was its adoption of the once heretical view that legal meaning
changes over time, the so-called living constitution. Examples are the decision
in *Brown* endorsing an evolving meaning of the Equal Protection Clause and
the application of the Eighth Amendment's cruel and unusual punishments
clause to the constitutionality of the death penalty.

A third influence on the Warren Court was its growing commitment to
democracy as a fundamental constitutional value. Justice William Douglas was

influential in elaborating an evolving conception of democracy. Though often exaggerated as an influence in shaping the character of the Warren Court, the resort to "higher law" arguments as a source of "rights" discourse does appear in some Warren Court decisions. Prominent illustrations appear in cases involving the right to privacy: Justice John Harlan's revival of substantive "due process" in his dissent in *Poe v. Ullman* and his concurrence in *Griswold v. Connecticut* as well as Justice Arthur Goldberg's separate concurrence in *Griswold*.

ACKNOWLEDGMENTS

I have incurred many debts during the long period in which this book has been in preparation.

To colleagues who have read and criticized some or all of the original manuscript: Stanley N. Katz, William E. Nelson, and Richard B. Bernstein.

To my wonderful assistant, Sandra Mays, and to Henry Shull, who provided outstanding short-term help.

To my research assistants over many years: first and foremost, Alan Gluck, without whose excellent support this book could not have been written; and Harvard Law students Nicolas Bowie, Jonathan Bressler, Jonathon Booth, and Dan Hamilton.

All of my Harvard Law School deans—Robert Clark, Elena Kagan, Martha Minow, and John Manning—have been extremely supportive.

I am grateful for financial support from the William Nelson Cromwell Foundation and the Rockefeller and Guggenheim Foundations.

1

EARL WARREN

Earl Warren took his oath of office as the fourteenth chief justice of the U.S. Supreme Court on October 1, 1953. Just three weeks earlier his predecessor, Fred Vinson, had died unexpectedly at age sixty-three. At that time, the newly installed Eisenhower administration was about to announce that Warren, serving in his third term as governor of California, would be nominated to be solicitor general, the official in charge of arguing on behalf of the government before the Supreme Court. Instead, just three weeks later President Dwight Eisenhower appointed Warren chief justice.

How Earl Warren came to be appointed chief justice is a story I confine to an appendix (see Appendix 1). Suffice it to say that the process of selection was not smooth. The president had earlier told Warren that he would appoint him to the first opening on the Supreme Court. It was presumably on this basis that Warren initially agreed to accept the relatively lowly position of solicitor general.

When the time came to fill the Vinson vacancy, the administration hesitated, claiming that Eisenhower's earlier pledge did not extend to the chief justiceship. But Warren stood firm, and the president agreed to submit the nomination.

There was another aspect of the Warren nomination that was unusual. The U.S. Constitution (Article II, section 2) provides that the president has the power to make appointments to fill vacancies that occur when the Senate is in recess. But it was highly unusual for presidents to appoint a Supreme Court justice to what might amount to a temporary appointment if the Senate should subsequently refuse to consent.

The administration was much criticized for the manner of the Warren appointment.[1] After all, a federal judicial appointee is granted life tenure precisely to protect against political retaliation. In the case of a recess appointment, moreover, the nominee knows that how he or she decides during this time may affect how the Senate treats the nomination.

Warren has often been praised for the manner in which he handled *Brown v. Board of Education* during his early months as chief justice. Instead of putting the decision to a vote, thereby potentially hardening positions, Warren succeeded in channeling the justices toward spending more time in informal deliberation before attempting to vote.

Viewed from another perspective, however, Warren's early treatment of *Brown* may have been dictated by a strategy of avoiding any vote that might arouse southern senators against him. From this perspective, self-preservation made it virtually inevitable that he would delay any vote on *Brown* until after the Senate confirmed his nomination.

The unanimous Senate confirmation vote took place exactly five months later on March 1, 1954. Two and a half months after confirmation the Supreme Court handed down its unanimous decision in *Brown*, which triggered widespread "massive resistance" in the South. I doubt that at this point southern senators would have been politically able to vote to confirm the author of that opinion.

Biographers of Earl Warren love to offer up John Gunther's probing estimate of Warren in his 1947 best seller *Inside USA*.[2] At that time Warren had just won the second of his three elections as governor of California, becoming the first candidate in the state's history to win the nomination of both parties and, after the legendary Hiram Johnson, only the second to be reelected to a four-year term.[3] "Immediately he began to be talked about as an obvious and weighty candidate for the Republican nomination for the presidency in 1948," Gunther observed. "What manner of man is Warren—how shall we add him up?"[4]

> Earl Warren is honest, likeable, and clean; he will never set the world on fire or even make it smoke; he has the limitations of all Americans of his type with little intellectual background, little genuine depth or coherent political philosophy; a man who has probably never bothered with abstract thought twice in his life; a kindly man, with the best of social instincts, stable, and well balanced; a man splendidly devoted to his handsome wife and six healthy children; not greedy, not a politician of the raucous, grasping kind that has despoiled so much in the United States, a "typical" American in his bluffness, heartiness, healthy apple-pie atmosphere and love for joining things; a man glad to carry a bundle for his missus in the neighborhood supermarket and have an evening out with the boys once in a while; a man with nothing of a "grand line" and little inner force to throw out centrifugal or illuminating sparks; a friendly, pleasant, average Californian; no more a statesman in the European sense than Typhoid Mary is Einstein; a man

who, quite possibly and with luck, could make a tolerable President of the United States. . . . Warren's dominant note is, to sum up, decency, stability, sincerity, and lack of genuine intellectual distinction. But how many American governors have genuine intellectual distinction?[5]

Gunther later acknowledged that his assessment of Earl Warren was "the most serious misjudgment of a personality I have ever made," and most of the commentators have left it at that.[6] Gunther was surely wrong in predicting that Warren "will never set the world on fire or even make it smoke." But it is still useful to consider both what he got right and what he got wrong about Earl Warren and why.

Gunther's description of Warren's all-American character—kindness, decency, stability, and sincerity—has stood the test of time, as has his attribution to Warren of "the best of social instincts, stable, and well balanced."[7] Yet, Gunther never mentioned what only later would become an increasingly dark shadow that spread over Warren's reputation: his participation after Pearl Harbor in the relocation and internment of more than one hundred thousand West Coast Japanese Americans,[8] which slowly came to be acknowledged as a major national disgrace.[9]

One biographer observed of Warren as attorney general of California that he "had played a pivotal role in the ultimate decision" to remove the Japanese from the West Coast.[10] Another concluded that Warren was "a vital moving force in the formulation of the Japanese relocation program. . . . He was the most visible and effective California public official advocating internment and evacuation of the American Japanese. . . . Warren not only participated in but can be said to have engineered one of the most conspicuously racist and repressive governmental acts in American history."[11] Having urged action based on the crudest of racial stereotypes, one year later replying to a letter from a longtime political ally who questioned the justification for the internment, Warren pursued the stereotype of the inscrutable oriental.[12] Warren claimed in 1943 that "the evacuation of the Japanese saved our state from terrible disorders and sabotage." To allow even Japanese American citizens to return from internment camps, he declared, "would be laying the groundwork for another Pearl Harbor."[13] There was no evidence to support Warren's claims.[14]

In truth, Warren's active participation in the Japanese American internment was rooted in what G. Edward White calls a "provincial, xenophobic racism" that Warren shared with many of his fellow white Americans.[15] The anti-Asian prejudices that were common among white Californians of his generation also made Warren a "typical" American, as Gunther had put it.[16] In light of his background, one wonders how to understand Earl Warren's leadership role in producing a unanimous decision in *Brown v. Board of Education*.

During his chief justiceship, Warren managed publicly to ignore the growing criticism of his active involvement in the Japanese internment. But privately, his early confidence that the internment was justified by military necessity began to erode.[17] As Warren was about to assume the chief justiceship a decade after the internments, a longtime friend reported that Warren expressed "nagging doubts" about his part in the removal.[18] Yet, five years later he still defended the decision to a law clerk as "the right thing to do."[19] And as late as 1962 Warren wrote an article defending the relocation on grounds of military necessity, as Justice Hugo Black, who wrote the opinion upholding its constitutionality, also continued to do.[20] At retirement, "only one issue seemed to dog [Warren's] conscience . . . the Japanese evacuation," and for the first time he expressed regret to some of his former clerks.[21]

Warren "felt bad about what happened," one former clerk observed.[22] "In retrospect, given what he had learned over the years, given his heightened sensitivity to racial discrimination and so forth, he recognized that as a very sad day in American history."[23] "Still, the stiff-necked Warren resisted any public acknowledgement of responsibility," his biographer concluded.[24] "That would be showing too much vulnerability," a former clerk speculated.[25] "Others had infuriated him with demands for abject apologies," his son recalled.[26] Only in his posthumously published memoirs did the chief justice offer an apology for his behavior, but its long delay in coming could not put to rest questions about whether it was anything more than a painful accommodation to winner's history.[27]

Part of John Gunther's 1947 portrait of Warren focused on his "lack of genuine intellectual distinction": the "little genuine depth or coherent political philosophy; a man who has probably never bothered with abstract thought twice in his life."[28] Gunther's conclusion that Warren was no Einstein is surely true even in its most metaphorical sense. Warren's academic record was never better than average, and his student activities revealed more talent for networking than for studies. However, his years in public office in California revealed not only a real capacity for administration but also an extraordinary talent for marshaling energy to achieve large and original policy goals. During Warren's tenure as governor, the population of California rose by almost 50 percent.[29] There are enough examples in other states of the disastrous consequences of rapid unregulated growth to highlight Warren's remarkable achievement in creating the infrastructure for California's postwar boom. From education to transportation to social welfare legislation, Warren expanded opportunity and laid the foundations for a wider distribution of social goods.

Warren never was regarded as among the intellectually powerful or legally accomplished justices on his court. Still, he was arguably one of the greatest justices in the history of the Supreme Court. It is important that Warren not

be judged by an unrealistic standard. Few justices other than the very greatest have had a "coherent political philosophy" or were "bothered with abstract
thought." In the law schools, certainly, greatness has been defined in terms of
the ability to develop a relatively coherent constitutional philosophy. By that
standard, Warren stood in the shadow of Justices William Brennan and Hugo
Black as well as of Justice Felix Frankfurter. (It is interesting to compare Justice
William Douglas with either Brennan or Black. The claims of the latter two to
greatness lay in their ability to embody their constitutional visions in a system
of legal doctrine that Douglas scorned. Though Douglas had a constitutional
vision that substantially overlapped with Brennan's and Black's, there are few
lasting traces of any special influence Douglas had in constitutional law.) What
distinguishes Warren most from Frankfurter is the evolution (or not) of their
constitutional visions. In the course of Frankfurter's twenty-three years on the
court, there is little evidence that changes in the world had any impact on what
he thought. Frankfurter never managed to develop his ideas of judicial restraint
beyond the views he had when he joined the court. These views were themselves the product of the previous generation's struggles against the Lochner
Court. By contrast, Warren's views substantially evolved and deepened during
his sixteen years as chief justice.

The publication of the court's conference notes sheds some new favorable
light on Chief Justice Warren's intellectual abilities.[30] One of the traditional
duties of the chief justice has been to speak first at conference, outlining the
legal issues presented by each case and suggesting a disposition. Performing
this task well is quite demanding and often represents the first evidence on
which a new chief justice is judged by his fellow justices. Warren's two immediate predecessors, Fred Vinson and Harlan Fiske Stone, had both been regarded
as failures in their leadership of the conference, as had Warren Burger, Warren's
successor as chief justice.[31] Vinson was never able to rise above his shallow
understanding of the legal issues presented.[32] His predecessor, Harlan Fiske
Stone, had a powerful enough intellect; his problem was that he presented the
cases in a one-sided way, precipitating an unnecessarily argumentative and
divisive discussion.[33] There is considerable evidence that Chief Justice Burger
was also a dismal failure in his leadership role in the conference.[34]

The Warren Court conference notes are unofficial diaries of the conference
discussion recorded by one or more of the justices. They portray a chief justice
who consistently mastered the often complex legal issues that the cases presented. He seemed always to be aware of the necessity of choosing between
broad and narrow decisions and, contrary to the stereotype, often steered the
court in the direction of a narrow holding. Unlike his two immediate predecessors, he often succeeded in orchestrating a serious discussion of the issues
before the court.

During roughly the second half of his tenure as chief justice, Warren regularly conferred with Justice Brennan the day before the weekly Friday conference,[35] causing "some grumbling among the other Justices,"[36] especially the usually mild-mannered Justice John Marshall Harlan, who resented what he perceived as Warren's effort "to organize conference votes in advance."[37] Whatever added depth Brennan brought to Warren's analysis, the fact remains that the chief justice was able intellectually to present the cases with an understanding and dexterity that neither of his two predecessors nor his successor ever managed to accomplish.

Where John Gunther seemed most completely to misread Warren was in his belief that Warren had "little inner force, to throw out centrifugal or illuminating sparks."[38] Gunther missed Warren's keen sense of justice and passionate commitment to an idealized version of the American creed. Warren's fundamental decency and his public spiritedness combined to give content to his own evolving version of a California progressive creed. This was the "inner force"—the gravitas—that almost instantly propelled him into the inner circle of presidential politics and later allowed him to confidently lead a court that included several clear intellectual superiors.[39]

There was another side to Warren's character that is often understated by those who wish to find a clear line of principle or character that, over a half century, connects the young Warren to the chief justice. Warren's life, however, was filled with contradictions of principle. While as district attorney he was unusual in his fidelity to the rules governing wiretapping and interrogation, no one would have mistaken him for the civil libertarian he was to become. As a Republican politician in the 1930s, he indulged in the sort of red-baiting that he later came to loathe especially in his fellow California Republican, Richard M. Nixon. Of all Warren's contradictions, his leadership in producing the unanimous decision in *Brown* is difficult to reconcile with the evident racism that propelled his active involvement in the internment of Japanese Americans.

Warren's ability to put his California racial past behind him in deciding on the constitutionality of racial segregation is an excellent example of Gunnar Myrdal's prediction as World War II was coming to an end that "typical" Americans would soon be forced to choose between their egalitarian ideals and the pervasive social reality of racial subordination. But it is also an example of an important character trait noticed by G. Edward White: a pronounced role morality.[40]

In his award-winning novel *The Remains of the Day*, Kazuo Ishiguro offers a complex meditation on the emotional and moral limits of professionalism.[41] He portrays Stevens, the chief butler in an aristocratic British household of the 1930s who devotes his life to serving the diplomat Lord Darlington just as Darlington begins to profess pro-Nazi sympathies. Stevens continues to find dignity in rigid adherence to his professional role, which, he emphasizes, "has to do crucially with a butler's ability not to abandon the professional being he inhabits."[42] "Throughout the years I served [Lord Darlington]," he later reflects, "it was he and he alone who weighed up evidence and judged it best to proceed in the way he did, while I simply confined myself, quite properly, to affairs within my own professional realm."[43]

All people, especially professionals, try to confine themselves "to affairs within [their] own realm" and screen out issues that they regard as within the proper role of other persons or institutions. President Thomas Jefferson's constitutional position on the national government's power to acquire the Louisiana Territory stood in marked contrast to his earlier pronouncements. Felix Frankfurter's shift from progressive law professor to Supreme Court justice may account for much of the difference in his views on constitutional law. There was a marked difference in Hugo Black's approach to racial issues and to questions of federalism after he left the U.S. Senate for the Supreme Court. Earl Warren's underdeveloped constitutional views before he became chief justice were shaped by the practical requirements of criminal prosecutor, or the policy-centered questions that dominated service as attorney general or governor.

Warren's political values were originally shaped by the California progressivism of Hiram Johnson, whose election as governor in 1910 initiated a far-reaching set of social and political reforms.[44] As a nineteen-year-old student at the University of California at Berkeley, Warren campaigned for Johnson and was caught up in the surge of reformist zeal that would produce a fundamental transformation of California political culture.[45] Johnson's reforms energized a powerful Good Government constituency that attacked corruption, promised "to kick the Southern Pacific Railroad out of politics," and severely weakened the power of boss-controlled political parties.[46] By introducing the initiative and the referendum and the cross-filing primary system, Johnson sought to weaken the political party system and institute "direct" democracy not beholden to the patronage of corrupt politicians.[47]

In his memoirs written almost seven decades later, Warren counted Hiram Johnson as one of two role models in his life. That Johnson took on the Southern Pacific Railroad had both personal and political significance, for Warren's other role model was his father who, except for one important interval, had devoted forty years to working as a car repairman for the Southern Pacific Railroad.[48] As a boy, Warren himself had been employed as a train caller by Southern Pacific.[49] In his memoirs, he introduced his father and the Southern Pacific Railroad in the same paragraph.[50] The railroad was "a giant corporation that dominated the economic and political life of the community. I saw that power exercised and the hardships that followed in its wake."[51] Warren did not say that his father had been blacklisted by the railroad for joining the Pullman strike of 1894.[52] Only after Matt Warren managed to secure a job with another railroad was he able to move back into a Southern Pacific job at a different site.[53]

In his first public office as Alameda County district attorney, Warren emphasized Hiram Johnson's Good Government legacy, devoting the resources of his office to attacking gambling, prostitution, and bootlegging, the source of much official corruption.[54] This anticorruption activity also expressed a deeply puritanical streak in Warren that would often resurface when as chief justice he confronted cases involving obscenity, immorality, or corruption.

By 1934 as the Great Depression ground on, California Republicans united to defeat the Democratic gubernatorial candidacy of the radical muckraker, Upton Sinclair. Warren now called for a "crusade of Americans and Californians against Radicalism and Socialism" and participated in a scurrilous red-baiting campaign.[55] "Take California out of the red; the Red out of California" a campaign billboard proclaimed.[56] He denounced Sinclair's program as un-American. "The battle is between two conflicting philosophies of government—one that is proud of our flag, our governmental institutions and our honored history, the other that glorifies the Red Flag of Russia and hopes to establish on American soil a despotism based upon class hatred and tyranny."[57] Warren channeled party money into an organization whose chairman asserted that Sinclair "would Russianize California and inflict on our people the curse of Communism."[58]

In 1936, Warren strengthened his anticommunist credentials by bringing first-degree murder charges against four militant union officials charged with killing the chief engineer of the freighter SS *Point Lobos*, one of several murders linked to union activity on the waterfront.[59] It was "the most controversial case of his thirteen-year career as district attorney."[60] The *Point Lobos* case "became another cause for embattled left-wing and labor activists," as a defense team funded by fifty unions declared the case a frame-up.[61] The jury returned a compromise verdict of second degree murder, casting some doubt on Warren's theory of the case.[62] For a long time thereafter, the political Left saw Warren as "the arch-enemy, a profoundly anti-union man" who had become "a reactionary Republican red-baiter."[63]

Elected California attorney general in 1938, Warren continued to lend his name to unrestrained red-baiting. In June 1940 when Governor Culbert Olsen nominated University of California law professor Max Radin to the California Supreme Court, his anticommunist demagoguery grew strident. Attorney General Warren, one of three members of the Commission on Judicial Qualifications, cast the deciding vote to block Radin's appointment.[64] The Radin vote, a Warren friend observed, cast a "black mark" on Warren's record and "soured his reputation with what remained of the Democratic New Deal."[65]

Before he ran for governor in 1942, Warren had absorbed various aspects of California progressivism: its good government, anticorruption strand; its racist, nativist xenophobic strand; and its antiparty, direct democracy strand. But until his second campaign for governor in 1946—the one that John Gunther had just written about—Warren could not have been considered a social or political progressive. In that year, however, he rolled out an elaborate social program, including health insurance and an expanded state college system.[66]

Warren's service as governor of California was interrupted in 1948 when Thomas Dewey, the Republican nominee for president, chose him as his vice presidential running mate. Warren reluctantly agreed to run only after he realized that any future chances he had for the presidency were dependent on his show of party loyalty in accepting the vice presidential nomination.

Four years later Warren did earnestly seek the Republican presidential nomination, which was captured by Dwight D. Eisenhower.

2

BROWN V. BOARD OF EDUCATION

If it had decided nothing else, the U.S. Supreme Court under Earl Warren would be remembered for its unanimous decision in *Brown v. Board of Education* (1954) declaring racial segregation in public schools unconstitutional.[1] It was perhaps the most important judgment ever handed down by the Supreme Court. Thurgood Marshall, at the time general counsel for the National Association for the Advancement of Colored People (NAACP), noted the sweeping nature of the decision: "In holding segregated public education unconstitutional, the Court eliminated one of the two primary pillars of the caste system (the other being disenfranchisement)."[2]

Because *Brown* has had such a pervasive influence on American history during the past half century and more, the process of recovering its historical significance involves untangling the multiple webs of meaning that sixty years of continuing racial strife has grafted onto the original decision. But above all, it requires a historical leap of understanding. As *Brown* has become one of the few constitutional "icons" to which every justice appointed since 1954 has paid special deference, it has been swept up into an older narrative of progressive historical evolution that sees *Brown* as but another virtually predestined step in the long-term expansion of liberty and equality that began with the Declaration of Independence.[3] But any close study of the circumstances under which *Brown* was decided underlines an opposite conclusion: just how unlikely it was that the final outcome would be a unanimous decision overruling *Plessy v. Ferguson* (1896), the constitutional foundation of the entire system of racial segregation in the South.[4]

INTRODUCTION

As late as 1910, when only about 10 percent of America's Black people lived outside the South, the "Negro problem" was still largely thought of as an exclusively southern problem.[5] The jobs made available by World War I, however, triggered the beginnings of the Great Migration of African Americans to the North and West. Between 1910 and 1940, an estimated 1.75 million Black people left the South; by 1940, about 24 percent of all African Americans lived beyond the reach of the former Confederate states.[6] Over the next two decades, the Great Migration became an exodus as several million more Black southerners, attracted by wartime jobs and postwar prosperity, migrated from the South. By 1950, about 33 percent of all African Americans lived in the North and the West. The proportion reached about 40 percent in 1960.[7] All told, Isabel Wilkerson estimated that during the six decades before 1970, six million Black people had fled the South.[8]

MYRDAL'S GRIM PORTRAIT OF A STAGNANT SOUTH

In *An American Dilemma* (1944), his monumental study of the position of Black people in American society, Swedish sociologist Gunnar Myrdal emphasized that after 1900, economic progress for Black southerners had stalled. At the time of Myrdal's writing more than forty years later, continuing economic decline had made African Americans' situation "grave."[9] Given the concentration of Black people in the rural South, the most important factor determining the economic condition of African Americans was the weakness of the southern agricultural economy and, in particular, the decline of cotton, its most significant commodity. "Negro farmers have always been dependent on the cotton economy to a much greater extent than . . . white farmers in the South."[10] Myrdal observed that "there was a time when it really looked as if the rural Negro had some chance" of eventually becoming a landowner.[11] By 1900, 25 percent of all Black farmers in the United States owned their own farms, a historic peak from which a long-term decline began.[12]

Even before World War I, world agricultural trends had slowly eroded America's more than 50 percent world market share of cotton. This shift of production to other countries became substantial after the war, and the trend of cotton prices continued downward during most of the 1920s.[13] During the 1920s, a series of "calamities" further undermined the economic viability of cotton production. Soil erosion took a third of land out of production,[14] and "the ravages of the boll weevil" wrought further devastation.[15] During the Great Depression, the cotton economy faced a further drastic decline as world demand dried up and competition from abroad increased. "The cotton economy suffered much more from the depression and recovered much less afterward than did American agriculture in general," Myrdal wrote.[16] "These changes are revolutionizing the whole structure of Southern agricultural economy. They have already rooted out a considerable portion of the Negro farmers and made the future of the remaining group extremely problematic."[17]

Despite his own grim evidence testifying to a steady, almost half-century decline in the economic position of Black people, Myrdal offered surprisingly "hopeful" and "optimistic" predictions of imminent progress in race relations. And he was not shy in offering a prophetic conclusion: "*not since Reconstruction has there been more reason to anticipate fundamental changes in American race relations, changes which will involve a development toward the American ideals.*"[18] Myrdal later noted that his "most important conclusion" in *An American Dilemma* was "that an era of more than half a century during which there had been no fundamental change was approaching its close."[19] This conclusion, he emphasized, attracted "little backing . . . in the contemporary literature on the Negro problem in America, nor could I feel myself to have much support from the social scientists then working in the field of race relations, whose views in the main were more static, fatalistic, and, more particularly, lacking in an appreciation of the importance for social change of the moral, ideological, and political forces in the nation."[20]

Caste was the central theoretical concept Myrdal used for portraying the system of racial subordination that had been reestablished in the South after Reconstruction. In the United States, he wrote, adding his own emphasis, "*a man born a Negro or a white is not allowed to pass from the one status to the other as he can pass from one class to another. In this important respect, the caste system of America is closed and rigid, while the class system is . . . always open and mobile.*"[21] The foremost expression of the caste system was laws on the books of thirty states forbidding interracial marriages.[22]

Myrdal was prescient in recognizing the early indicators of fundamental social change that others had not yet identified. He was justly proud of having avoided a "static" and "fatalistic" mindset about the race problem, a problem that, after all, had humbled many a previous optimist in American history. Yet, his own optimism about the possibilities of social change often obscured his bleak portrait of the material situation of the Negro in America in 1940. For many serious students of the race problem, there was not yet enough compelling evidence to lead them to agree with Myrdal's view that suddenly after more than a half century of soul-numbing fixity, the American system of racial subordination was drawing to a close.

Compared to the Supreme Court's fairly consistent rejection of the legal claims of Black people during the seventy-five years after the Civil War amendments were ratified, the period between 1944 and 1950 stands out for its unexpected string of victories for the cause of racial equality. In 1944, the court reversed itself and struck down the Texas all-white primary, one of the most successful devices in the South for disenfranchising African Americans.[23] It also held that the Railway Labor Act barred segregated labor unions from entering into labor contracts that discriminated against Black workers who had been excluded from the union.[24] In 1946, the court held that the Constitution's interstate commerce clause barred segregated seating for interstate passengers.[25] In 1948, the court unanimously overturned Oklahoma's refusal to admit a Black woman to its all-white law school, suggesting that, if the state refused to admit her it would have to choose between opening a Black law school and closing down the existing all-white law school.[26]

In *Shelley v. Kraemer* (1948), the court held racially restrictive real estate covenants unconstitutional.[27] The 6–0 ruling presented so loose a definition of the "state action" requirement of the Fourteenth Amendment that for a time it seemed possible that all judicial enforcement of discriminatory private contracts or wills might be barred by the Equal Protection Clause.[28] By 1950, the Supreme Court had clearly begun to back away from the inertia, passivity, and outright racism that had characterized virtually all but its recent decisions applying the Civil War amendments to former slaves and their descendants. On the last day of the 1949–1950 term, the court announced three unanimous decisions (known as the "1950 trilogy") that underlined the change.

The first of these cases, *Sweatt v. Painter*, raised the question of whether the State of Texas could satisfy the *Plessy* "separate but equal" standard by establishing a separate Negro law school.[29] In just three years, the new Black law school appeared to have become a credible educational institution. It had "a faculty of five full-time professors, twenty-three students, a library of 16,000 books serviced by a full-time staff, a practice court, and a legal-aid association."[30] Yet despite its arguably material equality, Chief Justice Fred Vinson, for a unanimous court, declared that he could not find "substantial equality in the educational opportunities offered white and Negro law students" by the State of Texas.[31] "[M]ore important" than these tangible factors, Vinson wrote, are "those qualities which are incapable of objective measurement but which make for greatness in a law school. Such qualities, to name but a few, include reputation of the faculty, experience of the administration, position and influence of the alumni, standing in the community, traditions and prestige."[32] These qualities, Vinson concluded, "the University of Texas Law School possesses to a far greater degree" than the new Black law school.[33] "It is difficult to believe that one who had a choice between these law schools would consider the question close."[34]

The nine lawyers on the Supreme Court understood that success at the bar often depended not only on what you know but also who you know. Though difficult to measure, the quality and prestige of a faculty in an established law school was surely of great significance. And while it was still more difficult to assess, the greater employment and networking opportunities offered at an established institution with generations of alumni who had achieved "position and influence" were also widely believed to be an important factor in achieving success in law.

From their own experiences, the justices knew that such factors did affect one's chances at the bar. If "greatness" in a law school depended on the steady accumulations of reputation and prestige over time, it meant that a new racially separate Black law school could never be equal to an established white institution.

In the second case, *McLaurin v. Oklahoma State Regents for Higher Education*, the NAACP successfully challenged the all-white University of Oklahoma's unequal treatment of an African American who, after being admitted to a PhD program in education "on a segregated basis" was required to sit all alone in an anteroom outside the regular classrooms and segregate himself in an isolated, assigned seat in the library.[35] Even more than in *Sweatt v. Painter*, the *McLaurin* case raised the question of whether segregated facilities could truly be equal. If McLaurin were deprived of equal protection of the laws, as the court unanimously decided, it was not because he was subjected to unequal material conditions but rather because racial separation produced intangible negative effects that interfered with his equal chance to learn.

In a third unanimous civil rights decision in *Henderson v. United States*, the Supreme Court declared racially segregated dining cars in interstate transportation illegal.[36] The three cases underlined a truth that had been all but ignored during the half century after *Plessy* promulgated its "separate but equal" standard. That standard, which declared that the Equal Protection Clause of the Fourteenth Amendment required that even racially segregated schools be otherwise equal, had almost never been conscientiously applied. Had it been, virtually all segregated schools would have failed even the *Plessy* test, for most Black schools in the South were not remotely equal to white schools by any comparative measure, whether the measure was physical facilities, the educational level of the teachers, or the per-student expenditure on teacher salaries and books.

Thus, when the Supreme Court signaled that it would no longer treat the separate but equal standard as an automatic formula for upholding segregation, it provided a possible future road map toward eliminating segregated schools. That is, if the real meaning of the new decisions was that the court would almost never find "separate" to be "equal," it seemed to lay the foundation for the gradual elimination of a dual school system in the South. Requiring equal expenditures on Black and white schools could mean that an economically backward South might not be able to sustain the extra fiscal burden necessary to maintain a segregated system.

INTERPRETATION OF THE TRILOGY: OPTIMISM OR PESSIMISM?

In 1950–1951, legal reformers were divided over the meaning of the trilogy. For some, it signaled the penultimate step before the Supreme Court overturned

Plessy v. Ferguson. For others, the court's conspicuous refusal to overrule *Plessy* signaled a future long, drawn-out struggle against segregation.

The NAACP exemplified this divide on the future of desegregation. The gradualists within the organization argued that a strategy aimed at equalizing material support offered at least the possibility of achieving more immediate tangible gains in the quality of Black schools, if not the sweeping goal of over-turning segregation. Those in favor of equalization in the NAACP also received support from Black educators, who worried about becoming the leading casual-ties of dismantling dual school systems.[37] "Where there are segregated schools," Myrdal observed, "the Negro teacher has usually a complete monopoly on the jobs in Negro schools. Where schools are mixed, Negroes have difficulty in getting in."[38]

Proponents of sweeping change, on the other hand, believed that racial segregation would not simply wither away because of economic strain on the system of separate but equal. Still, advocates of immediate change remained divided over whether it was realistic to pursue social change through the courts as an alternative to grassroots politics.

Thurgood Marshall's interpretation of the trilogy further illuminates the confusion—and ultimately the pessimism—among reformers about a near-term reversal of segregation. At one level, Marshall—then the chief counsel at the NAACP—depicted the trilogy to the NAACP membership as by no means foreclosing future equality. "The fact that the Court did not decide segregation to be unconstitutional per se or in all areas," Marshall wrote, "is not fatal. The *Sweatt* and *McLaurin* cases indicate the Supreme Court's conviction that seg-regation is a denial of equality, and these decisions are potent weapons with which to continue the fight against segregation."[39]

Some scholars have thus characterized Marshall as optimistic about the near-term overthrow of *Plessy.* They highlight a 1950 NAACP resolution in which Marshall led the call to challenge *Plessy* head-on as evidence of his enduring hopefulness that *Plessy* would soon be overturned as well as of his prescience in anticipating *Brown.*[40] In this version of events, Marshall inter-preted the 1950 trilogy as a signal that the Supreme Court was on the verge of overruling *Plessy* and, more important, that even in 1950 *Brown* was all but inevitable. All that was needed was a militant nudge by the NAACP.

But a closer reading of history defies these scholarly accounts. Whatever mea-sure of optimism existed prior to the trilogy seemed to evaporate as Marshall studied the Supreme Court opinions. The "road markings," as Marshall referred to them, pointed not to the imminent overthrow of *Plessy* but instead to the gradual tightening of the separate but equal standard on a case-by-case basis.

In this interpretation of the events of 1950–1951, Marshall ultimately viewed the trilogy as a setback. The court, Marshall reasoned, had addressed only isolated injuries to Black plaintiffs rather than having tackled the question of whether *Plessy* was constitutional. "The Court was content to solve only the specific problem presented, and explicitly refused to re-examine or reaffirm *Plessy v. Ferguson*."[41] Indeed, he read the cases as a deliberate decision by the court "to whittle away" at segregation and to refuse to entertain a frontal assault on *Plessy* in the near future. Marshall added, "The Court's present strategy may be to breach the pattern of segregation area by area by dealing with specific problems as they are presented. It may feel that in whittling away the legal foundation upon which segregation is based, in that fashion, the protection afforded to civil rights may be more palatable to the community and hence more lasting."[42] Here Marshall surprisingly seemed to endorse gradualism, a further sign that he did not see any immediate victory on the horizon.

JUSTICES WRESTLE WITH IMPLICATIONS OF OVERTURNING *PLESSY*

From the moment the justices heard the first modern challenge to school segregation in 1938,[43] they were deeply aware that the elimination of racially segregated schools would strike at the central nervous system of the southern way of life. While the Deep South might eventually acquiesce in desegregation of graduate and professional schools and the border states might even voluntarily desegregate the lower grades, it was difficult to imagine that the former Confederate states would ever yield, without a bitter struggle, to a decision to eliminate segregation in the public schools. It was never far from the justices' minds that overruling *Plessy* might ignite widespread social disorder.

It was common for those justices who wished to retain *Plessy* to warn of disaster. Anticipating the "serious practical problems" that the abolition of segregated schools would entail, Chief Justice Vinson from Kentucky emphasized the difficulties of immediate desegregation "when there are large numbers" of Black residents in a school district. "The situation is very serious and very emotional. We can't close our eyes to the seriousness of the problem in various parts of the country, although the problems are hotter in some parts of the country than in others. We face the complete abolition of the public school system in the South."[44]

As early as the *Sweatt* and *McLaurin* conference, Justice Robert Jackson warned that "these cases are fraught with great harm to the Court and the country. These cases can do this Court more harm than any other case."[45] Like Vinson, Jackson offered the prediction that segregation was dying because it created such economic strain. With the system poised to self-destruct, why should the court intervene? "Segregation is too expensive to whites. It is breaking down at the top [educational] levels. Maybe we will do the subject more harm than good [by intervening]."[46] Justice Stanley Reed, also of Kentucky, indicated clearly that he wished to affirm *Plessy*.[47] He also emphasized after the first argument in *Brown* that "segregation is gradually disappearing. . . . There has been great, steady progress in the South in the advancement of the interests of the Negroes. . . . We must allow time. Segregation in the border states will disappear in fifteen or twenty years. Ten years in Virginia, perhaps. Ten years would make it really equal. Every year helps."[48]

Justice Tom Clark also indicated that he might be prepared to affirm *Plessy*. In Texas, his home state, he noted that "the Mexican problem is more serious" and "more retarded" than for Black people.[49] Endorsing Jackson's call for delay, Clark added, "If we delay action . . . it will help. Our opinion should give the lower courts the opportunity to withhold relief in light of troubles. I would be inclined to go along with that."[50] Clark, one of President Harry Truman's poker-playing "cronies," had already begun to signal that he was prepared to bargain over *Plessy* if only he could be satisfied that implementation of desegregation would be gradual. In the next conference on *Brown* after Earl Warren joined the court, Clark repeated that "there is a danger of violence if this is not well handled. In some counties, it runs up to 60 per cent colored in Mississippi, and Alabama is much the same. . . . Violence will follow in the South. This is a very serious problem."[51] "If segregation is unconstitutional," Justice Clark reasoned, "it must be handled very carefully, or we will cause more harm than good."[52] Yet, he seemed to immediately reverse himself when he added, "I think that colored students in Texas get as good an education as the whites. Much progress has been made in voting there, in school boards, and so forth."[53]

Although he was unbending in favor of overruling *Plessy*, Justice Hugo Black also echoed the predictions of Vinson, Jackson, and Clark that "trouble" could be expected in the South. "There will be serious incidents and some violence if the Court holds segregation unlawful," Black told the conference after the first argument.[54] "There will be trouble," Sherman Minton also predicted as he announced that he too was prepared to overrule *Plessy*.[55]

THE THREE STAGES OF *BROWN*

Brown was one of five cases that had been consolidated in order to be heard together. The cases came from Kansas,[56] South Carolina,[57] Virginia,[58] Delaware,[59] and the District of Columbia.[60]

There were three stages in the Supreme Court's deliberations over *Brown*. The case was first argued on December 9–11, 1952, before a court presided over by Chief Justice Fred Vinson. After it became clear that the justices were badly divided, Justice Felix Frankfurter persuaded them to call for reargument on five questions submitted to the parties. By the time reargument took place a year later, Vinson had died of a heart attack, and President Dwight Eisenhower had appointed Earl Warren to replace him (for more on the Warren appointment, see Appendix 1). On May 17, 1954, the Supreme Court handed down its decision in *Brown v. Board of Education* (*Brown I*), unanimously declaring racial segregation in public schools unconstitutional.[61] After hearing further argument on the question of how to implement the desegregation decree, Warren announced one year later in a short seven-paragraph opinion (*Brown II*) that the cases would be remanded to federal district courts for implementation "with all deliberate speed."[62]

THE FIRST CONFERENCE IN *BROWN*

When the justices assembled at their conference after the first argument in *Brown*, it was clear that the court was badly divided. Four justices—Hugo Black, William O. Douglas, Sherman Minton, and Harold Burton—unequivocally favored overruling *Plessy*. Chief Justice Vinson and three other justices—Stanley Reed, Robert Jackson, and Tom Clark—seemed opposed. Though it has been assumed that Justice Frankfurter represented a clear fifth vote for overturning *Plessy*, there is no convincing evidence that this was so.

Chief Justice Vinson, according to custom, opened the discussion. He first turned to *Bolling v. Sharpe*, the case that challenged segregated schools in the District of Columbia.[63] "There is a body of law in back of us on separate but equal," he began.[64] History showed that Congress—even the Congress that passed the Civil War amendments—did not act to abolish segregation in Washington, DC.[65] "It is hard to get away from that contemporary interpretation of the Civil War Amendments. . . . I don't see in the District of Columbia case how we can get away from this Court's long and continued acceptance of these patterns of Congress ever since the Civil War Amendments."[66]

Though Vinson never said explicitly that he favored affirming *Plessy*, his view of the companion cases to *Brown* from Delaware and Virginia was that although "the schools here are not equal at the moment . . . they are moving toward it. I am inclined toward giving these states the time to make their facilities equal."[67] Burton ended his note of Vinson's presentation to the conference with "Affirm?," suggesting that he thought Vinson was inclined to affirm *Plessy*.[68]

But there were indications that even Vinson was far from set in his view. His statement that "boldness is essential but wisdom is indispensable," as Justice Clark heard it,[69] and Justice Burton's recorded version that "courage is needed, but also wisdom,"[70] would seem to point in the direction of overruling *Plessy*. And Vinson had been known to abruptly reverse himself. After announcing in conference that he would dissent in *Sweatt v. Painter*, Vinson changed his mind and eventually authored the court's unanimous opinion.[71] In *Terry v. Adams*

(1953), he again reversed himself in conference and joined an 8–1 majority overturning a second Texas effort to create an all-white primary.[72]

As the senior associate justice, Black spoke next. Already two years earlier with the support of Justice Douglas, he had boldly announced his willingness to overrule *Plessy*.[73] "Two roads are open," Black told his colleagues at the April 1950 conference that discussed the *McLaurin* and *Sweatt* cases.[74] The first road was to continue to decide under the *Plessy* standard while placing a "heavy . . . burden . . . on the state" to show the existence of equal facilities.[75] "The second road" was to overrule *Plessy*. The Fourteenth Amendment was designed "to prevent a caste system. . . . It is a hangover from the days when the Negro was a slave, and [whites felt] the racial humiliation of sitting together." The "premise" of the *Plessy* opinion "is not sound—it has been refuted by the facts and by history. . . . If I have to meet the issue, there is nothing to make me subscribe to *Plessy*. . . . It was Hitler's creed—he preached what the South believed. . . . The caste system, throughout the country, is the negation of the idea of the Fourteenth Amendment."[76]

Despite Black's eloquence, the court followed his "first road": unanimity in *McLaurin* and *Sweatt* was attained by stopping short of any consideration of overruling *Plessy*. Black was the only justice from the Deep South, and as such his early and unqualified declaration undoubtedly had a powerful effect on the future course of Supreme Court deliberations.

Two and a half years later at the first *Brown* conference, Black again spoke forcefully against legalized segregation. The Civil War amendments, he declared, "have as their basic purpose the abolition of such castes, and to protect the Negro against discrimination on account of color. . . . I can't go contrary to the truth that the purpose of these laws is to discriminate on account of color. The Civil War Amendments were intended to stop that. I have to say that segregation *of itself* violates the Constitution, unless the long line of decisions and stare decisis prevents such a ruling."[77] Black added, "*I have to vote that way*, to end segregation."[78]

Two real surprises at the first *Brown* conference were Justices Minton and Burton who, after Vinson, were the second and third of Truman's four weak appointments to the Court. At the outset, Burton declared straightforwardly that racial segregation in public schools was unconstitutional. "With the Fourteenth Amendment, states do not have the choice—segregation violates equal protection. The total effect is that separate education is not sufficient for today's problems. It is not reasonable to educate people separately for a joint life."[79] Minton's position was announced equally forcefully. "The hour is late," he proclaimed. The court had "chipped and chiseled" away at *Plessy*, but "classification by race does not add up." "There will be trouble," he predicted, "but this race grew up in trouble. The Negro is oppressed and has been in bondage for years after slavery was abolished. *Segregation is per se unconstitutional. I am ready to vote now."*[80]

The surprising positions of the normally ultraconservative Burton and Minton may be attributed, at least in part, to their ardent engagement as cold warriors. Much has been made of the relationship between the eventual outcome in *Brown* and the Cold War.[81] It is true that the brief for the U.S. government advocating the end of legalized segregation expressed concern over Soviet propaganda exploiting American racial segregation in the newly independent postcolonial nations.[82] But it is also striking that the subject appears never to have been mentioned in the published deliberations of the justices. While there is no direct evidence that foreign policy concerns had any effect on Burton and Minton, they were certainly the most likely candidates to be influenced by the government's brief.

Frankfurter spent most of his discussion time in conference advocating reargument. "This is *not* a delaying tactic," he told his skeptical colleagues.[83] But the goal of reargument shaped his argumentative strategy, which was to highlight uncertainties and ambiguities that could be clarified only after further reargument and research. "How does Black know what the framers of the Civil War Amendments meant?" he asked. "I have read all of its history, and I can't say that they meant to abolish segregation . . . or vice versa. . . . What justifies us in saying that what *was* equal in 1868 is not equal *now*?"[84] While he was prepared to immediately hold that segregation in the District of Columbia violated the Due Process Clause of the Fifth Amendment,[85] Frankfurter was unwilling to decide anything else "going to the merits."[86] "I can't say [now] that it is unconstitutional to treat a Negro differently than a white," he declared.[87]

With these provocatively contrarian expressions, Frankfurter managed to ignite the always-smoldering suspicions and resentments that Justice Douglas harbored toward him. One and a half years later on the very day that *Brown* was announced, Douglas dictated a "Memorandum for the File" in which he claimed that

> in the original conference there were only four who voted that segregation in the public schools was unconstitutional. Those four were Black, Burton, Minton and myself. . . . Frankfurter and Jackson viewed the problem with great alarm and thought that the Court should not decide the question if it was possible to avoid it. Both of them expressed the view that segregation in the public schools was probably constitutional. Frankfurter drew a distinction between segregation in the public schools [of the District of Columbia and segregation in the public schools] in the states. He thought that segregation in the public schools of the District of Columbia violated due process, but he thought that history was against the claim of unconstitutionality as applied to the public schools of the States.[88]

At almost exactly the same time, Justice Frankfurter made an equally bold effort to influence the historical record. In a letter to Justice Reed three days after the *Brown* decision, Frankfurter suggested that if a vote had been taken at the first conference there would have been five votes, including Frankfurter's, for overturning *Plessy*.[89] After a year and a half of Supreme Court deliberations over *Brown*, however, this is the first time that Frankfurter appears to have claimed that he had favored overruling *Plessy* at the initial conference.

WARREN REPLACES VINSON

When the justices reassembled in conference on December 12, 1953, after reargument of the case, almost exactly one year after their first discussion of *Brown*, Earl Warren had replaced Chief Justice Vinson, who had died of a heart attack three months earlier. Warren's opening statement to the conference, echoing Black's earlier pronouncements, set the tone: "The more I read and hear and think," Warren declared, "the more I come to conclude that the basis of the principle of segregation and separate but equal rests upon the basic premise that the Negro race is inferior. That is the only way to sustain *Plessy*—I don't see how it can be sustained on any other theory."[90] In a manner that would eventually become his judicial trademark, Warren framed the court's inquiry as a moral issue involving fundamental questions of justice.

Warren immediately turned to the problems of enforcement. Overruling *Plessy* "will perhaps cause trouble," he acknowledged:

> I recognize that the time element is important in the Deep South. We must act, but we should do it in a tolerant way. It would be unfortunate if we had to take precipitous action that could inflame the issue more than necessary. The conditions in the extreme South should be carefully considered by the Court. Kansas and Delaware are not much different from California. . . . But not so in the Deep South. It will take all the wisdom of the Court to do this with a minimum of commotion and strife. How we do it is important. At present, my instincts and tentative feelings would lead me to say that in these cases we should abolish, in a tolerant way, the practice of segregation in public schools.[91]

BROWN AND LEGAL REALISM

The justices who decided *Brown* demonstrated the powerful influence of the reform movement called legal realism on their approaches to law. It is difficult to imagine how without legal realism *Brown* could have been decided in the way that it was. There were three ways in which legal realism affected the outcome

in *Brown*. First was the powerful influence of sociological jurisprudence, a pre–
World War I early incarnation of realism.[92] Its most influential thinker, Dean
Roscoe Pound of the Harvard Law School, criticized the "mechanical jurisprudence" of the Supreme Court after its decision in *Lochner v. New York* (1905).[93]
The court, he argued, based its decision on a system of legal thought that had
lost touch with social reality. With his distinction between "law in books" and
"law in action," Pound invoked the new spirit of pragmatism to undermine the
legitimacy of the court's confident formalism.[94] The distinction spawned the
Brandeis brief, with which future Supreme Court justice Louis Brandeis won a
surprising unanimous decision upholding a maximum hours law for women in
Muller v. Oregon (1908).[95] The brief consisted of two pages of traditional legal
argument and ninety-five pages of economic and sociological data about the
conditions of working women in the factory system.[96] Like Pound, Brandeis's
message was clear: to apply abstract ideas such as "freedom of contract" justly,
the Supreme Court must take account of changing social reality.

The criticism of legal formalism by Pound and Brandeis was music to the
ears of NAACP lawyers planning their strategy to undermine *Plessy v. Ferguson*, one of the most representative decisions of the *Lochner* era.[97] To the
charge that the system of legally imposed racial segregation was based on an
unconstitutional assumption of the inferiority of Black people, the *Plessy* court
had responded with the dismissive counteraccusation that any such feelings
of inferiority arose "solely because the colored race chooses to put that construction upon it."[98] In reaction, much of the thinking among racial liberals
about how to challenge *Plessy* was devoted to showing that the formal equality
of racial separation ("the law in books") masked the social reality of systemic
racial subordination ("the law in action"). And with its gaping contradiction
between an egalitarian American creed and the social reality of a caste system, Myrdal's *American Dilemma* became the crown jewel in a generation of
social science studies expressing legal realism's vision of an alliance between
the social sciences and legal reform.[99] Within this context, NAACP lawyers
became adept at casting the race problem in a historical and sociological framework.[100] When during the *Sweatt* and *McLaurin* conference Justice Black first
declared in favor of overruling *Plessy*, he concluded that the "premise in *Plessy*
is not sound—it has been refuted by the facts and by history."[101] Two years later
during the first conference on *Brown*, Black added, "I am compelled to say for
myself that I can't escape the view that the reason for segregation is the belief
that Negroes are inferior. I do not need books to say that."[102] Yet despite this
backhanded dismissal of Myrdal's significance, the influence of *An American
Dilemma* is written all over Black's comments about race, especially his frequent appeal to the idea of "caste," one of Myrdal's signature concepts.[103] For
example, Black declared that "the Civil War Amendments have as their basic

purpose the abolition of . . . castes."[104] Above all, the idea, as Black put it, that *Plessy* could be "refuted by the facts and by history" seemed to acknowledge a Constitution whose meaning changes based on new understandings of the state of the world.

A second way in which legal realism affected the decision in *Brown* was through its influence in persuading a generation of New Dealers of the feasibility of social reform through law. Justice Douglas, who as a professor at the Columbia and Yale law schools, was one of the original group of realists, applied his ideas about corporate reform during his service on the Securities and Exchange Commission. Justice Abe Fortas, Douglas's student at Yale, advanced the cause of legal realism as a pro bono advocate in two famous cases, *Durham v. United States* (1954) and *Gideon v. Wainright* (1963).[105] Fortas's successful arguments for changes in the law of insanity in *Durham* and for a constitutional right to counsel in *Gideon* were infused with the legal realist ideal of progressive change through law. Increasingly, legal realists came to view law as a vehicle of social reform to be mocked as "transcendental nonsense," in Felix Cohen's words, unless it could be adapted to a "functional" or "instrumental" role in fostering social change.[106] Gunnar Myrdal coupled his advocacy of social reform through law with a denunciation of the guru of late nineteenth-century American sociology, William Graham Sumner, whose supine mantra—"stateways cannot change folkways"—became a formula for justifying social passivity in the emerging laissez-faire state.[107]

The third and most important respect in which legal realism affected the justices who decided *Brown* was their strikingly similar approaches to constitutional interpretation concluding in their agreement with the once heretical proposition that constitutional meaning changes over time.[108] Except perhaps for Justice Black, whose own views on constitutional meaning evolved into inflexible textualism much later, it is fair to say that all the other justices who decided *Brown* believed in some version of a "living Constitution." Though he came ardently to deny that his vote in *Brown* was based on an evolving Constitution,[109] Justice Black in his initial appeal to "facts and history" to refute *Plessy* may have indicated that even he had once subscribed to the legal realist claim that constitutional meaning varies with changing circumstances.

"A LIVING CONSTITUTION"

At stake in *Brown* was not simply the proposition that racial segregation was inherently unequal but also the notion that changing social conditions and realities had fundamentally altered the meaning of racial equality in America. The notion of a living Constitution owes its existence to an approach to the law developed during the New Deal. Justice Robert Jackson's unpublished draft

concurrences (discussed in Appendix 2), illustrate the extent to which committed New Dealers had come to take for granted the idea of a dynamic Constitution. "Of course," Jackson wrote, "the Constitution must be construed as a living
instrument and cannot be read as if written in a dead language."[110] "It is neither
novel nor radical doctrine that statutes once held constitutional may become
invalid by reason of changing conditions," Jackson continued, "and those [stat-
utes] held to be good in one state of facts may be held to be bad in another."[111]

Justice Harold Burton exemplifies the extent to which even a thoroughly
conventional judge had absorbed the constitutional lessons of the New Deal.
At the first argument in *Brown*, in response to a southern contention that for
seventy-five years state and federal courts and legislatures had reflected the
view that the Fourteenth Amendment did not bar racial segregation, Burton asked, "Don't you recognize it as possible that within seventy-five years
the social and economic conditions and the personal relations of the nation
may have changed, so that what may have been a valid interpretation of them
seventy-five years ago would not be a valid interpretation of them constitutionally today?"[112]

Frankfurter too rejected the notion of an unchanging Constitution, insu-
lated from the realities of a changing world. As a professor, he had helped to
shape the legal realist critique of a static Constitution.[113] In a two-page handwritten memo to himself composed while the court was deliberating over *Brown*,
Frankfurter gave voice to the idea of a changing constitution:

> The equality of laws enshrined in a constitution which was "made for an
> undefined and expanding future, and for a people gathered and to be gath-
> ered from many nations and of many tongues," *Hurtado v. California*, 110
> U.S. 516, 530, 531, is not a fixed formula defined with finality at a particular
> time. It does not reflect, as a congealed summary, the social arrangements
> and beliefs of a particular epoch. It is addressed to the changes wrought
> by time and not merely the changes that are the consequences of physical
> development. Law must respond to transformation of views as well as to
> that of outward circumstances. The effect of changes in men's feelings for
> what is right and just is equally relevant in determining whether a discrim-
> ination denies the equal protection of the laws.[114]

The centerpiece of the new approach was the way in which the court
treated the history of the Fourteenth Amendment. Four days before the reargument that had been ordered to answer the court's questions about history,
Frankfurter circulated to the justices a lengthy memorandum on the history
of the Fourteenth Amendment written by his law clerk, Alexander Bickel.[115]
Frankfurter declared that Bickel's memorandum showed that the legislative

history concerning whether the Equal Protection Clause barred segregated schools was "inconclusive, in the sense that the 39th Congress as an enacting body neither manifested that the Amendment outlawed segregation in the public schools or authorized legislation to that end, nor that it manifested the opposite."[116] In his memo Bickel, the future Yale constitutional scholar, also included his own conclusion about the proper scope of constitutional interpretation: "the Congress was on notice that it was enacting vague language of indeterminate reach." While congressmen entertained "hopes both for a broad and a narrow application of the general language being voted," in the end they "trusted to the future to solve future problems."[117]

The consequence of the Bickel memo was that by the time the cases were finally reargued on December 7–9, 1953, the court's focus on the historical background of the Fourteenth Amendment seemed to have vanished, and "the most pointed questions from the bench focused on remedy."[118] In the conference following reargument on December 12, 1953, further interest in the original meaning of the Fourteenth Amendment "appeared to be dead."[119] Chief Justice Warren's *Brown* opinion embraced Bickel's finding that the historical evidence was "inconclusive" as to whether the Equal Protection Clause was meant to bar racially segregated schools.[120] This freed Warren to declare that changing historical circumstances could justify a departure from *Plessy*. "We cannot turn the clock back to 1868 when the [Fourteenth] Amendment was adopted, or even to 1896 when *Plessy v. Ferguson* was written," the chief justice declared.[121] When the Fourteenth Amendment was adopted, only a rudimentary system of public education had been established in America. Since that time circumstances had changed, and widely available public education—especially in Warren's home state of California—had become one of the glories of American democracy. "We must consider public education in the light of its full development and its present place in American life throughout the Nation," Warren concluded.[122]

The most striking instance of how deeply the legal realist vision had penetrated the justices' consciousness is the example of Justice Reed, the last holdout in *Brown* and the one justice who may have thought that racial segregation could be morally justified. In spite of his announced opposition to overruling *Plessy*, he could not ignore the views on constitutional interpretation that he had absorbed during his own prior service as solicitor general defending New Deal constitutional innovations before the Supreme Court. "I agree that the meaning of the Constitution is *not* fixed," he told his fellow justices at the first conference on *Brown*.[123] At the second conference, he continued to "recognize that this is a dynamic Constitution, and what was current in *Plessy* might not be current now."[124]

Replying to Frankfurter's letter expressing "deep gratitude" to Reed for making *Brown* unanimous, Reed explained why he finally had agreed to join

Warren's opinion. "While there were many considerations that pointed to a dissent," Reed wrote, "they did not add up to a balance against the Court's opinion." Then he recited—sometimes in code—the names of a string of Supreme Court opinions, beginning in 1938, that had recognized a racially liberal Constitution. "From [*Missouri* ex rel. *Gaines v. Canada*] through *Smith* and *Allright, Sweatt, Morgan, Steele* to Jay Bird [*Terry v. Adams*], the factors looking toward a fair treatment for Negroes are more important than the weight of history,"[125] Reed declared. Myrdal could not have hoped for a more perfect expression of the triumph of the American Creed.

THE TRIUMPH OF GRADUALISM

It is not fully appreciated that by the time the justices agreed unanimously to overrule *Plessy*, they already had reached consensus on the idea that the implementation of any desegregation order would have to be gradual. Of the original holdouts, Jackson and Clark seem from early on to have been willing to join an overruling opinion if only they could be assured that implementation of desegregation would be gradual. "I won't be a party to immediate unconstitutionality," Jackson declared at the first conference. "Segregation is nearing an end. . . . We should perhaps give them time to get rid of it, and I would go along on that basis. I would not object to such a holding with a reasonable time element. There are equitable remedies that can be shaped to the needs."[126] Speaking next, Justice Burton, while declaring for overruling, agreed that "we can use time—I would give plenty of time in this decree."[127] Endorsing Jackson's views, Justice Clark declared, "If we delay action . . . it will help. Our opinion should give the lower courts the opportunity to withhold relief in light of troubles. I would be inclined to go along with that."[128] Even Justice Douglas, who favored immediately overruling *Plessy*, acknowledged that "the answer is simple, though the application of it may present great difficulties." Time, he agreed, was a relevant factor. "It will take a long time to work it out."[129]

All of this was in the background when on December 12, 1953, newly appointed Chief Justice Earl Warren initiated the second round of discussion of *Brown*. As we saw, after firmly declaring his conviction that racial segregation in public schools was unconstitutional, Warren added that he "recognize[d] that the time element is important in the Deep South. We must act, but we should do it in a tolerant way. It would be unfortunate if we had to take precipitous action that could inflame the issue more than necessary."[130] Five days later Justice Burton noted in his diary that "after lunch the Chief Justice told me of his plan to try [to] direct discussion . . . toward the decree—as providing . . . the best chance of unanimity in that [later] phase."[131] Both Kluger and Schwartz interpret this as meaning that Warren hoped that even if the court failed to achieve unanimity on the merits, it might still avoid dissent at the decree phase.[132] Yet, there was only a small step to a dramatically different conclusion that a seasoned politician such as Earl Warren could have been expected to understand: if he could reassure the potential dissenters that any remedy would be gradual, he might also be able to produce unanimity on the merits.

A month later, Justice Frankfurter sought to provide just such assurance. In a four-page memo circulated to the court on January 15, 1954, Frankfurter, who still "cagily" refused to tip his hand on the merits, made clear that he stood with the gradualists on the question of implementation of any desegregation order.[133] "A decree in this case in favor of the appellants of necessity would be drastically different from decrees enforcing merely individual rights before the Court," Frankfurter began. Instead, the remedy question more closely resembled cases under the Sherman Antitrust Act or the law of nuisance, where "so-called considerations of public convenience are balanced against the right of the plaintiff in molding an appropriate decree. Attention is paid to the element of time for obedience." Earlier cases involving segregation in higher education were also different, he continued, in that they involved only at most a few plaintiffs and were therefore "amenable to individual treatment." But "this is not so in the situations before us," Frankfurter observed, since the court was being "asked in effect to transform state-wide school systems."[134]

The justices reassembled to discuss *Brown* for a second time under Warren the day after Frankfurter circulated his memo. This meeting appeared to be an informal luncheon gathering, since none of the usual notetakers—Burton, Douglas, Clark, and Jackson—took notes of the discussion. Only Frankfurter, not usually a notetaker at conference, sketchily recorded the deliberations. His notes suggest that the nature of the decree was the only subject discussed.[135]

Opening the discussion, Warren outlined his ideas about the two elements of a decree that were designed to satisfy potential dissenters. The first stressed a decentralized approach in which implementation would be delegated to the district courts, which were presumably more familiar with local conditions; the second emphasized a flexible standard that would allow for gradual implementation of the court's order. The justices also reached agreement on scheduling another round of arguments to focus on the nature of the decree. Their reactions to Frankfurter's and Warren's ideas suggest that they already had forged a consensus on a gradualist decree. Oddly, Jackson appears to have remained silent, though in earlier discussions he had hardly ever missed a chance to insist on gradualism. His silence at this moment may be explained by the fact that he was still in the process, apparently unknown to his colleagues, of drafting a dissent, which would soon evolve into a concurrence. Yet even in the last of his five unpublished drafts, he remained vociferously against delegating the task of implementation to the district courts.[136] Since Jackson died during the one-year

interval between *Brown I* and *Brown II*, we will never know whether he would
have stood in the way of unanimity by holding out against this essential element
of the gradualist degree in *Brown II*.

There were no voices for immediate across-the-board desegregation. All
the justices, including Black and Douglas, endorsed gradualism. "Leave it to
the district courts," Black urged, while also endorsing a vague decree. "Vagueness is not going to hurt. . . . If necessary, let us have 700 [law]suits" to work
out the process. The meeting closed with a strong declaration by Justice Black
on the need for flexibility in enforcement. "Let it simmer. . . . Let it take time.
It can't take too long." He predicted that any politician in the Deep South who
supported desegregation "would be dead politically forever. . . . In Alabama
most liberals are praying for delay."[137]

It has often been suggested that the Supreme Court that decided *Brown* did
not foresee the backlash that would ensue. It has also been asserted that the
court never realized that its opinion in *Brown II* might encourage resistance in
the South. However, the process of decision presented here shows that from
the beginning of their deliberations, the justices had never failed to focus on the
potential for violent backlash. The opinion in *Brown II* was no casual effort at
phrase-making. Rather, the justices reached consensus on a gradualist decree
much earlier in their deliberations than we have heretofore realized, and the
phrase "all deliberate speed" was an apt summary of that gradualist consensus.
Indeed, it does seem clear that without this prior consensus there could not
have been unanimity in *Brown I*. The result reflected the justices' understanding that they were initiating a social revolution. The court feared that because
deeply entrenched southern attitudes and institutions were completely unprepared for immediate desegregation, anything more than a gradualist approach
would inevitably lead to violence.

Their worst fears were realized in *Cooper v. Aaron*, the Little Rock, Arkansas,
school desegregation case.

COOPER V. AARON:
THE LITTLE ROCK SCHOOL CRISIS

Even before the regular 1958 term got under way, the chief justice called the
justices back early to hear argument in *Cooper v. Aaron* (1958),[138] the Little
Rock, Arkansas, school desegregation case, the first such case to come before
the court since *Brown v. Board of Education*. In the interim, southern white
political leadership had turned bitterly against *Brown*. Already in March 1956,
virtually all of the senators and congressmen from the eleven states of the former Confederacy had endorsed the "Declaration of Constitutional Principles,"
known informally as the Southern Manifesto, which condemned *Brown* as

"unwarranted" and "contrary to the Constitution." The manifesto commended those states that declared their intention "to resist forced integration by any lawful means."[139]

The Southern Manifesto provided the constitutional basis for state pledges of "massive resistance" to desegregation. The court, in stunned efforts at reconciliation, had assiduously avoided deciding cases that would add fuel to the fire. The justices even went so far as to refuse to hear a case from Virginia, *Naim v. Naim* (1956), in which that state's highest court upheld a Virginia law barring interracial marriages while heaping scorn and derision on the *Brown* decision.[140]

The Little Rock case, however, was one the court could not avoid. It began in the fall of 1957, a still hopeful time when southern white "moderates" believed it was possible to gradually desegregate public schools, at least at the high school level, without generating white backlash. In this spirit, the Little Rock School Board voluntarily prepared a plan under which nine carefully chosen Black students would enter Central High School on September 3, 1957, the first day of the new school year. The day before, however, the demagogic governor of Arkansas, Orval Faubus, dispatched the state National Guard to Central High to prevent the students from entering. On September 24 President Eisenhower, invoking a threat of "anarchy," sent federal troops to Little Rock, who assisted the Black students in entering the school.[141] As the political climate grew more heated and white mobs surrounded Central High, the school board backed down from its desegregation plan and petitioned the federal district court for a postponement. After the district court judge granted a thirty-month delay, the court of appeals reversed pending appeal to the Supreme Court.[142] At this point, Chief Justice Warren abruptly ended the court's summer vacation more than a month and a half early by calling the justices back to an unusual special term he convened at the end of the hot Washington summer.[143]

Warren asked newly appointed Justice Brennan to draft a per curiam opinion.

BRENNAN'S OPINION

The message of Brennan's per curiam opinion in *Cooper v. Aaron* is twofold. First, the message seeks to demonstrate the continuing unanimity of the justices in support of *Brown*, and second, it expresses the court's determination not to back down on *Brown* in the face of threats of violence. The message is also an appeal to the rule of law and to the obligation of the white South to obey the law as declared in *Brown* regardless of personal disagreement.

In order to demonstrate that the rule of law requires obedience to judicial decrees, Brennan ventured enthusiastically into a contested area of constitutional theory. His pronouncement that "the federal judiciary is supreme in the exposition of . . . the Constitution"[144] is now widely cited in academic works as one of the relatively rare instances in which the Supreme Court has explicitly argued for "judicial supremacy."[145] For most of American history, a more limited "departmental theory" of judicial review has sought to restrict claims by the Supreme Court to judicial supremacy.[146]

DESEGREGATION AFTER LITTLE ROCK

The fall of 1958 brought major acts of defiance by the governors of Virginia and Arkansas. After the Supreme Court decision in *Cooper v. Aaron*, Arkansas governor Faubus closed the Little Rock public schools for the 1958–1959 school year.[147] The voice of Virginia's "massive resistance" strategy, Governor Lindsay Almond, also closed public schools in three of the commonwealth's counties.[148] Alongside these dramatic acts of defiance, all but one of the states of the former Confederacy also enacted so-called pupil-placement laws, an "elaborately conceived alternative to defiance" that stopped desegregation of public schools virtually in its tracks for another five or six years.[149] Pupil-placement laws were designed to freeze existing school placements by concentrating authority to transfer students in a state board. A student could be moved to another school only with the placement board's consent.

"The difference between pupil-placement laws and massive resistance was purely cosmetic,"[150] Lucas Powe bluntly concluded. "In practice," J. Harvie Wilkinson III observed, "pupil-placement laws suited segregationist aims quite nicely."[151] "They were an ideal delaying device, a maze of administrative hearings and appeals through which Negroes on an individual basis had to wind before reaching federal court. And the loose, multiple criteria in the statutes allowed officials to hold to an absolute minimum the number of blacks setting foot in white schools."[152] The laws, "functioning as intended," one commentator noted, "make mass integration almost impossible, place the burden of altering the status quo upon individual Negro pupils and their parents, establish a procedure that is difficult and time-consuming to complete, and prescribe standards so varied and vague that it is extremely difficult to establish that any individual denial is attributable to racial considerations."[153]

As these laws were being enacted, a perceptive *Washington Post* journalist noted that "hopeful liberal observers saw in [these laws] a means of effective selective gradualism in adjusting to the Supreme Court ruling," while the actual proponents of the pupil-placement laws simply sought "to make it possible to deny Negroes admission to white schools or to hold desegregation to a minimum when it could no longer be prevented."[154] For a time, each group found comfort in these laws.

As mounting evidence of the extent of southern white resistance continued to accumulate during the fall of 1958, the Supreme Court may itself have come to the grim conclusion that tokenism was the best that could be expected until things calmed down. In *Shuttlesworth v. Birmingham Bd. of Ed.*,[155] decided in November 1958, the court, in a curt one-sentence opinion, upheld the pupil-placement law in Birmingham, Alabama, against a claim that it was discriminatory "on its face." While the Supreme Court emphasized "the limited grounds" upon which it was affirming the lower court ruling, even this limited "facial" challenge ought to have enabled the Black plaintiffs to prevail. Like the lower federal court, however, the Supreme Court chose to ignore the plain discriminatory purpose written all over the Alabama pupil-placement law. The three-judge federal panel below had maintained, with a wink and a nod, that since there was nothing on the face of the school law that required a dual school system, the plaintiffs could prevail only if they undertook the time-consuming task of offering evidence of discrimination in the actual administration of the law.[156] While there was clear evidence that Alabama had passed the law as part of its strategy of massive resistance, Judge Richard Rives, writing for the three-judge panel, was not to be persuaded.

Rives acknowledged that the plaintiff had argued "with much force" that the resolution of interposition and nullification passed by a special session of the Alabama Legislature in 1956 had declared *Brown* "null, void, and of no effect" and vowed to maintain segregation in Alabama public schools.[157] Though both the resolution of nullification and the pupil-placement law were part of the same legislative package expressing open defiance of the Supreme Court's ruling, Rives reached the hypertechnical conclusion that because the legislative declaration was "a joint resolution" that "does not have the force and effect of law," it could not be taken as evidence that the pupil-placement plan was tainted and therefore discriminatory on its face.[158]

Four years later, Judge Rives's colleague on the Fifth Circuit, John Minor Wisdom, cut through this fog of legalism to observe that pupil-placement laws were a ploy "to maintain segregation by allowing a little token desegregation."[159] Had the *Shuttlesworth* court been similarly inclined, it would not have been difficult to decide that the Alabama pupil-placement law was discriminatory on its face. Instead, the justices apparently concluded that they had little choice but to acquiesce even in a school plan whose overt purpose was to resist *Brown*. Two months after *Cooper v. Aaron*, then, "the Court rehibernated."[160] With the court still under siege, the tactical retreat in *Shuttlesworth* foreshadowed a decade-long strategy of withdrawal from the school desegregation struggle itself.

As "it became clear" during the early 1960s that "the sole purpose of [pupil-placement] statutes was to frustrate desegregation," the U.S. Court of

Appeals for the Fifth Circuit enjoined their application.[161] Southern legislatures responded by enacting "freedom of choice" plans that permitted students to choose to transfer to any school within the school district that had space available. Initially, courts of appeal responded positively to the newly enacted freedom of choice plans although they did not ultimately result in any meaningful integration in the Deep South. The problem with freedom of choice plans was that "in theory, each child's school choice was free; in practice, it was often anything but. . . . [The] opportunity for pressure, covert and overt," from white employers and school officials "was built into every pore of the 'free' choice system. In the very communities where blacks were most disadvantaged and illiterate, freedom of choice would be least likely to work."[162]

In 1964–1966, the Fifth Circuit Court of Appeals, under the leadership of Judge John Minor Wisdom, moved vigorously to end judicial paralysis over school desegregation. In three opinions striking down important aspects of freedom of choice plans that had ensured no more than token integration, "wisdom transformed the face of school desegregation law. . . . [His] critical premise was that school boards had a positive duty to integrate, not merely to stop segregating."[163]

After a decade spent mostly on the sidelines, the Supreme Court in 1968 boldly reentered the fray, striking down a Virginia freedom of choice law in *Green v. County School Board.*[164] The case involved the school system of New Kent County, Virginia, which by 1967 had 115 African American students attending public school with white students, up from zero in 1964, 35 in 1965, and 111 in 1966. But 85 percent of African American students in the county were still enrolled in a school with no white students.[165] The Supreme Court, in *Green*, found this unacceptable. Justice Brennan, writing for a unanimous Warren Court, stated that "a plan that at this late date fails to provide meaningful assurance of prompt and effective disestablishment of a dual system is . . . intolerable. 'The time for more "deliberate speed" has run out,' *Griffin v. County School Board.* . . . The burden on a school board today is to come forward with a plan that promises to work and promises realistically to work *now.*"[166]

The change was dramatic. In 1964, the year of the enactment of the monumental Civil Rights Act and the tenth anniversary of *Brown*, only 1.2 percent of Black school children in the South attended school with whites. (Excluding Texas and Tennessee, the percent dropped to less than half of one percent.)[167] By 1971, a "judicial blitz" resulted in 44 percent of Black children in the South attending majority-white schools, compared to only 28 percent who did so in the North and West. The last three years of this "judicial blitz" (1969–1971) occurred despite the newly elected Nixon administration's reversal of the aggressive enforcement policies of the Department of Health, Education, and Welfare. "The Court that once badly needed executive support now moved in the face of executive opposition." The results were astonishing. "The South, seventeen years after *Brown* . . . , became America's most integrated region."[168]

LOVING V. VIRGINIA (1967)

In 1967 when sixteen states still had laws on the books barring interracial marriage, a unanimous U.S. Supreme Court declared Virginia's antimiscegenation law unconstitutional.[169] To the surprise of many, there was hardly any negative public reaction. Just eleven years earlier in *Naim v. Naim* (1956), five justices, led by Justice Frankfurter, had successfully erected procedural obstacles to deciding the constitutional status of Virginia's law prohibiting racial intermarriage.[170] While the Court was quick to apply *Brown* to desegregate public buses and beaches,[171] it abruptly stopped at intermarriage. The justices were no doubt aware that public opinion polls showed virtually unanimous disapproval of interracial marriage. In the late 1950s, Gallup reported, well over 90 percent of those polled disapproved of racial intermarriage.[172] Justice Clark, who had joined Justice Frankfurter in blocking consideration of *Naim*, explained what had moved him. "One bombshell at a time is enough," Clark declared.[173]

What changed? Acknowledging that he was offering an explanation "contrary to the usual view," Richard Delgado sought to explain the absence of any strong reaction to *Loving*. "By the time *Virginia v. Loving* came down" in 1967, he wrote, "interracial marriage was practically a moderate practice, even a conservative one."[174] But multiple polls show us that Delgado was not correct. If he had been, it would have represented an astonishing change in racial consciousness in the eleven years since *Naim*. In light of the known polling results, it does seem that Justices Frankfurter and Clark were right in believing in 1955 that striking down antimiscegenation laws would produce a "bombshell."[175]

Ironically, Professor Delgado's characterization of interracial marriage as having become "a moderate practice, even a conservative one," by the time *Loving* was decided—though plainly wrong for the year 1967—may have become accurate by 2012, when he published his article on *Naim*. By then, a Gallup Poll showed that 83 percent of whites approved of interracial marriage.[176] In 1968, only 17 percent of whites had approved.[177] "As recently as 1990," Pew reported, 63 percent "said they would be opposed to a close relative marrying a black person."[178] This share had been cut to 30 percent by 2000 and 14 percent by 2017. Pew thus announced an astonishing result. In the twenty-seven years after 1990, almost 50 percent of whites abandoned their opposition to Black and white people intermarrying.[179]

We are still searching for an explanation that fits the year 1967. A possible explanation for the mild reaction to *Loving* might go like this. It was not that marriage between races had yet found any more favor among whites than in the past. It was rather that due to southern political reversals since *Brown*,[180] opposition to interracial marriage had been drained of its symbolic power as a primary expression of white supremacy. The decision in *Griswold v. Connecticut* (1965) two years earlier also highlighted the desirability of resisting state intervention into marital privacy. In sympathy with that set of values, the symbolic representation of white supremacy had migrated to the public/political sphere, especially to public schools and the "massive resistance" movement. Having lost their symbolic significance, antimiscegenation statutes also lost their power to stir racist passions.

MEASURES OF CHANGED RACIAL CONSCIOUSNESS, 1961–1991

With the perspective of more than half a century, should the decision in *Brown* be regarded as a success or a failure? Gerald Rosenberg raised this question in his provocative 1991 book *The Hollow Hope*, which emphasized the Supreme Court's inability to produce any significant desegregation in the Deep South until Congress and the president collaborated in pressing southern school districts to comply.[181] If the measure of the success of *Brown* is to be found in the degree of public school desegregation it achieved, the decision must be judged a failure at least as of the time the Warren Court passed into history fifteen years after *Brown* was decided.

But perhaps the success of *Brown* should be understood from a different perspective. In initiating a challenge to the premises of white supremacy, the Supreme Court in *Brown* began a long-term process that eventually succeeded in fundamentally altering white racial consciousness and overthrowing the caste system. In order to make the case for this version of success, I shall offer several snapshots of the racial consciousness of white America over time.

Beginning with the earliest public opinion polls in 1939 on equality and race, it is possible to sketch white racial consciousness before World War II. While data from this inaugural period in the history of polling must be used cautiously, it does provide a fairly grim portrait of the racial attitudes of white Americans in the years immediately before and after World War II.

The available polling data during the fifteen years before *Brown* supports Myrdal's picture of a caste system built on the conviction of white Americans that African Americans were inferior. In September 1939, a Roper/Fortune survey reported that 71 percent of its respondents thought that Negroes generally were of lower intelligence than whites.[182] A July 1945 Office of Public Opinion Research survey asked respondents which among four statements best described their attitude toward Negroes. Thirty-three percent answered that Negroes should have either "more" (14 percent) or "the same" (19 percent) opportunities as white people—we might call them "racial liberals"—compared to the 64 percent who might be called "white supremacists." The latter answered either that "although Negroes should not be mistreated by whites, the white race should always keep its superior position" (44%) or "because Negroes are so different from white people as a race, I believe they should not be allowed to mix with whites in any way" (20 percent).[183]

In May 1944, a University of Chicago poll asked respondents whether, "as far as you know," "Negro blood" was different from "white blood." Thirty-two percent of the respondents replied that "Negro blood" was different, while 36 percent thought they were the same; 32 percent answered "don't know."[184] Separation of donated white and Black blood was standard operating procedure in the military during World War II.[185] This continued to be practiced in blood banks in postwar America,[186] expressing the still widespread belief among whites that African Americans were biologically inferior. A May 1948 Gallup poll reported that 63 percent of Americans opposed President Truman's plan to integrate the armed forces by executive order.[187]

Polling data on equality and race supported one of Myrdal's important observations about the structure of the southern system of racial segregation: the most intense support for separation of the races existed in those relationships that tested the boundaries of intimacy between Black and white people. As one moved from the private to the public sphere, the insistence on racial segregation diminished. This can be illustrated by poll reactions to various forms of legally imposed racial separation.

In realms such as marriage and social intimacy, poll respondents after World War II continued to be virtually unanimous in rejecting both intermarriage and social mixing across racial lines. In 1948, 83 percent of respondents to a Roper/Fortune poll declared themselves opposed to a close relative marrying a Negro, and 64 percent were opposed to having a Black person as a neighbor.[188] Housing was a major area where large majorities favored racial separation. A 1939 Roper/Fortune survey found overwhelming support among Americans for residential segregation by race. Only 13 percent believed that Black people should be allowed to live in whatever neighborhoods they wished. The remaining respondents divided between those who believed that Black people should be prevented by law from living in white neighborhoods (41%) and those who believed that there should be no laws but that "there should be an unwritten understanding, backed up by social pressure, to keep Negroes out of the neighborhoods where white people live" (42%).[189]

Even as late as 1963 when large majorities of Americans had shifted to support President Lyndon Johnson's civil rights bill, the old white racial animosities continued to persist in the area of housing. As large majorities of white Americans approved of public accommodation laws that would outlaw discrimination in public transportation, restaurants, and even schools, a larger number continued to resist fair housing laws. Still, a 1963 Gallup poll of white racial attitudes seems to show a significant decline in white resistance to Black neighbors. When asked whether they would move if "colored people came to live next door," 21 percent of white people answered that they would definitely move, and 24 percent said they "might move." But 55 percent of white people replied that they would not move, compared to the 83 percent in 1939 who believed that Black people should be prevented by law or custom from living in white neighborhoods.[190]

A series of surveys of northern opinion recorded other dramatic reversals of racial attitudes. Beginning in 1942, respondents were asked, "If a Negro with the same income and education moved into your block, would it make any difference to you?" In 1942, 42 percent of northern whites said it would make no difference; by 1963, this group had grown to 70 percent. "By similar numbers (40 percent in 1942; 75 percent in 1963)," white northerners approved of desegregated schools. If the racial caste system was based on the conviction that Black people were inferior, we can see dramatic evidence of its disintegration in the North over a quarter century. In 1939, we recall, 71 percent of respondents answered that African Americans were of inferior intelligence. In 1963, by contrast, four-fifths of northern whites agreed that "Negroes are as intelligent as white people."[191]

As one moved away from the more intimate realms of family, friends, and neighbors to the question of enforced racial separation in public accommodations, the responses grew more divided. In a 1944 survey Americans, by a margin of 51 percent to 42 percent, said they would eat in a restaurant that served both Black and white people. But when the 51 percent majority were pressed to say whether they would sit next to a Negro at a restaurant, 10 percent of them said no.[192] There does seem to have been somewhat more acceptance of desegregation in public transportation. Gallup polls in 1948 and 1949 revealed a small but consistent majority in favor of desegregating interstate buses and trains.[193]

Sharply ambivalent attitudes toward equal employment rights were recorded in the post–World War II era. In a May 1944 poll, 50 percent of respondents said it was "all right" with them if Black people "with the same kind of training" were hired to do "the same kind of job as you"; 43 percent replied that they "wouldn't like it." Yet, in the same set of polls 51 percent simultaneously asserted that "whites should have first chance" at such a job, while only 42 percent answered that Negroes should have "as good a chance."[194] Many polls recorded these sorts of conflicts or ambivalences over equal employment rights. Differently worded questions often produced dramatically different answers. A June 1945 Gallup poll asked about a proposed state law that "would require *employers* to hire a person if he qualified for the job regardless of his race or color"; 43 percent were recorded in favor, 44 percent opposed. A changed question that shifted the focus and asked about a proposed law that required *"employees* to work alongside persons of any race or color" was opposed by a margin of 56 percent to 34 percent. Simply shifting the focus of the question resulted in a 22 percent margin of opposition instead of 1 percent.[195] After President Truman's 1948 proposal for a fair employment practices act, most surveys focused on attitudes toward Truman's federal plan. As a 1952 Roper survey demonstrated, poll responses typically divided into three categories: those who favored the law (33%), those who opposed the law (32%), and those who believed that states, not the federal government, should decide whether a law was needed (26%).[196] It was never clear to what extent devotion to states' rights was simply a cover for opposition to any fair employment law. Another three-way split occurred in response to a Gallup question asking "how far" the federal government should go in requiring employers to engage in equal hiring. Thirty-three percent replied "all the way," 6 percent answered "part of the way," and 47 percent said "none of the way."[197] After *Brown*, many polls asked how long the respondent thought it would take to desegregate American public schools. The choices were again divided into three categories: immediate desegregation, gradual desegregation over a period of years, and never. It was hardly clear whether the large group of gradualists who predicted there would be a very long delay actually favored the delay or were simply pessimistic about whether an otherwise desirable goal could ever be reached.

It is difficult to generalize too broadly about these surveys of public opinion before *Brown*. They show that in most segregated areas of American life, a broad consensus of white Americans favored the status quo. In some areas involving the more intimate realms of family, friends, and neighborhood, whites were virtually unanimous in disapproving of social relations across racial lines. In areas involving public accommodations—restaurants and transportation— the public was equally divided over segregation, and the poll results show dramatic shifts depending on small changes in the wording of the questions. This last phenomenon may suggest not so much differences among white people in their racial attitudes as an internal conflict within most white Americans reflecting the chasm between the nation's ideals and its racial attitudes.

WHITE ATTITUDES TOWARD BLACK PEOPLE, 1954–1960

If one were looking for signs after *Brown* of progress in white racial attitudes, the regular Gallup surveys on approval/disapproval of *Brown* would seem to offer all that one needed. Between 1954 and 1959, *Brown's* approval rating increased steadily from 55 percent to 60 percent.[198] But for whatever reason, Roper surveys undertaken during the same period show a clear majority against

Brown. In three surveys between 1956 and 1958, Roper offered the respondent four choices. The first two asked whether the respondent was for immediate desegregation or desegregation in "a reasonable time."[199] The third and fourth choices were

3. "The time may come when Negro and white children should go to the same school, but it will take years in some places and it shouldn't be pushed."
4. "The Supreme Court decision was a mistake and white and Negro students should never be forced to go to the same schools."

In all three Roper surveys between 1956 and 1958, the percentage of respondents agreeing with statements 3 or 4 varied between 53 percent and 58 percent. By contrast, the percentage approving of *Brown* (choices 1 or 2) varied between 35 percent and 44 percent. In October 1958, Roper recorded only 44 percent approval of *Brown*, a still substantially higher number than the 35 percent recorded only two years earlier or the 37 percent who favored *Brown* only four months earlier.[200]

Why the Roper and Gallup polls differed so much is not easy to fathom. Among polling professionals, it has long been suspected that where there are binary choices, some percentage of people will always choose "approve" out of fear that they will otherwise be thought too negative. Others speculate that some respondents, regardless of their views on the merits, are reluctant to say they disapprove of a Supreme Court decision. Whatever the explanation, the dramatically different attitudes toward *Brown* recorded in the Roper and Gallup surveys should lead to caution in supposing that racial consciousness had progressed during a period otherwise known for successful resistance to the Supreme Court desegregation decision.

CHANGING RACIAL CONSCIOUSNESS, 1961–1991

After a period in which a Black man came almost out of nowhere to be elected president of the United States, it can be easy to forget that when *Brown v. Board of Education* was decided, only a utopian dreamer could have believed that a person of color would be elected president in his or her lifetime. As a delegate to the Democratic Convention that nominated Barack Obama replied when asked whether she ever thought that the dreams inspired by Martin Luther King Jr.'s great civil rights speech would come to pass in her lifetime, "About 10 years ago, I thought: I won't see this. This is something for my grandchildren."[201]

The rise of Obama to the presidency and the decision in *Brown* both came as surprises to most contemporaries. And because historians are trained to find those factors in the past that shaped the present, they have often treated the unexpected as, in retrospect, hardly surprising at all. "History," Philip Roth wryly observed, is "where everything unexpected in its own time is chronicled on the page as inevitable."[202] As Michael McFaul, former U.S. ambassador to Russia, wrote, "In retrospect, all revolutions seem inevitable. Beforehand, all revolutions seem impossible."[203] As I have indicated, my treatment of *Brown* is an effort to restore the sense of surprise, contingency, and historical discontinuity that the unanimous decision actually represented.

In August 1961, the same month in which Barack Obama was born, Gallup asked Americans whether they would vote for a Black person for president if their party nominated him. Forty-one percent said they would not, while 50 percent said they would, the first time that a majority of Americans said they would vote for an African American for president.[204] These polls themselves signified a shift in racial consciousness from just three or four years earlier. In September 1958 as the Little Rock crisis was unfolding, only 38 percent of the respondents said they would vote for an African American for president, while 54 percent said they would not.[205] A year later, 49 percent said they were prepared to vote for a Black person for president, while 46 percent said they were not.[206] To put the point another way, three Gallup polls between September 1958 and August 1961 showed that opposition to a Black president fell from 54 percent to 46 percent and then to 41 percent. Fortunately, various polling organizations continued to ask this same question seven more times between 1961 and 1978. The results provide us with one of the best measures of change in white racial consciousness available. Between 1958 and 1978, the percent of respondents who said they were prepared to vote for an African American for president grew from 38 percent to 76 percent.[207]

My goal now is to borrow from William Julius Wilson's perceptions in his *The Declining Significance of Race*.[208] Wilson argues that increased access to voting in the 1960s produced a "political resurgence for black Americans" that "increased their sense of power, raised their expectations," and provided the foundation for the "proliferation of demands" that "shaped the black revolt during the sixties."[209] Meanwhile, the growth of a Black middle class in the cities contributed to "expanding occupational opportunities," enabling "a small but significant number of blacks [to] upgrade their occupations, increase their incomes, and improve their standard of living."[210] As a result, Wilson argues, "the problem for blacks today . . . is no longer one of legalized racial inequality. . . . With the passage of equal employment legislation and the authorization of affirmative action, the government has helped clear that path for more privileged blacks, who have the requisite education and training to enter the mainstreams of American occupations."[211]

At this point, one would wish to invite into the discussion the cultural historian who might identify the actual mechanisms by which popular consciousness on the race question was transformed. Left to my own devices, unfortunately, it will be necessary to offer my own simple sketch of the process. There are two basic propositions. The first is that during the half century after *Brown*—in significant part as a result of *Brown*—the Black middle class grew substantially. Perhaps the best measure of Black entry into the middle class is the percentage of Black college graduates. From 1955 to 1990, the number of college students aged eighteen to twenty-four who were Black grew from 4.9 percent to 11.3 percent. Between 1987 and 2007, the percentage of Black adults with bachelor's degrees grew from 11 percent to 17 percent.[212]

The growth of a Black middle class was accompanied by a somewhat separate phenomenon: an increased acceptance and identification by whites of African American cultural figures. Nat King Cole, Sidney Poitier, Bill Cosby, and, in our own time, Oprah Winfrey were each influential in changing white perceptions of Black people. Through these figures, many white people arrived at the conclusion that "they're not that different from me," and in the case of Winfrey, large numbers of whites have actually treated her as a cultural prophet.[213]

If we look for signs of acceptance of Black people in public service, the first important gains came before *Brown* with President Truman's desegregation of the federal civil service. But mostly life continued as before *Brown*. By 1961, the year of Obama's birth, the only African American ever to be appointed to the federal bench, Judge William Hastie of the Third Circuit, continued to be the sole Black judge in the federal system.[214] He was joined in 1962 by President John F. Kennedy's appointment of Thurgood Marshall to the Second Circuit Court of Appeals.[215] Between the Hastie and Marshall appointments thirteen years had passed, including the entire eight years of the Eisenhower presidency, without a single Black nomination to the federal bench. When Obama was born, no African American had yet been elected a state governor or U.S. senator since Reconstruction, nor had any Black person served in the president's cabinet. The first Black ambassador was appointed in 1967. The first big-city Black mayors to be elected, both in 1967, were Carl Stokes in Cleveland, Ohio, and Richard Hatcher in Gary, Indiana. In 1961, just four African Americans served in Congress: from Chicago (since 1943), New York (since 1945), Detroit (since 1955), and Philadelphia (since 1958). In 2008, there would be forty-two Black members of the Congressional Black Caucus.

If these characterizations of major changes in white consciousness during the decades after *Brown* are correct, it should not be too difficult to show that *Brown* was a major factor in producing this change in consciousness. If that is so, then *Brown* was clearly a great success.

3

STANDING UP
TO MCCARTHYISM

When Senator Joseph R. McCarthy of Wisconsin delivered his notorious Wheeling, West Virginia, speech on February 9, 1950, claiming—but never proving—that there were a large number of communists in the U.S. government, he formally inaugurated what came to be called McCarthyism. It is misleading, however, to think of the anticommunist hysteria that gripped the United States during the 1950s as the work of any one person.[1] Though McCarthy was an appalling liar and a cynical manipulator of popular anxieties, it is wrong to simply demonize him. The historical explanation of the McCarthy era must acknowledge the broad social forces that were at work, beyond the influence of any single individual.[2] Without the active collaboration of many people—including future president Richard M. Nixon, then an unknown second-term congressman, as well as much of the conservative Republican establishment led by Ohio senator Robert A. Taft—and the passive acquiescence of many others, McCarthy could never have become the prominent and powerful demagogue after whom an entire era was named.[3]

Dated in terms of the life of the junior senator from Wisconsin, the McCarthy era would have ended not long after it began. McCarthy was unknown outside Wisconsin before his 1950 speech, and his political fortunes began to decline just four years later when he rashly attacked President Dwight Eisenhower and the U.S. Army for being "soft on Communism."[4] The resulting Army-McCarthy congressional hearings marked the end of McCarthy's period of greatest influence. From that time on, he was increasingly abandoned even by his own Republican Party. By the end of 1954 after the Senate had passed a resolution condemning McCarthy, he rapidly degenerated into acute alcoholism and died in 1957. As measured by McCarthy's own personal influence, then, the McCarthy era lasted hardly five years.

In fact, however, the anticommunist hysteria that bears the name McCarthyism began well before McCarthy's entry onto the scene and did not end until long after his death.[5] The hysteria led to a large number of attacks on the loyalty of individuals and organizations: on communists, former communists, and "fellow travelers"; on government and union officials; and on Hollywood actors, screen writers, and many other artists.[6] Numerous government officials were dismissed from their jobs without a hearing or any proof or documentation of their alleged "disloyalty," including many homosexuals who were dismissed as "security risks."[7] Dishonorable discharges of gays from the armed forces also greatly increased for the same set of specious reasons. Openly gay couples were dismissed for "bad moral character," while those whose secret sex lives were discovered were dismissed because they were vulnerable to blackmail. Many scientists and engineers had their professional lives destroyed by denial of security clearances necessary for working in defense-related industries.[8] High school teachers and university professors were thrown out of jobs, at times without knowing who had accused them or what they had been accused of. Some had refused as a matter of conscience to sign loyalty oaths, which rapidly proliferated as a condition of employment required by federal, state, and local governments.[9] Many people were denied passports to travel abroad. Others who had lived most of their lives in the United States but had never become American citizens were summarily expelled from the country without any formal legal proceedings. Foreigners were frequently barred from entering the United States to lecture, travel, or study.[10]

The origins of McCarthyism can be traced to the emergence of the Cold War as the World War II alliance against Nazism between the United States and the Soviet Union began to collapse. From the time of former British prime minister Winston Churchill's famous 1946 warning that an Iron Curtain was descending over Europe, the level of postwar American anxiety had begun to soar. Within a very short time, the Soviets set up puppet regimes in Eastern Europe and aided the communists in the Greek Civil War.[11] The announcement in 1949 that the Soviet Union had tested an atomic bomb, years before anyone in the West had thought possible, dramatically punctured the sense of security that two oceans had for so long provided and also encouraged demagogues such as McCarthy to contend that the Soviets had received the secret of the bomb from spies inside the American government.[12] McCarthy's cry that there had been "twenty years of treason" dating all the way back to the beginning of President Franklin Roosevelt's New Deal was initially greeted with enthusiasm by his fellow Republicans. The newly powerful discourse of American anticommunism was welcomed by the political Right as an avenue for attacking the New Deal and its legacy.[13]

The fall of China to the communists in 1949 and the invasion of South Korea by communist North Korea in 1950 magnified the feeling that the world was falling to the communists. The American-led defense of South Korea soon triggered a massive Chinese communist intervention in the Korean War and for a time raised the real possibility of an American military defeat.[14] Anticommunist hysteria spread throughout the United States as a "witch hunt" for domestic traitors and spies served the psychological function of displacing responsibility for foreign military and diplomatic disasters.

Though anticommunism had long been a feature of American political life, the new hysteria demanded ever more elaborate mechanisms for seeking out and destroying imagined enemies within. Much of the repressive machinery that had been put into place before World War II for rooting out Nazi and fascist spies was rapidly redeployed against communist and leftist opponents. To give three major examples:

- The House Un-American Activities Committee (HUAC), originally created in 1938 to monitor pro-German elements in the United States as well as communist activity, stepped up the pace of its investigations, turning all its force against suspected communists and "fellow travelers."[15]
- The Smith Act, passed in 1940 while Nazi Germany and Stalinist Russia were short-lived allies after having entered into a nonaggression pact, made it a criminal offense to advocate the violent overthrow of the U.S. government or to join any organization that advocated overthrow.[16] The Smith Act was used to prosecute members of the Socialist Workers Party as early as 1941 but was rarely used during World War II.[17] The Smith Act was dusted off in 1948 to prosecute eleven of the top leaders of the American Communist Party, who were sentenced to substantial jail terms.[18]
- The director of the Federal Bureau of Investigation (FBI), J. Edgar Hoover, quickly realized that he could massively expand his organizational and personal power by shifting from an anticrime to an anticommunist mission while using national security as an excuse to build files based on surveillance and wiretapping of domestic "security risks." Until his death in 1972, these files enabled Hoover to blackmail and terrorize politicians and public officials.[19]

Two highly publicized trials involving accusations of espionage heightened and focused anticommunist hysteria. After Alger Hiss was convicted of perjury in 1950 for denying that he had transmitted official documents to an admitted communist, Whittaker Chambers, the American public was prepared to believe that communist sympathizers and spies were everywhere. A graduate of the Harvard Law School and a law clerk to Justice Oliver Wendell Holmes, Hiss had risen to a high-ranking State Department position. There were no other proven examples of disloyalty at Hiss's level. Nevertheless, his conviction (in a second trial after a hung jury refused to convict in the first trial) seemed to confirm

McCarthyite accusations of pro-Soviet infiltration of the highest levels of the U.S. government and especially of widespread disloyalty among the privileged Eastern establishment. More recent evidence from post-Soviet intelligence files has strengthened the claim that Hiss was a Soviet agent.[20]

By 1953 when Julius and Ethel Rosenberg were executed after having been convicted of delivering the secret of the atomic bomb to a Soviet agent—an accusation apparently without scientific merit—Americans were experiencing a deep loss of control in a world that seemed to be turning against them. After Chief Justice Fred Vinson in an unprecedented move hastily reconvened the Supreme Court during its summer recess to overturn Justice William Douglas's stay of the Rosenbergs' execution, it appeared that even the high court had been swept up in the anticommunist hysteria.[21]

THE SUPREME COURT, MCCARTHYISM, AND THE FIRST AMENDMENT

In 1949, just as anticommunist fervor was approaching its peak, Justices Frank Murphy, age fifty-nine, and Wiley Rutledge, age fifty-five, died within two months of each other. During the previous six years, along with Justices Hugo Black and Douglas (and, until he died in 1946, Chief Justice Harlan Stone), they had formed the most solid pro–civil liberties bloc in the history of the Supreme Court. The deaths of Murphy and Rutledge, at a time when President Harry Truman was bending to congressional anticommunist demagoguery, allowed Truman to appease right-wing forces by appointing two conservative justices, Tom Clark and Sherman Minton. Clark and Minton substantially strengthened the conservative wing of the Supreme Court led by Justice Felix Frankfurter. During some of the worst infringements on civil liberties in American history, the Frankfurter wing was ready to uphold virtually every repressive governmental measure justified in the name of national security.

Frankfurter believed that judicial restraint was necessary in order for the court to retain its legitimacy in a constitutional democracy. He had developed these views in reaction to the so-called *Lochner* era of the early twentieth century, when the Supreme Court had intruded into the political process to strike down as unconstitutional laws that were designed to reform the economic and social system. It was Frankfurter's position that the court could retain its own influence and prestige only by deferring to legislative judgment except where the legislature had acted completely unreasonably. The result of these views during the McCarthy era was that the court simply rubber-stamped congressional and state laws that interfered with freedom of speech and expression.

The most notorious example of the court's capitulation to the forces of repression occurred in *Dennis v. United States* (1951),[22] in which the eleven top leaders of the American Communist Party were convicted under the Smith Act for advocating the violent overthrow of the U.S. government. The case raised the question of whether individuals could be convicted for mere speech and if so whether there were constitutional limits on the government's power to punish speech. By a 6–2 vote, the court upheld the convictions.[23] The leading opinion by Chief Justice Vinson, another of Truman's appointees, seemed to undermine thoroughly the "clear and present danger" test for determining under what circumstances government could interfere with speech.

Since the "clear and present danger" standard will preoccupy us throughout our study of Warren Court decisions involving freedom of expression, we should pause for a moment and try to understand the constitutional issues that the court faced. Justice Oliver Wendell Holmes originally formulated the clear and present danger test in *Schenck v. United States* (1919) for the purpose of distinguishing between constitutionally protected speech and speech that fell outside the protection of the First Amendment and could thus be punished.[24] Holmes's famous example of falsely shouting "Fire!" in a crowded theater was designed to illustrate the kind of speech that presented such a clear and present danger of causing injury that it could legitimately be punished.[25] As the clear and present danger test was refined during the 1920s in famous Holmes-Brandeis dissents in *Abrams, Gitlow,* and *Whitney,* the resulting formula meant that speech could not be punished under the test unless it raised the threat of substantial and imminent danger.[26] The clear and present danger standard, they argued, was the best means of encouraging a "free trade in ideas" while fostering democratic citizenship.[27]

When a New Deal majority was finally consolidated in 1937, it was forced to confront the status of the Holmes-Brandeis free speech dissents. The question of whether the U.S. Constitution accorded a "preferred position" to First Amendment protections of freedom of expression almost immediately split the new majority. Justices Rutledge and Murphy, along with Black and Douglas, favored increased protection of First Amendment freedoms. On the other hand, Justice Frankfurter, who had long opposed the *Lochner* majority's judicial activism in striking down social and economic legislation, maintained that consistency required equal judicial deference to legislation affecting freedom of speech.[28]

By the time the Supreme Court upheld the criminal convictions of the top American communist leaders in *Dennis* two years after the deaths of Rutledge and Murphy, Frankfurter's position prevailed. Only Justices Black and Douglas, the two dissenters in *Dennis,* still held the Holmes-Brandeis view that the Constitution accorded a preferred position to the First Amendment. *Dennis* was especially significant, because although it purported to adopt the Holmes-Brandeis version of the clear and present danger standard, it actually eviscerated that standard by reformulating it as a balancing test. Under the *Dennis* balancing test, the government's interest in suppressing speech in order to avoid danger was weighed against the individual speaker's First Amendment interest. Such a test gave the government much more leeway to enact measures repressive of political speech. *Dennis* marked the nadir of Supreme Court protection of free speech after World War II.[29]

Much of Frankfurter's concurring opinion in *Dennis* highlighted his opposition to according First Amendment freedoms a preferred position as well as to his insistence on deferring to the judgment of the legislature. He set forth briefly the preferred position argument he so vehemently opposed: "Some members of the Court . . . have suggested that our function in reviewing statutes restricting freedom of expression differs sharply from our normal duty in sitting in judgment on legislation. . . . It has been suggested, with the casualness of a footnote [i.e., *Carolene Products*], that such legislation is not presumptively valid . . . , and it has been weightily reiterated that freedom of speech has a 'preferred position.'"[30] He then proceeded at length to explain why this position was unacceptable.

Frankfurter also stressed the need to use a balancing test: "The demands of free speech . . . as well as the interest in national security are better served by . . . weighing of the competing interests," he declared, adding that "no matter how rapidly we utter the phrase 'clear and present danger,' . . . [it is] not a substitute for the weighing of values. . . . The complex issues presented by regulation of speech . . . [should be] resolved by scrutiny of many factors besides the imminence and gravity of the evil threatened."[31]

Frankfurter then proceeded at length to explain why even free speech cases should be subject to the balancing principle. "Free-speech cases are not an exception to the principle that we are not legislators. . . . How best to reconcile competing interests is the business of legislatures, and the balance they strike is a judgment not to be displaced by ours, but to be respected unless outside the pale of fair judgment."[32] He concluded, "We are to set aside [Congress's] judgment . . . only if there is no reasonable basis for it. . . . Above all we must remember that this Court's power of judicial review is not 'an exercise of the powers of a super-legislature.'"[33]

RED MONDAY, JUNE 17, 1957:
THE COURT PUTS LIMITS ON MCCARTHYISM

Until Justice William Brennan took his seat in mid-October 1956, the Frankfurter position dominated the court's free speech jurisprudence. But there was a dramatic shift during the 1956 term, Brennan's first on the court, as the Supreme Court handed down a series of decisions that began to turn the tide against

McCarthyite legislation. Within a few years, as we shall see, Justice Brennan became the major intellectual force on the court in shaping and extending constitutional protections of freedom of expression well beyond any point that Holmes, Brandeis, or Stone could ever have thought possible.

The most important case decided during the 1956 term was *Yates v. United States*,[34] in which the Supreme Court overturned Smith Act convictions of fourteen so-called "second string" communist leaders. *Yates* was one of several major cases decided on June 17, 1957, denounced by its opponents as "Red Monday," that appeared to signal that the court was finally prepared to move against McCarthyism.[35] Justice John Marshall Harlan, a conservative appointed two years earlier by President Eisenhower, delivered an opinion that cast doubt on whether the court would ever again sustain prosecutions of communists under the Smith Act.

Harlan first dismissed convictions under the "organize" clause of the Smith Act, holding that they were barred by the statute of limitations. He then focused on those counts, like those in *Dennis*, that charged the defendants with advocating the violent overthrow of the government and reversed all of the convictions based on advocacy. Introducing a distinction between constitutionally unprotected "advocacy of action" and constitutionally protected "advocacy in the abstract," Harlan concluded that the First Amendment protects advocacy of "abstract doctrine," as opposed to advocacy of direct action or "incitement" to illegal action against the government.[36] Holding that there was insufficient evidence of incitement—as opposed to abstract discussion—against the *Yates* defendants, Harlan reversed the convictions after concluding that the evidence was too weak to warrant a conviction.

In two other major decisions delivered on Red Monday, *Watkins v. United States*[37] and *Sweezy v. New Hampshire*,[38] the court set limits on the investigative power of legislative investigating committees. In *Watkins*, Chief Justice Earl Warren for the first time questioned the power of HUAC, which had developed into one of the central institutions for exploiting anticommunist hysteria. One can trace the rising curve of its influence. A decade earlier, few members of the House of Representatives had wanted to serve on the committee; by the time *Watkins* was decided, publicity-hungry congressmen were lining up for assignment to HUAC and similar investigative committees that had been established in the Senate.

HUAC's most notorious activity was to hold public hearings at which those who were willing to recant their communist-sympathizing past were required to engage in public repentance and self-humiliation. Sincere repentance was measured by witnesses' willingness to give the names of those who had participated with them in a suspect organization. For those whose consciences would not permit them to involve others, a very different ritual evolved. These unwilling witnesses typically pleaded the Fifth Amendment, claiming that their refusal to testify was based on the concern that they might incriminate themselves by offering testimony that could subsequently be used against them in a criminal trial. Senator McCarthy regularly denounced them as "Fifth Amendment Communist[s]," and many of them were fired from their jobs after invoking their constitutional rights.[39]

Those who did plead the Fifth Amendment before either HUAC or the multiplying number of other congressional committees that joined in the chase were faced with another dilemma. The legal rule that one could not answer some questions and plead the Fifth to others forced witnesses to invoke the Fifth Amendment from the beginning of their testimony. Congressional investigators made the most of the spectacle of witnesses who repeatedly claimed their Fifth Amendment privilege in answer to a series of innocent-sounding questions. Those witnesses who stood on their consciences by refusing to name names were portrayed as completely uncooperative and contemptuous of Congress. As the television era was dawning, the image of so-called Fifth Amendment communists who were unreasonably hostile to congressional inquiries reached the entire nation. While these witnesses might have been willing to testify about their own past activities, any cooperation might trap them into having to answer every question, which would inevitably involve others.[40]

Some witnesses who were unwilling to misrepresent their reasons for refusing to answer by claiming the Fifth, which could only be legitimately invoked out of personal fear of future prosecution, took the courageous step of claiming instead a First Amendment right of freedom of expression. Invoking the protection of the First Amendment was risky; many who did so were convicted of contempt of Congress and jailed. In fact, contempt citations were issued with hitherto unheard-of frequency during the McCarthy era. In the 150 years from 1792 to 1942, only 108 contempt citations were issued by the entire Congress, fewer than 1 per year; during the brief period 1945–1957, HUAC alone issued 135 contempt citations.[41] Playwright Arthur Miller was one of the many convicted of contempt of Congress (his conviction was later overturned) for declining on the ground of irrelevancy to answer some of HUAC's questions about people he had known in the past.[42] HUAC's power to issue contempt charges provided a major incentive for witnesses to comply with its demands.

Chief Justice Warren's opinion in *Watkins v. United States* marked the first time that the Supreme Court had interfered with the witch-hunting powers of a congressional committee. As a direct challenge to congressional power, his opinion represented a politically dangerous move by a Supreme Court already facing mounting "massive resistance" in the South to the *Brown* decision.

Warren did not deny a broad power in Congress to authorize any investigation into communist subversion that it wished. The problem in *Watkins*, he said, was that there was no clear authorization by the House of Representatives to HUAC to conduct this particular investigation.[43] "There is no congressional power to expose for the sake of exposure," Warren declared.[44] Thus, while it was still theoretically possible after *Watkins* for the House to simply authorize every future HUAC investigation, the decision required every member of Congress for the first time to take personal responsibility for the outrages committed by congressional witch-hunters. Barely a month after Senator McCarthy's death, Chief Justice Warren probably sensed that the tide had already begun to turn and that HUAC was becoming an embarrassment. In both *Watkins* and *Sweezy*, the four liberals (Warren, Black, Douglas and Brennan) voted to reverse the contempt convictions. They were joined, but on more limited grounds, by Frankfurter and Harlan.

The Warren opinion in *Watkins* offered a confusing blend of broad and narrow as well as constitutional and statutory grounds for reversal. Early in his opinion, the chief justice introduced the Bill of Rights and, in particular, the First Amendment as potential limitations on the otherwise "broad" authority of Congress to investigate.[45] He then shifted to a search for a "legislative purpose" behind the investigation, concluding that none was clearly shown in the vague resolution authorizing the committee's activities or in other committee communications.[46] At this point, Warren's opinion seems headed for the conclusion that without a clear authorizing resolution, HUAC had no authority to investigate, a conclusion that would have shut down the committee until Congress acted to produce a clear authorization. Instead, Warren turned to the federal criminal statute authorizing punishment for contempt and noted that it is conditioned on refusal to answer a "pertinent" question.[47] So, he rightly concludes that "pertinency" of a committee question is a precondition for holding in contempt a defendant who refuses to answer. Since the defendant in *Watkins* had raised the pertinency objection to the HUAC questions on his own from the beginning of his testimony, it was not necessary for Warren to emphasize the statute. But the chief justice did conclude that without knowledge of the purpose of the investigation, it was impossible for Watkins to determine whether the questions he was asked were indeed pertinent.[48]

Frankfurter penned an aggressively separate *Watkins* concurrence to Warren's opinion. It began with "I deem it important to state what I understand to be the Court's holding. Agreeing with its holding, I join its opinion."[49] He then proceeded to explicitly limit Warren's holding to the "pertinency" objection and to join Warren's opinion on that basis. Frankfurter was thus suggesting that Warren's broader pronouncements ought not to be binding on future courts.

But Frankfurter failed to mention that Harlan had silently joined Warren's opinion, thus providing the chief justice with a majority. Oddly, Harlan's join occurred soon after he was recorded as having stated in conference that he "agree[d] with Frankfurter on relevancy."[50] Nor did this prevent Frankfurter in a private letter to Harlan months later from referring to "that 'god-awful *Watkins* opinion,'"[51] as if Harlan had been with him all along. And it did not prevent Harlan, along with Frankfurter, from separating himself from Warren's opinion in *Sweezy v. New Hampshire.*

Warren's *Sweezy* opinion was no more expansive than his *Watkins* pronouncement had been except that it arose out of state legal proceedings and therefore drew on the justices' attitudes towards federalism. One year earlier in *Roth* and *Alberts*, two obscenity cases, Harlan introduced his notion that state power to punish obscenity was greater than federal power because the First Amendment acted directly on Congress, while the Due Process Clause of the Fourteenth Amendment provided for less federal intrusion on state decision-making. It may be that Harlan continued to make such a distinction in arriving at his surprisingly different votes in *Watkins* and *Sweezy.*

Frankfurter meanwhile not only wrote a separate opinion in *Sweezy*, as he had done in *Watkins*, but this time also refused to join Warren's opinion. Instead, Frankfurter delivered an analysis of why, even under the Fourteenth Amendment's Due Process Clause, *Sweezy* should not be held in contempt.

Paul Sweezy, a prominent Marxist economist, had been called before a New Hampshire investigating committee, where he testified that he had never been a communist and had never advocated violent political change. However, he refused to answer two sets of questions. The first set was related to his activities in the recently formed Progressive Party; the second set was related to a classroom lecture he had given at the University of New Hampshire.[52]

Frankfurter found in the Due Process Clause "principles" of political autonomy and academic freedom and, in one of his finest opinions, held that the state had failed to offer sufficient justification for its intrusions.[53] It has been noticed that the former professor was able to deliver a truly eloquent defense of academic freedom but never succeeded in producing a similarly powerful justification of freedom of speech.

One would have concluded at the time that Frankfurter had separated himself from Warren's *Sweezy* opinion, as he had from the *Watkins* opinion, primarily because it highlighted the vagueness of the authorization resolution. Frankfurter's analysis instead sought to demonstrate that the Fourteenth Amendment was rich enough to protect Sweezy's political and academic freedom without invoking the Bill of Rights. If anyone seemed bent on creating a watered-down First Amendment, it was Justice Harlan, who seemed ready to extend the application of his *Roth* and *Alberts* distinction beyond the obscenity field. But as we shall see in chapter 4, six months after his opinion in *Sweezy* Frankfurter did clearly embark on a campaign to water down the First Amendment when it was applied to the states through the Fourteenth. Though it was hardly noticed at the time, *Sweezy v. New Hampshire* may have been an early example of Frankfurter's effort to extend his anti-incorporation philosophy to the First Amendment.

1957–1962: THE COURT IN RETREAT

The Supreme Court's 1957 shift turned out to be temporary; it would be misleading to conclude that its Red Monday decisions constituted a sudden and lasting victory over McCarthyite legislation. Until 1962, when Arthur Goldberg's appointment finally did shift the balance of power on the court, a solid five-person majority continued to regularly uphold Cold War legislation.

One set of cases strikingly illustrates the court majority's continuing reluctance to interfere with repressive governmental action. In *Konigsberg v. State Bar of California* (1957) (*Konigsberg I*),[54] Justice Black reversed a decision of State Bar of California examiners refusing Raphael Konigsberg a license to practice law after he declined to answer questions directed at finding out whether he had ever been a communist. In a quite technical opinion based on rules of evidence, Black held that the bar examiners made unwarranted inferences of bad moral character from Konigsberg's failure to answer. He sent the case back to the examiners to reconsider their conclusion.

Four years later after the state bar once again rejected Konigsberg's petition for admission, the court, in a 5–4 opinion by Justice Harlan in *Konigsberg II* (1961),[55] upheld the bar examiners' continuing refusal to license Konigsberg to practice law. This time, the bar examiners defended their rejection on the slightly different ground that Konigsberg's refusal to answer had obstructed the committee's investigation, not that it directly illustrated bad moral character. This distinction may have been drawn from two other Harlan opinions delivered shortly after he joined the court.

In his first term on the court, Harlan confronted the clash between individual constitutional rights and the intrusive claims of legislative investigations to inquire into subversive activities. With Harlan dissenting in *Slochower v. Board of Education* (1956),[56] the court, by a 5–4 vote, struck down a New York City charter provision that required summary dismissal of any government employee who refused to answer a question concerning his official duties. Harry Slochower, a tenured professor of German and comparative literature at Brooklyn College, challenged his automatic dismissal after he pleaded the Fifth Amendment before the Senate Internal Security Committee.

When called before the committee in 1952, Slochower had stated that he was not a member of the Communist Party and indicated complete willingness to answer questions concerning his associations or political beliefs since 1941. But he refused to answer questions concerning his membership during 1940 and 1941 on the ground that the answers might tend to incriminate him.

For a five-person majority, Justice Clark—normally among the most fervent of the court's anticommunists—struck down the New York law requiring automatic dismissal. "The privilege against self-incrimination would be reduced to a hollow mockery," Clark wrote, "if its exercise could be taken as equivalent either to a confession of guilt or a conclusive presumption of perjury."[57]

Harlan dissented. The cases, he wrote, had already established that knowing membership in an organization dedicated to the forcible overthrow of the government was a ground for disqualification from public school teaching. Likewise, it was already established "that public school teachers shall furnish information as to their past or present membership in the Communist Party, [which] is a relevant step in the implementation of such a state policy, and a teacher may be discharged for refusing to comply with that requirement."[58]

Harlan then added a second justification: "Moreover, I think a State may justifiably consider that teachers who refuse to answer questions concerning their official conduct are no longer qualified for public school teaching, on the ground that their refusal to answer jeopardizes the confidence that the public should have in its school system."[59]

It was not too great a step from this statement in Harlan's *Slochower* dissent to his assertion in *Lerner v. Casey* (1958) that a New York City subway conductor who refused to answer an official investigator's question about whether he was a communist could be dismissed because of "doubtful trust and reliability,"[60] nor was it a great leap from his joining the five-person Supreme Court majority that held that a Philadelphia schoolteacher's refusal to answer an investigator's questions about whether he was a communist was grounds for dismissal. The court held that the questions were relevant to his fitness and suitability as a teacher, and his discharge was based on his insubordination and lack of frankness and candor in refusing to answer such questions, not on disloyalty or any of the activities inquired about.[61]

There was a profound irony in the Supreme Court upholding a person's dismissal for lack of "frankness and candor" in an opinion whose disingenuous effort to avoid First Amendment scrutiny was itself lacking in such frankness and candor.

Between 1955, when Harlan ascended the Supreme Court bench, and 1962, when punishments for contempt by committees investigating subversion began to diminish, Harlan voted regularly against the parties who claimed some constitutional right to refuse to answer. The only exceptions are Harlan's ambivalent votes in *Watkins* and *Sweezy*, which he himself did his best to undermine if not overrule only two years later. Similarly, in *Konigsberg II* (1959) the court backed away from Black's earlier effort to limit the personal damage that might result from youthful political decisions.

In three other major areas, a five-person Cold War majority continued to endorse politically repressive governmental measures during the years immediately before Arthur Goldberg replaced Justice Frankfurter in 1962. In 1961, the court reviewed two cases involving convictions under the "membership" clause of the Smith Act. Acknowledging that conviction for mere membership would raise serious constitutional questions, Harlan followed his earlier *Yates* strategy of limiting the "membership clause" to "active and purposive membership, purposive that is as to the organization's criminal ends."[62] The effort to prove "purposive membership" would require showing "specific intent," which would return the inquiry to the earlier *Yates* distinction between teaching and incitement. In *Noto v. United States*,[63] Justice Harlan refocused on the *Yates* distinction between "advocacy in the abstract" and "advocacy of action" and held that there was insufficient evidence of the latter to convict for "purposive membership."[64] But in *Scales v. United States* he did find enough evidence of advocacy of action to uphold a conviction of the chairman of the North and South Carolina Communist Party.[65] The widespread assumption that Harlan's earlier reversal of the convictions of the "second-string" leaders of the Communist Party in *Yates* had signaled the end of Smith Act convictions turned out to be mistaken. Instead, Harlan would be remembered for writing the last opinion to uphold a conviction under the Smith Act.

Harlan worked hard to woo newly appointed Justice Potter Stewart to join his opinion as the fifth vote. But Stewart was skeptical that there was any more evidence in *Scales* of active incitement to illegal activity than there was in *Yates*, where Harlan had reversed all fourteen cases for lack of evidence of active advocacy.

Harlan cited evidence in *Scales* of an FBI undercover agent who testified that Scales's school taught the students "how to kill a person with a pencil,"[66] thus offering requisite proof of "active and purposive membership."[67] Skeptical of the testimony of "paid undercover agents," who "were the principal source of evidence against Scales," Harlan's biographer, Tinsley Yarbrough, sees Harlan's *Scales* opinion as having made Junius Scales "a sacrificial lamb" to the "surgery" that Harlan felt he needed to perform on the "membership clause" in his "effort to avoid a direct challenge to Congress' authority in a very controversial field."[68] In the process, Harlan also affirmed Scales's sentence of six years, the longest sentence of any Smith Act defendant including the leaders of the Communist Party in *Dennis*.

Ironically, one can be confident that if the *Scales* case had come before the Supreme Court only one year later, the four dissenters in *Scales*—Warren, Douglas, Black, and Brennan—would have been joined by newly appointed

Justice Goldberg to overturn Scales's conviction. Moreover, the pipeline of convicted defendants would soon be emptied after newly appointed attorney general Robert Kennedy, upon taking office in 1961, announced that he was ending Smith Act prosecutions.

In a second 5–4 decision in 1961, *Communist Party v. Subversive Activities Control Board*,[69] Justice Frankfurter upheld the forced registration of the Communist Party under another McCarthyite law, the Internal Security Act or Subversive Activities Control Act of 1950 (generally known as the McCarran Act). Even though registration brought real potential harm to members of the party, including denial of tax exemptions, denial of passports, labeling of mail, possible self-incrimination, restrictions on employment in defense plants or labor unions, and disqualification from naturalized citizenship, Justice Frankfurter called these "abstract assertions of possible future injur[ies]," too hypothetical to consider in the present case.[70] Frankfurter's decision, however, would prove to be the swan song of the McCarran Act, just as *Scales* had been for the Smith Act. After Goldberg's appointment in 1962, the court never again upheld enforcement of McCarran Act provisions against an American citizen.

The court also reverted to Cold War orthodoxy after 1957 in cases that challenged the constitutionality of legislative investigations. In *Barenblatt v. United States* (1959),[71] the Cold War majority turned its back on the spirit of Chief Justice Warren's *Watkins* opinion. A 5–4 decision by Justice Harlan upheld a contempt citation against a university instructor who claimed First Amendment rights of freedom of speech and association in refusing to answer HUAC questions about his political beliefs and associations.

Harlan's opinion followed Frankfurter's earlier strategy of reading *Watkins* narrowly as a holding on pertinency.[72] Since Barenblatt had not made a pertinency objection, Harlan reasoned, *Watkins* could be ignored.[73] Though Harlan dismissed the pertinency claim in *Barenblatt* on the ground that Barenblatt had failed to make any formal objection during the legislative investigation,[74] he missed the point of Warren's reliance on pertinency in *Watkins*. Warren had found the pertinency standard contained in the federal criminal contempt statute. The standard put the burden on the state to establish pertinency as part of the definition of contempt.[75]

The next step in Justice Harlan's *Barenblatt* analysis represented the crucial moment at which the spirit of *Watkins* was abandoned. Warren had been emphatic that the Bill of Rights and especially the First Amendment stood as significant limitations on the power of congressional investigators to compel answers to their questions. In *Barenblatt*, by contrast, Justice Harlan virtually obliterated the First Amendment as a constitutional limitation on legislative power. Applying a balancing test, he concluded that the governmental interest in national security outweighed Barenblatt's First Amendment rights.[76]

Justice Black's powerful dissent, in which the chief justice and Justice Douglas joined, exposed Harlan's misuse of balancing tests. Black showed that Harlan had misapplied the test by weighing the state's interest in "self-preservation" against Barenblatt's right to free expression. "At most," Black wrote, Harlan's opinion "balances the right of the Government to preserve itself, against Barenblatt's right to refrain from revealing Communist affiliations. Such a balance . . . mistakes the factors to be weighed." Among those factors, "it completely leaves out . . . the interest of the people as a whole in being able to join organizations, advocate causes and make political 'mistakes' without later being subjected to governmental penalties for having dared to think for themselves."[77] By purporting to balance the state's interest—"vastly overstated and called 'self-preservation'"—against Barenblatt's individual rights, Black observed, Justice Harlan had stacked the deck against any First Amendment claims.[78]

Moreover, *Barenblatt* offered no way of predicting the outcome of a balancing test. "On the Court's own test," Black wrote, "the issue is whether Barenblatt can know with sufficient certainty, at the time of his interrogation, that there is so compelling a need for his replies that infringement of his rights of free association is justified. The record does not disclose where Barenblatt can find what that need is."[79]

Unlike his liberal brethren, who suspiciously reviewed all Cold War legislation on the assumption that it constituted a dangerous threat to civil liberties, Harlan accepted the legitimacy of Cold War measures aimed at the Communist Party. It was justifiable to single out the Communist Party for special persecution, Harlan declared in *Barenblatt*, noting that "this Court . . . has consistently refused to view the Communist Party as an ordinary political party, and has upheld federal legislation aimed at the Communist problem which in a different context would certainly have raised constitutional issues of the gravest character."[80] Perhaps another unspoken factor in Harlan's distinction between *Watkins* and *Barenblatt* was that Watkins had agreed to testify about his own past, while Barenblatt had refused to do so.[81]

In an abrupt reversal of another of its Red Monday decisions, the court in *Uphaus v. Wyman* (1959)[82] by a 5–4 vote, appeared to overrule *Sweezy v. New Hampshire*. In what can only be described as a heavy-handed application of the *Barenblatt* balancing test, Justice Clark was able to "distinguish" *Sweezy* and uphold a New Hampshire civil contempt conviction against Willard Uphaus, executive director of the World Fellowship Center, for refusing to turn over guest lists of those who had attended his organization's summer camp. Clark recited the *Barenblatt* formula: "the governmental interest in self-preservation is sufficiently compelling to subordinate the interest in associational privacy."[83] Both Harlan and Frankfurter joined Clark's dubious effort to distinguish *Sweezy* on the ground that "the academic and political freedoms discussed in [*Sweezy*] are not present here in the same degree, since World Fellowship is neither a university nor a political party."[84] Nor did they question Clark's inappropriate application of the "self-preservation" test to what clearly was not a "Communist-front" organization.

Justice Brennan wrote a lengthy dissent detailing the operation of the New Hampshire investigating committee. He showed that the authorizing statute, which empowered the committee to search for "subversive persons or organizations" in New Hampshire, had in fact been used to bring about "exposure . . . for the sake of exposure."[85] While disclaiming the accuracy of its published list, the committee's report to the New Hampshire legislature publicized the names, addresses, and other private details of thirty-six possibly "subversive persons."[86] In upholding Uphaus's civil contempt conviction, the Supreme Court permitted New Hampshire to sentence the sixty-eight-year-old Methodist minister to spend almost one year in jail.

How do we account for the tortuous process by which the court between 1959 and 1962 seemed to flee from its earlier anti-McCarthy initiatives? What induced Justices Harlan and Frankfurter, who in 1957 concurred in several of these anti-McCarthy decisions, suddenly to forge a solid and inflexible bloc of five that regularly rubber-stamped all manner of repressive governmental activity?

The explanation seems to be the Jenner-Butler Bill, a "drastic anti-Court measure" that represented the immediate congressional reaction to Red Monday.[87] During the summer of 1957, a coalition of McCarthyite legislators and southern opponents of *Brown* sought to retaliate against the Supreme Court by introducing legislation that would have brought about the most significant reduction in the court's appellate jurisdiction since the post–Civil War years, barring the court from accepting or deciding cases in areas where its rulings had angered conservative members of Congress. One year later, the proposal was defeated in the Senate by one vote.[88] As one commentator noted, "The Court had escaped by the skin of its teeth; the . . . bill was clearly the high-water mark of congressional hostility to the Warren Court."[89]

1962–1969: THE DEMISE OF MCCARTHYISM

With Frankfurter's retirement and Goldberg's appointment in 1962, the court once again had a pro–civil liberties majority. After 1962 the court never again upheld punishment of an individual for refusing to answer questions before a legislative committee investigating communist activities.

In a series of cases after Goldberg's appointment, the court also indicated it would no longer enforce provisions of the McCarran Act. Effectively overruling Frankfurter's opinion in *Communist Party v. Subversive Activities Control*

Board (1961),[90] the court, per Justice Brennan, refused on self-incrimination grounds to force Communist Party members to register under the act.[91] In a second opinion, this one by Justice Goldberg, the court in *Aptheker v. Secretary of State* (1964)[92] also struck down as a violation of the right to travel a provision of the act denying passports to party members. And in *United States v. Robel* (1967),[93] the court held that the act's provision barring all members of communist-front organizations, "without regard to the quality and degree of membership," from being employed in defense plants was unconstitutionally overbroad.[94]

By this time, it had become common for southern opponents of desegregation to accuse civil rights organizations of being infiltrated by communists. Perhaps the most dramatic immediate result of Goldberg's appointment was to prevent this strategy from ever being endorsed by the court. The outcomes of two specific cases in the 1962 term dealing with harassment of the National Association for the Advancement of Colored People (NAACP) as a "subversive organization," *Gibson v. Florida Legislative Investigation Committee* (1963)[95] and *NAACP v. Button* (1963),[96] were actually reversed when Goldberg replaced Frankfurter after the cases had already been argued and voted on. In *Gibson*, a Florida legislative investigating committee sought to harass the Miami branch of the NAACP by ordering it to turn over its membership list on the grounds that it had been infiltrated by communists. Reargument transformed what had been a 5–4 decision upholding the committee's power into a 5–4 opinion written by Justice Goldberg holding that the committee had violated the organization's First Amendment rights.[97]

In *NAACP v. Button* (1963), dealing with the Commonwealth of Virginia's attempt to ban the NAACP under a statute forbidding improper solicitation of legal business, Frankfurter had already prepared a draft majority opinion upholding the Virginia law. Reargument after his retirement resulted in a victory for the NAACP on First Amendment grounds, a decision Frankfurter bitterly criticized, saying it resulted from the appointment of "such wholly inexperienced men as Goldberg . . . without familiarity with . . . the jurisprudence of the Court either as practitioners or scholars or judges."[98]

The stunning speed with which the court reversed its free speech jurisprudence after 1962 is best captured by its unanimous decision in *Brandenburg v. Ohio* (1969).[99] In that case, the court overturned the conviction of a leader of the Ohio Ku Klux Klan who had been prosecuted under that state's criminal syndicalism statute, which barred "'advocat[ing] . . . the duty, necessity, or propriety of crime, sabotage, violence, or unlawful methods of terrorism as a means of accomplishing industrial or political reform'" and "'voluntarily assembl[ing] with any society, group, or assemblage of persons formed to teach or advocate the doctrines of criminal syndicalism.'"[100]

Criminal syndicalism laws were widely adopted between 1917 and 1920 as part of the Red Scare that swept America after the Russian Revolution and specifically targeted the Industrial Workers of the World, a radical labor group. In *Whitney v. California* (1927),[101] the Supreme Court had upheld California's criminal syndicalism law, which was very similar to Ohio's, ruling that "'advocating' violent means to effect political and economic change involves such danger to the security of the State that the State may outlaw it."[102] Holmes and Brandeis had dissented on the free speech issue,[103] invoking the clear and present danger test, which might have exonerated the defendant. In *Brandenburg*, the court decisively overruled *Whitney* and, adopting the reasoning of the Holmes/Brandeis dissents, rejected the line of cases culminating in *Whitney* as "thoroughly discredited."[104] *Brandenburg* marked the triumph of the Holmes-Brandeis position that First Amendment freedoms could be abridged only in the case of a clear and imminent danger. "The constitutional guarantees of free speech and free press," the court wrote, "do not permit a State to forbid . . . advocacy of the use of force . . . except where such advocacy is directed to inciting or producing imminent lawless action and is likely to incite or produce such action."[105]

4

FELIX FRANKFURTER'S
LOST LEGACY, 1957–1962

Felix Frankfurter's last five years on the Supreme Court were dominated by a growing realization that his legacy was under siege. As the court returned from its summer recess in 1957, it began to dawn on the justice that the unrivaled influence he had exercised since 1949 was being increasingly contested. During the previous term his former Harvard Law School student, William J. Brennan, was appointed to the court, and despite Frankfurter's active efforts to woo him, Brennan soon began to chart an independent course. By the end of 1958 as the long-standing animosity between Frankfurter and William Douglas ignited once again, Frankfurter's growing self-absorption and increasing eccentricity also antagonized Earl Warren, Hugo Black, and even the genial Brennan.[1] In December 1958, Frankfurter was stricken with a mild heart attack, which caused him to miss several conferences of the justices.[2]

As the 1957 term opened in the fall, the court itself was also under siege. As we have seen, a powerful white backlash had already begun to build in the South. Combined with this escalating "massive resistance," the so-called Red Monday decisions handed down in June had helped to promote a lethal alliance between southern segregationists and strident anticommunists.[3] In July, the American Bar Association Special Committee on Communism delivered one of many unqualified rebukes of the court for being "soft" on communism. "If the courts lean too far backward in the maintenance of theoretical individual rights," warned the committee at its annual meeting in London, "it may be that we have tied the hands of our country and have rendered it incapable of carrying out the first law of mankind—the right of self-preservation."[4] The report added,

> We desire to record emphatically our approval of the organization and functioning of . . . the Senate Internal Security Committee and the House Un-American Activities Committee. . . . [T]hey have rendered immeasurable

service to the American people and . . . their operations have been of ines-
timable value in the defense of our country against those who would undermine our basic institutions.[5]

Even more ominously, also in July powerful U.S. senators attacked the
Supreme Court by targeting its greatest constitutional vulnerability: the congressional power to modify the court's jurisdiction.[6] The move ultimately failed
in the Senate by one vote but only after majority leader Lyndon B. Johnson
devoted his iron will to blocking it.[7] It represented the most ominous threat to
the Supreme Court's jurisdiction in almost a century.[8]

Ever ready to invoke the "lessons of *Lochner*," Frankfurter returned from
his summer break even more inclined than usual to criticize the court for
overreaching and for ignoring his preachments about the necessity of judicial
restraint.

In a September 30 memorandum to the conference, Frankfurter delivered
a thinly veiled attack on the chief justice's administration of the court's docket.
Specifically pointing to Red Monday little more than three months earlier,
Frankfurter criticized a supposed practice of "massing" cases near the term's
end. He thus implied that Warren, by mismanaging the court's docket and presenting an easy target for congressional discontent, bore some of the responsibility for the growing congressional backlash against the court.[9] After the
chief justice one week later circulated an elaborate table of scheduled cases that
sought to demonstrate that Frankfurter's criticism was inaccurate, Frankfurter
responded the same day, writing to the conference "in order to dissipate a
wrong impression that I have evidently created . . . that we purposefully so
conduct our business that we hand down numerous important opinions near
the end of the Term."[10]

Frankfurter's careful unwillingness to withdraw the implied charge of
mismanagement must have added to the growing estrangement between
Frankfurter and the chief justice, discussed elsewhere.[11]

Frankfurter's memo also draws our attention to his special sensitivity to
hostile congressional reaction, which sometimes grew to a nearly phobic fear of
the country's turning on the court. It was a sentiment that had been implanted
into Frankfurter's consciousness a half century earlier as progressives accused
the *Lochner* court of losing touch with the country. The memo foreshadows his
shift during the next three years to a consistent willingness to uphold repressive
anticommunist governmental activity.

We learned in chapter 2 that even before the regular 1958 term got under way,
the chief justice called the justices back early to hear arguments in *Cooper v.
Aaron* (1958),[12] the Little Rock, Arkansas, school desegregation case, the first

such case to come before the court since *Brown v. Board of Education.* During the interim, the southern white leadership had turned bitterly against *Brown,* and the justices had conspicuously avoided deciding cases that would add fuel to the fire.

The Little Rock school crisis triggered an intense desire to reassert the court's institutional authority in the face of widespread southern white resistance. There were solemn expressions among the justices of the wish to deliver a unanimous opinion as in *Brown,* this time supporting desegregation in the face of official resistance and mob violence. In this spirit, Justice John Marshall Harlan proposed what became the hallmark of the decision in *Cooper v. Aaron*: the unprecedented step of each of the nine justices individually signing the court's opinion.[13] Harlan explained that as three new justices had joined the court since *Brown,* there should be no doubt that each of the new justices (Harlan, Brennan, and Charles Evans Whittaker) also supported that decision.[14] After the court heard arguments on September 11, Justice Brennan was assigned the task of drafting what would be delivered as a per curiam opinion.[15] Although Frankfurter had appeared to go along with this plan, on September 26—three days before the opinion was scheduled to be announced—he delivered what Justice Douglas called a "bombshell."[16] Frankfurter told the justices that in addition to his individual signature, he would also file a separate concurrence.[17] The "Conference could not dissuade him from writing separately," Justice Burton noted in his diary, "but he agreed not to file his separate opinion until a week or so after the court opinion is filed."[18]

Chief Justice Warren recalled in his memoirs that Frankfurter's announcement "caused quite a sensation on the court,"[19] an observation that Bernard Schwartz later termed an "understatement."[20] Schwartz notes that by this time Warren's relations with Frankfurter had become so "touchy" that Warren needed to ask others to speak to the justice about withdrawing his opinion. Justice Black spoke to Frankfurter but without success. According to Douglas, "Harlan had spent several hours with Frankfurter trying to get him to alter some phraseology."[21] The net result of the episode, Schwartz noted, was that "Warren, Black, and Brennan were furious."[22] Warren experienced Frankfurter's reversal as a personal betrayal and regarded the incident as the last straw in the slow two-year deterioration of their relationship.[23]

Frankfurter's odd behavior may be traced back to September 11, the day the court heard argument in *Cooper v. Aaron* and immediately voted unanimously to uphold the court of appeals' reversal of the district court's thirty-month delay. At the conference, Chief Justice Warren assigned Justice Brennan the task of writing an opinion.

In a strange letter to Justice Harlan the next day, Frankfurter indicated that something had gone wrong between him and Brennan in connection with

Brennan's prospective draft of an opinion in the Little Rock case. "After sleeping on it," Frankfurter wrote, "I have decided to curb my temperamental spontaneity and not talk to Bill Brennan." He continued:

> "Too much ego in his cosmos." When [Harvard law professor] Paul Freund was here recently—and Paul Freund is as wise as any member of the profession whom I know—he asked, "Is my classmate Bill as cocksure as his opinions indicate?" Cocksureness begets sensitiveness, and as his erstwhile teacher, I have to be particularly careful with Bill. He was plainly displeased at the thought of my writing anything before I saw what he will produce, on the assumption that he will take care of all there is to be said. Therefore, I do not think I ought to tell him what I think should be the conception and temper of our opinion. All of this has nothing to do with my personal relations with him, which are as pleasant as they can be.[24]

It turns out that on August 27, one day prior to the first argument in *Cooper*, Frankfurter already had drafted the substance of what would become his concurrence in *Cooper v. Aaron*.[25] This opinion presents the challenge of trying to understand what Frankfurter could have thought was so important about his concurrence to break ranks at a moment when the other justices were intent on bolstering the court's institutional legitimacy by emphasizing continued unanimity.

As the court reassembled at the end of August to deal with the Little Rock crisis, Frankfurter had become fixated on a theory of what the court needed to do in order to reduce its alarming rift with the white South. "My own view," Frankfurter wrote to Warren on September 11, just as the court was to resume argument in the Little Rock case, "has long been that the ultimate hope for the peaceful solution of the basic problem largely depends on winning the support of lawyers of the South for the overriding issue of obedience to the court's decisions."[26] Two weeks earlier he had sent a memorandum—constituting the gist of his eventual concurrence—to all of the justices.[27] The memorandum contained a direct appeal to southern white lawyers by praising their devotion to the rule of law. By contrast, Warren had publicly chastised the school board lawyers for caving in to the politicians and supporting the thirty-month delay granted by the district court.[28]

One searches Frankfurter's concurrence in vain for any trace of disagreement over principle that might have justified his separate opinion. One also doubts that at this particular moment, as southern lawyers were diving for cover amid the rising demagogic tide, that any pronouncement by the Supreme Court could have rallied the southern bar. From this perspective, Frankfurter's concurrence reads like an idiosyncratic essay, irrelevant to what the rest of the court believed truly needed to be said in a moment of institutional crisis. Several of the justices regarded it as being motivated by egotism and self-absorption. Frankfurter's bad interaction with Justice Brennan right after the judges' conference was probably triggered by Frankfurter's insistence on passionately sharing at length "what I think should be the conception and temper of our opinion."[29] As Frankfurter pressed his point of view, Brennan, not alone in this reaction, probably experienced Frankfurter as gradually passing over the line toward bullying, and he retreated from Frankfurter's suggestion as unhelpful and irrelevant. "When Felix didn't get his way," Brennan told an interviewer years later, "he was like a child."[30] But Brennan may not yet have realized that Frankfurter was in the midst of engaging in another sort of child-like behavior: launching one of his periodic idées fixes in order to temporarily relieve his central anxiety—the fate of "incorporation"—that was about to be reopened in *Bartkus v. Illinois*.[31] For more than a month before he suddenly announced his intention to the conference, Frankfurter seemed determined to write separately in *Cooper v. Aaron* regardless of the impact it would have on his colleagues.

As Frankfurter published his concurrence in *Cooper v. Aaron*, the Supreme Court returned to a case that challenged what he considered one of his most important legacies in constitutional law, his opposition to Justice Black's effort to "incorporate" the Bill of Rights into the Fourteenth Amendment, thereby extending the constitutional protections of the Bill of Rights wholesale to the states.

INCORPORATION

Before the American Civil War, there was little question that the first eight amendments to the Constitution were meant to restrict only the newly created federal government.[32] The promise extracted from the Federalists during the ratification debates that the First Congress would immediately pass a Bill of Rights was widely understood to be a concession to anti-Federalist fears about the powers of the new central government.

The question was reopened with the passage of the Civil War amendments, which expressly extended new constitutional restrictions to the states. In particular, both the Due Process Clause and the privileges and immunities clause of the Fourteenth Amendment had the potential for applying the restrictions of the Bill of Rights to the states. However, the first interpretation of the Civil War amendments by the Supreme Court in the *Slaughterhouse Cases* (1873) left the privileges and immunities clause virtually emptied of significant content and played little part in the subsequent debate over extending the Bill of Rights to the states. That role initially fell to the Due Process Clause.[33]

From almost the beginning of his service on the Supreme Court, Hugo Black began to suggest that as a result of the Fourteenth Amendment, the Bill of Rights was meant to be applied to the states. In his third term on the court, Black included a footnote in his eloquent coerced confession opinion in *Chambers v. Florida* (1940),[34] which observed that "there has been a current of opinion—which this court has declined to adopt in many previous cases—that the Fourteenth Amendment was intended to make secure against State invasion all the rights, privileges and immunities protected from Federal violation by the Bill of Rights."[35] By 1947 in *Adamson v. California*,[36] he came within one vote of persuading a majority of the court that all of the provisions of the first eight amendments to the Constitution were intended to be "incorporated" into the Fourteenth Amendment as restrictions on state power. Writing the most influential opinion for a 5–4 majority in *Adamson*, Justice Frankfurter upheld a California rule that allowed prosecutors to comment to the jury on a criminal defendant's decision not to testify at his trial.[37] Though it was agreed that such prosecutorial conduct in a federal case would violate the Fifth Amendment privilege against self-incrimination, Frankfurter rejected the proposition that the Due Process Clause of the Fourteenth Amendment incorporated the Fifth Amendment as a restriction on the states.

As Black had originally acknowledged, the Supreme Court precedents were weighty in their refusal to extend Bill of Rights restrictions on criminal trials to the states. One line of precedents narrowly construed the Due Process Clause to guarantee "sufficient notice and adequate opportunity . . . to defend" oneself.[38] Another somewhat more expansive line of precedents held that due process included fundamental principles of fairness, "the natural and inherent principles of justice," or a "principle of justice so rooted in the traditions and conscience of our people as to be ranked as fundamental."[39] Under these various formulas, the Supreme Court had ruled that states were not required to adopt a grand jury for criminal indictments or even trial by jury in criminal cases.[40] The court had also turned down arguments for extending to the states the right to counsel as well as rights against self-incrimination, double jeopardy, unreasonable searches and seizures, and cruel and unusual punishments.[41]

PALKO V. CONNECTICUT (1937)

The modern starting point for discussion of the scope of the Due Process Clause of the Fourteenth Amendment is Justice Benjamin Cardozo's opinion in *Palko v. Connecticut* (1937).[42] By the time Cardozo wrote *Palko*, several cracks had already appeared in the wall of resistance to incorporating the Bill of Rights. Early on, the Supreme Court did not hesitate to include in the Fourteenth

Amendment's guarantee of "due process" the just compensation requirement of the Fifth Amendment, thus sacrificing its claimed devotion to the diversity values of federalism to the greater goal of protecting property against state regulation.[43] Before turning down the freedom of speech claim in *Gitlow v. New York* (1925),[44] the court had assumed *arguendo* that the First Amendment applied to the states through the Fourteenth Amendment.[45] In *Moore v. Dempsey* (1927), the court overturned state convictions and concomitant death sentences imposed on five Black Alabama sharecroppers after a "mob-dominated" trial. And in *Powell v. Alabama* (1932), it held that due process included a right to counsel in capital cases, at least when a defendant, facing "circumstances of public hostility," was young and indigent as well as ignorant and illiterate.[46] While the court in *Powell* limited its holding to exceptional circumstances, the decision soon came to stand for a general right to counsel in death penalty cases. At this point, it was becoming increasingly difficult to understand why "due process" did not also extend the Sixth Amendment right to counsel to other serious state criminal charges, where, as any lawyer knew, a defendant without assistance of counsel was usually put at a major disadvantage in defending himself.[47] Nevertheless, in *Betts v. Brady* (1942),[48] a 6–3 majority refused to extend the right to counsel to noncapital offenses and rejected Justice Black's newly formulated contention that the Sixth Amendment was incorporated into the Fourteenth Amendment and was therefore a general constitutional requirement that states were obliged to meet.[49]

In *Wolf v. Colorado* (1949),[50] Justice Frankfurter, for a 6–3 majority, refused to extend the "exclusionary rule" to the states.[51] This meant that evidence illegally obtained by state authorities in violation of the Fourth Amendment's bar against "unreasonable searches and seizures" could still be admitted as evidence against a state criminal defendant. Acknowledging that such illegally obtained evidence would be excluded from a federal court, Frankfurter nevertheless maintained that only the "core" of the Fourth Amendment, which did not include the exclusionary rule, was absorbed into the Due Process Clause as a restriction on the states.[52]

After Justices Frank Murphy and Wiley Rutledge died and were replaced by Tom Clark and Sherman Minton in 1949, it seemed that Black's challenge to the Frankfurter position had been permanently thwarted. But in 1953 in his fourth year on the court, Justice Clark issued a surprising declaration of independence from Frankfurter by announcing in a concurring opinion that he was ready to overrule *Wolf v. Colorado*. Until there was a majority to overrule, Clark declared, he would continue to follow it as the established law. During the eight years leading up to *Mapp v. Ohio*, many of Clark's colleagues may have wondered whether he had forgotten his declaration. Even after Warren and Brennan joined the court and the issue was once again put into play, Clark gave no further hint of wishing to join an opinion that overruled *Wolf.*

Three weeks after the Little Rock opinion was issued, the court began its regularly scheduled 1958 term, hearing rearguments in *Bartkus v. Illinois*,[53] which had been put over from the previous term.[54] The case rekindled intense anxieties in Justice Frankfurter just two months before his heart attack.

Bartkus originally had been argued one year earlier, and it became the focal point of Frankfurter's early alarm over losing his majority. It involved an appeal from an Illinois criminal conviction for bank robbery by a defendant who had previously been acquitted of the same crime in a federal court. The case raised the question of whether the double jeopardy clause of the Fifth Amendment applied to consecutive trials in federal and state courts, which in turn may have depended on whether the Due Process Clause extended the protection against double jeopardy to state criminal trials. The case not only revived the *Adamson* debate between Frankfurter and Black over whether the Fourteenth Amendment incorporated the Bill of Rights but also challenged Justice Cardozo's earlier holding in *Palko v. Connecticut* (1937) that protection against double jeopardy was not sufficiently fundamental to be included in due process.

With newly appointed Justice Brennan not participating, the court in *Bartkus* originally divided 4–4,[55] leading the justices to put the case over for reargument.[56] But what must already have alarmed Frankfurter was that Justice Charles Whittaker, recently appointed and expected to be a compliant ally, had joined the chief justice and Justices Black and Douglas in voting to overturn the Illinois conviction.[57] After the case was reargued in October, Justice Brennan joined the liberal justices in voting to reverse, though on narrower grounds,[58] while Justice Whittaker, performing the first of many flip-flops for which he would soon become notorious, moved to the Frankfurter side. The power to break the tie now shifted to the newly appointed Justice Potter Stewart, who told the justices that he was undecided and not yet ready to vote.[59] It took four months before Stewart finally made up his mind to align himself with Frankfurter.[60] Meanwhile, with his anti-incorporation legacy hanging in the balance, Justice Frankfurter succumbed to a mild heart attack.[61] But even as Frankfurter finally secured Stewart's vote, one of his allies, Justice Tom Clark, came close to jumping ship after accusing Frankfurter of unnecessarily injecting the incorporation issue into the *Bartkus* deliberations.[62] "I see no necessity of burdening the opinion with the 'incorporation' problem," Clark wrote to Frankfurter, adding that narrower grounds for upholding the conviction existed.[63] Frankfurter could not have failed to remember Justice Clark's threat five years earlier to join a majority ready to overrule *Wolf v. Colorado.*

Now, at the very last minute after almost two years of silent acquiescence in *Bartkus*, Clark suddenly threatened Frankfurter with desertion on the broader incorporation issue.

Despite Clark's blunt accusation that his colleague was forcing the incorporation issue, Frankfurter was unapologetic. After pondering his answer for three weeks, he replied defiantly that "we have the relevant chance" of laying to rest the "evil ghost" of incorporation "as definitively as such a judicial ghost can be laid."[64] "What I have done in *Bartkus*," Frankfurter declared, "is to make the case against the 'incorporation' theory as devastatingly conclusive as possible."[65] Despite this tactless bombast, he concluded with an uncharacteristic personal plea to Clark not to break away and instead to "allow . . . the opinion to go as is, as the opinion for the court."[66] Clark had no trouble recognizing Frankfurter's plea for a personal favor, however much it surprised him. He wrote back reaffirming his vote—which made five—for the Frankfurter position. "Although I do feel that [incorporation] is not necessary to the decision, especially since Hugo barely touches on it . . . [y]our personal plea weighs heavily with me," so "I shall, reluctantly, join."[67]

His back to the wall, Frankfurter's defiant response seems at first glance self-defeating, given that Clark could no longer be assumed to agree with Frankfurter's position on incorporation. Yet, Frankfurter understood that personal pride and deference meant more to Clark than either consistency or any commitment to a particular theory of incorporation.

If the suspicion that Clark had been "all talk" in his original threat against *Wolf* was heightened by his vote in *Bartkus*, it seemed to have been completely borne out by his behavior the next year in *Elkins v. U.S.* (1960).[68] In that case, Clark silently joined Frankfurter's dissent in a case overruling the so-called silver platter doctrine. By a 5–4 vote, the court held that federal courts could no longer admit illegally obtained evidence that state officials had handed over to federal prosecutors as if "on a silver platter." Though the case could be distinguished from Frankfurter's holding in *Wolf v. Colorado*, Justice Stewart's opinion took clear aim at *Wolf*'s major premise by describing the exclusionary rule as "the only effectively available way" of deterring illegal police conduct "by removing the incentive to disregard it."[69] Just as Frankfurter's *Elkins* dissent made clear that he recognized the handwriting on the wall, Clark's silent agreement seemed to provide definitive evidence that he was prepared to join Frankfurter at the barricades in defending both *Wolf* and its anti-incorporation philosophy. It certainly left everyone unprepared for Clark's own dramatic shift one year later in *Mapp v. Ohio*,[70] in which he wrote the opinion that eventually led to the overthrow of Frankfurter's anti-incorporation legacy.

Clark had questioned Frankfurter's effort to use *Bartkus* to solidify his *Adamson* victory for posterity. Frankfurter's response to Clark made it clear that indeed nothing mattered more to Frankfurter than to accomplish precisely that goal before he left the court. To achieve that end, Frankfurter slaved over a ten-page appendix designed to deal a knockout blow to the incorporation theory.[71]

Roger Newman has suggested that Frankfurter's "personality changed" in the aftermath of his first heart attack in December 1958.[72] Yet, events before the heart attack, such as his strange behavior in *Cooper v. Aaron*, had already raised concerns about Frankfurter's emotional balance. During the several months before his heart attack, as we have seen, Frankfurter's erratic behavior poisoned his relationship with several of the other justices. If his earlier run-in with Justice Brennan over *Cooper* typified this early loss of perspective, a later encounter with Brennan over *Bartkus* proved even more explosive. On February 6, 1959, less than two months after Frankfurter's heart attack, Justice Brennan circulated a memorandum to the conference protesting Frankfurter's intemperate reaction to a Brennan draft opinion supporting a narrow ground for reversing *Bartkus*.[73] Frankfurter's response led Brennan to complain that "Brother Frankfurter not too delicately implies that my circulated dissent misrepresents the record."[74] At around the same time as *Bartkus* neared its climax, Frankfurter's audacious reply to Justice Clark revealed an unmistakable desperation about preserving his anti-incorporation legacy.

After the close call in *Bartkus*, Frankfurter grew ever more strident. He continued to fear that Justice Whittaker might switch back to the pro-incorporation position. On January 12, 1960, almost a year after *Bartkus* was decided, he wrote to Justice Harlan asking him to lobby Whittaker on the issue. "In addition to [Professor Charles] Fairman's destruction of the Black [incorporation theory]," wrote Frankfurter, "I suggest you ask Charlie to look at my supplementary materials in the Appendix to *Bartkus*. . . . Make Charlie consider what real hell would be raised in so many of our States by adoption of the incorporation theory."[75]

FRANKFURTER AND A "WATERED-DOWN" FIRST AMENDMENT

Frankfurter's obsession continued to grow even after his defeat in *Mapp v. Ohio* (1961). In 1965, three years after a severe stroke had forced Frankfurter to resign from the court, he published an anti-incorporation brief in the *Harvard Law Review*, now appealing to posterity even as the actual battle appeared to be lost.[76] The law review piece consisted mostly of a republication of Frankfurter's *Bartkus* appendix. Importantly, however, Frankfurter now added a new section at the beginning on incorporation of the First Amendment. Separate from the long-standing Black versus Frankfurter argument over the extent to which the Bill of Rights was incorporated into the Fourteenth Amendment, this new section publicly revealed for the first time that Frankfurter had extended his anti-incorporation philosophy to include a "watered down" First Amendment.[77]

Though during his last five years on the court Frankfurter had worked behind the scenes to bring about this shift, he never found the right case to directly argue in a judicial opinion that the First Amendment's constitutional restrictions were weaker against the states than against the federal government.

Frankfurter first floated this argument in a case that came before the court on November 19, 1957, the same day as the first inconclusive *Bartkus* argument. *Staub v. City of Baxley* involved a free speech challenge by a labor organizer to a Georgia municipal ordinance that required anyone seeking to solicit members for a dues-paying organization first needed to seek a permit from the mayor and the city council of the municipality in which the solicitation was to occur.[78] In what appears to be a crude legislative effort to block union organizing, the municipal officials were given complete discretion to deny the permit. Assigned to Justice Charles Whittaker, serving in his first year on the court, the case seemed to call for a straightforward application of precedents striking down similar efforts of municipal authorities to block labor picketing or to restrict religious proselytizing by Jehovah's Witnesses.[79]

That is precisely the way Justice Whittaker viewed the case, and he circulated a straightforward draft opinion holding that the exercise of unfettered municipal authority was a violation of the First and Fourteenth Amendments.[80] In a letter to Whittaker, however, Frankfurter objected. "I do not know why you mention the First Amendment," he wrote, "since it is not involved here and leads only to confusion of thought. . . . I deprecate strongly going into . . . contentious issues, such as the scope of free speech protected by the Fourteenth Amendment."[81] This was more than enough to unsettle the earnest and insecure Whittaker who, after having shown Frankfurter's letter to Justice Brennan, spent the next three days diligently reading the precedents. To Brennan, Whittaker expressed bewilderment at Frankfurter's objection, hardly believing that Frankfurter could have been unaware of the long line of cases holding that First Amendment rights were so fundamental that they were included in the Due Process Clause.[82]

What Whittaker could not have known was that Frankfurter had opened a new front in his defense against incorporation, one that would grow in stridency as he saw the possible triumph of Justice Black's position on the horizon. This became clear when almost a month later Frankfurter finally wrote to Whittaker informing him that he was dissenting on procedural grounds in *Staub*.[83] But Frankfurter could not resist lecturing Whittaker on the merits:

Of course, you are right in saying in some of the prior cases there was uncritical talk about the First and Fourteenth Amendments. I say uncritical because it was the *Adamson* case . . . which makes precision in regard to the nature and scope of the legal content of the Fourteenth Amendment important. In that case and its precursor, *Palko v. Connecticut,* the issue was sharply drawn between the Fourteenth Amendment as a self-contained and independently operating limitation upon state action and the minority view as set forth by Black in his dissenting opinion. . . . I would in this case, as in every other, keep out reference to the First Amendment in all cases where freedom of speech derives its shelter from the Fourteenth Amendment.[84]

Even though Frankfurter had never failed to emphasize that specific provisions of the Bill of Rights did not necessarily apply with equal force against the states when they were "absorbed" into the Due Process Clause, he does not ever before appear to have extended this analysis to the First Amendment.[85] There were at least two reasons why this was so. First, by the time he joined the court after several decades of being steeped in Progressive constitutional theory, Frankfurter had participated in the Progressive celebration of the Holmes-Brandeis dissents in free speech cases of the 1920s.[86] Second, while Frankfurter often approvingly cited Cardozo's opinion in *Palko v. Connecticut* (1937) for the proposition that only a limited class of fundamental rights was absorbed into the Due Process Clause, he could not have failed to notice that Cardozo in that very opinion was explicit in concluding that First Amendment rights were so fundamental that they were included within due process. "The Due Process Clause of the Fourteenth Amendment," Cardozo declared in *Palko,* "may make it unlawful for a state to abridge . . . the freedom of speech which the First Amendment safeguards against encroachment by the Congress. . . . [I]mmunities that are valid as against the federal government by force of the specific pledges of particular amendments have been found to be implicit in the concept of ordered liberty, and thus, through the Fourteenth Amendment, become valid as against the states."[87] Cardozo added that "freedom of thought, and speech[,] . . . is the matrix, the indispensable condition, of nearly every other form of freedom."[88]

Frankfurter's sudden shift on the First Amendment caught even some of his followers by surprise. Justice Whittaker's startled reaction in the *Staub* case to Frankfurter's misrepresentation of the precedents did not prevent the new justice from standing his ground and delivering a 7–2 opinion striking down the Georgia statute on free speech grounds.[89]

Staub represented the opening shot in Frankfurter's campaign to reverse the incorporation of the First Amendment into the Due Process Clause. In his next effort a few months later in the important case of *NAACP v. Alabama,*[90] he achieved some success. The case, discussed elsewhere,[91] involved one of the earliest legal challenges to the strategies of "massive resistance" adopted by southern states against desegregation. As part of a general campaign of intimidation against the NAACP, the Alabama attorney general required that the organization turn over—and thus make public—its membership lists. The first draft of Justice Harlan's opinion striking down the Alabama law as a violation of freedom of expression and association was almost as straightforward as Whittaker's had been in *Staub*.[92] "It is, of course, firmly established," Harlan initially wrote, "that the protection given by the First Amendment against federal invasions of such rights is afforded by the Due Process Clause of the Fourteenth Amendment against state action."[93] The draft produced two critical memos, one from Justice Frankfurter and another from Justice Douglas.

The Douglas memo accused Harlan of asserting that free speech protections were less restrictive of states than of the federal government. During the previous term, Douglas correctly pointed out, Harlan had explicitly taken that position in two companion obscenity cases, *Roth v. United States* and *Alberts v. California*.[94] But it is difficult to find any trace of Douglas's concern in the actual text of the initial draft that Harlan circulated in *NAACP v. Alabama*. Why Harlan circulated a draft that seemed to ignore his recent position remains something of a mystery. Perhaps he already knew, as Douglas warned him, that he would not be able to attract a majority to any opinion asserting that only a "watered-down" version of the First Amendment applied to the states. More likely, Harlan always meant to limit his differentiation between federal and state power to the area of obscenity.[95]

Whatever the explanation, Frankfurter bitterly criticized Harlan's draft for failing to say what Douglas had just condemned it for saying. "I am not happy about the opinion," Frankfurter wrote to Harlan on April 23, 1958.[96] Frankfurter pounced on Harlan's formulation, never once even acknowledging that Harlan's own recent pronouncements suggested that Harlan might be prepared to agree with him. Instead Frankfurter delivered a rant, which showed the extent to which he was now prepared to sacrifice the protections of the First Amendment to the purity of his anti-incorporation position. "Why in heaven's name must we, whenever some discussion under the Due Process Clause is involved, get off speeches about the First Amendment? Why can't you [discuss it] without all the rehash of *Doud* and that god-awful *Watkins* opinion."[97]

In a conciliatory letter to Harlan the next day, Frankfurter acknowledged his own "loose reference . . . years ago to the 'First Amendment' as a shorthand for freedoms protected against state action by the Fourteenth Amendment."[98] But things had changed, because according to Frankfurter, the First Amendment was becoming "lochnerized." Frankfurter wrote:

Little did I dream in my early days when we were dealing with explicit cur-
tailments of speech that loose rhetoric in the service of recently discovered
doctrinaire views by members of the Court would be snowballed into a tal-
ismanic mouthing of "First Amendment" in dealing with state action, which
only by the most indirect argumentation could be made to relate to utter-
ance or refusal to utter, i.e. speech and its withholding. It deserves repeating
that the loose talk of this Court is responsible for, because it encourages
and sustains, the kind of half-baked, flannel-mouthed talk that [civil liber-
tarians] dish up to us in the confident belief that they have to get only one
more "vote" to win their case. And so, by this process of building words on
words, we have reached with reference to "First Amendment" precisely the
same situation that led to . . . F.D.R.'s "Court packing plan," as a result of a
series of decisions based on the destructive employment of "liberty of contract" [for laissez-faire ends.][99]

In reaction to Frankfurter's onslaught, Harlan revised the draft to eliminate all references to the First Amendment, which produced a reaction by
Justice Black.[100] "As you know," Black wrote, "I think unanimity is essential in
opinions resolving problems in the [civil rights] field involved here. For that
reason, I am willing to go a long way to obtain such unanimity."[101] But he was
unwilling to agree to that part of Harlan's opinion that had ignored the First
Amendment:

The price is greater than I am willing to pay. Personally, I do not believe that
ignoring the First Amendment should be a *sine qua non* to unanimity here.
If [the First Amendment] is to be treated as having no effect in any cases,
I believe it would be better to do so frankly, openly and without leaving anything to implication. I am not willing to do it either expressly or impliedly.[102]

As a final expression of contempt for what he understood as Harlan's capitulation to Frankfurter, Black concluded by reiterating his refusal to agree "to
an opinion which I read as unnecessarily embracing the views of others which
I do not accept."[103]

In the end, however, Black signed on to Harlan's unanimous opinion after
Harlan included a citation to *Staub*, which, as we saw, Frankfurter already had
denounced as subversive of his anti-incorporation position. And perhaps as a
further sop to Black, Harlan's final opinion did introduce the Supreme Court's
state free speech precedents as based on "the Due Process Clause of the Fourteenth Amendment, which embraces freedom of speech."[104]

These early skirmishes in 1957–1958 represented Frankfurter's first recognition of a renewed threat to his anti-incorporation position in *Adamson*.

By February 1959, he was ready to do battle against the "evil ghost" of Black's incorporation theory.

Some might maintain that Frankfurter's sudden insistence on watering down the First Amendment in the name of establishing a consistent interpretative framework for the Due Process Clause is the very essence of the judicial craft. But in truth, the greater inconsistency was in his willingness to throw overboard a string of hard-won First Amendment precedents in order to heighten the defenses against Black's impending attacks. Frankfurter willingly watered down the First Amendment in order to craft an incorporation theory purified of any complex subcategories that might make it more difficult to defend. He chose to misrepresent the precedents, including some of his own earlier libertarian pronouncements on free expression, in order to present a single, consistent theory of incorporation. Frankfurter's decision to drag the First Amendment into the incorporation debate revived the broader battle between Frankfurter and Black that had inflamed the pre–Warren court.

Before Murphy and Rutledge died in 1949, the split between New Deal justices over "the lessons of *Lochner*" focused on whether the court could legitimately distinguish between protecting "personal" as compared to "property" rights. Frankfurter believed that one of the important "lessons of *Lochner*" was that the Supreme Court of the *Lochner* era became despised by the country because of its failure to exercise judicial restraint. When Justice Harlan Fiske Stone or Justice Black sought to argue that there was a difference between vindicating property rights and protecting personal rights, Frankfurter stridently replied that the only principled reaction to *Lochner* was across-the-board deference to legislative judgment.

After 1949, during the McCarthy era, just as state and federal legislation was succumbing to anticommunist hysteria, Frankfurter's philosophy came to dominate the court, resulting in a Supreme Court that rubber-stamped some of the worst violations of civil liberties in American history.

MAPP V. OHIO (1961)

Mapp v. Ohio originally came to the Supreme Court presenting entirely different legal issues than those that were ultimately decided. And what was finally decided included a surprising last-minute decision by Justice Clark to provide a fifth vote to overrule *Wolf v. Colorado,* one of the pillars of Justice Frankfurter's anti-incorporation philosophy.

Dollree Mapp was the victim of a coerced and unlawful police search of her residence that resulted in the discovery of obscene materials. Her conviction under Ohio law of mere possession of obscene materials was challenged in the Supreme Court as a violation of the First Amendment's right of free expression.

With one small exception, all of the briefs as well as the arguments before the court were directed to the First Amendment challenge.[105] In conference, Justice Douglas flagged the Fourth Amendment search and seizure issue as a possible alternative ground, with which the Chief Justice and Justice Brennan agreed, but it was dropped for lack of additional support. The justices then voted unanimously to overturn the conviction on First Amendment grounds, and Justice Clark was assigned the opinion.

According to Bernard Schwartz, "Clark . . . changed his mind just after the conference. On the elevator after leaving the conference room, the Texan turned to Black and Brennan and asked, 'wouldn't this be a good case to apply the exclusionary rule and do what *Wolf* didn't do?'"[106] Three weeks later, Clark circulated a draft overruling *Wolf.*

It took some additional work to bring Justice Black on board. Black had voted with the majority in *Wolf v. Colorado* after expressing his uniquely restrictive view that because the Fourth Amendment was limited to "unreasonable" searches and seizures, its application to the states was also limited. In *Mapp,* however, Black reversed himself and joined Clark's opinion after persuading himself that combining the self-incrimination provision of the Fifth Amendment with the Fourth Amendment was enough to overturn *Wolf.*

Clark's opinion for the court in *Mapp* was characteristically unclear about its grounds for decision. Although Frankfurter later identified *Mapp* as the case that overturned his anti-incorporation philosophy, this was by no means clear from the text of Clark's opinion. That opinion takes no stand on the general arguments for or against incorporation that had been debated by Black and Frankfurter ever since *Adamson.* Instead, Clark's entire justification for overturning *Wolf* rests on what he sees as a contradiction in Frankfurter's willingness to absorb the "core" of the Fourth Amendment into the Due Process Clause while refusing to apply the exclusionary rule to the states. For Frankfurter, citing Cardozo's famous *Palko* test, the exclusionary rule was not "of the very essence of a scheme of ordered liberty" and hence not worthy of absorption into due process protection.

From the time he first declared his willingness to overrule *Wolf,* Clark had emphasized how it violated common sense to recognize a constitutional right against illegal searches while admitting evidence that was the fruit of that illegal search. "The Constitution is not at war with common sense," Clark wrote in *Mapp.* He was insisting that *Wolf* was wrong on factual grounds, what Alexander Bickel called an "empirical judgment" that the "core" of privacy in the Fourth Amendment could not be protected without an exclusionary rule.[107]

From this perspective, *Mapp* can be read as a very narrow holding that in no way challenges Frankfurter's theory of the limited applicability of the Due Process Clause to the states. Clark's earliest denunciation of *Wolf* was coupled with criticism of Frankfurter's "shock the conscience" test for excluding illegally obtained evidence. On that occasion, Clark criticized as "ad hoc" Frankfurter's case-by-case determination of due process violations. But Clark never differed from Frankfurter's typically narrow reading of Cardozo's *Palko* formula. And he certainty never agreed with Black's claims for "total incorporation."

After he circulated the draft of his *Mapp* opinion, Clark received a critical reaction from Justice Harlan. "If you don't mind my saying so," Harlan wrote, "your opinion comes perilously close to accepting 'incorporation' for the Fourth A. and will doubtless encourage the 'incorporation' enthusiasts."[108] In a reply to Harlan's letter, Clark denied "that the opinion is a windfall to 'incorporation' enthusiasts. If it is, then *Wolf* brought it on."[109]

What Clark apparently meant was that his *Mapp* opinion was entirely compatible with only a slightly more liberal reading of Cardozo's "ordered liberty" test in *Palko v. Connecticut*. Indeed, there was nothing in *Mapp* that suggested that Clark had strayed from Frankfurter's anti-incorporation methodology. It was Frankfurter in *Wolf*, after all, who first extended the "core" of the Fourth Amendment to the states. Clark believed that Frankfurter's common sense had abandoned him as he ignored the "empirical" truth that without the exclusionary rule any right against unreasonable searches and seizures was an empty formality. Clark had every right to think that Frankfurter's head was in the clouds when he discussed the exclusionary rule. Anyone familiar with how the world of prosecutors and police actually worked understood that the exclusionary rule was the only practical remedy that might deter illegal searches by the police.

After achieving success in the difficult task of persuading Justice Black that the Fourth and Fifth Amendments, taken together, could justify a constitutionally required exclusionary rule, Clark's opinion generated further doubts in Black about whether he was about to sign on to a Frankfurtarian opinion after all. Only four days before the *Mapp* opinion came down, Black wrote to Clark expressing second thoughts about his concurrence:

> I am disturbed by the sentence . . . in your opinion that "Since the Fourth Amendment's right of privacy has been declared enforceable against the States through the Due Process Clause of the Fourteenth, it is enforceable against the Federal Government." This, I think, makes it necessary for me to say that my agreement to your opinion depends upon my understanding that you read *Wolf* as having held, and we are holding here, that the Fourth Amendment *as a whole* is applicable to the States and not some imaginary and unknown fragment designated as the "right of privacy."[110]

His concurrence in Clark's opinion, Black insisted, was based on this reading:

If I am wrong on this and your opinion means that the Fourth Amendment does not apply to the States *as a whole,* I am unwilling to decide the crucial question in this case. . . . In other words, I am agreeing to decide this question in this case and agreeing to yours as the opinion of the Court on the basis of my understanding that the holding and the opinion mean that hereafter the Fourth Amendment, when applied either to the states or federal governments, is to be given equal scope and coverage in both instances. If this is not correct, I think the case should be set down for reargument as the dissenters suggest.[111]

The uncharacteristically repetitive manner in which Black made his point to Clark suggests the depths of Black's doubts about whether he and Clark were in fact in agreement. But Clark immediately responded that "the gist of the opinion is that *Wolf* held the entire Fourth Amendment to be carried over against the states through the Fourteenth, and therefore the exclusionary rule which *Weeks* applied to the federal cases must likewise be made applicable to state prosecutions." Apparently this was enough to satisfy Black, even though he could not have been entirely reassured by Clark's failure to make any of this clear in his opinion.

SELECTIVE INCORPORATION

Mapp v. Ohio (1961) initiated a rapid extension of most of the provisions of the Bill of Rights to state criminal trials. Just seven years later in *Duncan v. Louisiana* (1968),[112] Justice Byron White could already observe that "many of the rights guaranteed by the first eight Amendments to the Constitution have been held to be protected against state action by the Due Process Clause of the Fourteenth Amendment."[113] He offered a list, which included earlier decisions incorporating the "just compensation" provision of the Fifth Amendment and the guarantees of freedom of expression and religion in the First Amendment.[114] Summarizing the further changes that had taken place since *Mapp*, he continued his list: "the right guaranteed by the Fifth Amendment to be free of compelled self-incrimination; and the Sixth Amendment rights to counsel; to a speedy and public trial, to confrontation of opposing witnesses, and to compulsory process for obtaining witnesses."[115]

Then there was *Duncan* itself, which extended to the states the federal requirement of a jury trial in criminal cases. Yet, the struggle between Black and Frankfurter over the reach of the Fourteenth Amendment hardly came to a close with *Mapp*. Justice Clark's swing opinion in *Mapp*, characteristically free of any systematic discussion of the theory of incorporation, left open exactly how revolutionary a change the decision represented.

During the next two years without explicitly taking sides between Frank-furter and Black, the Supreme Court extended two other provisions of the Bill of Rights to the states. In *Robinson v. California* (1962),[116] the court for the first time applied to the states the clause of the Eighth Amendment barring cruel and unusual punishments, though it did not articulate any general the-ory of incorporation. Similarly, in *Gideon v. Wainwright* (1963),[117] an opinion by Justice Black extended the Sixth Amendment guarantee of counsel to state criminal trials but also without being explicit about its theory of incorporation.

This truce was broken in *Ker v. California* (1963),[118] another search and seizure opinion written by Justice Clark. "We said in *Mapp*," Clark asserted, that the Fourth Amendment is enforceable against the states "by the applica-tion of the same constitutional standard prohibiting 'unreasonable searches and seizures'" as are applied against the federal government.[119] This was enough to bring Justice Harlan back into the fray.

It is difficult to disagree with Harlan's contention in dissent that *Mapp v. Ohio* "did not purport to change the standards by which state search and sei-zures were to be judged," which is only to underline the point that the result in *Mapp* could have been reached without adopting Justice Black's incorpora-tion theory. "Heretofore," Harlan insisted, echoing Frankfurter, "there has been a well-established line of demarcation between the constitutional principles governing the standards for state searches and seizures and those controlling federal activity of this kind. . . . Today this distinction in constitutional prin-ciples is abandoned. Henceforth state searches and seizures are to be judged by the same constitutional standards as apply in the federal system."[120] It fell to Justice Brennan to develop such a theory of "selective incorporation" to express this new reality.

From the time that he joined the court, Justice Brennan was unwilling to subscribe to Black's total incorporation position. Brennan's primary objection to Black's position was a practical one: total incorporation swept both signif-icant and insignificant provisions of the Bill of Rights into the Due Process Clause.[121] It was easy, for example, to see how one might hesitate before extend-ing to the states the administratively costly provision of the Seventh Amend-ment requiring jury trials in all civil cases in which the amount in controversy exceeded $20. Because it remains a mystery how the Framers—familiar in their own time with rampant inflation—could have saddled the federal system for all eternity with a fixed dollar amount, there is considerable justification for not regarding such a constitutional provision as fundamental.

On the other hand, Brennan rejected Frankfurter's *Adamson* formulation because in its determinations of what was "fundamental" to "ordered liberty," it showed little concern or respect for the Framers' vision of preventing the crim-inal justice system from becoming an instrument of governmental oppression.

Frankfurter could declare in *Adamson* that extending the restrictions of the Bill of Rights to the states would only serve to "imprison" them "in what are merely legal forms even though they have the sanction of the Eighteenth Century."[122] He relied on Cardozo's *Palko* opinion, which similarly declared that it was "narrow [and] provincial" to insist that in criminal cases a grand jury indictment and jury trial were part of "the very essence of a scheme of ordered liberty."[123] The Fourteenth Amendment, Frankfurter concluded in another case, "did not mean to imprison the states into the limited experience of the eighteenth century."[124] Frankfurter's opinion in *Adamson,* Justice Rutledge critically observed, viewed the Bill of Rights as "a strait jacket of Eighteenth Century procedures rather than a basic charter of personal liberty."[125]

In *Malloy v. Hogan* (1964),[126] Brennan was finally ready to craft a compromise position between Black and Frankfurter that came to be known as "selective incorporation." For a 5–4 majority, Brennan reversed not only a three-year-old precedent—*Cohen v. Hurley* (1961)—but also a longer line of decisions, including *Adamson,* to hold that the Fifth Amendment guarantee against self-incrimination was "absorbed" into the Due Process Clause as a limitation on the states. Unlike Black, Brennan was prepared to follow *Palko,* at least in deciding whether a particular provision of the Bill of Rights was sufficiently fundamental to be "absorbed" into the Due Process Clause. As early as 1960, he had stated that "the Palko opinion refers to 'a process of absorption,' . . . of specific Bill of Rights guarantees [into] the Fourteenth Amendment's [due process] standard. It is not a license to the judiciary to administer a watered-down, subjective version of the individual guarantees of the Bill of Rights when state cases come before us."[127] Unlike Frankfurter, therefore, Brennan was content to recognize most of the Bill of Rights as fundamental. Brennan's selective incorporation approach thus highlighted the fact that in hands other than Frankfurter's, *Palko* could always have supported a much broader program of incorporation than Frankfurter (or Harlan) was ready to entertain.

In *Duncan v. Louisiana* (1968), Justice White also realized that a reformulated *Palko* test could bring the incorporation debate nearly to a close. He decided for the court that the Sixth Amendment guarantee of a jury trial in criminal cases that are more serious than so-called petty offenses was absorbed into the Due Process Clause and thus applied to Louisiana and other states that had failed to require jury trials. Declaring that *Mapp v. Ohio* initiated a "new approach" to determining the content of "due process," White showed how since then the court had revised the *Palko* formula so as to decide not whether "the limitation in question is . . . necessarily fundamental to fairness in every criminal system that might be imagined" but instead whether it "is fundamental in the context of the criminal processes maintained by the American States."[128] Under this new formula, by the time the Warren Court drew to a close, only a handful of arguably insignificant provisions of the Bill of Rights had failed to be incorporated into due process protection.[129]

But the position Justice Brennan thought he had finally secured in *Malloy*—that once a provision of the Bill of Rights is absorbed into "due process" it may not be "watered down" when it is applied to the states—was subtly challenged once again in *Duncan*.

Justice White's opinion left open the question of whether requiring a criminal jury in the states also meant that the states were required to follow the federal rule that a unanimous vote of a twelve-person jury was necessary in order to convict. Justice Fortas explicitly denied that *Duncan* also extended to the states what he called these "ancillary" features of the criminal jury. After the Warren Court had come to a close, the justices initially refused to hold that either jury unanimity[130] or a twelve-person jury[131] was constitutionally required of the states under the Fourteenth Amendment. Recently, the Supreme Court reversed itself and held in *Ramos v. Louisiana* (2020) that jury unanimity is constitutionally required.[132]

As the Warren Court drew to a close, Justice Black was ready to claim qualified victory in his twenty-five-year campaign for total incorporation. "I have been willing to support the selective incorporation doctrine . . . as an alternative, although perhaps less historically supportable than complete incorporation," Black declared in his concurring opinion in *Duncan v. Louisiana*:

> The selective incorporation process, if used properly, does limit the Supreme Court in the Fourteenth Amendment field to specific Bill of Rights' protections only and keeps judges from roaming at will in their own notions of what policies outside the Bill of Rights are desirable and what are not. And, most importantly for me, the selective incorporation process has the virtue of having already worked to make most of the Bill of Rights' protections applicable to the States.[133]

5

THE REAPPORTIONMENT CASES

When the Supreme Court was asked to hear challenges to the fairness of state legislative apportionment in *Baker v. Carr* (1962),[1] the maldistribution of legislative districts had become a national disgrace. As the shift in population from rural to urban areas accelerated during the twentieth century, entrenched state legislators simply refused to redraw election districts to reflect population changes. In Tennessee, the state whose apportionment was under attack in *Baker*, legislators for sixty years had ignored a state constitutional requirement that they apportion every decade.[2] In the lower house of Tennessee's two-house legislature, election districts had been drawn so that less than 40 percent of the population could elect a majority of representatives.[3]

The situation was much worse in other states. In eleven state senates, a legislative majority could be elected by less than 20 percent of the population, including California (10.7%), Florida (14.1%), and Nevada (8%). In only seventeen states was as much as 40 percent of the population required to attain majority control. In the lower houses, there were four states in which potential majority control was in the hands of fewer than 20 percent of the voters, while only seventeen states required at least 40 percent for such control.[4]

As a result, state legislatures dominated by rural interests regularly refused to provide cities a fair share of state funds.[5] Indeed, cities faced disproportionate needs, since the poor and underprivileged, who were especially dependent on government services, were concentrated in urban centers. Nor was it lost on the Warren Court justices that over the past half century there had been a major migration of Black citizens from southern rural areas to the large urban industrial centers of the Northeast and Midwest. Legislative malapportionment served as another device for diluting the political power of urban Black voters.

Over the course of his career on the Supreme Court, Felix Frankfurter had embodied his ideas of judicial restraint in a series of doctrinal categories that expressed his most fundamental beliefs about the constitutional limitations on the judiciary. Two areas of constitutional law that especially bore Frankfurter's stamp were abruptly disavowed by the court in 1961–1962. As we saw in chapter 4, in *Mapp v. Ohio* (1961),[6] with Frankfurter sitting, a majority reached out beyond the parties' briefs to overturn one of the monuments to Frankfurter's jurisprudence, *Wolf v. Colorado* (1949).[7] The broader issue involved the extent to which the states were immune from the constitutional restrictions of the Bill of Rights and whether the Fourteenth Amendment's Due Process Clause incorporated the provisions of the Bill of Rights as restrictions on the states.

So, when the court in *Mapp* reached out with incorporationist language to overturn *Wolf* and apply the exclusionary rule to the states, Frankfurter saw that his anti-incorporation philosophy was being dismantled; the edifice of constitutional doctrines he had crafted to limit the reach of the Bill of Rights was about to collapse.

Moreover, Frankfurter began to insist for the first time that his anti-incorporation views extended to limit the application of the First Amendment to the states. The result was that by the time he retired from the court in 1962, he had endorsed a more restrictive view of the reach of First Amendment constitutional protections than at any time since he began service as a Harvard law professor nearly five decades earlier.

If *Mapp* foreshadowed the decline of Frankfurter's intellectual dominance on the court, he understood the challenge to legislative malapportionment in *Baker v. Carr* (1962) as an effort to undo everything he stood for in constitutional jurisprudence. Ten days after delivering his bitter dissent in that case, Frankfurter was stricken with a debilitating stroke that led him to resign four months later. *Baker v. Carr* thus became his "last great judicial battle."[8]

Soon after taking office in January 1961, the new attorney general, Robert Kennedy, began to lean on his solicitor general, Archibald Cox, to endorse the claims of Supreme Court petitioners who were mounting an equal protection challenge to grossly unequal state legislative districts. For Cox to agree to file an amicus curiae brief supporting the claim would involve him in both personal and professional dilemmas.

The case that would have to be overruled in order to recognize the court's power to hear challenges to legislative districting was a Frankfurter opinion in *Colegrove v. Green* (1946), which held that the drawing of congressional districts by a state was a matter "of a peculiarly political nature and therefore not meet for judicial determination."[9] He warned the court against being drawn into a "political thicket."[10] For Frankfurter, the doctrine of "political questions" stood at the core of his philosophy of judicial restraint.

As a professor at Harvard Law School, Frankfurter had been one of Cox's most important mentors. Twenty-five years earlier Frankfurter had helped to launch Cox on a distinguished academic career by choosing him for a much-coveted clerkship with his friend, the celebrated Judge Learned Hand. By the time Cox became solicitor general, Frankfurter and Hand had spent two decades elaborating ever more dogmatic versions of the limits of judicial power, which Hand long before had already framed as a struggle between the "principled" proponents of judicial restraint and their "opportunistic" opponents.[11]

Cox was not only personally indebted to Frankfurter but had also absorbed much of the Frankfurter-Hand viewpoint during his fifteen years of teaching at Harvard Law School. Indeed, as he began his service as solicitor general, Cox was "lukewarm and leery" about getting involved in the reapportionment cases.[12] When he finally decided to submit an amicus brief urging the court to hear challenges to reapportionment, Cox denied, perhaps even to himself, that he had embarked on a course that would end in a rule of "one person, one vote." All that he had committed to, he insisted, was to seek to overturn a decision that prevented the court from even considering the constitutionality of arbitrarily drawn legislative districts.[13] But even in victory, Cox's biographer noted, he was "tormented over his role" in bringing it about.[14]

Cox's ambivalence was mirrored among the justices of the Supreme Court, who struggled to find a formula for limited judicial intervention into the electoral process. Inside the court, following what had become an annual practice, Justice William Brennan's clerks prepared a chronological account—presumably with the justice's blessing—of the important cases in which the justice was involved during their term of clerkship.[15] Roy Schotland's colorful account of the maneuvering among the justices leading to the decision in *Baker v. Carr* provides us with an insider's perspective on the dynamics of forging a majority opinion in an intensely contested case.

"Since the end of the 1957 Term," Schotland began, "it had been fairly clear that soon the Court was going to take a legislative apportionment case and test the vitality of *Colegrove v. Green.*"[16] Schotland based his conclusion on a recent lawsuit attacking the Georgia county unit system in which four justices (Earl Warren, Hugo Black, William Douglas, and Brennan) were already on record as being willing to entertain constitutional challenges to apportionment.[17]

Baker v. Carr was first argued in April 1961 and then, at Justice Potter Stewart's request, was put over for reargument the next term. Schotland reported (what he could only have learned from Justice Brennan) that at the first conference

> Justice Frankfurter unleashed a brilliant tour de force, speaking at considerable length, pulling down Reports and reading from them, and powerfully

FIGURE 1. Official Supreme Court portrait of Chief Justice Earl Warren. 1977-13-MASTER-1, Collection of the Supreme Court of the United States.

FIGURE 2. Studio portrait of Earl Warren, likely taken when he joined the Supreme Court in 1953. 2002.56.26, Collection of the Supreme Court of the United States.

FIGURE 3. John Birch Society billboard calls for the impeachment of Supreme Court Justice Earl Warren, Mississippi, June 1966. Bob Fitch Photography Archive, Department of Special Collections, Stanford University Library.

FIGURE 4. Lawyers George E.C. Hayes (left), Thurgood Marshall (center), and James M. Nabrit join hands as they pose outside the U.S. Supreme Court on May 17, 1954, after the ruling that segregation is unconstitutional. Associated Press.

FIGURE 5. Justice Felix Frankfurter in his chambers, 1957. 1990.7.1, Bachrach, Collection of the Supreme Court of the United States.

FIGURE 6. Portrait of Justice Felix Frankfurter by Gardner Cox, 1960. Harvard Law School Library, Historical & Special Collections.

FIGURE 7. Official Supreme Court portrait of Justice Potter Stewart. 1983-6-MASTER-1, Collection of the Supreme Court of the United States.

FIGURE 8. Potter Stewart standing in front of a bookcase, 1958. Wikimedia Commons.

FIGURE 9. 1962 photograph of Justice Arthur Goldberg inscribed for Justice William Brennan. The inscription reads, "To Bill Brennan, who in his core feels 'the sacred stir for justice' and in whose keeping the torch burns brightly. With high regard and esteem of his friend and colleague." 1998.9.3, Harris & Ewing, Collection of the Supreme Court.

FIGURE 10. Official Supreme Court portrait of Justice Hugo Black, painted by his grandson, John Black. Wikimedia Commons.

FIGURE 11. Studio photograph of Justice William Brennan, 1956. 1956.5.1, Collection of the Supreme Court of the United States.

FIGURE 12. Photograph of Justice William Brennan, taken in his chambers in the 1980s. Wikimedia Commons.

FIGURE 13. Photograph of Justice Thurgood Marshall at his desk, circa 1977. Science History Images / Alamy Stock Photo

FIGURE 14. Official Supreme Court portrait of Justice Thurgood Marshall. 1993-83-MASTER-1, Collection of the Supreme Court of the United States.

FIGURE 15. Photograph of Justice William Douglas at his desk in his chambers, circa 1961–65. 2003.31.9, Peter Ehrenhaft, Collection of the Supreme Court of the United States.

FIGURE 16. Photograph of Abe Fortas seated behind his desk at his Washington law offices in September 1965, shortly before joining the Supreme Court. 2003.31.12, Peter D. Ehrenhaft, Collection of the Supreme Court of the United States.

FIGURE 17. Portrait of Justice Byron White. Wikimedia Commons.

FIGURE 18. Official Supreme Court portrait of Justice John Marshall Harlan II by Gardner Cox. Wikimedia Commons.

FIGURE 19. President Lyndon B. Johnson giving Justice Abe Fortas "the treatment" in 1965. Wikimedia Commons.

arguing the correctness of *Colegrove*. Justice Stewart was not persuaded, but could not yet see his way to voting to reverse. Justice Whittaker disagreed with Justice Frankfurter on the law (as newspapers had inferred from his questioning at the argument), but felt that *Colegrove* should not be abandoned by a majority of five. . . . In this posture and at Justice Stewart's urging, the case was put over for re-argument.[18]

By the time of the first conference on *Baker*, Justice Frankfurter, ever on the lookout for "opportunists," already concluded that Cox, in placing the weight of the government behind overruling *Colegrove*, had succumbed to political pressure from the Kennedy administration.[19] In conference, both Frankfurter and his only eventual ally in dissent, Justice John Marshall Harlan, denounced Cox in unusually strong and personal language. Frankfurter called him "irresponsible." The usually mild-spoken Harlan added that he thought that Cox was "reckless in his desire to inject the judiciary into this field."[20]

The depth of Frankfurter's anger can be measured by an account of a public humiliation inflicted by Frankfurter on Cox at a Washington dinner party shortly after the first argument. Cox had joked out loud about having to reargue the case. As Gormley writes, a "voice trumpeted back across the table: 'Archie!' The entire room fell silent. It was Justice Felix Frankfurter. 'Archie!' he repeated. 'I will tell you why *Baker v. Carr* was set for reargument. When the case was reached in our conference, one of my colleagues said, 'The new solicitor general doesn't argue very well in [April], does he? Let's have him come back and see if he can do better in October.'" As Gormley observed, "the bonds that had sealed their relationship for three decades now seemed to be dissolving."[21]

What Frankfurter and Harlan managed to ignore was that Cox's predecessor in the previous administration, Solicitor General Lee Rankin, serving under President Dwight Eisenhower, had decided that the United States would submit an amicus brief supporting judicial review of apportionment.[22] Knowledge of Rankin's position seemed to have strongly influenced Justice Stewart's eventual decision to vote to overturn *Colegrove*.[23] The day after reargument, Justice Frankfurter circulated a sixty-page memorandum that later became, with minor changes, his dissent. At the conference, according to Roy Schotland's account, Justice Frankfurter "deferred" to Justice Harlan, "who argued with most intense emotion" that reversing *Colegrove* would be a mistake. In addition, "Justice Clark was as firm in the Frankfurter view of the law as F.F. himself." Clark "emphasized that what really was at stake here was, at least in the South, the whites' control of the power structure" and that he believed "it was impossible . . . for the court to get into that." Justice Stewart said he saw much in Frankfurter's arguments but "went on to say that he had to agree entirely with Justice Brennan's analysis of this case." Whittaker took the same stand as he had at the first conference, asserting that "the law called for a reversal" but that he "was not prepared to vote that way." With Stewart's apparent agreement, the tentative vote at the close of the conference was 5–4 for reversal.[24]

Chief Justice Warren "gave long thought to the assignment of the opinion" before choosing Brennan over Stewart. Given the familiar practice of assigning opinions to maximize the likelihood of a majority decision, Stewart, the still tentative fifth vote, seemed to be the natural choice for the assignment. Indeed, Justice Black, after talking to Stewart, advised the chief justice that Stewart "was so much at the outer edge that unless he were to write the opinion, he mightn't be held" for the majority. But Douglas told Warren that he felt he might be "unable to join a Stewart opinion" because of Stewart's remarks in conference about the severe burden of proof voters would have to meet to challenge an apportionment scheme. After conferring "repeatedly with Justice Black, as well as with Justice Douglas," over the next two weeks, the chief justice finally assigned *Baker* to Justice Brennan. After six years on the court, it was arguably Brennan's first major assignment.[25]

Brennan immediately expressed his delight by writing to Douglas to inform him that "the Chief told me this morning he's giving me . . . Baker v. Carr & that your view expressed to him yesterday had decided him. Thanks so much." Douglas returned the memo, scrawling at the bottom "He was going to give it to Potter [Stewart] but I urged him to talk first with you."[26]

All of Brennan's energies were devoted to forging an opinion that would hold Stewart for the majority. This meant above all that the opinion needed to be limited to the question of the justiciability of an equal protection challenge to legislative districting while postponing any consideration of the contentious issue of what substantive standards of apportionment should apply. And following *Brown*'s two-stage process, Brennan also put off to the future the question of framing an appropriate remedy, refusing to be drawn into the sensitive question of how any judgments could be enforced against state legislatures.

Three months after being assigned the opinion, Brennan circulated a draft to Stewart, who phoned Brennan "to say he was entirely satisfied." Brennan then sent a draft to Warren, Black, and Douglas, noting that Stewart was on board, which caused Justice Black to phone Brennan at home "to say that he was surprised Stewart was in the fold on this opinion." The chief justice was "wholly delighted."[27]

But "Justice Douglas sent in a series of questions and objections [that expressed] his unhappiness with anything that seemed to approve the [earlier] political question decisions which the opinion considered." Despite some "sharpening and tightening" to accommodate Douglas, the new draft "differed in no major way from [its predecessor]." While Douglas agreed to join, he "was not entirely mollified by the changes . . . and said he would have to write independently, on the political question doctrine in general [but] not on standards of apportionment."[28]

On the last day of January, Brennan circulated his opinion to the entire court. The next day Justice Frankfurter circulated his dissent, which except for a few opening pages was essentially the same as his original October memo. Thus, Brennan was able to recirculate his opinion after making "merely three changes" in response to Frankfurter. "Justice Stewart sent his note of concurrence and the majority was solid." Brennan was confident that the court was ready to act. But Justice Clark requested that the decision be delayed because he wished to add to Frankfurter's dissent. His own draft would have to await his return from a ten-day judicial conference in Puerto Rico, which both Brennan and the chief justice were also scheduled to attend.[29]

"Justice Brennan returned to face two of the most tense days that might occur in the process of any decision." A recirculation of Frankfurter's dissent noted that Justices Clark and Harlan had joined it. Douglas, mistakenly believing that this meant that the case would come down the following Monday, with Whittaker undecided, immediately circulated his own concurrence that, "contrary to his earlier private statement, did discuss standards of apportionment. . . . The Douglas opinion much disturbed Justice Stewart, who decided that he too would write separately."[30]

Confronting an unraveling majority, "Justice Brennan got Stewart to agree to a private circulation to the majority first." Meanwhile, having learned of Stewart's reaction, Justice Douglas phoned Brennan the next morning to say "he was willing to make any necessary changes in his separate opinion in order to keep Stewart from writing [separately]." Brennan suggested changes, which Douglas "accepted and went beyond." Just as Brennan was showing the changed Douglas opinion to Stewart, Harlan circulated his dissent. "While this did not switch Stewart, and while the Douglas revisions appeared significant to him, he refused to refrain from going ahead and moreover, as a result of the Harlan opinion, said he would go beyond his current circulation and state that on the merits, in other cases, he agreed with Justice Harlan. Justice Brennan was able to persuade him to circulate no more than he had already written, but still, Stewart's writing at all left Douglas very displeased."[31]

The following day, Stewart's concurrence did circulate as did another Frankfurter draft, which indicated that Justices Harlan, Clark, and Whittaker had concurred. But "curiously," Justice Clark had not also joined Justice Harlan's separate dissent. "At the time we assumed Justice Clark had simply not yet sent his note of concurrence. And for the next 20 days, everyone simply waited and we, at least, got tenser, while Justice Clark worked on his dissent."[32]

Instead, Clark delivered "an astounding surprise." He sent Brennan a draft of a concurring opinion. "It seemed that Justice Clark had been unable to sustain his grounds of dissent." He originally had intended to simply join the Frankfurter opinion, but Frankfurter had urged him to write and elaborate on certain themes he had mentioned during the conference deliberations. One of the subjects was "exhaustion of remedies."[33] Clark set out to "show that the Tennessee plaintiffs had not exhausted their remedies—that they had other ways to cure the unfair apportionment of which they complained."[34] Before long, however, Clark "found he had to come out for a reversal."[35] It was not the first time that Clark had shifted his vote at the last minute. One year earlier in *Mapp*, he provided the fifth vote for another successful last-minute assault on Frankfurter's legacy.

Amid the elation in Brennan's chambers at the news of Clark's reversal, "never to be forgotten" was the phone call Brennan received at home from Chief Justice Warren, who "just laughed happily" during the first few minutes of the conversation. Throughout the tense effort to assemble a majority, the chief justice "was Gibraltor like in his support of Justice Brennan." Now, Warren said "that in spite of Stewart's having lost his indispensability, he firmly believed that the majority opinion must not be changed more than Stewart was willing." With Stewart agreeing to minor changes, the opinion was ready to come down. As Brennan read his opinion from the bench, the chief justice passed a note to him that said "It is a great day for the country."[36]

Archibald Cox reluctantly recalled a painful encounter with Frankfurter in the corridor of the Supreme Court shortly after his stroke. Though the justice was "weak" and "in a wheelchair" and "wasn't able to speak very clearly," Cox remembered that Frankfurter "said something that conveyed in substance the message that it had been *Baker v. Carr* that had been responsible for the breakdown in his health. And it seemed to me . . . that somehow he linked some of that responsibility to me."[37]

Frankfurter's health was not the only casualty resulting from *Baker v. Carr*. Justice Charles Whittaker, tormented by chronic indecisiveness from the day he arrived at the court five years earlier, broke under the strain of deciding *Baker*. He explained in conference that he had gone back and forth after drafting "memos diametrically opposed to each other."[38] In the end, he checked into Walter Reed Hospital twenty days before announcement of the decision and did not participate in the vote. Archibald Cox, who paid Whittaker a courtesy call after the justice announced his resignation, found him in a "state of emotional tension that made him very talkative."[39] Whittaker "launched into a soliloquy on *Baker v. Carr*, confessing, in effect, 'It just about killed me . . . I couldn't make up my mind.'"[40]

Of President Eisenhower's five appointments to the court, only Whittaker failed to raise its average quality.

BRENNAN'S OPINION IN *BAKER V. CARR*

Baker v. Carr was Brennan's first influential assignment for the court. His opinion was a great scholarly tour de force whose impact extended well beyond the reapportionment cases. Its central focus was on the "political questions" doctrine, which Frankfurter had previously invoked in *Colegrove v. Green* to reject all challenges to legislative malapportionment.[41]

Colegrove, as Justice Black put it in conference on *Baker v. Carr*, was "a weak reed on which to hang any notion of an established rule."[42] Decided by only a seven-person court,[43] the vote was 3–1–3 that reapportionment constituted a nonjusticiable political question. While Justice Rutledge provided the fourth vote to dismiss the lawsuit, he was very clear that he considered the case justiciable. He voted to dismiss based on equitable principles.

Brennan concluded in *Baker* that the central problem with Frankfurter's formulation of the political questions doctrine was that he had failed to ground the doctrine in the text or structure of the U.S. Constitution. Frankfurter's warning against entering the "political thicket" of reapportionment was derived from a much broader and vaguer conception of political prudence that tended to be thought of as an extraconstitutional limitation on judges that was not grounded directly in the Constitution.[44] Brennan, however, sought to derive the political question limitations from the structure of the Constitution itself. "The nonjusticiability of a political question is primarily a function of the separation of powers," Brennan wrote. "Deciding whether a matter has in any measure been committed by the Constitution to another branch of government . . . is itself a delicate exercise in constitutional interpretation," which inescapably requires a case-by-case inquiry.[45] He then undertook such an analysis of each of the categories of cases that had previously invoked the political questions doctrine, concluding that every case involved

> a textually demonstrable constitutional commitment of the issue to a coordinate political department; or a lack of judicially discoverable and manageable standards for resolving it; or the impossibility of deciding without an initial policy determination of a kind clearly for nonjudicial discretion; or the impossibility of a court's undertaking independent resolution without expressing lack of the respect due coordinate branches of government; or an unusual need for unquestioning adherence to a political decision already made; or the potentiality of embarrassment from multifarious pronouncements by various departments on one question.[46]

Finally Brennan declared, with some exaggeration, that because "judicial standards under the Equal Protection Clause are well developed and familiar," the court would not be called on in the reapportionment cases "to enter upon policy determinations for which judicially manageable standards are lacking."[47]

Brennan's opinion presented an impressive reformulation of a tighter and more rigorous political questions doctrine. With the exception of cases involving foreign relations, in the half century since *Baker* was decided the Supreme Court has invoked the political questions doctrine only three times to refuse to hear a case.[48] Some would argue that the failure of the Supreme Court to invoke the doctrine in *Bush v. Gore* (2000) is evidence that judicial supremacy has consumed any remaining limitations on judicial power, outside of foreign affairs, once derived from the political questions doctrine.[49] Indeed, some would argue that *Bush v. Gore* vindicates Justice Frankfurter's warnings against the Supreme Court entering the "political thicket" of elections.[50] As for foreign relations, Brennan, while questioning "sweeping statements" in prior cases "to the effect that all questions touching foreign relations are political questions," nevertheless conceded that "such issues frequently turn on standards that defy judicial application, or involve the exercise of a discretion demonstrably committed to the executive or legislature . . . [or] uniquely demand single-voiced statement of the Government's views."[51]

Because the struggle over *Baker v. Carr* centered on the political question doctrine, it was hardly noticed that it also represented a major expansion in the application of the Equal Protection Clause to an area outside of race. Together with *Brown v. Board of Education*, *Baker v. Carr* became one of the twin foundations of the Warren Court's revival of the Equal Protection Clause.

As we saw, when Archibald Cox agreed to file an amicus brief in *Baker v. Carr*, he was convinced that the eventual outcome would not be a "one person, one vote" rule that would mandate equal legislative districts in both houses of a state legislature.[52] Any such result, he insisted, would be "revolutionary" and difficult for the court to accept.[53] "The position is at variance with our entire Constitutional history," he wrote to Attorney General Robert Kennedy as the Justice Department was considering its stance toward the first post-*Baker* group of apportionment cases to be brought to the court. Besides, he told Kennedy, if he now advocated a "one person, one vote" standard, "the government would be going back on the position which it urged . . . in *Baker v. Carr*."[54] Indeed, the majority in *Baker* was forged by agreeing to postpone the divisive question of which substantive standard would govern. Justice Stewart thought that the equal protection challenge would only apply to "utterly arbitrary" or "irrational" legislative apportionments. Justice Clark was willing to reverse only when a "crazy quilt" apportionment scheme was held to be "irrational" because it amounted to "invidious discrimination."[55] Originally, then, there were at most only four potential votes (Warren, Black, Douglas, and Brennan) for a one person, one vote rule, and it seemed highly unlikely that only two years later a large majority would arrive at precisely this "revolutionary" result. Certainly, Archibald Cox was determined to steer the Supreme Court as far away as he could from a one person, one vote rule.

Baker v. Carr was decided in 1962. One year later, the composition of the court had changed after Frankfurter and Whittaker were replaced by President John F. Kennedy's only two appointments, Arthur Goldberg and Byron White. And while Goldberg and White soon tended toward aligning themselves with opposing wings of the court, they were agreed on the principle of equal legislative apportionment. The result was that the carefully negotiated majority supporting *Baker v. Carr* was immediately transformed into a solid majority behind the one person, one vote principle. It was a final irony that the personal tragedies that struck Justices Frankfurter and Whittaker as a result of *Baker* had cleared the path for the revolutionary result that even they could not have foreseen a year earlier.

There were four cases that marked the court's rapid march to the one person, one vote rule. *Gray v. Sanders* (1963),[56] an opinion by Justice Douglas, demonstrated the abrupt shift in the court's balance of power with the arrival of White and Goldberg. The case involved a challenge to the Georgia county unit system for counting votes in Democratic primaries. While the system gave every voter one vote, rural counties were given much greater weight than urban counties in determining the final result.

Douglas delivered a formally narrow holding. "Once the geographical unit for which a representative is to be chosen is designated, all who participate in the election are to have an equal vote," he wrote. The case, Douglas maintained, did not involve the *Baker* issue of whether designated legislative districts could vary in population. "Nor does it present the question, inherent in the bicameral form of our Federal Government, whether a state may have one house chosen without regard to population."[57]

This narrow holding, enough to bring Justices Stewart and Clark aboard with limited concurrences, was contained in an opinion otherwise filled with the sort of broad language that Douglas loved and that, given the changing alignment, Stewart and Clark no longer had the power to insist upon deleting. So, Douglas was able to write for a six-person majority: "The conception of political equality from the Declaration of Independence, to Lincoln's Gettysburg Address, to the Fifteenth, Seventeenth, and Nineteenth Amendments can mean only one thing—one person, one vote."[58] This statement seems to have signaled that six justices were prepared to settle on a one person, one vote standard.

Only Justice Harlan dissented. Though he found it "hard to take seriously" Douglas's analogy between unequally drawn legislative districts and "dilution" of a person's vote,[59] it was precisely that analogy that foreshadowed the future one person, one vote standard.

The next year in *Wesberry v. Sanders* (1964),[60] the court adopted a one person, one vote rule for congressional districts. Writing for the same six-person majority, Justice Black held that Article I, section 2, of the Constitution, which provides that the House of Representatives "shall be composed of Members chosen . . . by the People," required that state legislatures, as nearly as practicable, draw congressional electoral districts containing equal populations.[61]

In dissent, Justice Harlan launched a textual and historical counterattack against the conclusion that Article I, section 2, required equal voting districts for the House of Representatives. He noted that since the Constitution authorized the states to set voting qualifications, "the people" could not have meant that the states were required to implement universal male suffrage.[62] Black did not presuppose universal suffrage. Following Douglas's *Gray v. Sanders* formulation, Black held that once the qualified voting population is designated by a state, it then must be apportioned in equal districts.[63]

Harlan also argued that the Constitution explicitly conferred exclusive power on Congress to supervise legislative apportionment.[64] Whatever the merits of Harlan's reading, the "political question" decision in *Baker v. Carr* had already held that the Constitution did not exclusively commit supervision of apportionment to the legislature.

Omitted from Harlan's approach was any recognition that the lower house in Anglo-American constitutional theory had generally been understood to reflect population, more or less. Though history may have thrown up counterexamples of both theoretical and practical deviations from the norm of equal representation in the lower house, Black's majority opinion did manage to convey more accurately than Harlan's the essence of the role of the lower house in the constitutional theory of the Framers.

The real historical challenge to a one person, one vote standard was not the lower house, which generally was thought to be based on population, but rather the composition of the upper house in state legislatures. To rule that the upper house in the state legislature was also required to have equal districts was precisely the "revolutionary" position that Archibald Cox believed was "at variance with our entire Constitutional history."[65] Yet, just two years after *Baker v. Carr*, the Supreme Court in *Reynolds v. Sims* (1964) extended the requirement of equal districting to both houses of state legislatures.[66]

Reynolds, the first case before the court since *Baker* to challenge state legislative apportionment, involved an equal protection suit brought against both houses of the Alabama legislature, each of which had substantial inequalities in districting.[67] Despite shifts in population, which magnified the original rural advantage, there had been no reapportionment for over sixty years.[68] In the

Alabama House of Representatives, population variance was sixteen to one, ranging between Bullock County, whose 13,462 inhabitants were entitled to two seats, and Mobile County, which received only three seats with a population of 314,301.[69] Although the constitutional provision invoked in *Wesberry v. Sanders* to require equal congressional districts was different from the present equal protection claim, the chief justice had no difficulty in adopting Justice Black's view that the lower house in American constitutional theory was based on the principle of equal voting.

The truly revolutionary part of *Reynolds v. Sims* was its holding that even the upper house of a state legislature was required to be based on equal districts under the Equal Protection Clause. Because the Alabama Constitution provided that no county could be awarded more than one senatorial seat, population variance among senatorial districts was forty-one to one, ranging from Jefferson County, with 600,000 people, to Lowndes and Wilcox counties, with populations of 15,286 and 18,739 inhabitants, respectively.[70] In the most famous passage of Warren's opinion, he disposed of the claim that the upper house was meant to reflect values and interests that were different from population: "Legislators represent people, not trees or acres. Legislators are elected by voters, not farms or cities or economic interests. . . . Diluting the weight of votes because of place of residence impairs basic constitutional rights under the Fourteenth Amendment just as much as invidious discriminations based upon factors such as race or economic status."[71]

Alabama's primary defense of its upper house was to analogize it to the U.S. Senate, where each state is entitled to two senators regardless of population. Rejecting the "federal analogy," Warren emphasized that the composition of the Senate was "conceived out of compromise and concession indispensable to the establishment of our federal republic." It arose "from unique historical circumstances" under which thirteen independent states agreed to surrender some but not all of their sovereignty. "A compromise between the larger and smaller States . . . averted a deadlock in the Constitutional Convention which had threatened to abort the birth of our Nation."[72]

Because the structure of the Senate was the result of "unique historical circumstances," Warren was surely correct in characterizing the federal analogy as "inapposite." But his concentration on the expedient origins of the U.S. Senate led him to ignore a still deeper tradition among the Framers that modeled the upper house in Anglo-American constitutional theory on the English House of Lords, at least to the extent of serving as a check on the potential democratic excesses of the lower house.[73]

Robert Caro has highlighted the hostility to democracy that was a central element in the Framers' vision of the Senate. "In creating a Senate for the new nation, its Founding Fathers had tried to create within the government an institution that would speak for the educated, the well-born, the well-to-do, that would protect the rights of property, that would not function as an embodiment of the people's will but would stand—'firmly'—as a great bulwark against that will."[74]

Citing the words and actions of the Framers, Caro shows that they were virtually unanimous in supporting a Senate that would be independent of the popular will. "The use of the Senate," said Madison, "is to consist in its proceeding with more coolness, with more system, and with more wisdom, than the popular branch," the House of Representatives. It should be "an anchor against popular fluctuations." That the "long-lived" republics of antiquity, where senators served for life, had avoided "the fugitive and turbulent existence of other ancient republics," Madison concluded, were "very instructive proofs of the necessity of some institution that will blend stability with liberty." In addition, the Senate would be much smaller than the House. Large assemblies, Madison explained, have a propensity "to yield to the impulse of sudden and violent passions, and to be seduced by factious leaders into intemperate and pernicious resolutions."[75]

For these reasons, senatorial terms were designed to be six years as compared to two for members of the "democratic branch." And until the passage of the Seventeenth Amendment in 1913, senators were chosen by state legislatures, whose members themselves had often been elected by a restricted electorate consisting of property-owning white males. When at the Constitutional Convention, James Wilson of Pennsylvania rose to suggest that the Senate be directly elected by the people, not one other delegate supported him. Instead, they warned of the "evils . . . flow[ing] from an excess of democracy" and praised the system for achieving a "filtration" and "refinement" of the popular will. "The object of this second branch," Edmund Randolph concluded, "is to control the democratic branch."[76]

There was no way that Warren could accurately have claimed that the Framers actually believed in the principle of one person, one vote for the upper house of a bicameral legislature. Only some version of a "living Constitution" that, developing over time, could be understood to reverse the Framers' hostility to democracy might have justified *Reynolds v. Sims*. This was precisely what Justice Douglas had in mind when he declared in *Gray v. Sanders* that "the conception of political equality from the Declaration of Independence, to Lincoln's Gettysburg Address, to the Fifteenth, Seventeenth, and Nineteenth Amendments can mean only one thing—one person, one vote."[77] It was a fair statement of the evolution of American political ideals away from the Framers' equation of democracy with mob rule and toward a belief in universal suffrage and popular control of government as a citizen's fundamental right.[78] But it entailed the still controversial view that constitutional meaning changes over time, which as we have already seen in *Brown* was a major—though hotly contested—theme of the Warren Court. We shall soon return to this theme.

The final reapportionment case, decided with *Reynolds v. Sims* on the last day of the 1963–1964 term, was *Lucas v. Colorado* (1964),[79] which presented a factual setting that compelled the court to explain more deeply the basis of its newly adopted one person, one vote rule.

In the November 1962 general election by a vote of almost two to one, the Colorado electorate adopted a constitutional amendment that essentially maintained the state's unequal senatorial districts. A majority of voters in every county approved the amendment, though it likely diluted the vote of some counties. At the same time, the voters defeated by more than a two to one vote a constitutional amendment that provided for equal districts in both houses.[80]

A divided three-judge federal court held that the constitutional amendment did not violate the Equal Protection Clause.[81] The majority opinion stated the dilemma:

> The contention that the voters have discriminated against themselves appalls rather than convinces. . . . [A] proper recognition of the judicial function precludes a court from holding that the free choice of the voters between two conflicting theories of apportionment is irrational or . . . arbitrary. . . .
>
> By majority process the voters have said that minority process in the Senate is what they want. A rejection of their choice is a denial of the will of the majority. If the majority becomes dissatisfied with that which it has created, it can make a change at an election in which each vote counts the same as every other vote.[82]

For a 6–3 majority, the chief justice held that the Colorado constitutional amendment violated the Equal Protection Clause. Warren first observed that the electorate "was hardly . . . presented [with a] clear-cut . . . choice," since the two competing amendments before the Colorado electorate contained other "undesirable features" besides whether they provided for equal senatorial districts.[83] But the most crucial premise of Warren's opinion was his insistence that "the rights which are here asserted are the rights of the individual plaintiffs to have their votes counted equally with those of other voters." By framing the claim against unequal legislative districts as a deprivation of "personal rights which are to be protected against the will of the majority,"[84] Warren was able to move effortlessly to his conclusion. "An individual's constitutionally protected right to cast an equally weighted vote," Warren declared, "cannot be denied even by a vote of a majority of a State's electorate."[85]

After he retired, Chief Justice Warren expressed the conviction that the reapportionment cases were his court's most important legacy. In his *Memoirs*, Warren praised *Baker v. Carr* as "the progenitor of the 'one man, one vote' rule." "The reason I am of the opinion that *Baker v. Carr* is so important," Warren declared, "is because I believe so devoutly that, to paraphrase Abraham Lincoln's famous epigram, ours is a government of *all* the people, by *all* the people, and for *all* the people."[86] Warren was adopting what Garry Wills in his study of the Gettysburg Address, saw as Lincoln's revolutionary statement of democratic principles. "Lincoln was a revolutionary . . . for—he not only put the Declaration [of Independence] in a new light as a matter of founding *law*, but put its central proposition, equality, in a newly favored position as a principle of the Constitution."[87] In emphasizing "all" the people, Warren was further allying himself with a dynamic view of the Constitution as changing to reflect a new era of universal suffrage, one with which the Founders would certainly have been horrified.

CODA

When the one person, one vote rule was promulgated in *Reynolds v. Sims*, it seemed to provide an administratively simple barrier to the most partisan forms of legislative districting. With the new constitutional constraint of equal districting, there seemed to be little room left for legislatures to engage in partisan gerrymandering.

Computers changed all that. By making it possible to surgically draw district lines that were equal in population while maximizing partisan advantage, the challenge to democratic representation has shifted. The rise in the number of politically uncompetitive one-party districts has replaced numerical inequality as the foremost challenge to representative democracy. So far, the Supreme Court has refused to hear challenges to politically partisan legislative districting in part because no clear administratively simple test for measuring partisanship has yet been developed.[88]

Many commentators, however, fault the decision in *Reynolds v. Sims* for a too limited understanding of the variables that make a legislative district representative. While time clearly has shown that the requirement of population equality will not alone come close to ensuring representative districts, there is no good reason why the equality requirement should not continue to be a necessary though not sufficient condition for fair districting.

The real problem, the critics maintain, is that the individual rights-based theory of districting articulated in *Reynolds* and *Lucas v. Colorado* is difficult to apply to partisan gerrymandering in which there often is systemic or design failure even when no particular voter is harmed. The rights-based framework articulated in the reapportionment cases, it is argued, has stood as an obstacle to shifting the court's focus to the macroquestion of whether a district is representative or whether the election outcome is unfair, not whether a particular voter has been deprived of her constitutional rights.[89]

This is a good opportunity to attempt to make sense of the sometimes inscrutable votes of Justice Clark in *Mapp v. Ohio* and *Baker v. Carr*. In both of these cases, he not only departed from his quite consistent loyalty to Frankfurter's positions but also was willing to provide the fifth vote for reversing one of the centerpieces of Frankfurter's constitutional jurisprudence.

In *Baker*, Justice Clark angrily refers to Frankfurter's dissenting opinion as "bursting with words that go through so much and conclude with so little."[90] The core of his disagreement with Frankfurter turned on the important question of whether there were practical alternatives to a judicial remedy that held out hope of reversing malapportionment. Initially in conference, as we saw, Clark had sided with Frankfurter and added that the plaintiffs had failed to exhaust their remedies.[91] After Frankfurter urged Clark to elaborate on this point, he apparently was unable to write a draft, which caused him to change his mind. In his concurrence, Clark emphasized that the people of Tennessee "have no practical opportunities" to correct the existing malapportionment. "I would not consider intervention by this Court into so delicate a field if there were any other relief available to the people of Tennessee."[92] Clark's practical, down-to-earth instincts were offended by Frankfurter's pie-in-the-sky promise of political remedies when the reality was that entrenched legislatures could block all change.

In *Mapp*, Clark had a similar reaction to Frankfurter's unrealistic list in *Wolf v. Colorado* of alternative remedies for deterring police misconduct. This time he could appeal to his own contrary experience of how, in practice, the exclusionary rule worked.

6

CIVIL RIGHTS AND
THE FIRST AMENDMENT

From the beginning of the American republic, the activity of groups was viewed with much greater suspicion than individual action. James Madison's classic analysis in the *Federalist Papers* of why "factions" needed to be tolerated followed from his belief that their suppression could only be achieved by using means that were inimical to a free society. Groups represented a necessary evil, tolerated but never really embraced.

Many legal doctrines expressed the view that group action presented a greater threat to order than that of individuals. Laws barring criminal conspiracies were frequently explained in these terms and occasionally were even held to apply to group conduct for which an individual could not be punished.[1] In the nineteenth century, the regulation of both corporations and labor unions was often justified on grounds of the greater danger to the public interest that organized groups represented.

In almost every decade of the twentieth century, some group was singled out by legislation for special scrutiny. After the Russian Revolution, state criminal antisyndicalism statutes targeting anarchists, socialists, and communists were widely adopted. In the 1920s, many states passed anti–Ku Klux Klan laws. The large number of cases involving Jehovah's Witnesses that came before the Supreme Court during the 1930s and 1940s reflected public hostility to the religious group's recent adoption of aggressive modes of proselytizing—including offensive anti-Catholicism—combined with charges of disloyalty due to its religiously based refusal to salute the flag.[2] In the 1950s, the target was the Communist Party and "communist-front" organizations. And after *Brown v. Board of Education*, many southern states, as part of their campaign of "massive resistance" to school desegregation, sought to deploy the legal system to destroy the National Association for the Advancement of Colored People (NAACP).

Just one year after the decision in *Brown II*, Alabama began its effort to suppress the NAACP. Proceeding in the Alabama courts under the state's corporation law, the state attorney general first obtained a temporary restraining order prohibiting the organization from registering or conducting any activities within the state until there could be a determination on the merits. In addition, he persuaded the trial court to issue an order requiring the organization to turn over its membership lists. The civil rights organization appealed on the ground that the order interfered with its First Amendment rights of speech and association, but the Alabama Supreme Court refused on procedural grounds to decide the merits of the constitutional claim, holding that the NAACP should have brought the appeal by seeking a writ of certiorari.

The Alabama Supreme Court had hoped to foreclose an appeal to the U.S. Supreme Court. Ordinarily, state court rulings on procedural questions are treated as independent state grounds not constitutionally subject to review by a federal court. In the ordinary case, a dismissal on procedural grounds would have foreclosed the Supreme Court from reviewing the federal constitutional claim. In this case, however, it was easy for Justice John Marshall Harlan to show that Alabama had not followed its own long-standing procedural rules. An abrupt change in procedures, he held, could not be permitted to foreclose federal constitutional review.

The trial judge then imposed a $10,000 fine for contempt of court for failing to comply with his order. He gave the organization five more days to comply, subject to an increased fine of $100,000. The organization again appealed, and this time it did seek a writ of certiorari. But again, the Alabama high court declined to adjudicate the merits, this time holding that mandamus, not certiorari, was the proper writ.[3]

The case was appealed to the U.S. Supreme Court in *NAACP v. Alabama* (1958). In an opinion by Justice Harlan, a unanimous court overturned the Alabama order as a violation of the constitutional rights of speech and association of the group's members.

While Justice Harlan carefully avoided putting it this way, the performance of the Alabama high court could only be explained as a bad faith attempt to prevent constitutional review of the state's strategy of intimidation of the NAACP. The Alabama court's performance was not unique. During the next decade, southern judges regularly used their authority to defend segregation and support state efforts to put the NAACP out of business. As in *NAACP v. Alabama*, they often threw their weight behind efforts to thwart constitutional adjudication of civil rights claims by the Supreme Court. We shall see in a moment how even after the decision in *NAACP v. Alabama*, the state judges managed to resist implementation of the ruling for another three years.

The Supreme Court decision in *NAACP v. Alabama* introduced a First Amendment right of association that would probably never have happened but for the struggle over civil rights. Modifying its long-standing practice of deferring to state regulation of organizations, the Supreme Court established an organization's constitutional right to be free from state interference with its activities.[4]

Typical of the change, Harlan distinguished a 1928 case that upheld a New York law requiring compulsory disclosure of Ku Klux Klan membership. In that case, the court had justified singling out the Klan by underlining the group's "manifest tendency . . . to make the secrecy surrounding its purposes and membership a cloak for acts and conduct inimical to personal rights and public welfare."[5] In the present case, Harlan noted, Alabama had offered no evidence of similar abuses of secrecy by the NAACP. Given "that compelled disclosure of affiliation with groups engaged in advocacy may constitute [an] effective . . . restraint on freedom of association," Alabama, unlike New York in the Klan case, had "fallen short of showing a controlling justification for the deterrent effect on the free enjoyment of the right to associate which disclosure of membership lists is likely to have." Alabama failed to justify its action by showing "a subordinating interest of the State [that is] compelling.[6]

The collaboration of the Alabama judiciary in the state's efforts to suppress the NAACP did not end after *NAACP v. Alabama*. On remand, the Alabama Supreme Court defied the U.S. Supreme Court by reaffirming the trial judge's contempt order and reinstating the $100,000 fine. The state court ruled that the U.S. Supreme Court had acted on a "mistaken premise" in asserting that except for its failure to disclose its membership, the organization had otherwise complied with the injunction.[7] In a per curium opinion written by Justice Harlan, the high court emphatically reaffirmed its decision, but it again, out of deference to the state court, left the temporary restraining order in effect until the state could consider its legality on the merits.[8] As a result, without even a determination on the merits, Alabama had thus far succeeded in shutting down NAACP operations in the state for more than five years.

But the case did not end here. Following the second remand, Alabama's judicial system went into what historian Del Dickson called "a four-corner stall."[9] The trial judge refused to schedule a hearing on the merits, "and the state appellate courts sat mute, effectively making [the] 'temporary' restraining order permanent."[10] The NAACP then brought suit in federal court to force the issue, and in 1961 the U.S. Supreme Court ruled that if the state did not hear the case by January 2, 1962, the federal district court itself would rule on the merits.[11] At last, the Alabama trial judge scheduled a hearing, and just four days before the federal trial was scheduled to begin, he ruled against the NAACP and issued a permanent injunction prohibiting the organization from ever again doing business in the state. The Alabama Supreme Court then failed to hear the NAACP's appeal for almost a year. When it finally did, the court again refused a decision on the merits and again held that the organization had failed to follow state procedures. Finally in 1964, after a unanimous U.S. Supreme Court ruled that the state's failure to decide on the merits was unwarranted, the Alabama Supreme Court yielded and dissolved the injunction.[12] Without ever deciding on the merits of the case, it had managed to prevent the NAACP from operating in Alabama for eight years.[13]

Though recognition of the bad faith behind these illicit southern judicial strategies rarely appears on the face of U.S. Supreme Court opinions, it cast a long shadow over all the decisions of the civil rights era. For example, in *New York Times v. Sullivan* (1964), to be discussed shortly, there was wide agreement among the justices on the principle that a libel judgment against the *New York Times* violated the First Amendment. But the justices circulated a seemingly endless round of memos concerning the procedural disposition of the case. Initially Justice Harlan, taking a position completely out of character, proposed reversing the Alabama judgment without even giving Alabama the customary opportunity to hold a new trial. After he was persuaded that a provision of the Judicial Code he had relied on was inapplicable, he reversed his position with a vengeance, insisting that because he was no longer willing to foreclose a new trial, he would dissent from Justice William Brennan's draft opinion holding the evidence insufficient. This led Chief Justice Earl Warren—who had learned his lesson over almost a decade of Alabama intransigence—to write to Brennan insisting that under no circumstances should the case be sent back for a new trial. "Otherwise we would merely be going through a meaningless exercise. The case would be remanded, another improvisation would be devised and it would be back to us in a more difficult posture."[14]

This squabble over procedure reflected the justices' accumulated frustrations with the Alabama judiciary. As Justice Harlan would have been the first to acknowledge, a federal system, with only occasional review by the Supreme Court, depended for its basic integrity on being able to accept at face value the state judges' grounds of decision. Yet, rarely did a set of state decisions offer as unequivocal evidence of judicial bad faith as did the Alabama NAACP cases. Much of the stretching and reaching by the Supreme Court during the civil rights era was actually an effort to find traditional grounds for reversing state court decisions without openly questioning the motives of the state judges.

Conversely, as Justice Harlan's toing and froing indicated, there was always professional pressure among the judges to revert to the traditional presumption of good faith, however much it was at odds with reality. In 1967, a majority of the Supreme Court upheld Alabama's imprisonment of Dr. Martin Luther King Jr. for disobeying another presumably unconstitutional state court injunction without even trying to overturn it on appeal. Despite more than a decade of accumulated experience with the Alabama courts' treatment of civil rights litigation, Justice Potter Stewart held that King should have appealed. "It cannot be presumed," he declared, "that the Alabama courts would have ignored [his] constitutional claims."[15]

Arkansas was next in the parade of southern states that sought to eliminate the NAACP as part of their "massive resistance" campaign. In *Bates v. Little Rock* (1960), the Supreme Court heard a challenge to a Little Rock ordinance passed in 1957 that required corporations to disclose, among other things, the purpose of the organization, the names of its officers, and "dues, fees . . . and contributions paid, by whom, and the date thereof."[16] Again, a unanimous court, in an opinion by Justice Stewart, reversed the fines imposed on the NAACP for failure to comply with the law. Quoting at length from Harlan's opinion in *NAACP v. Alabama*, Stewart presented an unusually realistic assessment of the devastating consequences likely to befall members of the NAACP if it turned over its financial records. The constitutional rights of speech and association, he declared, "are protected not only against heavy-handed frontal attack," such as direct attempts to shut down the organization, "but also from being stifled by more subtle governmental interference." Stewart then restated the balancing test that Justice Harlan had originally formulated in the Alabama case. The case, Stewart wrote, must finally turn on whether Little Rock has such a need to see the NAACP membership lists as to justify substantial abridgment of associational freedom that such disclosures would affect. "Where there is a significant encroachment upon personal liberty, the State may prevail only upon showing a subordinating interest which is compelling."[17]

A second case from Arkansas challenged a state law that sought to undermine the NAACP with a different strategy of enforced disclosure. The law required that all Arkansas schoolteachers disclose the organizations to which they belonged in the previous five years. "The Court [was] thus at the threshold of a genuine difficulty, for the state's nominal interest [was] persuasive—a concern with teacher qualifications and dedication. Hence the formula of *Alabama* and *Bates* [would] not work. . . . The dilemma [split] the Court."[18]

Shelton v. Tucker (1960) was one of the first civil rights decisions after *Brown* to be decided on the merits by a nonunanimous Supreme Court. For a bare 5–4 majority, Justice Stewart overturned the Arkansas law while conceding that *Alabama* and *Bates* did not control the case. Instead, he formulated what has come to be known as the "least restrictive alternatives"[19] standard in First Amendment jurisprudence:

> Even though the governmental purpose be legitimate and substantial, that purpose cannot be pursued by means that broadly stifle fundamental personal liberties when the end can be more narrowly achieved. The breadth of legislative abridgment must be viewed in light of less drastic means for achieving the same basic purpose. . . . The statute's comprehensive

interference with associational freedom goes far beyond what might be justified in the exercise of the State's legitimate inquiry into the fitness and competency of its teachers.[20]

Justice Harlan and Justice Felix Frankfurter both wrote dissenting opinions whose stylized innocence about the motives of the Arkansas legislature would surely have struck an informed layperson as willfully blind to social realities. Justice Harlan acknowledged that the court faces "an unusual statute that touches constitutional rights whose protection in the context of the racial situation in various parts of the country demands the unremitting vigilance of the courts." He conceded that "there can be little doubt that much of the associational information called for by the statute will be of little or no use whatever to the school authorities" and agreed that more limited inquiries, "more consonant with a decent respect for the privacy of the teacher," would not be "unworkable." Yet, he dissented from Stewart's "least restrictive alternative" analysis on the ground that it is "impossible to determine a priori the place where the line should be drawn between what would be permissible inquiry and overbroad inquiry in a situation like this." "If it turns out that this statute is abused . . . ," he concluded, "we would have a different kind of case."[21]

Frankfurter ended his dissent on a similar note. Though he acknowledged that the Arkansas disclosure law constituted "crude intrusion by the state" into the private lives of teachers, that was not enough to render it unconstitutional. If it turned out that the disclosed information was "used to further a scheme of terminating the employment of teachers *solely* because of their membership in unpopular organizations, that would run afoul of the Fourteenth Amendment. It will be time enough, if such use is made, to hold the application of the statute unconstitutional." By that time, he failed to note, many teachers would have been intimidated into resigning from the NAACP, and many others would not have been able to prove that they were dismissed "solely" because of the information they provided.[22]

It is surely difficult to find in these dissenting opinions any trace of "the unremitting vigilance of the courts" that Justice Harlan had promised for the constitutional rights of Arkansas schoolteachers "in the context of the racial situation in various parts of the country." This pitiful paralysis in response to a facially neutral statute whose illicit purpose everyone understood gave rise to Justice Brennan's historic reformulation of First Amendment doctrine in *NAACP v. Button* (1963).

The state that initiated the "massive resistance" campaign after *Brown* deployed a still different strategy in its effort to suppress the civil rights organization. In 1956, Virginia enacted five new laws expanding prohibitions against various kinds of legal practice, known by their ancient English names as barratry, champerty, and maintenance. As part of the campaign of "massive resistance," similar laws regulating legal practice were also passed after *Brown* in Arkansas, Florida, Georgia, Mississippi, South Carolina, and Tennessee.[23] The new Virginia laws barred the solicitation of legal business by any organization that was neither a party to nor had a pecuniary interest in a case; they also prohibited individuals and organizations from soliciting business for an attorney. Finally, the statutes placed new limits on "racial litigation" and required all organizations that participated in such litigation to register with the state and disclose their membership lists.[24]

After the NAACP filed a lawsuit in federal court seeking a declaratory judgment that the state laws were unconstitutional, a three-judge federal court held three of the statutes unconstitutional and enjoined their enforcement. They sent the two remaining statutes to state court for an authoritative interpretation of their meaning. Virginia appealed, arguing that the federal court should have abstained from taking any action until the state courts had construed the meaning of each of the five laws. In *Harrison v. NAACP* (1959), Justice Harlan agreed with Virginia, holding for a 6–3 majority that the lower federal court should have abstained from ruling on any of the five laws until the state courts were given an opportunity to construe them.[25] Though it was not a decision on the merits of the constitutional claim, it was the first time after *Brown* that the Supreme Court had divided on a civil rights case. At conference, Justices Black and Frankfurter, though initially inclined to affirm the lower court, had each urged unanimity and switched their votes to Harlan's opinion in order to produce the largest possible majority.[26]

After the case was sent back to Virginia, the trial court struck down three of the statutes but affirmed two others prohibiting solicitation and advocacy of lawsuits against the state. On appeal, the Virginia high court struck down the antiadvocacy law but upheld the antibarratry law barring solicitation of legal business.[27]

In *NAACP v. Button* (1961), the civil rights organization appealed the ruling upholding the antibarratry law to the Supreme Court. In conference, the justices voted 5–4 to uphold the Virginia law, the first time after *Brown* that a majority was prepared to reject on the merits a constitutional claim in a civil rights case. Their discussion, recorded by Justice Brennan, revealed a widening chasm over race cases between the opposing wings of the court.

Chief Justice Warren saw "these laws [as] intended to put [the NAACP] out of business. Publishing their membership lists would put them out of business. It is not a question of motives, but of avowed legislative purpose." He concluded that "the purpose of the statute is obviously to circumvent *Brown*."[28] Justice Black added, "This law was one of a group of laws designed as a package to thwart our segregation decision in *Brown*. This is part of a scheme to defeat the Court's order." Douglas and Brennan agreed. But the remaining five justices saw the case very differently.[29]

"I can't imagine a worse disservice than to continue being the guardians of the Negroes," Justice Frankfurter declared. "This act does not deal with more than fomenting litigation. There is nothing in the record to show that this statute is aimed at Negroes as such!!!!!" (The exclamation marks in Brennan's notes were designed to underline his astonishment at Frankfurter's oblivious— and incorrect—statement.)[30]

"Colored people," Frankfurter continued, "are now people of substance. Colored people now have responsible positions."[31] They can take care of themselves, he seemed to be suggesting, and they no longer needed the NAACP to protect them.[32]

Frankfurter's views were echoed by Justices Tom Clark and Charles Whittaker. "To strike this law down," Clark declared, "we would have to discriminate in favor of Negroes." Whittaker added, "This law, if applied to the white supremacy group, would be constitutional. We should be color blind on this law." Justice Harlan also voted to affirm. "Virginia applies in its statute the proper standards for law practice," he concluded. "This law was aimed at the NAACP and the school problem, but a state has that right."[33]

The post-*Brown* unanimity over race that, despite three new appointments, had been emphatically reaffirmed as recently as in *Cooper v. Aaron* (1958) had begun to unravel.

Frankfurter prepared a lengthy majority opinion, but before the decision could be announced, Justice Whittaker retired, leaving the court evenly divided. The case was put over to the next term for reargument, but by then Justice Frankfurter himself was forced to resign due to a stroke. When the case was reargued the next term, Byron White and Arthur Goldberg had replaced Whittaker and Frankfurter.

After reargument, the justices in conference voted to reverse on First Amendment grounds, with the remaining three justices of the old majority—Clark, Harlan, and Stewart—now dissenting. It is noteworthy that the votes of both of the new justices, White and Goldberg, contributed to the new majority. The chief justice assigned the court's opinion to Justice Brennan, causing his law clerks to speculate on Warren's reasons: "Perhaps because [Brennan's] special interest in the case was known, perhaps because of his demonstrated concern [citing *Speiser v. Randall* (1958), *Smith v. California* (1959), and *Marcus v. Search Warrant* (1961)] with so-called 'indirect' restraints on freedoms protected by the First Amendment, or perhaps simply because The Chief Justice felt that Justice Brennan stood the best chance of winning a majority consensus on a tenable ground for reversal."[34]

According to the law clerks, Brennan circulated a draft opinion that quickly won the assent of Justices Douglas and Goldberg and of the chief justice. Justice Black, however, had serious reservations. His problem stemmed from the fact that the majority opinion, as written, did not go so far as to hold that the NAACP had a constitutional right to pay and maintain a legal staff for the purpose of assisting nonindigent civil rights litigants. The opinion was predicated instead on the overbreadth of the statute.[35] In short, Justice Brennan in the first circulation shied clear of actually propounding a First Amendment right to furnish litigation assistance.

"Justice Black, however, felt that the majority opinion as drafted was an open invitation to the Virginia authorities to employ a narrow statute against the NAACP's legal staff to accomplish the same purpose as the instant statute—thus provoking further litigation and compelling an eventual confrontation by the Court of the vexing constitutional issue sought to be avoided by reliance on the overbreadth rationale."[36]

Because "Justice White had remained ominously silent" after Brennan's circulation, the law clerks added, "it was deemed preferable to accommodate Justice Black's views than to risk delivery of a merely plurality opinion, . . . and so the majority opinion was rewritten to intimate most strongly that [Virginia's] activities . . . were [unconstitutional]." The law clerks "confessed that the addition of Justice Black's suggestions in the majority opinion may have caused a certain tension to be visible in the opinion, since the overbreadth rationale remained." Eventually, Justice White filed a separate opinion insisting on limiting the grounds of the majority opinion to the overbreadth rationale, "just the ground on which the majority opinion had originally rested prior to Justice Black's intervention. Had Justice White espoused this view of the case to Justice Brennan earlier, it is possible that the original draft would never have been revised in conformity with Justice Black's objections."[37]

Despite the evident "tension" in Justice Brennan's opinion, *NAACP v. Button* (1963) represents a historic decision on both First Amendment rights and constitutional overbreadth. The opinion expresses a much more robust recognition of the relationship between public interest litigation and First Amendment rights than any of the preceding NAACP cases. Brennan reframes the private litigation orientation that in the first consideration of the case had led the Harlan/Frankfurter majority to approve application to the NAACP of traditional restrictions on solicitation of clients.[38] "In the context of NAACP objectives," Brennan now responded,

> litigation is not a technique of resolving private differences; it is a means
> for achieving the lawful objectives of equality of treatment . . . for the mem-
> bers of the Negro community in this country. It is thus a form of political

expression. Groups which find themselves unable to achieve their objectives through the ballot frequently turn to the courts. . . . And under the conditions of modern government, litigation may well be the sole practicable avenue open to a minority to petition for redress of grievances. . . . For such a group, association for litigation may be the most effective form of political association.[39]

Brennan's reformulation of the overbreadth doctrine, which came to play a major role in Warren Court jurisprudence, is even more striking. The court, he wrote, does not need "to decide whether the activities of [the NAACP] deemed unlawful by [Virginia] are constitutionally privileged. If the line drawn . . . between the permitted and the prohibited activities of the NAACP . . . is an ambiguous one, we will not presume that the statute curtails constitutionally protected activity as little as possible." If the Virginia statute is vague,

[it] may be invalid . . . whether or not the record discloses that the petitioner has engaged in privileged conduct. . . . The objectionable quality of vagueness and overbreadth does not depend upon absence of fair notice to a criminally accused . . . , but upon the danger of tolerating, in the area of First Amendment freedoms, the existence of a penal statute susceptible of sweeping and improper application. . . . These freedoms are delicate and vulnerable, as well as supremely precious in our society. The threat of sanctions may deter their exercise almost as potently as the actual application of sanctions. . . . Because First Amendment freedoms need breathing space to survive, government may regulate in the area only with narrow specificity. . . . It is enough that a vague and broad statute lends itself to selective enforcement against unpopular causes. We cannot close our eyes to the fact that the militant Negro civil rights movement has engendered the intense resentment and opposition of the politically dominant white community of Virginia; litigation assisted by the NAACP has been bitterly fought. In such circumstances, a statute broadly curtailing group activity may easily become a weapon of oppression, however evenhanded its terms appear. Its mere existence could well freeze out of existence all such activity on behalf of the civil rights of Negro citizens.[40]

Justice Brennan's great achievement in *NAACP v. Button* was that he managed to completely reformulate the issues in First Amendment jurisprudence. First, he transcended the two-decade-long deadlock between Frankfurter and Black over whether the First Amendment occupied a "preferred position" in the constitutional scheme. Second, he created a new middle ground that overcame the court's growing polarization over the NAACP cases. After the first argument in *NAACP v. Button*, the justices seemed stuck over how to proceed without attributing unconstitutional motives to the Virginia legislature. Five judges, led by Frankfurter and Harlan, were prepared to acquiesce in Virginia's campaign against the NAACP rather than break professional norms by ascribing bad motives to state courts or legislatures.

Brennan's opinion in *NAACP v. Button* introduced four new concepts into the court's analysis of free speech issues: the idea of "chilling effects," the "void for vagueness" doctrine, the notion of an overbroad statute ("overbreadth"), and the legitimacy of a so-called facial challenge to statutes affecting First Amendment rights.

Chilling effects. In his second term on the Supreme Court, Brennan began his reformulation of how the court should deal with so-called indirect restraints on First Amendment rights. In *Speiser v. Randall* (1958), he struck down a California loyalty oath that was made a precondition for a tax exemption on the ground that it put the burden of proof on the person seeking the exemption to swear, under threat of perjury, that he was not disloyal. "Where the transcendent value of speech is involved," Brennan wrote, challenged statutes must receive strict scrutiny. "The man who knows that he must bring forth proof and persuade another of the lawfulness of his conduct necessarily must steer far wider of the unlawful zone than if the State must bear these burdens."[41] Brennan further elaborated this idea in *NAACP v. Button*, noting that First Amendment freedoms "need breathing space to survive."[42] And in his great opinion a year later in *New York Times v. Sullivan* (1964), involving a challenge to Alabama's defamation law, to be discussed shortly, Justice Brennan emphasized what Justice Goldberg, in his concurring opinion, referred to as "the chilling effect."[43]

The chilling effects doctrine thus focused attention on the wider consequences of laws restricting speech. Statutes could now be challenged even when the particular application at issue might survive a balancing test of the sort Justice Harlan had deployed in *NAACP v. Alabama*, since the mere presence of such laws on the books would still tend to discourage others from exercising their First Amendment rights to the fullest extent.

Void for vagueness. The "void for vagueness" doctrine followed from Brennan's analysis of the chilling effects created by laws that threaten free expression. If a statute is vague about the offense it is proscribing or about the persons it is meant to reach, individuals might refrain from legitimate speech out of fear that the statute might be construed against them. For that reason, Brennan wrote in *Button*, "it does not follow that the Court now has only a clear-cut task to decide whether the [defendant's] activities . . . are constitutionally privileged. If the line drawn . . . between permitted and prohibited activities of the NAACP . . . is an ambiguous one," that is enough to invalidate it. "The objectionable quality of vagueness . . . does not depend on the absence of fair notice" to the defendant but rather on its chilling effect on the rest of society.[44]

The void for vagueness doctrine reintroduced an old criminal law idea but gave it a new meaning. It had always been true that a criminal defendant could claim that he or she should not be punished under a law so vague that the individual had no advance notice whether the conduct was criminal. Under the traditional view, however, if the trial court "construed" the words of the statute to give it a clear meaning that unambiguously covered the defendant's conduct, then this "narrowing" interpretation saved the statute from constitutional challenge for vagueness.

Traditionally, a defendant could not successfully challenge a law on the grounds that it could be unconstitutionally applied to other people. A defendant had no "standing" to raise the claims of others. If those other individuals wished to challenge the statute, they could do so only after they were indicted for violating it.

After Brennan redefined the evil of ambiguous statutes by emphasizing their chilling effects, however, the void for vagueness doctrine was transformed. Its primary focus shifted from whether the particular defendant before the court had received adequate notice that his or her behavior was criminal to whether anonymous individuals might have engaged in what Brennan called "self-censorship" out of fear that the vague statute might eventually be applied to them.

To appreciate how widely accepted the void for vagueness doctrine became, let us turn to the majority opinion in *Baggett v. Bullitt* (1964) by Justice White, not otherwise known for his strong defense of civil liberties. The case challenged loyalty oaths for University of Washington teachers, who had been required to swear that they were not "subversive persons" or members of "subversive organizations." Quoting from Brennan's opinion in *Speiser*, White held that the loyalty oaths were unconstitutionally vague because of their potential chilling effect on oath takers, who might be forced to "steer far wide of the unlawful zone." "Those with a conscientious regard for what they solemnly swear or affirm, sensitive to the perils posed by the oath's indefinite language, avoid the risk of loss of employment, and perhaps profession, only by restricting their conduct to that which is unquestionably safe," White wrote. "Free speech may not be so inhibited."[45]

Overbreadth. Brennan's use of the chilling effects doctrine also drastically affected the treatment of "overbroad" laws. Under the traditional view, if a defendant was indicted under a statute that was overbroad—that is, the law potentially covered both conduct that was constitutionally protected and conduct that could constitutionally be punished—then the only question was whether this particular defendant's conduct could be punished under the

Constitution. Again, a defendant had no standing to raise the constitutional claims of others.

But Brennan's reformulation permitted the defendant to act as a so-called private attorney general who could raise a claim on behalf of the rest of society that the law produced a chilling effect on the public's right of free expression. As Brennan put it in *NAACP v. Button*, "The objectionable quality of vagueness and overbreadth does not depend upon the absence of fair notice to a criminally accused . . . but upon the danger of tolerating, in the area of First Amendment freedoms, the existence of a penal statute susceptible of sweeping and improper application."[46]

"Facial" challenge. All of this meant that it was now possible to launch what is known as a "facial" challenge to vague and overbroad laws that interfered with free expression. It was no longer necessary to wait and see how these laws would actually be applied; they could be held unconstitutional "on their face." Whereas under the traditional view the statute might be "saved" through a later narrowing interpretation by a court, the chilling effects analysis showed that such an interpretation would come too late in the process to undo the harm to free expression.

This point was especially important in cases involving Supreme Court review of statutes passed by southern legislatures for the purpose of harassing or suppressing the civil rights movement. Under traditional doctrine, the Supreme Court was bound by a state high court's interpretation of its own laws. In addition, the Supreme Court was bound to rely on a state court's own assessment of the facts in the particular case. The overbreadth doctrine thus freed the high court from dependence on trial and appellate records created and interpreted by hostile southern judges. It was no longer necessary to attempt to decide whether in the specific case, filtered through the findings of state judges, the particular defendant could be constitutionally punished. Instead, a law could be held unconstitutional and invalid on its face, freeing civil rights defendants from the crushing burden of litigating many individual constitutional challenges.

Dombrowski v. Pfister (1965) carried this logic to its ultimate conclusion. A suit brought by the Southern Conference Educational Fund, a Louisiana civil rights organization, to enjoin enforcement of the Louisiana subversive activities and communist control law and the communist propaganda control law alleged that the laws were overbroad on their face and "susceptible of sweeping and improper application" abridging First Amendment rights. An opinion by Justice Brennan held that a federal court could enjoin enforcement of the Louisiana criminal statutes without waiting to see whether a state court would issue a narrowing interpretation that might save its constitutionality.[47] The opinion overruled a divided three-judge federal court whose majority had dismissed the suit, declaring that federal intervention "truly . . . would be a massive emasculation of the last vestige of the dignity of sovereignty."[48] Indeed, Brennan's extremely controversial 5–2 decision went to the verge of denying a state any control over interpretation and enforcement of its own laws.

Because Justices Black, Stewart, and initially Goldberg had all withdrawn from *Dombrowski* for various reasons, Justice Brennan had needed to convince Justice White to join his opinion. According to Justice Brennan's law clerks,

> Justice Brennan's original drafts reasoned that the justifications for the vagueness doctrine dictated that there be no prosecution for conduct occurring prior to an acceptable narrowing construction. . . . [But] Justice White found this inconsistent with the traditional vagueness doctrine, which permitted the use of a narrowing construction arrived at in the course of a state criminal prosecution and allowed the application of such a construction to prior conduct. Justice Brennan resolved the inconsistency by expressly disapproving these cases, but this proved too much for Justice White. A compromise was finally worked out permitting retrospective application of a permissible construction, in the absence of surprise, but requiring that the construction itself, if not readily apparent, be arrived at in noncriminal proceedings.[49]

Three years later, under the threat that *Dombrowski* might itself be overruled, Justice Brennan introduced a still more limited reading of the case, holding that it applied only to allegations of "impropriety of (state officials) invoking [an overbroad] statute in bad faith."[50] Given the reluctance of the justices to ever overtly find bad motives, it was tantamount to eliminating the effectiveness of *Dombrowski* in preventing state harassment of civil rights activists.[51] Two years after the Warren Court ended, this was made perfectly clear in *Younger v. Harris* (1971), which effectively overruled *Dombrowski*.[52]

NEW YORK TIMES V. SULLIVAN (1964)

The most dramatic illustration of the intersection of the First Amendment and the civil rights movement was the decision in *New York Times v. Sullivan* (1964),[53] subjecting state libel laws for the first time to First Amendment scrutiny. The case demonstrated that the southern policy of massive resistance extended well beyond localized efforts to destroy the NAACP.

The *New York Times* case arose from a campaign of harassment by Alabama officials to prevent civil rights organizations from raising funds in the North for, among other things, the legal defense of Dr. Martin Luther King Jr., who had been indicted for perjury in Montgomery. The officials brought a libel suit in the Alabama courts against the *New York Times* for several misstatements of fact that appeared in a fundraising advertisement the newspaper had published. A state court imposed $500,000 in damages (about $3.7 million in 2019 dollars) against the newspaper, but there were also eleven other pending libel suits by other officials seeking an additional $5.6 million (about $41 million in 2019 dollars) against the *New York Times*. Five other lawsuits had also been brought against the CBS television network seeking $1.7 million ($14 million in 2019 dollars) due to its news broadcasts about the advertisements.[54]

There were two separate sets of lawsuits brought against the *New York Times*. The first (potential liability of $3 million) was for the advertisement. The second (potential liability of $3.1 million) was for a series of articles by *New York Times* reporter Harrison E. Salisbury. (The $6.1 million total potential liability against the newspaper was worth $45 million in 2019 dollars.) In addition, five libel suits against CBS News (potential liability of $1.7 million) were worth $14 million in 2019.

The threat was clear. If local judges and juries could impose millions of dollars in damages on the preeminent national newspaper for failure to check the factual accuracy of each statement in every advertisement it ran, then no newspaper could ever afford to risk publishing controversial material.

Justice Brennan was assigned the opinion in the case. As his law clerks observed, "The Court's deliberations . . . were marked by a notable harmony on basic principles and an equally notable disharmony on less important points. The disagreement over relatively minor issues made it questionable until almost the last minute whether the Brennan opinion could command a majority of the Court."[55]

At the conference, the justices voted unanimously to reverse the damage award, but the majority were "inclined to do so on virtually the narrowest possible ground." Given the historic opinion that eventually did emerge, it is striking that at first Justice Brennan rested his vote on a quite technical view of the appropriate evidentiary standard.[56]

Justices Black and Douglas unsurprisingly declared that all discussion of public affairs or criticism of official conduct was protected against libel by the First Amendment. As Black observed, "These kinds of cases provide a method to put newspapers out of business. The amount of the verdict reflects the local feeling that the *Times* belongs to a foreigner who is an enemy of Alabama."[57]

Justice Harlan's declaration that "we must lay down new constitutional rules for state libel laws" set the tone for the remainder of the discussion. All of the justices except Black, Douglas, and Goldberg agreed with Harlan's view that "the First Amendment does not outlaw [all] state libel laws, even in the field of public affairs." Moreover, Alabama's eight-year delay in the *NAACP* case appears to have moderated even Harlan's usual deference to state decision-making. "We should finally dispose of this case," he continued. "The rule must not permit retrial of this case, [and] should not leave loopholes for other cases." On the merits, he proposed a "two-pronged test in the public affairs field": a high standard of proof and an "*actual* malice" test for punitive damages. He indicated that he might even "go so far" as to eliminate punitive damages entirely in civil libel suits.[58]

Justice Brennan indicated that he was "not far" from Harlan, following Brennan's suggestion that a "clear, convincing and unequivocal" standard of proof be borrowed from "our expatriation cases." But Justice Goldberg declared that "we should not go on standards of proof" and agreed with Black and Douglas that "in the public domain," libel suits should be entirely barred by the First Amendment.[59]

In his first circulated draft, Justice Brennan went beyond the consensus of the conference majority and for the first time applied the "actual malice" standard not to punitive damages but instead to the evidence required before a public official could successfully bring a libel action against a critic of his official conduct. Within three weeks he had secured agreement from the chief justice and Justice White, but Justices Black, Douglas, and Goldberg held out for the position that the First Amendment barred all libel judgments resulting from criticism of a public official for his official conduct. (Black nevertheless sent Brennan a note stating "You know of course that despite my position and what I write, I think you are doing a wonderful job in the *Times* case and however it finally comes out it is bound to be a very long step toward preserving the right to communicate ideas.")[60] "With [these] three Justices alienated from the Brennan position, it was evident that, if the Brennan position was to have a majority, it could not lose more than one vote from the group consisting of the Justices Clark, Harlan and Stewart. The reaction of Justice Harlan was awaited with some trepidation." Soon after, "a letter from Justice Harlan . . . showed this fear to have been amply warranted."[61]

Harlan began his flip-flop, discussed above in *NAACP v. Button*,[62] over the question of a new trial. He first declared that the Judicial Code authorized a reversal without sending the case back to the Alabama courts for a new trial. Brennan then reluctantly included Harlan's analysis in his next draft.[63] But when this analysis was shown to be faulty, Harlan completely reversed course and not only agreed that a new trial could not be foreclosed but also insisted that this meant that Brennan should eliminate his lengthy analysis of why the evidence in the record was insufficient to warrant a new trial.[64] Brennan now agreed to discard the passages that he had included to satisfy Harlan's original wish to bar a new trial but refused to acquiesce in Harlan's further insistence that he eliminate his analysis of the evidence. As expected, Harlan wrote that he would have to dissent. "The question now was whether anyone would agree with Justice Harlan."[65]

Justice Stewart did not agree and instead sent Justice Brennan a note of agreement. Although Justice Clark had previously also sent a note of agreement, "it was known," probably from his clerks, that he "was now seriously attracted to the Harlan point of view, and it was also suspected that Justice White might be wavering from his earlier agreement. There was thus a very real doubt about whether the entire Brennan opinion could command a majority of the Court." With Brennan's "worst fears . . . being realized" about Justice Clark's position, Justice White also "got into the act" and separated himself from the Brennan opinion. "The fight was thus apparently over," and Brennan turned to an "unsatisfactory . . . hybrid . . . compromise" proposed by Justices Douglas and Goldberg that would indicate that the Harlan forces agreed with the actual malice standard but not the analysis of the evidence, while they did not agree with the malice standard but agreed with the evidentiary analysis.[66]

But one day later Justice Clark, who the day before "had suddenly produced his sharp separate opinion, just as suddenly notified Justice Brennan that he had decided to withdraw it" if Brennan would justify his analysis of the evidence in terms of "effective judicial administration." Brennan promptly complied, and Justice White then also returned to the fold. With the agreement of the chief justice and Justice Stewart, "who expressed the view that the entire battle smacked of quibbling," a majority was finally consolidated. "The final move took place" on the evening before the opinion was announced, "when Justice Harlan telephoned Justice Brennan to inform him that he was withdrawing his separate opinion and unreservedly joining the Brennan opinion."[67]

In one of the great opinions of American constitutional law, Justice Brennan brilliantly reviewed the history of the First Amendment. He focused on the infamous Sedition Act of 1798, which had been enacted by President John Adams's administration. "Although the Sedition Act was never tested in this Court," Brennan declared, "the attack upon its validity has carried the day in the court of history."[68] He thus concluded that the First Amendment bars libel laws from being used to discourage criticism of public officials. "We consider this case against the background of a profound national commitment to the principle that debate on public issues should be uninhibited, robust, and wide-open, and that it may well include vehement, caustic, and sometimes unpleasantly sharp attacks on government and public officials," Brennan wrote in one of his most quoted statements.

After his two historic opinions in *Baker v. Carr* (1962) and *NAACP v. Button* (1963), Brennan, for a third consecutive term, had written a historic opinion that completely recast an entire area of constitutional law. As a result, the mantle of intellectual leadership of the liberal bloc had begun to pass from Justice Black to Justice Brennan. For a quarter century, Black had stood at the head of that sometimes powerless bloc. From his early lonely insistence that the Fourteenth Amendment incorporated the Bill of Rights as a limitation on the states, he had managed to persuade a Warren Court majority to adopt substantially all of this once revolutionary position. In the darkest periods of the Cold War, his almost religious belief in the First Amendment cast him as a protector of unpopular minorities and as a heroic prophet of the values underlying self-government. But nothing revealed his nobility of spirit better than his ability to transcend his own background and lead the court in overturning racial segregation and discrimination in American life.

New York Times Co. v. *Sullivan* is a dramatic example of a consciousness-raising phenomenon that occurred quite often during the Warren Era. The struggle over civil rights in the South repeatedly raised questions involving the boundaries of political struggle as well as the parameters of legitimate criticism of government actions. It was one of the rare periods in American history in which the Supreme Court largely sympathized with the substance of antigovernment criticism. In these circumstances, it was much easier to appreciate the deepest meaning of the constitutional guarantees of freedom of speech and association, which through most of its history the Supreme Court had managed to ignore.

7

THE REVOLUTION
IN CRIMINAL JUSTICE

The Warren Court efforts to reform criminal procedure focused on both police methods and protection of criminal defendants. The impetus for the court's dramatic intervention in the criminal justice system was a growing recognition of the pervasiveness of racism and brutality in the states' administration of the criminal law.

Two major factors focused the Warren Court's attention on the operation of the criminal justice system: first, a growing recognition that the criminal law was a major instrument for preserving the structure of racial hierarchy in the South, and, second, the realization that the police in many large cities both in the North and the South had regularly deployed "the third degree" to extract confessions from criminal suspects.

Before the late nineteenth century, the Supreme Court jurisdiction to review criminal convictions was almost nonexistent. In the federal courts, "there was no review at all until 1879, while serious crimes could not be reviewed as a matter of right before 1891."[1] Indeed, most of the leading cases of Supreme Court review of state criminal convictions occurred after 1931.[2]

As a result of the Criminal Appeals Act of 1907, the Supreme Court's review of criminal cases somewhat increased.[3] During the next seventeen years, the Supreme Court heard appeals in 137 criminal cases.[4] These cases forced the justices for the first time to engage with the nature of criminal justice in the South, which soon contributed to the dissolution of the web of denial that had become a prominent feature of Supreme Court encounters with the South.

Beginning in 1923 and increasing in momentum during the 1930s, the court intervened to apply the Due Process Clause to overturn criminal convictions of Black defendants sentenced to death in proceedings that displayed all the characteristics of a "legal lynching."[5] *Moore v. Dempsey* (1923) marked the first occasion in which the justices overcame their long-standing reluctance to overturn a state criminal conviction.[6] In a 6–2 opinion, Justice Oliver Wendell Holmes recited an appalling set of facts in which five Black defendants were convicted of murder and sentenced to death in the midst of mob violence that had led local Arkansas officials to "promise . . . that if the mob would refrain . . . they would execute those found guilty in the form of law." African American witnesses were "whipped and tortured" until they would testify against the defendants. Black people were "systematically excluded from both grand and petit juries," and the defendants were assigned counsel only on the morning of the trial. At the trial, which lasted less than an hour, counsel for the defendants did not even call one witness, challenge any juror, or seek to move the trial to a less hostile venue. The all-white jury took only five minutes to return a guilty verdict.[7]

Justice Holmes held that "if . . . the whole proceeding is a mask—that counsel, jury and judge were swept to the fatal end by an irresistible wave of public passion," there was a failure of constitutional due process.[8]

During the 1930s, the death sentences imposed by Alabama on all but one of the so-called Scottsboro Boys (nine young black males accused of raping two white women) aroused national and international protest.[9] The legal proceedings had taken place "from beginning to end . . . in an atmosphere of tense, hostile and excited public sentiment."[10] In two separate cases, the Supreme Court made new law in overturning their convictions.

In *Powell v. Alabama* (1932), the court held that failure to appoint counsel in a capital case—at least "where the defendant is unable to employ counsel, and is incapable adequately of making his own defense because of ignorance, feeble mindedness, illiteracy, or the like"—was a ground for reversal.[11] In *Norris v. Alabama* (1935), the court held that where there was a "long-continued, unvarying, and wholesale exclusion of negroes from jury service," whether at the grand or trial jury stage, the conviction was unconstitutional.[12] In another case, *Brown v. Mississippi* (1936),[13] the court, after finding that the confessions of three Black sharecroppers, convicted of murdering their white landlord, had been extracted through torture, reversed their death sentences.[14]

Michael Klarman summarizes the circumstances of the four cases:

[They] arose from three similar episodes. Southern blacks were charged with serious crimes against whites: rape or murder. The defendants were nearly lynched before trial. Mobs consisting of hundreds or thousands of whites surrounded the courthouses, demanding that the defendants be turned over for execution. No change of venue was granted, except in the Scottsboro retrial. Lynchings were avoided only because state militiamen armed with machine guns surrounded the courthouses. Serious doubt existed—at the time of the trials, not just in retrospect—as to the guilt of the defendants. The defendants in *Moore* and *Brown* were tortured into confessing. Lawyers were appointed only a day or even less before trial, without adequate opportunity to consult clients, interview witnesses, or prepare defense strategy. Trials took place soon after the crimes to avoid lynchings—less than a week in *Brown*, twelve days in *Powell*, and a month in *Moore*. Trials lasted only a few hours—forty-five minutes in *Moore*—and juries, from which blacks were intentionally excluded, deliberated only a few minutes before imposing death sentences.[15]

By 1940 as Western Europe lay prostrate under Adolf Hitler's boot, Supreme Court opinions began to highlight the differences between democracy and tyranny. In *Chambers v. Florida* (1940),[16] a unanimous Supreme Court reversed a death sentence for murder and extended *Brown v. Mississippi* to cases involving defendants whose confessions had been extracted under coercive circumstances, short of the torture condemned in *Brown*. Justice Black, whose appointment to the court three years earlier had been tainted by revelations of his earlier membership in the Ku Klux Klan, delivered a powerful opinion that signaled to the white South that he could not be relied on to defend its system of racial subordination. "Tyrannical governments," he wrote, "had immemorially utilized dictatorial criminal procedure and punishment to make scapegoats of the weak, or of helpless political, religious, or racial minorities and those who differed, who would not conform and who resisted tyranny."[17] "Over the next two years," Klarman writes, "the Court decided four more similar cases. Each involved the murder of a white man or the rape of a white woman, followed by a police roundup of numerous blacks, without any particularized suspicion. Each defendant was held incommunicado for up to a week and relentlessly interrogated until he confessed. . . . [T]he confessions were the only direct evidence of the defendants' guilt." In two of the four cases, the justices reversed the death sentences on the basis of *Chambers* "without even bothering to hear oral arguments—a virtually unprecedented procedure at that time."[18]

By the time World War II ended, then, the Supreme Court had clearly served notice on the South that its system of criminal justice as applied to Black defendants would be subjected to serious constitutional scrutiny by the court.

Just as capital sentences imposed on African Americans triggered Supreme Court scrutiny for the first time, a major critical report in 1931 on the operation of the criminal justice system shed light on widespread police corruption and brutality throughout the nation. The report of the National Commission on Law Observance and Enforcement, popularly known as the Wickersham Commission after its chairman, former attorney general George W. Wickersham, highlighted the widespread prevalence of police brutality and corruption, magnified after a decade of often corrupt or inept enforcement of Prohibition laws.[19]

The Wickersham Commission report focused on the use of "the Third Degree" by American police. The report defined "the Third Degree" as "the employment of methods which inflict suffering, physical or mental, upon a person in order to obtain information about a crime." The report concluded that the existence of the third degree "is widespread throughout the country" and that "physical brutality is extensively practiced."[20]

> The methods are various. They range from beating to harsher forms of torture. The commoner forms are beating with the fists or with some implement, especially the rubber hose, that inflicts pain but is not likely to leave permanent visible scars. . . . The method most commonly employed is protracted questioning . . . so protracted that the prisoner's energies are spent and his powers of resistance overcome. At times such questioning is the only method used. At times the questioning is accompanied by blows or by throwing continuous straining light upon the face of the suspect. At times the suspect is kept standing for hours, or deprived of food or sleep, or his sleep is periodically interrupted to resume questioning.[21]

The Wickersham Commission surveyed police practices in fifteen American cities, only two of which, Dallas and El Paso, were in the South. "The third degree is widely and brutally employed in New York City," the report declared. It quoted a former New York district attorney who observed that "the third degree has now become established and recognized practice in the police department of the city of New York. Every police station in the city is equipped with the instruments to administer the torture incident to that process."[22]

In Buffalo, the commissioner of police displayed open contempt for constitutional rights of criminal suspects. "If I have to violate the Constitution or my oath of office, I'll violate the Constitution," he declared. "A policeman should be as free as a fireman to protect his community. Nobody ever thinks of hedging a fireman about with a lot of laws that favor the fire. . . . Shysters have turned the Constitution into a refuge for the criminal. . . . I'm going to protect the community. If in so doing I make a mistake and trespass on somebody's rights, let him sue."[23]

The Wickersham Commission report noted that in Chicago, police used various methods, including "the application of rubber hose to the back or the pit of the stomach, kicks in the shins, beating the shins with a club, blows struck with a telephone book on the side of a victim's head." It added that "the Chicago telephone book is a heavy one and a swinging blow with it may stun a man without leaving a mark." The report especially remarked on "the frequent participation of prosecuting attorneys in the third-degree sessions." "Illegal detention and detention *incommunicado* are said to be common" in Chicago, the report observed.[24]

A few cities had restricted or even eliminated the third degree. "The third degree exists in Newark but subject to control," the report noted. "The use of pressure in various forms to get confessions is frequent, but it is kept within bounds, so that there are no outstanding flagrant cases and public attention, therefore, is not directed to the practice."[25] In addition, "The decision to employ force is made, it is said, only after a protracted period of questioning without violence has failed to 'break' a man. This long questioning may involve two or three nights of wakefulness, with more or less constant pressure upon the suspect by relays of detectives. There is reason to believe that food is sometimes denied and that threats are made during the process."[26]

In Boston, "the third degree and related types of police illegality are at a minimum . . . , though they are not quite nonexistent."[27]

"There was a good deal of third-degree practice in Philadelphia" until just over two years earlier, when a new director of public safety and a chief of detectives were named. "Having been acquainted with an earlier regime which permitted brutal third-degree practices," the new chief of detectives, William B. Connelly, "believe[d] that these practices harden the criminal and make more work for the police in the end. In his opinion, it is necessary for the reduction of crime that the detectives should have a reputation among the criminals for squareness and decency. He insists without qualification that third-degree practice is unnecessary and does not get results."[28]

Despite this evidence of change, the report concluded that in ten of fifteen cities studied "there was no doubt of the existence of the third-degree practices at that time." And it named another sixteen cities as well as the District of Columbia in which during the previous decade "there have been proven instances" of the third-degree practice.[29]

The Wickersham Commission report, which appeared just as many of the future justices of the Warren Court were arriving at early professional success, shaped their generation's expectations of how the criminal justice system actually operated. The report's portrait of an out-of-control police system was part of the background one generation later as the Warren Court began its encounter with criminal justice in America. Combined with their growing dismay over a criminal justice system in the South that worked to support white supremacy, the Warren Court justices were already disposed to bring about a revolution in criminal law.

We saw in chapter 4 that under the influence of Justice Hugo Black's call for "total incorporation" of the Bill of Rights, the Warren Court finally settled on "selective incorporation," by which most provisions of the Bill of Rights were extended to the states. Therefore, by the time the Warren Court ended, the rules governing criminal trials in America, which for most of American history had varied widely from state to state, had suddenly become virtually uniform throughout the nation.

THE PUBLIC REACTION TO WARREN COURT CRIMINAL DECISIONS

As the Supreme Court began to restrain the power of the police during the 1960s, no one could have known that its actions would coincide with the most troubled period of violent crime and racial unrest in twentieth-century America. As it turned out, wrote Fred Graham, the Supreme Court reporter for the *New York Times*, the cycles of legal reform and rising crime and racial tensions moved in "uncanny rhythm." In 1962, the Federal Bureau of Investigation's crime index swung upward after several stable years. By the mid-1960s, "record crime increases were being registered each year and waves of Negro riots were raking the cities each summer."[30] "The Supreme Court's reform campaign eventually encountered a monumental incongruity—the Court had announced the most rigid legal limitations that any society had sought to impose on its police at a time when the United States had the most serious crime problem of any so-called advanced nation in the world."[31]

For the American public, three cases decided between 1961 and 1966 highlighted the revolution in criminal law initiated by the Warren Court. Together, they became the focus of Richard M. Nixon's attacks on the court during the 1968 presidential campaign for "hamstringing the peace forces in American society and strengthening the criminal forces."[32] The three cases were

- *Mapp v. Ohio* (1961),[33] which extended the federal exclusionary rule for illegally seized evidence to state criminal proceedings;
- *Gideon v. Wainwright* (1963),[34] which extended the Sixth Amendment right to counsel to state criminal proceedings; and
- *Miranda v. Arizona* (1966),[35] which required that state criminal suspects be informed of their right to remain silent and to request counsel—the famous Miranda warning—before they could be interrogated by police. Failure to give the warning resulted in exclusion of the confession from evidence, which often produced an acquittal.

MAPP V. OHIO (1961)

We saw in our earlier discussion of the controversy over incorporating the Bill of Rights that *Mapp v. Ohio* arrived at the Supreme Court as an obscenity case challenged under the First Amendment and, after a last-minute switch by

Justice Clark, emerged from the court as a 6–3 decision.[36] Five justices overruled *Wolf v. Colorado* (1949) and extended the exclusionary rule to the states,
while Justice Stewart concurred on other grounds.[37]

Applying the exclusionary rule to the states—where the vast majority of
criminal trials take place—produced a revolution in police practices. Realizing that evidence derived from an illegal search would now be excluded at
trial, police and prosecutors reluctantly adapted to a new reality that usually
made it necessary to seek search warrants before conducting a search. When
seven years later in *Katz v. United States* (1967)[38] the Supreme Court overruled
Olmstead v. United States (1928)[39] and held that wiretapping without a warrant was an unconstitutional search and seizure, the potential field of operation of the exclusionary rule suddenly expanded dramatically to include the
vast realm of newer technological communications that would be introduced
by the internet.

The *Mapp* decision was never popular. Newspaper editorials regularly
expressed shock that a concededly guilty defendant could go free because the
police had produced evidence of his guilt by improper means. It meant, as
Judge Cardozo had put it years earlier, allowing the criminal to go free "because
the constable has blundered."[40]

A further objection to *Mapp* focused on its scope. Did *Mapp*'s reversal of
Wolf v. Colorado also entail releasing all those who had been previously convicted with the aid of illegally seized evidence allowed at their trials?

The Supreme Court itself made important moves to restrict the potentially sweeping consequences of *Mapp*. In *Linkletter v. Walker* (1965),[41] the
court took the unprecedented step of limiting the application of *Mapp* to future
cases, so-called prospective overruling.[42] The opinion distinguished *Mapp* from
other cases, such as coerced confession cases, in which an unreliable confession admitted at trial might have been the basis for a wrongful conviction. By
contrast, cases involving illegally seized evidence, Justice Clark reasoned in
Linkletter, should only be excluded prospectively because the illegally seized
evidence continued to be reliable evidence of guilt. Prospective overruling is
appropriate in these cases, Clark declared, because the exclusionary rule is
designed only to affect future police conduct, not to determine whether the
defendants have been reliably convicted.[43]

Prospective overruling thus became a technique for introducing revolutionary changes into criminal law while limiting the public backlash that a traditional retrospective application of the rule changes might have triggered. In
two other cases, *Tehan v. Shott* (1966)[44] and *Johnson v. New Jersey* (1966),[45] the
justices also refused to extend a new constitutional ruling to benefit those who
had been jailed under the old rule.[46]

The court's highly unusual disposition in these prospective overruling cases could be seen as a gesture of appeasement to those who complained that Warren Court decisions were throwing open the prison gates to free those who had been convicted with the help of illegally obtained evidence. In his dissent in *Linkletter*, Justice Black specifically called attention to this motive: "one of the great inherent restraints upon this Court's departure from the field of interpretation to enter that of lawmaking has been the fact that its judgments could not be limited to prospective application."[47]

GIDEON V. WAINWRIGHT (1963)

In *Gideon v. Wainwright*,[48] the Supreme Court unanimously decided that the Sixth Amendment right to counsel extended to the states, thereby overruling *Betts v. Brady* (1942),[49] the case that held that the right to counsel did not apply to the states through the Due Process Clause of the Fourteenth Amendment. Justice Black wrote the opinion, providing him with the satisfaction of overturning the case that had originally spawned his outrage at the court's refusal to apply the Bill of Rights to the states.

Unlike *Mapp* and *Miranda*, the decision in *Gideon* did not spark public outrage. At the time it was decided, only five southern states (Alabama, Florida, Mississippi, North Carolina, and South Carolina) failed to provide counsel for the poor in other than capital cases. Thirty-seven states already assured counsel to defendants as a matter of right in felony cases, while in another eight states the practice of appointing counsel had developed without the benefit of any statute or rule of court.[50]

Appraisals of the *Gideon* case in the South were surprisingly favorable, Anthony Lewis observed. In Florida, whose legislature had long refused to address the problem of the unrepresented indigent, the state legislature reversed course and acted quickly to create a public defender office in each of the state's sixteen judicial circuits. The four other southern states that had not provided counsel for noncapital defendants also acted quickly to comply with the new requirements.[51]

Despite these widespread constructive efforts by states to adapt to the decision, Chief Justice Earl Warren warned that the *Gideon* case might soon "amount almost to a revolution in some states."[52] Though hardly anyone in the public continued to defend the justice of denying counsel to the poor, the institutions for delivering legal services were still widely understaffed and underfunded. Chief Judge J. Edward Lumbard of the Second Circuit Court of Appeals captured the inadequacy of representation even in those states that offered legal services to the poor:

When advised that an indigent needs counsel, the judge usually picks out some lawyer who happens to be in the courtroom. . . . The lawyer then spends a few minutes with his new client at the side of the courtroom. . . . In most of such assignments, after a few minutes of conference, the defendant is advised to plead guilty and he feels he has no choice but to do so. . . . This mock assignment of counsel and the cursory hurry-up job of a busy uncompensated lawyer makes a farce of due process of law and our Bill of Rights. Everyone who participates in the farce knows this—the judge, the district attorney, the assigned lawyer, the bailiff, and of course the defendant himself.[53]

The ultimate success of *Gideon* turned on whether the criminally accused could be provided an appointed lawyer who took the job just as seriously as if he or she were being compensated by the defendant. Unfortunately, even in most of the thirty-seven states that assured counsel to indigent criminal defendants, the process of providing uncompensated lawyers continued to display many of the elements of farce that Judge Lumbard had identified in New York.

Most of the reformers seemed to recognize that some public financial support was necessary to create an adequate system of criminal defense, but they were deeply divided over whether the effort should result in full-time state-employed public defenders or instead in private legal aid societies even if they were subsidized by public funds. A half century later, the argument has hardly abated. As the *New York Times* reported on the fiftieth anniversary of *Gideon v. Wainwright*, legal reformers were continuing to argue over whether public or private legal aid best served the needs of poor criminal defendants.[54] And the question that *Gideon* had answered fifty years earlier has evolved into another related question: Does the U.S. Constitution also require the Supreme Court to determine whether convicted criminal defendants had received adequate assistance of counsel?[55]

MIRANDA V. ARIZONA (1966)

Except for *Brown v. Board of Education* and the two cases in which the Supreme Court struck down the recital of school prayers in public schools,[56] no other decision of the Warren Court generated such a volume of hostility as its ruling in *Miranda v. Arizona.*[57]

Miranda represented the culmination of a generation of criticism of police and prosecutors for extracting and relying on coerced confessions. In one set of cases from the South, police used confessions to buttress the system of white supremacy; in another set of cases, mostly from urban areas, the Wickersham

Commission report had exposed the widespread use of the third degree to extract confessions.

In *Brown v. Mississippi* (1936),[58] the Supreme Court for the first time reversed a capital sentence on the grounds that the Black defendant's confession was involuntary based on the totality of the circumstances. In the thirty years since, various justices had expressed dissatisfaction with the totality of circumstances test, arguing that it provided no guide for determining involuntariness.[59] Chief Justice Warren began his discussion of *Miranda* in conference by rejecting the totality of circumstances approach.[60]

The totality of circumstances standard had been reaffirmed just two years earlier in *Escobedo v. Illinois* (1964).[61] In that case, the defendant was arrested and interrogated for the fatal shooting of his brother-in-law. While in custody he repeatedly asked to see his lawyer, and even though his lawyer was present in the police station, police told Escobedo that he did not want to see him. On the basis of statements he made, Escobedo was convicted of murder. By a 5–4 vote, the Supreme Court reversed the conviction and held that Escobedo's Sixth Amendment right had been violated and that Escobedo's statement was coerced as judged by a totality of the circumstances standard. This set the stage for *Miranda* two years later.

Unusually, Chief Justice Warren opened the conference discussion of *Miranda* by reading from a prepared text. As we saw, he began by rejecting the totality of circumstances test. He then declared:

> Basically, the issue is under the Fifth Amendment and "being a witness against himself." It also might be under the Sixth Amendment, in case there was a lawyer being sought [as in *Escobedo*]. The right against interrogation involves the Fifth Amendment. Talking to the police is different from being interrogated by the police. The right to counsel commences at least when a man is taken into custody, or when police undertake to put him there. Our system is accusatory; there is no right to arrest for investigation, only on probable cause or with a warrant. His right to counsel commences at that moment—the case commences then. This does not mean that a lawyer must be appointed then, but later—interrogation is such a "later" time.[62]

At this point in his presentation to the conference, the Chief Justice offered a six-point statement that closely resembled the eventual Miranda warning.[63] Item 3 reads "[he must be advised] that in time the court may appoint a lawyer."[64]

Justice William Brennan's clerks showed little restraint in claiming that Brennan was in large measure responsible for having the *Miranda* decision turn on the Fifth Amendment rather than on the Sixth Amendment, that is, to rest on Brennan's opinion in *Malloy v. Hogan* (1964)[65] rather than on *Escobedo*.[66]

Warren's opening statement in conference, however, raises doubt about the accuracy of the Brennan clerks' efforts to assign credit to Brennan for the eventual Fifth Amendment approach of Warren's *Miranda* opinion. In that statement, Warren more or less dismisses a Sixth Amendment approach. After declaring that "basically, the issue is under the Fifth Amendment," Warren does digress to acknowledge that "it also might be under the Sixth Amendment, in case there was a lawyer being sought."[67] But there was no evidence that a lawyer was being sought, and Warren immediately returned to a Fifth Amendment analysis.

The decision to rest *Miranda* on the Fifth Amendment, not the Sixth Amendment, had major implications for the chief justice's approach to determining what was required when a person was held for what Warren called "incommunicado interrogation."[68] A Sixth Amendment analysis could lend itself to a narrow rule that a criminal suspect's statement is excludable only if he or she had already retained and requested counsel.[69] Since few felony suspects were in any financial condition to afford retained counsel, a Sixth Amendment analysis might end up only benefiting a small group of wealthy defendants or those connected to organized crime. Escobedo, who was not wealthy but had retained counsel before he was arrested, was a clear exception to the usual pattern.

But the Sixth Amendment might also lead to an expansive rule that no interrogation could take place without counsel being present. Many predicted at the time that this latter interpretation of *Escobedo* would eventually become the rule for police interrogations. In its *Miranda* argument, the American Civil Liberties Union unsuccessfully pressed the court to require the actual presence of a lawyer at any interrogation.[70]

There were constant warnings that any requirement of the presence of a lawyer at the interrogation stage would mean that "there may be no effective, immediate questioning" by the police. "That is not a rule that society will long endure," warned Henry Friendly, the widely respected judge of the Court of Appeals for the Second Circuit.[71]

Brennan also appears to have been concerned that an absolute requirement of counsel would eliminate all confessions. He seems to have believed that a Sixth Amendment analysis would eventually result in a requirement of counsel at the interrogation stage, effectively shutting down confessions. Such a result, he may have concluded, had a good chance of producing backlash against the court.

A Fifth Amendment analysis, by contrast, lent itself to a rule that a suspect must be warned that he had a right to counsel while avoiding the conclusion that the Fifth Amendment required the actual presence of a lawyer in order to render any confession admissible.

All of these reservations were rolled into Justice Brennan's "principal concern": the failure of the opinion to leave any room for legislatures, state or federal, to devise alternative procedures for safeguarding the privilege. His response to Warren's draft sought to persuade the chief justice to acknowledge that Miranda warnings were only one among many possible arrangements for protecting against involuntary confessions.[72] At Brennan's urging, Warren did include the following: "It is impossible for us to foresee the potential alternatives for protecting the privilege which might be devised by Congress or the States in the exercise of their creative rule-making capacities. Therefore, we cannot say that the Constitution necessarily requires adherence to any particular solution for the inherent compulsions of the interrogation process as it is presently conducted."[73]

Though he didn't say so, Brennan was perhaps looking to technology to provide future "potential alternatives" to the *Miranda* rule. For example, a rule might require that any confession would be admissible only if the entire interrogation process had been recorded by video. This might, in Brennan's words, have served to "eliminate the possibility of . . . contests of veracity between the police and the accused." But most police stations did not yet have such technology available.

Despite Brennan's concession, Justice John Marshall Harlan, in dissent, criticized Warren's opinion for imposing a rigid set of requirements on police interrogations. This led Brennan to draft a concurrence in order to respond to Harlan's claim.[74] It concluded with "nothing we hold today prevents the States from devising and applying similar prophylactic means for avoiding the dangers of interrogation which at the same time eliminate the possibility of such contests of veracity between the police and the accused."[75]

Brennan showed this draft concurrence to the chief justice prior to circulation. "The Chief Justice expressed deep concern," Brennan's clerks noted, "not only at the prospect of a separate concurrence, but also at the content of the concurrence—at the proposition that the warnings need not be given if alternative safeguards are created." Although Brennan explained to Warren "that the proposition expressed in the concurrence was already embodied in the Court opinion and that the concurrence was being written solely for emphasis," Warren remained opposed. "Finally, the Justice agreed not to file the concurrence."[76]

Warren's negative reaction to Brennan's draft suggests that Warren actually regarded Brennan's concurrence, which further emphasized the possibility of alternative safeguards, as a threat to his Miranda warning. Warren may have agreed to include Brennan's quite similar earlier language about alternatives in order to demonstrate that he was open-minded and not subject to the inflexibility that the dissenters had claimed. But Brennan's insistence that he was writing solely for emphasis could not overcome Warren's firm conviction that he did not want possible alternatives to be further emphasized.

Warren may have been prescient. The passage that Brennan persuaded Warren to include came back to haunt him years later when it cast doubt on the constitutional standing of Warren's own *Miranda* formula. As Professor Kamisar observed, the Supreme Court, subsequently increasingly populated by justices unfriendly to *Miranda*, undertook a mission of "downsizing" the case. The most active justice in the campaign to undermine *Miranda* was William Rehnquist, who succeeded in downsizing *Miranda* on the premise that a violation of *Miranda* is a violation not of a constitutional right but instead only of a prophylactic rule designed to implement a constitutional right. It followed that the court was free to replace the Miranda warning with another rule that might do the job better. And citing the passage on alternatives that Brennan had championed, Rehnquist claimed that the Warren Court itself had recognized that alternatives to the Miranda warning were constitutionally permissible.[77]

Brennan later told his biographers that in retrospect, he was relieved that Warren had persuaded him not to file his concurrence. He contrasted what had become the standardized version of the Miranda warning "to the confusing medley of fifty different state formulations his concurrence might have encouraged." "'Obviously, it would have been just dead wrong,'" Brennan told his interviewer. "'Thank heavens I woke up.'"[78]

Still, if the "alternatives" that Brennan originally contemplated were "technological alternatives" as with the video, designed to monitor the process of producing a valid confession, he may have been right after all. One might test this idea with a thought experiment. What if the Supreme Court in *Miranda* had possessed the power to order Congress to pay for installing videos in every police station in the land and such technology were available? Would we choose to promulgate the *Miranda* rule or instead to institute the requirement that to be admissible, the interrogation process resulting in a confession must be videorecorded? Which path would have been more likely to reduce, as Brennan had put it, a "contest of veracity between the police and the accused"? But unfortunately, Brennan never did argue that the future "alternatives" he sought to champion were primarily technological advances.

TERRY V. OHIO (1968)

In 1967 and 1968, the Supreme Court faced mounting criticism for decisions protecting criminal suspects' constitutional rights. By the fall of 1967 Richard Nixon, the leading Republican presidential candidate, had linked the Supreme Court to "shocking crime and disorder" in the cities, blaming "the cumulating effect of many decisions, each one of which has weakened the law and encouraged the criminal."[79] Nixon would repeat the charge that "some of our courts have gone too far in weakening the peace forces as against the criminal forces" in nearly every campaign speech throughout the next year.[80] Meanwhile, in what the *New York Times* called "the most crippling Congressional attack aimed at the Court in its history," a coalition of senators proposed anticrime legislation that would have reversed some of the court's decisions on suspects' rights and stripped the court of jurisdiction to hear certain future appeals.[81]

The "stop and frisk" case *Terry v. Ohio* was argued in December 1967 and decided the following June. The court's deliberations show that it took notice of the growing public opposition to its criminal procedure decisions.[82] Earl C. Dudley Jr., Warren's principal clerk for the *Terry* decision, later reported that the justices were unwilling to be perceived as tying the hands of the police in dealing with dangerous situations on the streets.[83] In *Terry*, a white police officer had stopped two Black men in downtown Cleveland whom he suspected of preparing to rob a store (but lacked probable cause to arrest), questioned them, and frisked them for weapons. He found a pistol on Terry, who was convicted of carrying a concealed weapon. Terry challenged the lawfulness of the search and seizure.[84]

During oral argument and in conference, Warren stressed the police officer's right to protect himself, and all nine justices initially voted to affirm.[85] Warren assigned himself the opinion, and his early drafts emphasized the need to protect the police. "A police officer," he declared, "is not required to sacrifice his life on the altar of judicial scholasticism which ignores the deadly realities of criminal investigation and law enforcement."[86] Brennan's chambers thought that Warren's early drafts were "written in a rhetoric often almost embarrassingly sympathetic to the plight of the policeman" and "read dangerously much like an apology for past decisions which have been charged with having overly restricted the police."[87]

Brennan and others feared that the court's tone could inadvertently legitimize the "aggressive patrol" police tactics used in urban ghettos that had been recently criticized in a report from the President's Commission on Law Enforcement and the Administration of Justice.[88] This concern was only heightened when Judge George Edwards, the former police commissioner of Detroit, told Brennan at a judicial conference that the police would view *Terry* as a mandate in their favor to stop and frisk at will.[89] Brennan relayed this fear to Warren:

> I've become acutely concerned that the mere fact of our affirmance in *Terry* will be taken by the police all over the country as our license to them to carry on, indeed widely expand, present "aggressive surveillance" techniques which the press tell us are being deliberately employed in Miami, Chicago, Detroit + other ghetto cities. This is happening, of course, in response to the "crime in the streets" alarums being sounded in this election year in the Congress, the White House + every Governor's office. . . . It will not

take much of this to aggravate the already white heat resentment of ghetto Negroes against the police—+ the Court will become the scape goat.[90]

Wishing to downplay the race and criminal justice issues engulfing the nation, the court took the unusual step of reversing its decision to grant the NAACP Legal Defense Fund oral argument time,[91] and it would almost entirely eliminate any mention of race from the final opinion.[92] Some justices even considered delaying the opinion so that it would not be handed down just before the summer when stop-and-frisk problems were greatest.[93]

In addition to the problem of tone, Warren encountered conceptual and analytical difficulties in explaining why the *Terry* stop was constitutional. The justices had originally agreed to decide the case on "probable cause" rather than "reasonable suspicion" grounds.[94] Yet, their question was not the familiar one of whether there was probable cause to arrest, which all agreed was absent in this case. The justices sought to avoid a rigid rule that would prevent the police from doing anything unless the officer had what a court would later determine to be probable cause for arrest. So, they reframed the question into one of whether there was probable cause to investigate suspicious behavior by asking the suspect to give an account of himself—in other words, probable cause to "stop" the suspect—and probable cause to believe that the suspect might be armed and dangerous, or probable cause to "frisk."[95] Instead of focusing on the suspect's behavior, Warren tried to frame the new probable cause inquiry in terms of the police conduct at issue: the less intrusive the police officer had been, the less probable cause he would need to show a judge.[96] This balancing model, though, was vague and uncertain, and it seemed to turn probable cause into a reasonableness test. The best Warren could say was that the officer in *Terry* had acted reasonably on facts that fit some model of probable cause.[97]

After several justices expressed dissatisfaction with Warren's drafts, Harlan proposed rejecting probable cause in favor of the reasonable suspicion formula approved by the American Law Institute.[98] Contending that a stop was fundamentally different from an arrest, Harlan argued that the traditionally objective probable cause standard did not work in on-the-street investigation situations, where stop-and-frisk questions came down to the officer's allegation that the suspect had aroused reasonable suspicion.[99] Brennan, who agreed that Warren's confusing probable cause standard was a mistake, considered the alternatives of agreeing with Harlan's reasonableness standard or completely changing his view on the case's holding and finding that no *Terry* stop is constitutional absent the traditional probable cause to arrest.[100] Deciding that the probable cause to arrest rule went too far in holding unreasonable as a matter of law conduct that in fact a judge would find reasonable,[101] Brennan rewrote Warren's draft, changing the constitutional standard from "probable cause" to the "reasonableness" of the search and deleting much of the propolice language.[102] Warren accepted most of Brennan's revisions, and the chief justice's ghostwritten opinion won near unanimity.[103]

In the final weeks, however, Douglas changed his mind and decided to dissent on the ground that probable cause to arrest was the constitutionally required standard. "There have been powerful hydraulic pressures throughout our history that bear heavily on the Court to water down constitutional guarantees and give the police the upper hand," he observed. "That hydraulic pressure has probably never been greater than it is today."[104] He suggested that the political environment had pressured the court into watering down the Fourth Amendment's "probable cause" requirement into a standard of mere "reasonableness."

The dissent completely surprised the justices,[105] but the Warren Court's liberals would soon come to sympathize with Douglas's fear that *Terry* had watered down Fourth Amendment rights. In 1972 Justice Thurgood Marshall, who had joined the *Terry* majority, acknowledged "just how prescient" Douglas had been and bemoaned the fact that "the delicate balance that *Terry* struck was simply too delicate, too susceptible to the 'hydraulic pressures' of the day."[106] Brennan, quoting Judge Henry Friendly, also recognized that *Terry* may have "opened the sluicegates for serious and unintended erosion of the protection of the Fourth Amendment."[107] Justices who had preferred a flexible standard to a fixed rule found that such standards were much more susceptible to being watered down.

It should be noted that the revolution in criminal justice for which the Warren Court became famous was remarkably short-lived. It took place between 1961 and 1966. By the time the court encountered *Terry v. Ohio* during the 1968 presidential campaign, the Supreme Court encountered backlash and began its retreat.

8

CITIZENSHIP,
CAPITAL PUNISHMENT,
AND CRUEL AND
UNUSUAL PUNISHMENT

It seems astonishing in retrospect that it took almost 170 years before anyone on the U.S. Supreme Court ever suggested that capital punishment was unconstitutional. Until Justice Arthur J. Goldberg wrote the first draft of his 1963 "Dissent from a Denial of Certiorari," maintaining that the death penalty was itself an unconstitutional cruel and unusual punishment, no attorney before the court appears to have argued that this practice, so deeply rooted in Anglo-American legal history, could violate the U.S. Constitution. Yet, only six years after the Goldberg memo during the waning months of the Warren Court, eight of the nine justices seemed prepared, on one ground or another, to overturn a capital sentence as unconstitutional. Despite their unprecedented level of agreement, the justices were so sharply divided on the grounds of decision that the case, *Maxwell v. Bishop*, was put over until the next term. By then, both Chief Justice Earl Warren and Justice Abe Fortas had resigned, and the new court, led by Chief Justice Warren E. Burger, reversed the death sentence without breaking any new ground.[1]

It remained for the Burger Court, by a 5–4 vote, to declare existing systems of capital punishment unconstitutional in *Furman v. Georgia* (1972).[2] By 1976 as the Supreme Court upheld these new laws restoring capital punishment, the death penalty had returned to American law.[3]

Two earlier surprises had prepared the way for the Supreme Court's deliberations in *Maxwell v. Bishop*. First was Justice Arthur Goldberg's 1963 declaration, out of the blue, that the death penalty was an unconstitutional cruel and unusual punishment. Second, almost as surprising, was a 6–3 decision in *Witherspoon v. Illinois* (1968) striking down as unconstitutional a capital sentence handed down by a jury from which opponents of the death penalty had been excluded, the so-called death qualified jury.[4]

Three separate challenges to constitutional orthodoxy unexpectedly converged during the Warren era, producing revolutionary changes in constitutional law. Almost from out of nowhere, the Eighth Amendment prohibition against cruel and unusual punishments suddenly emerged from a long sleep to become a significant arbiter of the fate of men and women. This development immediately merged with two other unanticipated movements: a new recognition by the Supreme Court of an irrevocable right of citizenship and the first moves by the Supreme Court to constitutionalize abolition of the death penalty.

At issue in *Trop v. Dulles* (1958) was the revocation of the U.S. citizenship of a deserter from the armed forces, who could otherwise have been subject to capital punishment.[5] In a plurality opinion, Chief Justice Warren declared that the cruel and unusual punishments clause of the Eighth Amendment barred Congress from revoking U.S. citizenship as a punishment.[6] *Trop* marks the convergence of two separate strands of development in the law involving dramatic changes in both the idea of citizenship and the meaning of the Eighth Amendment's ban on cruel and unusual punishments.

THE RIGHT OF CITIZENSHIP

Democracy emerged as the foundational value of the Warren Court's constitutional jurisprudence in the expatriation cases, in which the concept of citizenship underwent revolutionary change as the court tied it to values underlying democratic theory. In these cases, the court made clear that citizenship in a democracy is a basic right—superior to any governmental interest—that cannot be destroyed except by the will of the citizen.

The expatriation cases concerned the constitutionality of congressional statutes that deemed certain citizens to have forfeited their citizenship if they performed particular acts. Although the Fourteenth Amendment defined who citizens are, it did not expressly address whether or how citizens might forfeit citizenship. For almost the next century, it was assumed that Congress could create rules for forcible denationalization. The Expatriation Act of 1907 provided that a citizen would be "deemed to have expatriated himself" or herself through certain acts including naturalization in a foreign state, taking an oath of allegiance to a foreign state, or marriage to a foreign man. Congress later expanded the list to include voting in a foreign election, desertion in wartime, and departure from the United States in wartime to avoid military service. Two older Supreme Court cases had upheld the denationalization of a woman who married a foreigner[7] and that of another woman who obtained foreign citizenship.[8]

The Warren Court struck down many of these statutory provisions, ultimately asserting that citizenship is a constitutional right that Congress has no power to take away and that the only means of expatriation is a citizen's voluntary relinquishment of citizenship.

The first of the Warren Court's key expatriation cases arrived during the 1956 term but was not decided until 1958 because the court was closely divided, with several justices changing their votes over the course of deliberations.[9] In *Perez v. Brownell* (1958),[10] one 5–4 majority affirmed Congress's power to strip a person of citizenship for voting in a foreign election, but in *Trop v. Dulles*,[11] decided on the same day, a different 5–4 majority held that Congress had no power to denationalize a citizen for wartime desertion from the military. Justice William Brennan was the swing vote. Concurring separately in *Trop*, he reasoned—unpersuasively—that expatriation for foreign voting was rationally related to Congress's power to supervise foreign affairs but that expatriation for desertion was not a rational exercise of Congress's war power.[12]

Chief Justice Warren took a particular interest in these cases. His powerful dissent in *Perez* charged that Congress lacked the power to denationalize anyone without his or her consent.[13] His opinion for the court in *Trop* reiterated this constitutional argument and added, for the first time, that involuntary expatriation was also a cruel and unusual punishment because it amounted to "the total destruction of the individual's status in organized society."[14] Famously reasoning that the Eighth Amendment "must draw its meaning from the evolving standards of decency that mark the progress of a maturing society,"[15] the chief justice succeeded in importing an evolutionary perspective to Eighth Amendment jurisprudence, one to which Justice Goldberg would turn five years later as he mounted an Eighth Amendment challenge to the death penalty.

But in *Trop*, Warren's Eighth Amendment argument failed to sway Justice Brennan and thus to win a majority of the court. Indeed, the chief justice's Eighth Amendment argument would never win a majority and was to have no further influence in the expatriation field for which it was originally revived. Instead, its greatest influence was in shaping the emerging constitutional attack on capital punishment.

Eventually, Justice Brennan came over to Chief Justice Warren's position that Congress lacked authority over involuntary denationalization, enabling Warren to win a series of victories. In 1963, a 5–4 majority held that in the absence of criminal due process Congress could not impose expatriation on draft dodgers who left the United States,[16] and the next year the court held that the forced denationalization of a naturalized American citizen residing in a foreign country unconstitutionally discriminated between naturalized and native-born citizens.[17] Finally, in the all-important case of *Afroyim v. Rusk* (1967),[18] the court once again considered a challenge to the statutory provision that in *Perez* had resulted in loss of citizenship for voting in a foreign election. This time, a 5–4 majority formally overruled *Perez* and also struck down the same statutory provision that had authorized revocation of Afroyim's citizenship for voting in an Israeli election. The court per Justice Hugo Black adopted the theory of Warren's dissent and held in the broadest language that citizenship was a basic right guaranteed by the Fourteenth Amendment that, under the citizenship clause, Congress wholly lacked power to terminate. Citizenship could be lost only if voluntarily and intentionally relinquished. Chief Justice Warren's view finally prevailed.[19]

The concept of dual citizenship, which had long been opposed by the U.S. government, has become more accepted in the years since *Afroyim* was decided. In 1980, the administration of President Jimmy Carter concluded that the Bancroft Treaties—a series of bilateral agreements formulated between 1868 and 1937 that provided for automatic loss of citizenship upon foreign naturalization of a U.S. citizen—were no longer enforceable, due in part to *Afroyim*, and gave notice terminating these treaties.[20] In 1990, the State Department adopted new guidelines for evaluating potential loss-of-citizenship cases, under which the government is required to assume that Americans do not intend to give up their citizenship unless they explicitly indicate this intention to a U.S. official. As explained by Peter J. Spiro, "In the long run, *Afroyim*'s vision of an absolute right to retain citizenship has been largely, if quietly, vindicated. As a matter of practice, it is now virtually impossible to lose American citizenship without formally and expressly renouncing it."[21]

On its surface, the court's shift from the position that Congress could take away citizenship contrary to a citizen's will to the view that Congress could never take away citizenship in the absence of voluntarily relinquishment was a victory for the language of rights. Citizenship, Chief Justice Warren declares in his *Perez* dissent, is a right in itself: it is "man's basic right for it is nothing less than the right to have rights."[22] Much of his *Trop* opinion may be seen as a rights-based defense of citizenship against a republican-style vision of citizenship as civic duty. Even shirking the basic responsibilities of citizenship, such as wartime desertion, could not result in deprivation of a person's citizenship because "the deprivation of citizenship is not a weapon that the Government may use to express its displeasure at a citizen's conduct, however reprehensible that conduct may be."[23] The idea that basic rights turn on an evaluation of civic virtue—or lack thereof—may have seemed too closely associated with contemporary persecution of the "un-American." Reconceptualized from being an expression of civic virtue within the citizenry, citizenship became enshrined in the framework of constitutional rights.

For Chief Justice Warren, citizenship was the "priceless right" because it formed the essence of the individual.[24] In *Perez*, he found nothing more abhorrent than the "stateless person, disgraced and degraded in the eyes of his countryman."[25] Indeed, in *Trop* he wrote that statelessness was a fate worse than death, and hence it should be barred as punishment by the Eighth Amendment even as the death penalty was not. Denationalization, he wrote, "is a form of punishment more primitive than torture, for it destroys for the individual the political existence that was centuries in the development."[26] In a democracy, a man without citizenship was relegated to utter nothingness.

Yet, underneath this language of individuals Chief Justice Warren's theory of citizenship also drew on the democratic nature of American government. The essence of his theory was that a government of the people has no power to sever the citizen relationship that itself forms the government. Denationalization in a democracy was a simple impossibility. "What is this government, whose power is being asserted?" he asked in *Perez*.[27] He found the answer within the first principles of American government, ones antecedent to even the Constitution and the Fourteenth Amendment. Quoting from the Declaration of Independence, he reminded us that "Governments are instituted among Men, deriving their just powers from the consent of the governed."[28] It was citizenship that empowered government, not government that regulated citizenship. "This Government was born of its citizens, it maintains itself in a continuing relationship with them, and, in my judgment, it is without power to sever the relationship that gives rise to its existence."[29] He concluded that "the power to denationalize is not within the letter or the spirit of the powers with which our Government was endowed."[30]

In his opinion for the court in *Afroyim*, Justice Black built upon the chief justice's theory of citizenship, invoking the specter of "a man without a country."[31] True to his textualist faith, Black's opinion, unlike Warren's pronouncements, was primarily derived from the citizenship clause of the Fourteenth Amendment. Yet, it too drew strength from the first principles of American government. "In our country the people are sovereign," Justice Black wrote, "and the Government cannot sever its relationship to the people by taking away their citizenship."[32] The expatriation cases thus stood for the principle that the essence of the American polity is the people, not the government. In Justice Black's words, "Its citizenry is the country and the country is its citizenry."[33] The people themselves decide whether they are to belong; their government cannot decide for them.

By ultimately deriving the right of citizenship from the democratic nature of American government, Chief Justice Warren also reframed the Supreme Court's role in safeguarding American democracy. During the *Perez* and *Trop* deliberations, the issue for Justice Felix Frankfurter was not whether citizenship was a fundamental right nor whether Congress lacked the power to denationalize but rather whether the Supreme Court had any role in protecting citizenship. "The ultimate determinant," Frankfurter declared, "is not what we find in the Constitution, but our conception of what is the job of the judge."[34] His dissent in *Trop* was a paean to judicial restraint. Judicial power, he asserted, "must be on guard against encroaching beyond its proper bounds."[35] To uphold the act providing for denationalization "is to respect the actions of the two branches of our Government directly responsive to the will of the people."[36]

Chief Justice Warren instead wrote that the court must enforce the "rules of government."[37] The court, in other words, would protect the citizens who were out of power from those in power. "The very nature of our free government," Justice Black would add in *Afroyim*, "makes it completely incongruous to have a rule of law under which a group of citizens temporarily in office can deprive another group of citizens of their citizenship."[38] Just as the court had found a new role in protecting democratic voting rights in the reapportionment cases, so too did it become a champion of democratic citizenship rights in the expatriation cases.

CRUEL AND UNUSUAL PUNISHMENTS

Before *Trop*, the Supreme Court had interpreted the Eighth Amendment's "cruel and unusual punishments" provision only a handful of times and only once to strike down a punishment. In 1892, the court denied that the Eighth Amendment applied to the states.[39] But in *Weems v. United States* (1910),[40] the court dramatically departed from the traditional interpretation of the cruel and unusual punishments clause, which had focused the Eighth Amendment inquiry on whether a method of punishment—for example, death by firing squad or electrocution—was tantamount to torture.[41] While the traditional approach boiled down to asking whether a particular punishment was similar to or different from those forms of grotesque punishment known to the Framers, in *Weems* the Supreme Court for the first time struck down a punishment on a proportionality theory, holding that a sentence of fifteen years' hard labor for document falsification was "cruel and unusual" because it was disproportionate to the offense.[42] Moreover, the opinion by Justice Joseph McKenna, reflecting the sociological jurisprudence of the era, for the first time recognized an evolving conception of the Eighth Amendment: "Time works changes, brings into existence new conditions and purposes. Therefore a principle to be vital must be capable of wider application than the mischief which gave it birth. This is peculiarly true of constitutions."[43]

But when the court next considered the cruel and unusual punishments clause, it reverted to the traditional interpretation. In *Louisiana* ex rel. *Francis v. Resweber* (1947),[44] the court refused by a 5–4 vote to hold that after a bungled first attempt, a second attempt at electrocuting a capital defendant was cruel and unusual punishment.[45] Justice Stanley Reed, writing for the court, suggested a return to the narrow method-based analysis employed prior to *Weems*. He stated, "The cruelty against which the Constitution protects a convicted man is cruelty inherent in the method of punishment, not the necessary suffering involved in any method employed to extinguish life humanely. . . . There is no purpose to inflict unnecessary pain nor [is] any unnecessary pain involved in the proposed execution."[46]

The case was caught up in the growing division between the two wings of the court led by Justices Frankfurter and Black over whether the Due Process Clause "incorporated" the Bill of Rights. Reed's holding that the second electrocution was not a cruel and unusual punishment was one way of avoiding a direct confrontation over the incorporation question. Justice Black contributed the fifth vote on the understanding that the incorporation issue did not need to be reached because the second electrocution did not constitute a cruel and unusual punishment.[47]

In 1958, Chief Justice Warren reinvigorated the *Weems* conception in his plurality opinion in *Trop v. Dulles*, suggesting that the Eighth Amendment could be dynamically interpreted in light of the "evolving standards of decency that mark the progress of a maturing society."[48] He continued: "The provisions of the Constitution are not time-worn adages or hollow shibboleths. They are vital, living principles that authorize and limit governmental powers in our Nation."[49]

Robinson v. California (1962)[50] was among the first surge of cases extending provisions of the Bill of Rights to the states that began the previous year with *Mapp v. Ohio*. In *Robinson*, the Supreme Court decided that the cruel and unusual punishments provision of the Eighth Amendment also applied to the states. The case involved the question of whether drug addiction was a "status" and whether the state could create "status crimes" under which people were punished not for "what they did" but for "who they were."[51] Deciding the case "in the light of contemporary human knowledge," the court struck down the law and reiterated the evolutionary framework of *Weems* and *Trop*.[52]

The great intellectual difficulty with the position of the majority in *Robinson* was that the justices did not seem entirely aware that they were grappling with some of the deepest philosophical dilemmas about how to draw a line between conduct and status or free will and determinism. Everyone agreed that the state could punish all of the prior activity of buying and using drugs that had made the defendant an addict; that was "conduct" for which he could be punished. But once he became addicted, the court held, it was a "status" for which he was protected from the reach of the criminal law. Six years later in *Powell v. Texas* (1968),[53] the court reversed course and refused to extend *Robinson* to forbid the criminal prosecution of chronic alcoholics for public drunkenness.[54]

Whatever the merits of *Robinson*'s application of the cruel and unusual punishments clause to status crimes, it sparked a bold effort by newly appointed Justice Arthur Goldberg to extend the clause to capital punishment. At the start of the next term, Goldberg's second, the Supreme Court voted to deny certiorari in *Rudolph v. Alabama* (1963), involving a capital sentence of a convicted rapist. But

Goldberg dissented, declaring a willingness to apply the Eighth Amendment to abolish the death penalty for "a convicted rapist who has neither taken nor endangered human life."[55] He was joined by Justices William Douglas and Brennan.

Goldberg's published dissent was based on a more extensive memorandum that he had drafted with his law clerk, Alan Dershowitz, during the summer of 1963 as the court faced petitions for certiorari in six capital cases.[56] The memorandum originally addressed the broader question: "Whether, and under what circumstances, the imposition of the death penalty is proscribed by the Eighth and Fourteenth Amendments to the United States Constitution."[57]

As Justice Brennan later observed, Goldberg's dissent, "although not unheard of," was "highly unusual" because an individual justice had unilaterally decided to write at length and prior to conference on an issue that was neither argued nor set for argument.[58] Furthermore, until that time the constitutionality of the death penalty had received "relatively little attention," and neither the litigants nor the press had focused on it.[59]

But public opinion had begun to shift against the death penalty. As late as 1953, a substantial majority in a Gallup poll had approved the death penalty by a margin of 68 percent to 25 percent.[60] This 43 percent margin of approval had shrunk to 17 percent in 1960 (53% to 36%), and to just 2 percent (45% to 43%) in 1965.[61] In 1966, a slight plurality (47% to 42%) was recorded against capital punishment, the only time in more than a half century of polling (1953–2006) that more Americans were recorded against the death penalty than in favor.[62] In 1963, Justice Goldberg might well have believed that public opinion was in the process of expressing those "evolving standards of decency that mark the progress of a mature society."

The Goldberg memorandum was a comprehensive assault on the death penalty, and its legal arguments resurfaced and were used to attack capital punishment for the next decade. The memorandum viewed *Weems* as the "turning point" in Eighth Amendment jurisprudence, as the moment at which the court switched from a methods-based to a proportionality or excessiveness standard.[63] Goldberg derived from *Weems* three tests under the Eighth Amendment: whether the punishment offended a contemporary standard of decency, whether a less severe punishment could effectively achieve the purported ends for which the death penalty was imposed, and whether the punishment was disproportionate.[64]

Justice Goldberg reaffirmed the analysis of *Trop* and *Robinson* that the court's stance toward the death penalty should be based on "evolving standards of decency that mark the progress of [our] maturing society."[65] This was another major step toward elaboration by a Warren Court majority of the idea of a "living" or dynamic Constitution, one of the signature concepts of the Warren Court.[66]

At the time, the Goldberg memorandum was so potentially explosive that Chief Justice Warren exhorted Goldberg not to publish it.[67] Warren expressed concern that it would be a blow to the court's credibility and thus might undermine the court's desegregation rulings as well as decisions on other controversial issues.[68] The decisions in the school prayer case and the reapportionment case during the previous term had already triggered vocal opposition to the court.

The scope of Goldberg's published dissent in *Rudolph v. Alabama* was more modest than the original memo on which it was based. His dissent avoided a general attack on capital punishment per se and instead focused on the less demanding task of questioning the constitutionality of capital punishment for rape. Unlike the memo, the dissent avoided all discussion of the issue of racial discrimination, which, after all, was at the heart of the death penalty for rape.[69] Virtually all capital sentences for rape came from the South in cases of Black men accused of raping white women.[70] Goldberg's dissent not only skirted this theme, which might otherwise have highlighted the volcanic relationship between race and sex in the South, but also represented one the first examples of an unfolding pattern: that the racial issue in capital sentencing would never be addressed explicitly in any Warren Court case on the death penalty.

Goldberg's dissent, joined by Justices Douglas and Brennan, was the original inspiration for the decision of the NAACP Legal Defense Fund to begin its campaign to abolish the death penalty.[71] The dissent signaled to opponents of capital punishment that a significant faction of the court was having doubts about its constitutionality.[72] As Professor Meltsner put it, "No longer did a direct attack in the courts on capital sentencing seem doomed to failure."[73] Quite the opposite. Just five years later in *Witherspoon v. Illinois* (1968),[74] the Supreme Court went to the brink of abolishing the death penalty.

In an opinion by Justice Potter Stewart for four other justices (Warren, Brennan, Marshall, and Fortas), the court held that it was a violation of a capital defendant's right to a representative jury to automatically bar a potential juror who declared conscientious objections to the death penalty. Justice Douglas wrote an even stronger separate concurrence. In a subsequent case one year later, the court per Justice Douglas made it clear that unless a potential juror "states unambiguously that he would automatically vote against the imposition of capital punishment no matter what the trial might reveal," he could not be barred from serving on the jury.[75]

The *Witherspoon* decision was widely received as the "first hard evidence that abolition" of the death penalty "was on the Supreme Court's agenda."[76] Though Goldberg's 1963 memo had first indicated abolitionist stirrings within the court, in the interim Goldberg himself had resigned and was replaced by Justice Fortas. In addition to the votes of Douglas and Brennan, who had already tipped their hands by joining Goldberg's 1963 dissent, *Witherspoon* revealed for the first time that there might be a six-person majority for abolition: that not only Warren, Marshall, and Fortas but also Stewart might be willing to join Douglas and Brennan along an abolitionist path.

At the time it was decided, many believed that *Witherspoon v. Illinois* (1968) was tantamount to de facto abolition of capital punishment.[77] Public opinion polls, after all, showed a nation more or less evenly divided over the death penalty. The one thing *Witherspoon* certainly stood for was that the half of the population with conscientious doubts about the death penalty could no longer be automatically excluded from serving on a jury in a capital case. Under such circumstances, critics complained, it might become all but impossible to assemble a unanimous jury for imposing a death sentence.

Though large numbers of public officials, especially prosecutors, lamented the decision and declared it the end of capital punishment, the lower courts, especially the state courts, spent their energy creating improbable distinctions that would allow them to ignore *Witherspoon* and maintain the death penalty. Clearly contrary to the rule, one state supreme court declared that there was no *Witherspoon* violation when "an excluded juror's attitude toward capital punishment was ambiguous."[78] But the most typical misapplication of *Witherspoon* occurred when prosecutors during the voir dire rephrased a potential juror's answer, beginning with "in other words" or "did you mean?" The resulting question encouraged an unqualified "yes," misleadingly suggesting that the potential juror would never vote to impose the death penalty. This widespread misuse of the voir dire often succeeded in avoiding the constraints of *Witherspoon*.[79]

MAXWELL V. BISHOP (1969)

In *Maxwell v. Bishop*,[80] the Supreme Court heard an appeal from a death sentence imposed by an Arkansas jury on a Black defendant convicted of raping a white woman. In granting certiorari, the Supreme Court limited the grounds of appeal to two procedural questions while refusing to hear challenges to either capital punishment per se or the death penalty for rape on the grounds that it was imposed in a racially discriminatory manner.[81]

The first question the court agreed to decide was whether in a state such as Arkansas that permitted a jury to choose between sentences of life imprisonment and death due process required a "bifurcated" jury, that is, separate jury proceedings to determine guilt and punishment. The second question was whether there needed to be clear legislative or judicial standards guiding the jury's discretion. At the conference, which took place on March 6, 1969, eight justices seemed ready to reverse the conviction, though on different grounds, while Justice Black stood alone in voting to uphold the capital sentence.[82]

As Justice Douglas was assigned the opinion, he realized that the eight justices willing to reverse divided three ways. Justices Stewart and White were
prepared to reverse only on *Witherspoon* grounds even though the defendant
had never previously raised the issue of a "death qualified" jury. The remaining
six justices split between reversing on the issue of bifurcation and reversing for
lack of jury standards.[83]

For a short twenty-four-hour period, Justice Harlan counted himself among
the six. The day after the conference, however, he wrote to the chief justice
that he was having second thoughts "on my yesterday's vote to reverse this
case on the basis of the 'split-trial' issue."[84] Without Harlan, there still were five
votes to reverse on bifurcation—the chief justice, Douglas, Brennan, Fortas, and
Marshall—but the latter two would not agree to reverse for lack of jury standards.[85] Douglas, whose initial draft of April 4 had reversed on both grounds,
circulated a second draft limited to the issue of bifurcation, while on May 14
Justice Brennan, joined by the chief justice and Justice Douglas, circulated a
concurrence that addressed both issues.[86] Meanwhile, that same day Justice
Fortas submitted his resignation, and the vote of the wavering Justice Harlan
became essential for a majority on the bifurcation question.[87] But on April 9,
Harlan had already told Douglas that "while I continue to think a split trial on
the issue of punishment [is] constitutionally required, I have not yet come to
rest on the precise scope of what due process would require in this regard." He
therefore "[could] not at this time say whether I would be able to join" you on
bifurcation.[88] With the possibility of assembling a majority having vanished, the
justices voted to put *Maxwell v. Bishop* over for reargument in the next term.

The deliberations in *Maxwell v. Bishop* revealed the fault lines in the court
over capital punishment during the last months of the Warren Court. Only Justice Black was unwilling to reverse the death penalty. "This country has managed to get along without the constitutional requirement of [bifurcated] trials
for around 180 years and it seems late in the day for this Court to announce
such a constitutional rule," he wrote.[89] Justices Stewart and White were not
willing to go further than reversing on the basis of *Witherspoon*.[90]

But the objection to a unitary jury seemed unanswerable. As Justice Douglas
wrote in his initial draft, there is an inherent conflict between the right against
self-incrimination in the guilt-determining phase and the need to explain or
seek mercy in the punishment phase.

"In an attempt to obtain mercy rather than complete exoneration," Douglas
wrote, the defendant's

> efforts to obtain a lesser punishment may only worsen his position on the
> issue of guilt. . . . It may be that only by presenting his mitigating evidence
> may an accused make an impact on the jury's determination of the penalty.

Yet he may not dare exercise his right [to seek mitigation] at the unitary trial, lest he suffer irreparable harm on the guilt issue. He thus purchases a fair trial on the issue of guilt at the cost of sacrificing his right to a fair trial on the issue of punishment.[91]

Justice Harlan initially agreed with Douglas on the bifurcation issue. "I do have trouble with the split trial in light of the burden on the privilege against self-incrimination," Harlan wrote. The defendant "[has] got a tough choice to make on whether to take the stand."[92]

The split over standards between Warren, Brennan, and Douglas, on one hand, and Fortas and Marshall, on the other, was surprising. Douglas introduced the standards issue as inseparable from protecting the defendant against jury discrimination:

Where there are no guidelines or relevant evidence one jury may decide that one defendant is not "fit to live" . . . because he is a black who raped a white woman, while another defendant is "fit to live" because he is a white who raped a black. Or whatever the race of the defendant one jury may be seized by the spirit of the mob, while another, dealing with the same quality of offense, may be more reasoned and compassionate. . . . We know from our own observations that the death penalty is seldom suffered by the affluent member of society; it is reserved, in practice, for the indigent and those otherwise inferior or somehow incapacitated, whether by education or mental instability.[93]

Justice Fortas replied that he could not agree with Douglas on standards. "The basic fact," he wrote in his concurrence, "is that it is impossible, as far as I am concerned, to state standards which would justify capital punishment. . . . Further, I think that if standards are legislated, the result will be substantially to increase the number of cases of [mandatory] imposition of the death penalty."[94]

If the court called for legislatively mandated standards, Fortas warned, state legislatures were more likely to replace jury discretion with mandatory capital punishment. By this time, however, it seemed unlikely that there was any majority even for bifurcation standing alone.

CAPITAL PUNISHMENT AND RACE

A deafening silence on the relationship between capital punishment and race is one of the most distinctive features of Warren Court death penalty opinions. Until Justice Douglas alluded in his *Maxwell v. Bishop* draft to jury discretion over whether to impose the death penalty for interracial rape, the court had struggled mightily to avoid linking capital punishment to racial discrimination. In *Maxwell v. Bishop* itself, even though the court below had decided and rejected the claim of racial discrimination, the Supreme Court narrowed the appeal so as to avoid hearing argument over whether the death penalty for rape was racially discriminatory.

Maxwell's claim of racial discrimination had been rejected by the Eighth Circuit in an opinion by Judge Harry Blackmun,[95] soon to be elevated to the Supreme Court. Despite statistical evidence showing that in Arkansas a Black man convicted of raping a white women had a 50 percent chance of receiving a death sentence, compared to 14 percent if the rape victim were Black, Justice Blackmun refused to upset the death sentence "on the basis of broad theories of social and statistical injustice."[96] Sitting on the Supreme Court almost twenty years later, he changed his mind and dissented from a 5–4 decision that turned down a similar claim of racial discrimination in Georgia's administration of the death penalty for murder. Despite a statistical study showing that those who kill whites were 4.3 times more likely to receive the death penalty than those whose victims were Black, in *McCleskey v. Kemp* (1987) the court refused to find racial discrimination.[97]

It took major acts of denial for the court to avoid the simple racial facts of how the death penalty operated in the South. "Most of the southern states' capital crimes on the eve of the Civil War were still capital nearly a century later," Stuart Banner observed.[98] As of 1954, capital punishment for rape still existed in eighteen states: all eleven states of the former Confederacy, five border states, and Nevada and West Virginia.[99] In the Deep South, capital punishment for rape replaced antebellum legal penalties that had openly applied the death penalty for rape and other capital offenses only to slaves. Instituted under the attractive banner of mitigating the mandatory death sentence, jury discretion over capital punishment in reality permitted white juries to restore an antebellum system of separate criminal codes for Black people and white people.

The result was that "of the 771 people of identified race known to have been executed for rape between 1870 and 1950, 701 were black."[100] All but a handful of the executions for robbery and burglary during this period were also imposed on Black southerners. And even the death penalty for murder was carried out with astonishing disproportionality. In Virginia, for example, between 1870 and 1950, executed Black defendants outnumbered executed white defendants 217 to 57; in Texas, it was 301 to 135.[101] "Throughout the South, for all crimes," Banner concluded, "black defendants were executed in numbers far out of proportion to their population. The death penalty was a means of racial control."[102]

Even though it was hard to avoid the conclusion that capital punishment supported and was supported by a culture of racial subordination, the opponents of capital punishment on the Warren Court struggled to find a non–race-based theory that would sharply reduce or eliminate the death penalty. Justice Goldberg's suggestion that the death penalty for rape was cruel and unusual punishment emphasized the disproportionality of imposing the death penalty where human life had not been taken, downplaying the racially discriminatory way in which it was administered.[103] *Witherspoon*'s refusal to bar jurors who had conscientious scruples about capital punishment also circumvented the discrimination issue. The moves in favor of jury bifurcation and standards in *Maxwell* were likewise procedural changes that avoided dealing directly with the question of race. All of the justices understood that any race-based theory would eventually have to confront the likely truth that the entire criminal justice system—capital as well as noncapital offenses in the North as well as the South—was inescapably tainted by systemic racial discrimination.

9

THE SIT-IN CASES

The second phase of the civil rights movement was launched in Greensboro, North Carolina, on February 1, 1960, as four Black college students challenged segregation in public accommodations by sitting-in to demand service at an all-white lunch counter. Before the sit-in movement ended four years later with the passage of the Civil Rights Act of 1964, it had spread throughout the South, causing hundreds of mostly Black civil rights activists to be fined, sentenced to jail, or both for refusing to leave segregated public facilities. Many of these convictions were appealed to the U.S. Supreme Court, producing an emotional division and bitter feelings among the justices. In particular, the sit-in cases led Justice Hugo Black to break with the new liberal majority and align himself with the four conservative justices.

The first set of cases to come before the court in 1961 involved student sit-ins at segregated lunch counters in Baton Rouge, Louisiana. In *Garner v. Louisiana* (1961) and two companion cases, sixteen Black students were fined and sentenced to jail for violating a state law that prohibited disturbing the peace by acting "in such a manner as to unreasonably disturb or alarm the public."[1] After circling around broader constitutional issues in conference, the court unanimously reversed the convictions, with seven justices finding a lack of evidentiary support.[2]

The discussion in conference was spread over two sessions.[3] At the first session, formally devoted only to the question of whether to grant certiorari, the justices already began to stake out their constitutional positions. The most significant statement came from Justice Black, who foreshadowed how he would come out on the ultimate constitutional question. "The owner of a store," he declared, "has the right (absent an act of Congress or state statute) to say who can and cannot come into his store or stay there." Frankfurter agreed: "If a merchant wants to serve only one race, he can follow it. . . . The owner need not call in police, and the police need not wait until there is a fracas."[4] On the opposite side, Justices William Douglas and William Brennan declared that *Shelley v. Kraemer* controlled the case.[5] This meant that they were prepared to apply that controversial decision to hold that police or judicial enforcement of even private discrimination was "state action" under the Equal Protection Clause of the Fourteenth Amendment.

But Black sought to draw a sharp line between public and private discrimination. "The convictions are based upon state policy, not employer policy. This is not a trespass ordinance—this is a public alarm statute. They can sit there whether the state wants them there or not. . . . The law in this field has to be drawn precisely and narrowly as a trespassing statute to be constitutional."[6]

These early discussions took place against a constitutional background that highlighted the Supreme Court's decision in the *Civil Rights Cases* (1883),[7] holding unconstitutional the Civil Rights Act of 1875 in its effort to ban racial discrimination in public accommodations and transportation. This early Supreme Court interpretation of the Equal Protection Clause of the Fourteenth Amendment as requiring "state action" and therefore unable to reach private discrimination had not subsequently been challenged before the court. Indeed, the unanimous—though highly controversial—decision in *Shelley v. Kraemer* (1948) stood as one of the rare successes in skirting the precedent established in the *Civil Rights Cases*. Representing virtually the final act of the Reconstruction Congress, the passage of the ill-fated Civil Rights Act took place at the last moment a congressional majority could be mustered for transforming southern social practices. As southern whites reasserted exclusive control over their state political systems, they were also able to deploy the seniority system in Congress to retain disproportionate influence. And for almost a century, they invoked the rules of the Senate to filibuster any legislation that threatened the southern way of life. The success of southern senators in blocking congressional legislation that restricted private discrimination meant that there had been no occasion to judicially challenge the precedent established in the *Civil Rights Cases*.

The second round of sit-in cases—from five southern states—was appealed to the Supreme Court during the 1962 term.[8] Again, Black took the lead in the conference discussions. "I am ready to meet these cases on their merits," he began.

The Court would have to assume or pass on the constitutionality of a store owner choosing his own customers. We have a system of private ownership of property—we should not turn down these rights by constitutional construction. I believe that a store owner, the same as a homeowner, has a right to say who can come on his premises and how long they can stay. A store owner, like a house owner, can tell a customer to leave. If he has that right, he cannot be helpless to call the police and get help to throw the customer out. One man on another man's property [without permission] can be thrown off with force, if necessary. That rule is necessary if private property is to be protected. I would rank stores along with homes, although there is, of course, a difference in history and sentiment. I would have no difficulty [despite the *Civil Rights Cases*] in sustaining a state law or a federal law under the Fourteenth Amendment that would prevent racial discrimination and require a retailer to serve all people. But [without a statute] it cannot make a constitutional difference.[9]

Yet, once more, as in the previous term, Black declared that "it was not shown that it was the owner's choice, not the state's, that they leave." The state has "the burden . . . to show that the owner exercised free choice. . . . [I]f the state has a law that makes it illegal for the races to eat together, it is unconstitutional. . . . I would try to work out an opinion to reverse . . . all of these cases" on grounds of state involvement.[10] Through a combination of grounds, some fairly tenuous, Chief Justice Earl Warren was able to reverse all of the convictions, with all but Justice Harlan in accord with his reasoning.[11]

In the conference discussion of this second set of sit-in cases, more of the justices took positions on the ultimate constitutional issue. In what may have been the first time after almost a quarter century together on the court that Justices Black and Douglas parted company on a major constitutional issue, Douglas declared, "My views are in diametric opposition to Hugo's—that retail stores cannot segregate constitutionally."[12] Justice Arthur Goldberg added "that there is a lot to what Bill Douglas says, especially in light of *Shelley v. Kraemer*. However, it is not necessary to face the broad issues. I would like to have unanimity."[13] On the opposite side, Justices Harlan, Tom Clark, and Potter Stewart now lined up behind Black's position.[14] Justice Brennan, who had agreed with Douglas in the previous term's discussions, this time took the middle position: "We need not deal with the broad problem discussed by Hugo and Bill Douglas." Justice Byron White declared, "I stand with Bill Brennan."[15]

The chief justice's narrow opinion managed once again to postpone the ultimate confrontation to the next term. "The great battle of the [next] Term . . . was fought . . . over the Sit-In Cases," Justice Brennan's clerks, Stephen R. Barnett and Stephen J. Friedman, recalled. The third round of these cases was "argued on the first day of the [1963] Term and decided on the last, and [the cases] were the subject of fierce debate for much of the time in-between."[16]

The court had agreed to review five cases—two from Maryland, two from South Carolina, and one from Florida—"for the express purpose of deciding the Equal Protection issue that had been avoided" the previous term:

In view of the prevalence of sit-in demonstrations throughout the country and the heated emotions aroused by the issue of racial discrimination in places of public accommodation, the Court, led by Justice Black, thought it imperative that a definitive constitutional ruling be announced as to whether such demonstrators could constitutionally be convicted of trespass. The fact that a Civil Rights Bill banning such discrimination had been sent to Congress . . . did not divert the Court from its determination to decide this issue. . . . Determined as it was to decide the broad issue, the Court was surprised to receive . . . a brief *amicus* from the Solicitor General [Archibald Cox] arguing that this Term's cases, no less than last Term's, could be disposed of on narrow grounds.[17]

At its first conference the court rejected Cox's view, though it did vote 5–4 to reverse one Maryland conviction (*Griffin*) "because of the participation of a deputy sheriff in the exclusion of the demonstrators," and the two South Carolina cases were reversed on "void-for-vagueness" and "lack of fair warning" grounds. In both *Bell v. Maryland* and *Robinson v. Florida*, however, "the Conference did reach the basic issue, and it voted 5 to 4 to affirm the convictions." Justice Black was joined by Justices Clark, Harlan, Stewart, and White for the majority; the chief justice and Justices Douglas, Brennan, and Goldberg voted to overturn the convictions.[18]

The Conference discussion was very heated, not only because of the importance of the issue and the fervor with which views were held on both sides, but also because the minority Justices feared that the affirmance might have a crippling effect on the prospects for Congressional passage of the Civil Rights Bill. For this reason, and in the heat of verbal battle, the statement was made by some members of the minority, including Justice Brennan, that they would do their utmost to delay the decision as long as possible, in the hope that Congress would meanwhile have acted favorably on the bill or that, if it had acted unfavorably, some member of the then-prevailing majority—in particular, Justice White, who was considered the least firm of the five—might be led to change his vote. The suggestion of delay caused a certain amount of hard feeling among the Justices.[19]

In the discussion of the merits, Chief Justice Warren for the first time sided with Douglas's position. "I had hoped that we could take these cases step by step, not reaching the final question until much experience had been had," Warren began. "That course [now] seems to me to be impracticable." Most of the cases could be decided on narrow grounds, Warren declared, but in *Bell v. Maryland* "I hit hard bottom." So, he turned to the ultimate constitutional question. "If you have a private property for private use, you can call on the state to throw people off. A person can keep anyone out of his home, or hog pasture, or warehouse, provided that it is strictly private." But "in the field of public accommodations," Warren continued, "the owner is advertising to the world for customers without restriction. He gives up some rights of privacy. . . . This certainly meets the principle of *Shelley v. Kraemer*."[20]

Justice Black reiterated the constitutional position he had taken the previous term, "reportedly," according to the Brennan clerks, "basing his position, at least partially, on his inability to believe that his 'Pappy,' who ran a general store in Alabama, did not have the right to decide whom he would or would not serve."[21] Black refused to decide the two remaining cases, *Robinson v. Florida* and *Bell v. Maryland*, on narrow grounds. "I will go the whole way to protect [against] discrimination by government, but not discrimination by private people. I think that the right of association is vital to American life, and reversal here would endanger it. Colored people want to be treated . . . like the rest of us. Perhaps Hitler could make [forced association] come to pass, but I will not foist it on people."[22]

At a subsequent conference three days later, the argument continued, "and an all-day discussion ensued." Justice Goldberg made what the Brennan clerks called "an elaborate and moving attack on the proposed affirmance."[23] "This is the most serious problem before the Court in recent years," he began.

> "This will be the first time in the history of the country [*sic*!] where if we say that the [demonstrators] are not entitled to their rights, we legitimize racial discrimination. If we say that these stores have a right to discriminate, we will have to overrule *Shelley v. Kraemer*, and repudiate the basis of the majority in [the] *Civil Rights Cases* and embrace the majority opinion in *Plessy v. Ferguson*. I agree with the first John Marshall Harlan's dissent in the *Civil Rights Cases*."[24]

"We have progressively implemented the policy of desegregation," Goldberg continued. "Now we are receding—why? . . . I fear the results of an affirmance in these cases. . . . The Fourteenth Amendment does not give a right to discriminate in the public area. . . . It is shocking to me beyond words to predicate the decision on that ground. . . . [It] will take the Court very far back."[25]

Perhaps there was no way for Goldberg to avoid directly referring to Justice Harlan's revered grandfather, John Marshall Harland I, who was the sole dissenter in the *Civil Rights Cases*. Yet, given that the case would be directly relevant only if Congress passed a public accommodations law, it is hard to avoid concluding that Goldberg was impolitic in personalizing the difference between the grandfather and the grandson. Then Goldberg went one step further.

"I believe that Hugo Black's views are colored by Alabama's background of slavery. My family also had a store in Elgin, but they served all comers because Illinois never knew slavery."[26] One can only imagine how this must have offended Black, whose position in *Brown v. Board of Education* had turned him into a pariah in Alabama.

Bell v. Maryland left personal scars within the liberal majority that never healed. After the first argument of the case, Black voted with the four conservatives to uphold the protesters' convictions; he then wrote and circulated a draft majority opinion.[27] In his draft dissent, Justice Goldberg further offended Black by comparing his opinion to the Dred Scott case, the notorious decision supporting slavery that pushed the nation to the brink of the Civil War.[28] Distrust grew. Black felt that Brennan was delaying release of Black's final opinion out of fear that, as Elizabeth Black put it in her private diary, "Hugo's enormous prestige would work adversely on the [civil rights] bill's passage."[29] In fact, Black's "scant and scared majority" (in Mrs. Black's words) unraveled, and Justice Brennan managed to produce a 6–3 decision reversing the convictions.[30]

Six months later in *Cox v. Louisiana* (1965),[31] Black once again broke with his former liberal allies in a civil rights case. The case began in December 1961 after twenty-three Black students were arrested in Baton Rouge, Louisiana, for picketing stores that maintained segregated lunch counters. The following morning Reverend B. Elton Cox led a march to the courthouse, where two thousand student protesters gathered across the street from the courthouse and jail to protest the arrests. The protesters sang, prayed, and listened to a speech by Cox without incident. However, when Cox urged the crowd to sit in at uptown lunch counters, the sheriff ordered the crowd to disperse, and the police almost immediately fired tear gas shells into the crowd. Cox was arrested the following day.[32] Writing for a 5–4 majority, Justice Goldberg overturned Cox's one-year sentence for "picketing near a courthouse" on the ground "that our constitutional command of free speech and assembly is basic and fundamental and encompasses peaceful social protest."[33]

Goldberg originally had voted in conference to uphold Cox's conviction on the ground that Louisiana was entitled to protect its courts from coercion. But after viewing television film of the march, Goldberg changed his mind apparently because the local sheriff had seemed at first to permit the protesters to gather in the area near the courthouse.[34] Even so, Goldberg wrote, "the rights of free speech and assembly" do not protect marches "in the middle of Times Square at the rush hour." But granting the police "unfettered discretion" to decide when a peaceful march can take place, he concluded, violates the First Amendment.[35]

Once more at the last moment, Black lost his majority. His dissent raised the fear that the decision would open the door to "fanatical, threatening, lawless mob[s]" applying "coercive pressures" on the courts. "Minority groups in particular," he declared, "need always to bear in mind that the Constitution . . . does not take away the State's power, indeed its duty, to keep order and to do justice according to law."[36] In private Black went even further, denouncing "government by demonstrations and marching."[37] "He remembers Hitler took to the streets before he took over," Mrs. Black recorded in her diary.

Four months after *Cox*, Black reported to his wife that Justice Brennan, among the friendliest and most cordial of justices, "was really mad with him because of one of his opinions and dissents and was very snippy to him in Conference."[38] By the summer of 1965 as terrible riots broke out in the Black ghetto of Watts in Los Angeles, Mrs. Black wrote, "Hugo has been saying that the demonstrations would lead to riots and anarchy and he is borne out, to some extent, already." "Part of the lawless spirit of the times," she added two days later, observing that the Los Angeles riots were still going on after three days, with "about 37 killed and 750 wounded and stores burned and looted. Horrible!"[39] The Watts riots exacerbated the fear of Black and others that the civil rights demonstrations were leading only to disorder and unrest. That same summer, Justice Douglas warned newly appointed Justice Abe Fortas that "the majority of the Court [is] moving toward the anti-Negro side," presumably referring to Black's increasing distrust of the civil rights movement.[40] His words were to prove prophetic. "You can now see what I meant last summer," Douglas told Fortas early in 1966[41] when Black announced his dissent in another sit-in case, *Brown v. Louisiana*.[42] In *Brown*, Fortas led the court in overturning the breach-of-peace convictions of protesters who sat in at a public library to protest segregated library services. In his impassioned dissent, Black maintained that

> it is high time to challenge the assumption in which too many people have too long acquiesced, that groups that think they have been mistreated or that have actually been mistreated have a constitutional right to use the public's streets, buildings, and property to protest whatever, wherever, whenever they want, without regard to whom such conduct may disturb. . . . But I say once more that the crowd moved by noble ideals today can become the mob ruled by hate and passion and greed and violence tomorrow. . . . The peaceful songs of love can become as stirring and provocative as the Marseillaise did in the days when a noble revolution gave way to rule by successive mobs until chaos set in.[43]

Black was brought up in Alabama during its darkest decades of racial oppression, and his views on race had for a long time been the subject of intense public scrutiny. No sooner had he been confirmed by the Senate in 1937 than it became public that he had once been a member of the Ku Klux

Klan in Alabama.[44] While Black continued to leave the impression that he had been only marginally involved with the Klan over a short period of time, Roger Newman concludes that Black "did more—much more."[45] There is no question that he could not have won his Senate seat in 1926 without the active backing of the Klan.[46] It seems quite likely that if his membership in the Klan had been made public before the Senate voted, he would not have been confirmed.[47]

Though he was the only justice from the Deep South, Black was among the minority of justices who were completely committed to overruling *Plessy v. Ferguson* even before Earl Warren became chief justice.[48] Black never doubted that there would be turmoil and bitterness when segregation was outlawed.[49] Though he warned Warren that his *Brown* opinion needed to avoid blaming the South, he appears never to have wavered in his view that racial segregation could not be justified under the Fourteenth Amendment. There are many stories involving the personal price Black paid among longtime southern friends, especially old political friends, who shunned him after *Brown*.[50]

While Black's courageous stand in *Brown v. Board of Education* was never in doubt, his support for the civil rights movement a decade later was not unqualified. In the sit-in cases he suddenly became a spokesman for the rights of private property, a role that markedly diverged from the populist rhetoric that originally brought him to the U.S. Senate. It also seemed incongruous with his former position that personal rights were more central to democracy and thus were entitled to greater protection than property rights, which he had argued while battling Justice Frankfurter over the appropriate scope of judicial review.[51]

The Civil Rights Act of 1964 and the Voting Rights Act of 1965 marked the high point of success of the civil rights movement. Thereafter the public's tolerance of social protest began to wane, especially after Congress seemed to have agreed to the demands of the movement. As Black's dissents illustrated, a continued strategy of civil disobedience triggered fears of lawlessness, just as the challenge to property rights invoked dread of radicalism. Mass marches, especially by Black protestors, touched deep fears of mob rule.

During the summer of 1964, Congress approved the Gulf of Tonkin Resolution supporting President Lyndon Johnson's escalation of the Vietnam War. The war soon drew energy away from domestic concerns and reversed a decade-long cycle of social reform. During the summer of 1965, as Mrs. Black noted, several days of rioting broke out in the Watts section of Los Angeles, leaving about thirty-five dead and at least seven hundred wounded.[52]

The changing national mood affected the Supreme Court.[53] After another summer of widespread urban riots in November 1966, the court—for the first time since *Brown v. Board of Education*—decided a civil rights case against Black people. In a second case in mid-June 1967—at the beginning of a "long hot summer" in which over 150 riots erupted in the nation's ghettos—the court upheld criminal convictions against the leadership of the civil rights movement, including Dr. Martin Luther King Jr.[54]

In *Adderley v. Florida* (1966),[55] Justice Black was finally able to muster a majority in a sit-in case. He aligned himself with the four conservative justices to affirm the convictions of thirty-two students from Florida A&M University in Tallahassee who had protested outside the county jail against segregation and the arrest of their comrades.[56] The depth of the split within the court became clear, as Black's defection left his four former liberal allies in dissent. Justice Douglas wrote in the dissenting opinion that "conventional methods of petitioning [for the redress of grievances] may be, and often have been, shut off to large groups of our citizens. . . . Their methods should not be condemned as tactics of obstruction and harassment as long as the assembly and petition are peaceable, as these were. . . . [B]y allowing these orderly and civilized protests against injustice to be suppressed, we only increase the forces of frustration which the conditions of second-class citizenship are generating amongst us.[57]

In the notorious case *Walker v. City of Birmingham* (1967),[58] Black again broke with his four liberal colleagues to uphold a contempt of court conviction of Dr. King and other prominent civil rights leaders for disobeying a judicial injunction that barred engaging in a civil rights demonstration.

The events that led to the decision in *Walker* began in April 1963, when King led a nonviolent campaign to end segregation in public accommodations in Birmingham, Alabama. Birmingham was a particularly dangerous place for the boycott, sit-ins, and marches that King proposed, since its commissioner of public safety, Eugene "Bull" Connor, was a passionate segregationist who was expected to respond violently to any civil rights demonstrations.[59] But King hoped to draw the nation's attention to the persistence of segregation nearly ten years after *Brown*. After sit-ins and marches in early April resulted in numerous arrests, the City of Birmingham obtained an injunction from an Alabama lower court judge forbidding any further demonstrations.[60] Believing that the injunction was both unconstitutional and immoral, King and the other demonstrators went ahead with marches planned for Good Friday and Easter Sunday.[61] King was promptly convicted of contempt of court for violating the injunction and jailed. While in jail, he learned that eight white Alabama clergymen had issued a statement urging the Black community to stop demonstrating and work within the system for reform. In response, King wrote his famous "Letter from Birmingham Jail" outlining his theory of civil disobedience. Explaining his reasons for defying the injunction, he wrote, "I submit that an individual who breaks a law that conscience tells him is unjust, and who willingly accepts the penalty of imprisonment in order to arouse the conscience of the community over its injustice, is in reality expressing the highest respect for law."[62]

The injunction had been issued by the Alabama judge at a time when much of the state judiciary remained hostile to all civil rights activity. The case was argued before the U.S. Supreme Court four years later on the assumption that if King had immediately appealed, the injunction would have been overturned as an unconstitutional limitation on First Amendment rights. Therefore, the only question before the court was whether King was entitled to disobey a concededly unconstitutional judicial order without bringing an appeal.[63]

There was a long history of bitterness by progressives against the use of the injunction by the judiciary to suppress social protest. For almost half a century, the federal courts had issued injunctions against labor union activities until the practice was barred in 1932 with the passage of the Norris-LaGuardia Act. Widely regarded as the most potent and notorious weapon available to a conservative judiciary hostile to union organizing, the labor injunction provided many advantages to employers.[64] It could be issued ex parte, meaning that an employer could ask a court to issue an injunction without even initially hearing the employee's position. While the union was free to appeal the injunction, this took time and money. The injunction thus had the effect of cooling down the energy, solidarity, and shared sense of injustice that may have taken a long time to build. Employers quickly realized what an effective instrument the injunction was for demobilizing social protest movements. Equally important, disobedience to an injunction could be punished as contempt of court by a judge without a jury, thus eliminating any restraint that juries drawn from a community may have exercised on unpopular criminal convictions.

The use of the injunction against the demonstrators in *Walker v. City of Birmingham* brought to mind the history of partisan uses of the injunction to squelch labor unions. "One would expect this Court particularly," wrote Justice Brennan, "to remember the stern lesson history taught courts in the context of the labor injunction, that the ex parte injunction represents the most devastating of restraints on constitutionally protected activities."[65] Moreover, the Supreme Court justices could not have failed to remember that for more than a decade they had struggled against southern—and most prominently Alabamian—intransigence.[66] To appeal an injunction through a hostile state judiciary could take years. The appeal in *Walker* itself took four years. Could the Supreme Court have expected civil rights protesters to suspend their activities during that period? The Supreme Court ruling in *Walker* empowered local southern judges to tie up the civil rights movement in the expensive and time-consuming task of overturning illegitimate court-ordered injunctions.

"It cannot be presumed," Justice Stewart declared for the majority, "that the Alabama courts would have ignored the petitioners' constitutional claims."[67] Once again—as it had often done during the previous decade—the court refused to acknowledge that southern judges were doing their best to crush the civil rights movement.

As Chief Justice Warren declared in dissent, "The ex parte . . . injunction has a long and odious history in this country. . . . As a weapon against strikes it proved so effective in the hands of judges friendly to employers that Congress . . . remov[ed] from federal district courts the jurisdiction to issue injunctions in labor disputes." The majority opinion, Warren added, was providing its "seal of approval to . . . a gross misuse of the judicial process. . . . This injunction was such potent magic that it transformed the command of an unconstitutional statute into an impregnable barrier" that could be challenged only through "protracted legal proceedings."[68] The civil rights marchers, he wrote,

> were in essentially the same position as persons who challenge the constitutionality of a statute by violating it, and then defend the ensuing criminal prosecution on constitutional grounds. It has never been thought that violation of a statute indicated such a disrespect for the legislature that the violator always must be punished even if the statute was unconstitutional. . . . Indeed, it shows no disrespect for law to violate a statute on the ground that it is unconstitutional and then to submit one's case to the courts with the willingness to accept the penalty if the statute is held to be valid.[69]

Justice Brennan wrote in his dissenting opinion that "we cannot permit fears of 'riots' and 'civil disobedience' generated by slogans like 'Black Power' to divert our attention from what is here at stake."[70] *Walker* suggests that by 1967 a majority of the Supreme Court had been affected by those fears. The court was no longer willing to presume that the civil rights movement's acts of civil disobedience were on the side of the angels and should be treated with impunity. The country at large had become more intolerant of social protest as it faced the prospect of a long drawn-out war in Asia. Widespread rioting in Black ghettos during the "long hot summer" of 1967 led to the realization, in the words of the Kerner Commission on Civil Disorder, that racial polarization was dividing the country into "two societies." The hope that had led to a decade of social reform was replaced by growing despair that the United States would ever be able to overcome the heritage of slavery.[71] On April 4, 1968, less than five years after delivering his "I Have a Dream" speech, Martin Luther King lay dead, the victim of an assassin's bullet.

CIVIL DISOBEDIENCE

Martin Luther King Jr.'s famous justification for civil disobedience in his "Letter from Birmingham Jail" has engendered considerable confusion. "I submit," he wrote, "that an individual who breaks a law that conscience tells him is unjust, and who willingly accepts the penalty of imprisonment in order to arouse the conscience of the community over its injustice, is in reality expressing the highest respect for law."[72] This statement raises the question of why King appealed his contempt conviction to the Supreme Court instead of "willingly accept[ing] the penalty" by staying in jail "to arouse the conscience of the community."

King's justification of nonviolent civil disobedience was influenced by two quite different schools of thought. First, he frequently cited the example of the successful anticolonial political campaign instituted by Mahatma Gandhi to rid India of its British colonial rulers.[73] This depended above all on a realistic assessment of the likelihood of "arous[ing] the conscience" of the British rulers by willingly accepting the penalties that they meted out.[74] But it was a strategy whose success was always contingent on an accurate prediction that a particular community's conscience could be aroused. Could anyone have doubted that deploying a strategy of civil disobedience in Nazi Germany would have ended in abject failure?

A second tradition that King appealed to was medieval natural law thinking, whose leading exponent, Thomas Aquinas, had declared that a positive law that conflicted with divine natural law was not law and therefore did not authorize punishment.[75] In America, this higher law justification for disobedience was highlighted by Thomas Jefferson's appeal in the Declaration of Independence to the "Laws of Nature and of Nature's God."[76] It also became a prominent part of abolitionist thought, most notably in William Lloyd Garrison's denunciation of a slave constitution that he believed could be legitimately disobeyed with impunity.[77]

King's statement in his "Letter from Birmingham Jail" has been regularly cited as a justification for imposing punishment on those who engage in civil disobedience. Had not even Dr. King agreed that these protesters should be prepared willingly to accept the penalty for their disobedience to law? In his book *Concerning Dissent and Civil Disobedience*, written shortly after *Walker v. Birmingham* was decided, Justice Fortas, one of the dissenters in *Walker*, wrote, "I have no moral criticism to make of Dr. King's action in this incident, even though it turned out to be legally unjustified. . . . Dr. King went to jail and served his time. . . . [He], without complaint or histrionics, accepted the penalty of misjudgment."[78]

King's failure to distinguish between the different bases of disobedience in Gandhian and Thomistic thought has led to profound confusion about its real justification. Gandhi regarded willing acceptance of the penalty for civil disobedience as a tactical move, necessary for appealing to the conscience of the community. Where there was no chance of arousing the conscience of the rulers or the broader community, there was no more fundamental reason why a protestor was required to willingly accept punishment. Natural law thinkers such as St. Augustine declared that "an unjust law is no law at all." He regarded any law that conflicted with higher law as an illegitimate basis for imposing punishment. Imagine Thomas Jefferson declaring that he would willingly accept punishment for his disobedience to the British crown.

Accepting the penalty for civil disobedience was, for Gandhi, a political tactic designed to arouse the conscience of unjust rulers, not a universal statement about what is right under all circumstances. By contrast, Thomistic philosophy directly supported disobedience to unjust law by declaring that it was not law that needed to be obeyed. In such a case, any imposition of a penalty would constitute a lawless act.

We can shed further light on King's views by asking why he even appealed his Alabama contempt conviction to the U.S. Supreme Court if he was willing to accept the penalty by staying in jail. Here it is important to distinguish further between King's positive and higher law claims. King's judicial challenge to the constitutionality of the Alabama injunction was not based on higher law arguments. Rather, it was a claim that positive law itself did not authorize punishment, because if the injunction was unconstitutional, it was not law. Only if the injunction itself was held to be constitutional would it even be necessary to appeal above the U.S. Constitution to higher law. At that point, it would be essential to unravel the confusion that King's failure to distinguish between the different bases of philosophical justification has engendered.

10

FEDERALISM

Federalism, along with separation of powers, has stood as one of two perennial subjects of constitutional debate for more than two centuries. Compared to other sections of the U.S. Constitution whose influence has waxed and waned over time—such as the Bill of Rights or the Civil War amendments—there never has been a time when debates over the proper understanding of federalism has not been a major contested constitutional issue.

From the beginning, federalism showed two contradictory faces. On one hand, it was the product of the idealism and creative imagination of late eighteenth-century Western political thinkers who sought to develop institutional forms that might reverse Europe's three-century marriage between centralization and tyranny. As a result, unlike most other Western nations since the French Revolution, America developed a mainstream political culture that identified decentralization with freedom.

Yet, from the time of the founding the federal system also embodied the grossest concessions to expediency. It was in part adopted to reassure the slave states that they would not have to fear a distant, unitary central government that might eventually turn hostile to slavery. Therefore, federalism spawned the doctrine of states' rights, which continued to serve as the principal constitutional slogan that justified both slavery and, after the Civil War, white supremacy. Until quite recently, the expedient appeal to federalism in defense of racial supremacy tainted what might otherwise have been legitimate arguments in favor of localism and decentralization in public policy.

Race is but one of two fault lines in society that the expedient face of American federalism has always highlighted. The other is political economy. A federal structure establishes a competitive system of state regulatory regimes that strives to attract businesses by offering regulatory concessions that reduce the cost of doing business. The result is a "race to the bottom," by which businesses move from states with high taxes or strong labor and public interest regulations to lower-cost states that have minimized tax and regulatory burdens.[1] Except for those cases in which industries support uniform national rules out of concern that the "balkanization" of the economy will multiply the costs of obeying potentially contradictory state rules, American business has generally favored federalism for creating a competitive political market that tends to reduce governmental regulation.

The Civil War and the constitutional amendments it spawned offered the opportunity for a vast expansion of national power at the expense of the states. Yet, once Reconstruction ended, the entrenched decentralistic bias of American political culture reasserted itself. As David Brion Davis observed, though the South lost the Civil War, it won the ideological debate after the war by exporting states' rights ideology, which came to dominate both constitutional and political discourse. Until it was rejected by the New Deal Supreme Court, the constitutional theory of dual federalism, promulgated just as the country was turning against Reconstruction, sought to minimize the far-reaching potential of the Civil War amendments to reverse the decentralistic structure of the prewar constitutional system.[2]

The eight New Deal justices appointed by President Franklin Roosevelt shared to different degrees the basic New Deal economic critique of the federal system as an anachronistic barrier to economic recovery. Felix Frankfurter presents a somewhat more complicated case. When he was appointed to the court, he certainly shared the basic New Deal critique of federalism. Though his enthusiasm for federalism grew during his tenure on the court, it is also true that even before he joined the court, Frankfurter had been influenced by Louis Brandeis's decentralistic views. The New Deal more or less marginalized the Brandeisian decentralistic position in progressive politics.

Of the other liberal justices. Earl Warren also did not fit into the New Deal paradigm. Unlike the Roosevelt justices and the other Warren Court liberals, whose orientation to national power was shaped by the New Dealers' belief that states were an obstacle to a just and efficient economic system, Warren's experience led him to believe that the states were by no means passé. As governor of California during its years of spectacular post–World War II growth, he demonstrated how vision and leadership could turn state government into a dynamic force for progressive social change.

The New Dealers instituted sweeping reversals of constitutional doctrines that had long limited national power over the economy. The interstate commerce and taxing powers of the national government were suddenly reinterpreted with a breadth previously unimaginable.[3] Perhaps most symbolic of the dramatic change was the swift elimination after 1937 of the constitutional theory of dual federalism, which interpreted the Tenth Amendment as independently establishing states' rights that limited the powers of the federal government.[4] Justice Stone's blunt dismissal of the Tenth Amendment, as stating no more than a mere "truism that all is retained which has not been surrendered," foreshadowed more than half a century during which, with one eccentric exception,[5] no congressional law was declared unconstitutional in violation of either the commerce clause or the Tenth Amendment.

All of the justices of the Warren Court accepted the New Deal settlement by which federalism came to be regarded a political rather than constitutional doctrine. During his Senate career, Justice Hugo Black had delivered his share of standard southern states' rights speeches in opposition to federal antilynching legislation and other civil rights measures. Yet, these views rarely affected Black's strongly nationalist positions on most New Deal economic legislation. As a justice, he remained a leading supporter of national power even during the bitter struggle over the sit-in cases, where he made it clear that he was prepared to overrule the *Civil Rights Cases* and recognize congressional power under Section 5 of the Fourteenth Amendment to bar "private" discrimination. When Congress finally did outlaw such discrimination in the Civil Rights Act of 1964, Black reiterated his view that but for the fact that Congress had chosen to justify its power under the commerce clause, he would have considered upholding the act under Section 5 of the Fourteenth Amendment.[6]

That the court was unanimous in upholding the Civil Rights Act under the commerce clause highlights the persistence of the New Deal settlement.[7] In *Heart of Atlanta Motel v. United States* (1964)[8] and *Katzenbach v. McClung* (1964),[9] the justices subjected the act to a minimalist "rationality review," thereby reaffirming the post-1937 consensus that an act of Congress promulgated under the commerce clause would not be overturned by the court.[10] Indeed, the facts of both *Heart of Atlanta* and *McClung* underline the truth that even the most tenuous connection to interstate commerce had become sufficient to invoke the commerce power. As if to make this point clear, Justice Tom Clark rejected the McClungs' claim that their restaurant was local and had no effect on interstate commerce by observing that 46 percent of the food they served had moved in interstate commerce.[11] Clark cited *Wickard v. Filburn* (1942),[12] the triumphal New Deal decision that is often thought to stand for the expansive proposition that in an interdependent economy virtually every economic activity can be treated as affecting interstate commerce.[13]

Congress had explicitly invoked the commerce clause to justify its power to bar "private" discrimination in the Civil Rights Act precisely because that justification had become impregnable. The act thereby avoided pressing the controversial question of the powers of Congress to pass "appropriate" enforcement legislation under Section 5 of the Fourteenth Amendment. Justices William Douglas and Authur Goldberg had wanted to uphold the Civil Rights Act under Section 5 in *Heart of Atlanta* and *McClung*, but they failed to enlist a majority behind that position.[14] The question finally did come before the court in *Katzenbach v. Morgan* (1966),[15] testing the power of Congress to bar literacy tests under the Voting Rights Act of 1965. Writing for a 7–2 majority, Justice William Brennan offered an extremely expansive definition of congressional power under Section 5 to enforce the provisions of the Fourteenth Amendment and, in particular, the Equal Protection Clause.[16] Justices John Harlan and Potter Stewart dissented. Harlan observed that the court had previously unanimously held that fairly administered voter literacy tests did not raise an equal protection problem.[17] Therefore, in the present case Congress was giving equal protection a more expansive meaning than the court had, raising the question of whether in addition to "ratcheting up," as occurred in this case, Congress might also have the power to dilute or "ratchet down" the meaning of equal protection.[18] "Congress can't define the Equal Protection Clause—that is for us to say," Harlan declared in conference. "Congress could not restore state poll taxes, for example, now that we have struck it down."[19] In a footnote, Justice Brennan declared that Congress had the power under Section 5 only to expand the definition of equal protection, not to contract it.[20] But it was never entirely clear how he arrived at this asymmetry.[21]

In concluding his dissent, Harlan made sure to warn of the diminution of state power that might occur in light of the court's opinion in *Morgan*:

> To hold, on this record, that § 4(e) overrides the New York literacy requirement seems to me tantamount to allowing the Fourteenth Amendment to swallow the State's constitutionally ordained primary authority in this field. For if Congress by what, as here, amounts to mere *ipse dixit* can set that otherwise permissible requirement partially at naught I see no reason why it could not also substitute its judgment for that of the States in other fields of their exclusive primary competence as well.[22]

The decisions upholding the Civil Rights Act of 1964 and the Voting Rights Act of 1965 meant that the Warren Court had not only reaffirmed virtually unchecked congressional power under the commerce clause but also acknowledged for the first time a new source of potentially expansive congressional power under Section 5 of the Fourteenth Amendment.[23] It was certainly the high point of judicial recognition of national power since 1937. The Rehnquist Court gutted Section 5 and virtually overruled Brennan's opinion in *Katzenbach v. Morgan*. It also placed restrictions on the congressional commerce power.[24]

On federalism issues, the Warren Court conservatives were led by Justice Harlan, whose unwavering reverence for "our federalism" demonstrated the continuing power of the traditional ideal. Yet, it is worth reiterating that even Justice Harlan showed not a trace of a wish to return to the pre-1937 doctrine of dual federalism or to cut back on the New Deal commerce clause decisions. Among the other Warren Court conservatives, Justice Byron White tended to an even more positive view of national power than did Harlan. Not only had White's legal education at Yale immersed him in New Deal constitutional values, but his almost two-year stint with the Kennedy administration's Justice Department reinforced his commitment to national regulatory power, especially in the area of civil rights. The most important influence on Justice White's view of federalism was the questions of racial justice that pressed on the Kennedy Justice Department while he served as second-in-command.

Economics originally shaped the New Dealers' low regard for the federal system. But beginning with the worldwide outrage at the conviction and capital sentence in 1931 of the youthful black Scottsboro defendants for the alleged rape of two white woman, the Supreme Court began to focus attention on a series of southern criminal convictions of Black men that amounted to "legal lynching[s]."[25] These appeals presented a picture of the southern system of criminal justice as a major support for white supremacy and of the federal system as a principal means of legitimating white southerners' use of the criminal system to support racial subordination. In addition, in the 1936 presidential election, a majority of African Americans voted for the Democratic presidential candidate for the first time.[26]

If almost all of the Warren Court liberals arrived on the court with an already formed skepticism about the virtues of a federal system, their experience with enforcing the school desegregation decision led them to grow even more impatient with continuing deference to state authority. In the process, they substantially relocated a series of constitutional markers that had previously helped define the boundaries of the federal system.

One of the most important areas of change involved the relationship between federal and state courts. As the massive resistance campaign against *Brown v. Board of Education* spread to include virtually all elected southern officials, many southern state judges also succumbed to a strategy of resistance to federal rulings. The Alabama effort to shut down the National Association for the Advancement of Colored People (NAACP) included a series of delaying tactics by the Alabama Supreme Court designed to thwart review by the U.S. high court. Despite a series of unfavorable rulings by the U.S. Supreme Court, Alabama succeeded in barring the civil rights organization from practicing in the state for eight years.

Justice Harlan's approach to the Alabama NAACP cases, discussed above, offers an example of the difficulties that state court resistance to school desegregation created for even a devoted admirer of the federal system. While Harlan refused to be bound by Alabama's claim that an abrupt change in its rules of procedure constituted an "independent state ground" barring Supreme Court review, he continued to presume in other less transparent cases that state judges were acting in good faith. Even after he reversed the Alabama Supreme Court for its bad faith refusal to hear the civil rights organization's constitutional claims in *NAACP v. Alabama*, he nevertheless, out of comity, permitted the Alabama injunction to remain in force pending the Alabama high court's decision on the merits. This move allowed Alabama judges, by delaying a ruling on the merits, to continue to prevent the NAACP lawyers from practicing in the state. All told, more than six years had passed since Justice Harlan's original decision declared the Alabama injunction unconstitutional.[27]

The struggle with Alabama appears to have brought Justice Harlan to the realization that his assumption of good faith in the Alabama courts had only provided more opportunities for continued delay and resistance. During the conference discussion of *New York Times v. Sullivan* (1964),[28] Harlan, fresh from his recent experiences with Alabama, initially took the unorthodox position that the Supreme Court should foreclose the possibility of another new trial in Alabama in order to eliminate further opportunities for delay or resistance.[29] Though he eventually abandoned the effort,[30] it did underline Harlan's frustration at realizing that the degree of trust essential for a working federal system was being sacrificed by the Alabama judiciary to the cause of preserving segregation.[31] Brennan's opinion, in which Harlan joined effectively if not expressly, foreclosed Alabama from holding a new trial.[32]

If Harlan's experience with the massive resistance of the Alabama judiciary led him to temporarily hesitate before deferring to state judicial authority, his liberal Warren Court colleagues felt no strong ideological attachments to federalism in the first place. For them, southern state judges were acting, as they had long acted, to protect white supremacy. Even so, the justices were unprepared for the depth, breadth, and persistence of southern judicial resistance.

Many Warren Court decisions upsetting one or another postulate of federalism were actually dictated by the mutual distrust, unleashed by the desegregation struggle, between the Supreme Court justices and their state judicial colleagues from the South.

Two major examples of the Supreme Court's expansion of the powers of the federal courts vis-à-vis those of the states are *Fay v. Noia*[33] and *Dombrowski v. Pfister.*[34]

In *Fay v. Noia*, Justice Brennan produced a significant expansion of the jurisdiction of the federal courts to review state criminal convictions in which the defendant had claimed a denial of federal constitutional rights. In a lengthy and controversial opinion, Brennan took aim at one of the major strategies deployed by southern judges seeking to insulate criminal convictions from Supreme Court review. As we saw, under ordinary circumstances the Supreme Court would not review state criminal convictions that were based on "independent state grounds" not involving any claim of constitutional deprivation. In many post-*Brown* cases, southern judges had deployed state rules of procedure in a highly questionable manner to frustrate review of state criminal convictions.

Brennan reviewed the history of the Habeas Corpus Act to conclude that the act authorized federal "collateral" review even in state cases where federal claims could not otherwise be heard on direct review because a procedural default below had furnished "an adequate and independent ground" of state decision. Given the Supreme Court's limited resources, direct review of state criminal decisions could only have covered a handful of cases. *Fay v. Noia* thus made it possible to bring a claim of denial of federal rights before any federal trial judge despite procedural error by the defendant's lawyer below.[35]

Fay v. Noia produced a major expansion of federal review of state criminal convictions, an especially important development in light of the Warren Court's simultaneous extension of the protections of the Bill of Rights to state criminal proceedings. By authorizing lower federal court judges to entertain constitutional challenges to state criminal convictions even when state courts had expressly based their opinions on state law grounds, *Fay v. Noia* provided a federal forum that could monitor state court deprivations of constitutional rights. What also made a great deal of difference was whether the Supreme Court heard an appeal based on a record developed in a sympathetic federal forum, as opposed to an often hostile state judicial system.

Without the decision in *Fay v. Noia*, it would therefore have been administratively impossible for the Supreme Court to institutionalize its revolutionary expansion of the rights of criminal defendants. Because of the many other cases ordinarily pressing for review, it would have meant that as a practical matter, the court could only hear a handful of criminal appeals in any year.

Like most of the federalism decisions of the Warren Era, *Fay v. Noia* can only be understood in the context of the struggle over civil rights that began with resistance to *Brown* and continued through extension of the provisions of the Bill of Rights as a restriction on the power of the states. Judicial behavior in these cases compounded long-standing liberal skepticism about whether southern judges could be devoted to the rule of law when race was a factor.[36] It also heightened the determination of liberals to assure that federalism should not continue to serve as an institution for entrenching racial hierarchy.

It is hard to imagine that *Dombrowski v. Pfister* could have been decided in any other era in Supreme Court history.[37] *Dombrowski v. Pfister* represented the amplification of the Warren Court's First Amendment ideas amid the deep suspicions engendered between the Supreme Court and southern state courts during the civil rights struggles. In its "determination to protect the civil rights movement," Owen Fiss observed, the court in *Dombrowski* put forth "a new vision of federalism."[38]

We saw in our previous discussion of the "void for vagueness" and "overbreadth" doctrines that the Warren Court, for the first time, had permitted "facial" challenges to the constitutionality of criminal statutes that exerted a "chilling effect" on First Amendment rights. In the context of the struggle over civil rights, the Supreme Court had learned that southern state courts were not, Professor Fiss delicately put it, "as prone as federal courts to vindicate constitutional rights promptly and effectively."[39] Facial challenges enabled civil rights activists during the civil rights era to launch an immediate challenge in federal court to state criminal laws that were being deployed for the purpose of resisting civil rights activities.

Facial challenges represented a major innovation in the relationship between federal and state courts. This permitted federal courts to avoid the traditional rule that a "narrowing" interpretation by a state court of even a constitutionally vague statute could "save" the statute from constitutional infirmity. Instead, it was now possible to bypass state courts in challenging a state criminal law on its face. Virtually all of these facial challenges involved the civil rights struggle in the South.

Though *Dombrowski* followed from the logic of facial challenges, it went one step further in enjoining a state court from enforcing—and thereby from interpreting—its own laws. Even before *Dombrowski*, the Supreme Court had provided a new federal path for avoiding a narrowing construction by state courts, but now it could actively prevent a state court from even hearing criminal cases that could have provided the opportunity to offer a narrowing reading to its own statute. Such an extreme departure from the traditional premises of the federal system could have occurred only in the unprecedented situation in which the Supreme Court felt abandoned by southern state judges in enforcing federal constitutional rights. Still, shortly after the Warren Court ended, the justices neutralized *Dombrowski* in *Younger v. Harris* (1971).

11
DEMOCRATIC CULTURE

The Reapportionment Cases showed that the Warren Court took democracy seriously as a constitutional ideal. Its decisions involving freedom of expression show the court trying to make democracy a practical reality. The free speech cases allowed the court to formulate the necessary conditions for achieving popular self-government through the ballot box. Beyond free and equal voting, there needed to be "uninhibited, robust, and wide-open" debate on public issues that would "assure unfettered interchange of ideas for the bringing about of political and social changes desired by the people."[1] More than any U.S. Supreme Court in American history, the Warren Court was seriously attentive to the political culture that underlay democracy.

What is still more amazing is that the Warren Court did not limit its understanding of the preconditions for democracy to the narrowly political. It was the first Supreme Court to realize that there was a close connection between democratic political institutions and culture and that, indeed, there was such a thing as democratic culture. Beyond the political freedoms most obviously necessary to democracy, the court recognized that self-government required citizens to be able to express themselves artistically without the overhanging threat of vague obscenity laws and to engage in symbolic speech-actions that could potentially communicate more than mere words. What is more, democratic culture required that citizens form their beliefs and live their lives free from both the stultifying imposition of religious doctrine and unnecessary government intrusion into their private lives.

OBSCENITY

Perhaps the best place to begin examining this development is through the court's decisions involving obscenity. The story begins with the decision in *Roth v. United States* (1957), written by Justice William Brennan in his first term on the court.[2] Holding that obscenity is not protected by the First Amendment, *Roth* nevertheless offered the most permissive definition of obscenity ever proposed until that time by any court. Material was not obscene unless it was "utterly without redeeming social importance." "All ideas having even the slightest redeeming social importance," Brennan wrote, "—unorthodox ideas, controversial ideas, even ideas hateful to the prevailing climate of opinion— have the full protection" of the First Amendment.[3]

"Sex and obscenity are not synonymous," Brennan declared in the midst of a decade known for its postwar resurgence of puritanism and its determination to censor movies and prevent Americans from reading books such as D. H. Lawrence's 1928 novel *Lady Chatterley's Lover* and Henry Miller's long-suppressed *Tropic of Cancer*.[4] "Obscene material is material which deals with sex in a manner appealing to prurient interest," Brennan announced. "The portrayal of sex, e.g., in art, literature and scientific works, is not itself sufficient reason to deny material the constitutional protection of freedom of speech and press. Sex, a great and mysterious motive force in human life, has indisputably been a subject of absorbing interest to mankind through the ages; it is one of the vital problems of human interest and public concern."[5]

The test for whether material is obscene, Brennan declared, is whether "to the *average* person, applying contemporary community standards, the *dominant* theme of the material *taken as a whole* appeals to prurient interest."[6]

In light of the enormous changes that have taken place in American law and culture in the seven decades since Brennan delivered his *Roth* opinion, it is easy to underestimate both the importance and the wisdom of his brilliant formulation. Only by locating *Roth* in its historical context can we fully appreciate its significance.[7]

When *Roth* was brought before the Supreme Court, a respectable body of opinion, led by the distinguished civil libertarian Alexander Meiklejohn, sought to restrict the scope of free speech protections to speech about the "public welfare." In this view, the First Amendment was absolute but limited to protecting speech related to political freedom and democratic self-government. Private speech, in contrast, received only the minimal protection of the due process requirement of the Fifth Amendment. The Meiklejohn thesis thus drew a sharp distinction between political and cultural forms of expression.[8] *Roth* was among the first Supreme Court opinions to reject this distinction and to acknowledge a relationship between culture and politics.

Justices Hugo Black and William Douglas dissented in *Roth* on the "absolutist" ground that the First Amendment bars all restrictions on speech, even obscene speech. None of the rest of the justices, including Brennan, was ever willing to accept that proposition. Whatever one may say in defense of the Black-Douglas position, it is important not to forget that in *Roth* Brennan was able to assemble a majority behind a constitutional formula that was more protective of artistic expression than any that had been previously proposed.

By the time the Warren Court ended, however, Brennan's *Roth* formula had unraveled as the difficult task of applying its various elements to a society undergoing unprecedented changes in sexual mores became increasingly evident. By 1964, it had already become apparent that Brennan had failed to rally a majority around a coherent and consistent application of his *Roth* formula. In *Jacobellis v. Ohio* (1964), a splintered court produced seven different opinions, including Justice Potter Stewart's memorable pronouncement about hard-core pornography: "I know it when I see it."[9]

The justices divided over such questions as how to define "community" in *Roth*'s phrase "contemporary community standards"—whether, for example, whether there should be a national or local test of obscenity.[10] A local test would mean that more straitlaced communities would be allowed greater leeway to suppress books, magazines, movies, theatrical productions, paintings, and other forms of artistic expression. A national standard would mean that uniform criteria would prevail throughout the United States, which in practice would mean that the more cosmopolitan assumptions of the cultural elite would be applied. In a period when television, dominated by national networks, was emerging as the leading influence over popular culture, the questions might already have become moot.

Another problem that emerged with Brennan's formulation was whether the phrase "utterly without redeeming social importance"[11] incorporated unconscious prejudices in favor of "highbrow" as opposed to "lowbrow" culture. Shortly before *Jacobellis* came to the court, Brennan drafted a memorandum to his colleagues that set out his main views on pornography. "The basic point of this memorandum," he concluded, "is that no bona fide work of art or information may be suppressed in the name of obscenity, even if it is deeply repulsive to the dominant current thought of the community."[12] This view, critics noted, led the court to embark on a misleading search for artistic merit from the vantage point of "highbrow" culture.[13] In a period in which some of the most creative cultural achievements—such as the music of the Beatles—were directed at a mass audience, Justice Brennan's search for "bona fide" works of art left the impression that he was concerned only with protecting masterpieces—such as the Renaissance painter Titian's nudes—from the scorn of the philistines.

The truth is that in 1957 the Supreme Court justices were totally unprepared for the sexual revolution that was about to burst onto the scene and thoroughly transform the most intimate aspects of American life. Themselves largely the products of a puritanical middle-class culture, the justices were surprised by the emergence of sexuality into mainstream popular culture that began in the

1950s with the Kinsey Reports in 1948 and 1953 on male and female sexuality, the appearance of *Playboy* in 1953, and such scandalous best-selling novels as *Peyton Place* (1956). And if the justices were unprepared for the increased frankness of the 1950s, still less were they prepared for the developments of the 1960s and 1970s. With the emergence of an increasingly self-confident gay culture, celebrating homosexuality through books and magazines, Justice Brennan's well-meant effort to define obscenity in terms of material that "appeals to prurient interest" itself came to seem positively puritanical.

The shift to the Burger Court after 1969 produced decisions that sought to narrow Brennan's standard. In turn, Brennan grew more and more skeptical about whether any satisfactory formula would work, eventually rejecting his own approach in *Roth*. His dissent in a pornographic film case, *Paris Adult Theatre* I (1973), announced his new position: "I am forced to conclude that the concept of 'obscenity' cannot be defined with sufficient specificity and clarity to provide fair notice to persons who create and distribute sexually oriented materials, to prevent substantial erosion of protected speech as a byproduct of the attempt to suppress unprotected speech, and to avoid very costly institutional harms."[14]

In a 1986 interview, Brennan acknowledged that the court's failure to find "a solution to the definitional horror of obscenity" was one of his major disappointments on the court and that maybe "it has been my fault."[15] Still later, he confided that he "had put sixteen years into that damn obscenity thing. . . . I tried and I tried, and I waffled back and forth, and I finally gave up."[16] Perhaps Brennan's concession demonstrates that Justices Black and Douglas were right all along and that their absolutist position on obscenity had anticipated the impossibility of reaching a consensus on a question that was in the midst of such dynamic cultural change.

One element of this dynamic change that totally shifted the ground of the debate over pornography was the emergence of the feminist movement soon after the Warren Court had come to a close. The writings of Catharine MacKinnon and Andrea Dworkin made it painfully clear that much pornography was addressed to male fantasies about the degradation of women by men.[17] Suddenly there was a split in the progressive, cosmopolitan coalition over the question of pornography, as some feminists called for greater regulation of hardcore pornography on the grounds that it created a culture harmful to women. Equally important was a serious debate over the effects of culture on action—on the effects of cultural images and symbols on the behavior of men toward women—a debate that did not necessarily carry the ancient baggage of puritan discomfort with sexuality.[18]

In the end, it would be mistaken to dismiss the court's efforts to deal with the constitutionality of obscenity as a failure. It may have been naive to believe that any legal formula could adequately capture the values affecting so complex a subject, especially in a period of such dynamic social change. Yet, as in so many other areas of constitutional law, the Supreme Court did manage to create an educational dialogue about fundamental values that no other institution was capable of producing. By the time the Warren Court ended, there was no longer any substantial body of opinion that sought to exclude artistic expression from First Amendment protection by sharply distinguishing the political from the literary or cultural realms. In the midst of the social and cultural upheaval of the 1960s, it was no longer possible to suppose that cultural expression has no effect on political action. But this also meant that one of the central organizing ideas of First Amendment jurisprudence—positing a sharp distinction between speech and action—began to collapse.

SYMBOLIC SPEECH

The sit-ins against segregated public facilities in the early 1960s first raised the question of whether it was possible to distinguish between speech and action. But it was the symbolic protests against America's growing involvement in the war in Vietnam that challenged the very foundations of the speech-action distinction.

The distinction was especially important for Justice Black's absolutist view of the First Amendment. Once something was categorized as speech, Black insisted that no state interest, however compelling, could justify its suppression. Thus, as we have seen, Black rejected any use of a "balancing test" to decide First Amendment questions.[19] Instead, he relied on a bright-line distinction between speech, which could never constitutionally be punished, and action, which could be. If one had asked Justice Black whether the state could punish a person for falsely shouting "Fire" in a crowded theater, he would have replied that it was not speech but rather action that was being punished.

Three symbolic speech cases involving antiwar protests strained the speech-action distinction to the breaking point. In *United States v. O'Brien* (1968), Chief Justice Earl Warren relied on the distinction to uphold the conviction of Vietnam War protesters for burning their draft registration cards.[20] "When 'speech' and 'nonspeech' elements are combined in the same course of conduct, a sufficiently important governmental interest in regulating the nonspeech element can justify limitations of First Amendment freedoms," the court ruled in a decision from which only Justice Douglas dissented.[21] *O'Brien*'s patriotic fervor alarmed civil libertarians, who realized that almost any act of speech could be said to include a nonspeech element.

In a contrasting decision, *Tinker v. Des Moines* (1969), the court moved to protect symbolic speech, overturning the Des Moines School District's decision to suspend students who wore black armbands protesting the Vietnam War.[22] Justice Black dissented on the ground that the students were engaged in action, not speech. In his *Tinker* dissent, Black seemed overtaken by the fears of growing lawlessness that had first surfaced five years earlier with the sit-in cases, as he painted a dark picture of judicially sanctioned anarchy:

> I repeat that if the time has come when pupils . . . can defy and flout orders of school officials to keep their minds on their own schoolwork, it is the beginning of a new revolutionary era of permissiveness in this country fostered by the judiciary. . . . [S]tudents all over the land are already running loose, conducting break-ins, sit-ins, lie-ins, and smash-ins. Many of these student groups, as is all too familiar to all who read the newspapers and watch the television news programs, have already engaged in rioting, property seizures, and destruction.[23]

The speech-action distinction to which Black clung in *Tinker* received perhaps its greatest blow in the 1971 case *Cohen v. California*. In *Cohen*, the court in a 5–4 decision overturned the breach-of-peace conviction of a man who had walked through a Los Angeles courthouse wearing a jacket emblazoned with the words "Fuck the Draft."[24] The dissenters, including Black, declared that "Cohen's absurd and immature antic . . . was mainly conduct and little speech."[25] In fact, "speech" and "action" were inextricably intertwined in Cohen's behavior. *O'Brien, Tinker,* and *Cohen* all revealed that First Amendment jurisprudence had failed to acknowledge that the very concept of symbolic speech was incompatible with a clear distinction between speech and action.

CHURCH AND STATE

Judged by the handful of Supreme Court opinions delivered during the Warren Court era, the two decades after World War II represent an unusually harmonious period in interreligious relations. The key Establishment Clause cases that did arise involved the application of the First Amendment to schools. The period began with *Everson v. Board of Education* (1947) that challenged New Jersey's school transportation program, whose benefits were extended to parochial school students. The harmony ended shortly after the Supreme Court's 7–1 decision striking down school prayer in *Engel v. Vitale* (1962).

The sudden focus on the schoolroom in postwar Supreme Court cases was triggered by an unexpected development in the constitutional doctrine of the 1940s. Deriving from Justice Black's efforts to claim that the Fourteenth Amendment incorporated the Bill of Rights, it meant that suddenly the religion clauses of the First Amendment would, for the first time, serve as restrictions on the states. The Establishment Clause of the First Amendment, originally designed primarily to prohibit the establishment of a national church, was now potentially called upon to adjudicate the legitimacy of every religious ceremony in every public school in the land.[26]

Since 1940, the free exercise clause had also been successfully deployed by nonmainstream religions—frequently the Jehovah's Witnesses—to challenge community restrictions on their proselytizing.[27] Justice Robert Jackson relied on First Amendment freedoms to strike down West Virginia's compulsory school flag salute in 1943.[28]

The Establishment Clause was activated just as the Roman Catholic Church in the United States had begun to shift from a defensive posture vis-à-vis Protestant America. Until the Supreme Court held in *Pierce v. Society of Sisters* (1925) that the Due Process Clause forbade the State of Oregon from shutting down its Catholic schools, much of the church's constitutional energy had been channeled into resisting such overtly anti-Catholic policies.[29] Yet, by the time *Everson* was decided just twenty-two years later, the Catholic Church had not only succeeded in persuading the New Jersey legislature to support transportation for Catholic students; it had also successfully defended this practice before the Supreme Court.[30]

Justice Black's statement for the majority in *Everson* expresses what perhaps had become a postwar consensus on the proper relationship between religion and the state. It also reflected Hugo Black's own religious upbringing. In his youth, Black had been deeply drawn to his family Baptist church. His beloved mother, who gave birth to Hugo just five days after burying her two-year-old daughter, spent most of Hugo's childhood battling depression. She died the month that Hugo turned nineteen. "The Bible was the only book my mother read to me," he recalled. "She made me study it." As a young man, he preached Baptist doctrine in Sunday school at his local church.[31]

This early immersion in his mother's evangelical religion seems to have shaped Black's views on the proper relation between church and state. "Ever since the days of Roger Williams and John Leland, separation of church and state and freedom of religious conscience had been central to the Baptist tradition."[32] Baptists, as "staunch defender[s] of church-state separation, . . . were historically reluctant . . . to see religion play a more direct and visible role in public affairs."[33] This all began to change in the 1960s as northern Baptists joined the widespread religious backlash against the school prayer decisions. Initially, "Southern Baptist leaders . . . dissented from the northern evangelical consensus," and the Southern Baptist Convention held firm in its opposition to all attempts to water down the religion clauses of the First Amendment.[34] It was not until the 1980s that Southern Baptists engaged in "a monumental shift" away from the earlier strict separationist views of Baptist leaders and founders.[35]

While Justice Black appears to have shed his earlier religious commitments long before he joined the court, he continued to espouse separatism as if nothing had changed. If he was any longer interested in sectarian religious doctrine, he might have noticed the emerging split between northern Baptists and Southern Baptists. Whether or not he any longer found sustenance in religious doctrine, he might have been proud to notice that Southern Baptists continued to uphold the separatism of his youth. When they finally did abandon their commitment to a strict separation of church and state in the 1980s, Black had long passed from the scene.

As we saw, *Everson* involved a challenge to the constitutionality of a New Jersey law that reimbursed students and their parents for the cost of public transportation needed to attend school, including parochial school. In 1947, almost all parochial school students in New Jersey attended Roman Catholic schools. Justice Black's opinion for five justices upheld the New Jersey policy while articulating an extremely rigorous test for judging whether the separation between church and state had been breached:

> The "establishment of religion" clause of the First Amendment means at least this: Neither a state nor the Federal Government can set up a church. Neither can pass laws which aid one religion, aid all religions or prefer one religion over another. Neither can force nor influence a person to go to or to remain away from church against his will or force him to profess a belief or disbelief in any religion. No person can be punished for entertaining or professing religious beliefs or disbeliefs, for church attendance or non-attendance. No tax in any amount, large or small, can be levied to support any religious activities or institutions, whatever they may be called, or whatever form they may adopt to teach or practice religion. Neither a state nor the Federal Government can, openly or secretly, participate in the affairs of any religious organizations or groups and vice versa. In the words of Jefferson, the clause against establishment of religion by law was intended to erect "a wall of separation between Church and State."[36]

We should note that Black's confident appeal to Jefferson's "wall of separation" as the basis for strictly interpreting the Establishment Clause was also agreed to by all four dissenters in *Everson*, who differed from Black only in believing that Black's own principles should have led him to strike down the New Jersey law.[37] Remarkably, then, in 1947 all nine justices were willing to agree that the metaphor of a "wall of separation" should frame the reach of the Establishment Clause.[38]

Justice Black had little reason to expect that much had changed when in 1962, over Justice Stewart's sole dissent, he struck down the required reading of an official New York school prayer as a violation of the Establishment Clause. Much to his surprise, *Engel v. Vitale* turned out to be among the most unpopular decisions rendered by the Warren Court.[39] One year later in *Abington School District v. Schempp*, the Supreme Court followed *Engel* and struck down a Pennsylvania law requiring that "at least ten verses from the Holy Bible shall be read, without comment, at the opening of each public school . . . day."[40] One imagines that the Pennsylvania law begat a slew of Bible readings whose ten verses were so lacking in context as to be incomprehensible to many students. The controversy over mandatory school prayer would soon be overshadowed by the results of the court's privacy jurisprudence.

THE RIGHT TO PRIVACY

In addition to the Warren Court's expansion of constitutional freedom in the public sphere, it also bolstered freedom in the most private realms of decisions about sexuality and birth control. The court recognized that a zone of privacy immune from intrusion by government was a necessary precondition for individual self-realization in a democratic society. The dystopias of *1984* and *Brave New World* suggested what society might be like if privacy and sexuality were sacrificed to the greater good of the state. It soon came to be recognized that democracy requires that citizens retain a measure of autonomy in not only public speech but also the private choices they make about their own bodies.

In *Griswold v. Connecticut* (1965), one of the Warren Court's most controversial and far-reaching decisions, the court first recognized a constitutional right to privacy, barring the State of Connecticut from enforcing its statute forbidding use of contraceptives even by married couples.[41]

By the time the Connecticut birth control law was challenged, public attitudes toward contraception had undergone a 180-degree change from early in the twentieth century, when Margaret Sanger had begun her battle against laws barring doctors from offering birth control advice. At that time, the federal Comstock Law forbade the mailing, interstate transportation, and importation of contraceptive materials and information; twenty-two states also had "little Comstock laws," of which the most restrictive was Connecticut's absolute ban on the "use" of birth control devices.[42]

Through the 1920s, Sanger scored very few successes in her effort to appeal to courts to relax the severity of these laws. But the educational efforts of the Planned Parenthood Federation, supported by First Lady Eleanor Roosevelt, brought the movement to "a new phase" during the 1940s "in which birth control began to enjoy substantial social and official acceptance."[43] Yet, political stalemate or inertia kept most of the old anti–birth control laws on the books so that they continued to threaten law-abiding citizens, even though prosecutors rarely enforced them.[44] And in the way that all laws are symbolic of community values, the anti–birth control laws conveyed a message about sexuality and the legitimacy of governmental intrusion into a person's most intimate realms.

By the time *Griswold v. Connecticut* was decided, then, a substantial consensus had emerged on the desirability of family planning through contraception. Even Justice Stewart, who believed that Connecticut's anti–birth control statute should be upheld, called it an "uncommonly silly law."[45] The question to be decided in *Griswold* was whether there was a constitutional basis for striking down such laws. Writing the opinion of the court, Justice Douglas found that the Connecticut law unconstitutionally interfered with "notions of privacy surrounding the marriage relationship."[46] The law intruded into "an intimate relation of husband and wife and their physician's role in . . . that relation."[47]

But where did the Constitution provide for any right to privacy? Various interpretations of the Fourth and Fifth Amendments by the court, Douglas declared, have created "penumbral rights of 'privacy and repose.'"[48] A "zone of privacy [has been] created by several fundamental constitutional guarantees."[49] Cases interpreting these specific provisions "suggest that specific guarantees in the Bill of Rights have penumbras, formed by emanations from those guarantees that help give them life and substance."[50]

As if Douglas's talk of "penumbras" and "emanations" was not provocative enough, Justice Goldberg (with the support of Chief Justice Warren and Justice Brennan) added an even more controversial note to the question of how to locate the right to privacy in the text of the Constitution. He invoked the long-dormant Ninth Amendment, which states that "the enumeration in the Constitution, of certain rights, shall not be construed to deny or disparage others retained by the people."[51] Goldberg acknowledged that the amendment had played no role in almost two hundred years of constitutional history. Its words had always been thought of as no more than what Justice Harlan Fiske Stone, referring to similar words in the Tenth Amendment, had dismissed as a "truism that all is retained which has not been surrendered."[52]

All of these intellectual gymnastics, it should be recognized, were devoted to avoiding Justice Harlan's more straightforward approach of holding that the "right to privacy" was included within the Fourteenth Amendment's Due Process Clause. For the liberal justices, however, who had spent years criticizing the *Lochner* Court for supposedly illegitimately changing from a "procedural" to a "substantive" interpretation of due process, nothing could have been worse than deriving a right to privacy from the Due Process Clause.

Though it is beyond the chronological scope of this book, we should note here that *Griswold v. Connecticut* became the leading precedent for the court's extension of the right to privacy to include a woman's right to an abortion in *Roe v. Wade* (1973), the most controversial Supreme Court decision in many years, just recently overruled.[53] Until that moment, the result in *Griswold* was quite popular even if its methodology was widely criticized within the legal profession.[54]

Justice Black's dissent in *Griswold* was a direct criticism of its methodology. One year after the first sit-in cases split the new liberal majority, *Griswold* represented another major step in Black's alienation from his former allies. Stating that the Connecticut law "is every bit as offensive to me as it is" to the majority, Black nevertheless denied "that the evil qualities they see in the law make it unconstitutional. . . . I like my privacy as well as the next one," Black continued, "but I am nevertheless compelled to admit that government has a right to invade it unless prohibited by some specific constitutional provision."[55] Both the Ninth Amendment grounds of Justice Goldberg and the due process grounds of Justice Harlan, Black declared, "turn out to be the same thing— merely using different words to claim for this Court and the federal judiciary power to invalidate any legislative act which the judges find irrational, unreasonable or offensive."[56]

Black here reiterated a view that he had expressed as long ago as *Adamson v. California* (1947), when, as we saw in chapter 4, he first crossed swords with Justice Felix Frankfurter's effort to base due process on ideas of fundamental fairness in criminal procedure.[57] Anything short of total incorporation of the Bill of Rights into the Due Process Clause Black then denounced as a subjective appeal to "natural law."[58] Yet, on the basis of his own controversial reading of the original intent of the Framers of the Fourteenth Amendment that seemed equally arbitrary to some critics, Black maintained that history justified total incorporation.

Black's increasing devotion to rigid originalism and textualism reduced every complex interpretative argument to a one-dimensional test: whether an interpretation was "objective" or "subjective." Here he was echoing arguments developed by Protestant fundamentalist ministers, arguments that he had surely heard in church in his youth. Southern evangelicals had traditionally opposed all biblical interpretation and insisted on finding a "plain meaning" in the biblical text.[59] We should recall that Black referred to the Constitution as "my legal bible" and "cherish[ed] every word of it, from the first to the last[,] . . . personally deplor[ing] even the slightest deviation from its least important commands."[60] Black followed his ancestors in seeking the original meaning of their sacred texts and refusing to acknowledge that those texts might change with changing times.

Using the twin criteria of textual literalism and historical originalism, Black righteously claimed objectivity for his own dogmatic readings of the Constitution, yet his position enmeshed him in contradiction. Though he was ardently opposed to the idea of a "living Constitution," he had been able to conclude that the Equal Protection Clause originally barred racial segregation as well as unequal apportionment in both houses of state legislatures, propositions that could only be defended on the basis of a dynamic view of evolving constitutional meaning.

As Black grew older and more disillusioned with the freewheeling interpretative style of his former allies, he became even more rigid in his denunciation of constitutional interpretation designed "to bring [the Constitution] into harmony with the times."[61] In another privacy case, he took this opposition to the point of absurdity.

Katz v. United States (1967) involved wiretapping by agents of the Federal Bureau of Investigation who had attached an electronic listening and recording device to the outside of a public telephone booth from which the defendant had placed his calls. The government insisted that unless there was a trespass onto the defendant's own property there could be no "unreasonable search and seizure" in violation of the Fourth Amendment. Rejecting this view, Justice Stewart held for an eight-person majority that the amendment was meant to protect not the defendant's property but rather his privacy.

Justice Black was the lone dissenter. "A conversation overheard by eavesdropping," he wrote, "whether by plain snooping or wiretapping, is not tangible and, under the normally accepted meanings of the words, can neither be searched nor seized."[62] Black's rigid literalism was not far from Chief Justice William Howard Taft's original refusal in *Olmstead v. United States* (1922) to include wiretapping under the Fourth Amendment because the Framers could not have intended to cover this unknown technology by the protection against unreasonable searches and seizures.[63] Justice Louis Brandeis had the better of the argument in dissent, emphasizing that the Fourth Amendment's underlying principle of protecting privacy from intrusion by the state would apply even to previously unknown technology.

Though the Douglas and Goldberg opinions in *Griswold v. Connecticut* were stated in more untraditional language, they were making the same point as Brandeis made in *Olmstead*. Courts frequently search for the underlying principle of a rule before deciding whether to apply it to new situations. And not infrequently when they are asked to extend a rule to a new situation, they find support for the extension in the fact that many different existing rules were supported by the same underlying principle.

This was what Justice Douglas meant when he found converging "penumbras" and "emanations" of the right to privacy in various constitutional rules such as the Fourth and Fifth Amendments. Even Justice Goldberg's invocation of the Ninth Amendment was more traditional in its methodology than has often been acknowledged. "I [do not] mean to state that the Ninth Amendment constitutes an independent source of rights," Goldberg emphasized but rather that it "shows a belief of the Constitution's authors that fundamental rights exist that are not expressly enumerated in the first eight amendments and an intent that the list of rights included there not be deemed exhaustive."[64]

Like its protection of artistic expression, the court's privacy decisions were based on an understanding of the multiple layers of human personality and self-expression that constitute a thriving democratic culture. The protection of human sexuality independent of procreation was the foundation of *Griswold*; protection of such spontaneous intimate relationships lies at the basis of an autonomous democratic culture.

CONCLUSION

The Jurisprudence of the Warren Court

In order to successfully generalize about the jurisprudence of the Warren Court, one first needs to recognize the key moments that shaped the Warren era, 1953–1969. Two moments especially stand out. First was the decision in *Brown v. Board of Education*, which exerted a powerful influence on the agenda of the Warren Court during the entire sixteen years of its existence. Decided during the first year of Earl Warren's chief justiceship, *Brown* ignited a wave of race-centered litigation that would otherwise surely have taken many more years (if ever) to emerge.

Almost every subject area in constitutional law was directly or indirectly reshaped by the decision in *Brown*. At its most direct, *Brown* inspired a more active reading of the Equal Protection Clause, which was soon applied to legislative apportionment as well as to a broadened recognition of the rights of "outsiders" (e.g., aliens and out-of-wedlock children). Shortly after the Warren Court ended, the momentum generated by equal protection challenges was, carried over to *Reed v. Reed* (1971), which initiated a new era of legal attacks on gender discrimination.

The southern massive resistance fueled by *Brown* generated, in reaction, a separate body of constitutional law that sought to shield civil rights organizations from state attack. Among the most important developments was the creation of a body of federal constitutional law protecting freedom of association, which brought about a reversal of the long-standing presumption that states possessed virtually unchallenged power to regulate incorporated organizations.

Brown affected legal doctrine in many seemingly unrelated areas. As we saw, questions of racism were embedded in the decisions involving legislative reapportionment or rights of criminal suspects.

A second key moment was the appointment in 1962 of Arthur Goldberg to the seat vacated by Felix Frankfurter after his stroke. Goldberg's appointment shifted the court's balance of power and especially changed the court's relationship to McCarthyite anticommunist legislation. Many of the dramatic changes in constitutional law for which the Warren Court would become well known occurred after Goldberg replaced Frankfurter. And Goldberg's surprising "dissent from a denial of *certiorari*" in 1963 triggered the slow march of the Supreme Court to temporary abolition of the death penalty.

Brown also introduced radical change in traditional jurisprudential ideas. The idea of a "living constitution" was perhaps the most important idea institutionalized by the Warren Court. It appeared in several variations. We saw that in *Brown* itself all but Justice Hugo Black clearly supported the once heretical proposition that constitutional meaning ought to change to accommodate social change. (As we saw, it is not entirely clear whether Black did oppose this idea at the time.) Another variation can be seen in Chief Justice Warren's introduction of an evolutionary perspective into the Expatriation Cases. The Eighth Amendment's protection against cruel and unusual punishments, Warren wrote in his dissent in *Trop v. Dulles*, "must draw its meaning from the evolving standards of decency that mark the progress of maturing society." Justice Goldberg incorporated Warren's evolutionary perspective into his 1963 dissent challenging the constitutionality of capital punishment.

The Warren Court also introduced the idea that democracy was a foundational value in interpreting the U.S. Constitution. As I have shown elsewhere,[1] the use of "democracy" and its variations in Supreme Court opinions was virtually nonexistent before the 1940s. During the Warren era the appeal to democracy as a foundational constitutional value multiplied and was widely proclaimed in both majority opinions and dissents. In one of the Reapportionment Cases, Justice William Douglas clearly expressed the idea of a constitution that had evolved over time into a democratic document. "The conception of political equality from the Declaration of Independence to Lincoln's Gettysburg Address to the Fifteenth, Seventeenth and Nineteenth Amendment can only mean one thing—one person, one vote," Douglas declared.

Chief Justice Warren surprises the reader of his memoirs by declaring that the Reapportionment Cases, not *Brown v. Board of Education,* were the most important decisions of his court. "The reason I am of the opinion that [the Reapportionment Cases are] so important is because I believe so devoutly that, to paraphrase Abraham Lincoln's famous epigram, ours is a government of *all* the people, by *all* of the people and for *all* of the people."

AFTERWORD

The Legacy of the Warren Court

Erwin Chemerinsky

The Warren Court has become a powerful symbol, with almost mythological significance, for both the Left and the Right. For liberals, the Warren Court was the epitome of what the U.S. Supreme Court should be in expanding constitutional protection of equality and freedom. Progressives glorify the Warren Court as the one time in history when the court had a liberal majority and for decades since have attempted to create a jurisprudence based on its precepts. But conservatives have railed against liberal judicial activism ever since Earl Warren was chief justice, even though the court has had a conservative majority appointed by Republican presidents since 1971. Originalism was developed in response to the Warren Court and though it started as a fringe theory, it flourished among conservatives as the antidote to liberal judicial decisions and now has substantial influence in constitutional law.

Professor Morton Horwitz's superb account of the Warren Court shows that the reality is far more nuanced and much more complicated than the popular and even scholarly characterizations of the Warren Court. The question that Horwitz ultimately leaves with the reader is what the legacy and long-term impact of the Warren Court have been.

After 1969, the Supreme Court quickly became profoundly more conservative when Richard Nixon was able to appoint four justices in his first two years as president, replacing Chief Justice Earl Warren and Justices Abe Fortas, Hugo Black, and John Marshall Harlan. Never again has there been a majority of the justices appointed by Democratic presidents. In fact, between 1960 and 2020, there have been thirty-two years with Republican presidents and twenty-eight years with Democratic presidents, almost exactly even. But during this time Republican presidents picked fifteen justices, while the Democrats selected only eight. And for political reasons, most of the Republican-appointed justices have been very conservative.

Nowhere are the effects of this more apparent than with regard to race and especially schools. A crucial theme in Professor Horwitz's account is how much racial justice was a central focus of the Warren Court. His examination of the Warren Court's decisions, as would be expected, starts and finishes with *Brown v. Board of Education.* Ending government-mandated segregation in schools and in American society was a central focus and enormous achievement of the Warren Court. In a country that protected slavery in its Constitution and lived with Supreme Court–approved apartheid after *Plessy v. Ferguson* in 1896, the Warren Court was the first to deal with racial justice in a serious way. In an initial chapter, Horwitz shows how much *Brown* was a product of the legal realism movement that began in the early twentieth century. In a concluding chapter, he explains how *Brown* affected virtually all aspects of constitutional jurisprudence. Horwitz also shows that the Warren Court's focus on race was much broader than the urgency of desegregation. Issues of racial justice were at the core of many areas of the Warren Court's jurisprudence and are part of almost every chapter of this book.

The Warren Court's most long-lasting legacy was the end of government-mandated segregation in every area of life in southern states and in other parts of the country as well. Of course, the court was not alone in bringing this about. Activism, such as the sit-ins and the civil rights marches, were essential, and the Civil Rights Act of 1964 was crucial too. But the Warren Court played an essential role in ending the regime of separate but never equal. Congress and southern state legislatures and courts would not have come to that on their own for a much longer time without the leadership and rulings of the Supreme Court.

Ironically, the place where the promise of the Warren Court has least been fulfilled is for public schools, the focus of *Brown v. Board of Education.* Schools remain separate and unequal in every major metropolitan area. Tragically, racial segregation in American schools has been increasing. A study by the National School Boards Association found "a pattern in which impressive progress toward school integration among blacks and whites during the 1970s petered out in the 1980s."[1] A study by Harvard professor Gary Orfield found that in the South "from 1988 to 1998, most of the progress from the previous two decades in increasing integration in the region was lost. The South is still more integrated than it was before the civil rights revolution, but it is moving backwards at an accelerating rate."[2]

Most children in the United States are educated only with children of their own race. A General Accounting Office study found that in 2020–2021, more than a third of students attended a predominantly same-race/ethnicity school, where 75 percent or more of the student population is of a single race/ethnicity, and 14 percent of students attended schools where 90 percent or more of the students were of a single race/ethnicity.[3] In most major metropolitan areas, the city public schools are about 10 percent white students and 90 percent students of color, while there are suburban schools and charter schools with dramatically different demographics.

The explanation for this is complicated, but the successors to the Warren Court deserve a great deal of the blame. Two 5–4 decisions just a few years after the end of the Warren Court contributed significantly to the separate and unequal schools of today. In *San Antonio Board of Education v. Rodriguez*, in 1973 the court held that disparities in school funding within a metropolitan area do not violate equal protection.[4] Despite the majestic language in Chief Justice Warren's opinion in *Brown* about the enormous importance of education, the court in *Rodriguez* held that education is not a fundamental right. A year later in *Milliken v. Bradley*, the court held that there virtually never can be interdistrict remedies for segregation where suburban students are brought into city schools and city children are taken to suburban ones.[5] The result in most urban areas is city schools that are overwhelmingly students of color surrounded by predominately white suburbs that are wealthier and spend much more on education. Both of these decisions had a majority composed of the four Nixon appointees to the court (Warren Burger, Harry Blackmun, Lewis Powell, and William Rehnquist) joined by Eisenhower appointee Potter Stewart. No one believes that these cases would have been decided the same way if the Warren Court had lasted for several more years.

In subsequent cases, the court has made it ever harder for school districts to pursue desegregation. For example, in *Parents Involved in Community Schools v. Seattle School District No. 1*, in 2007 the Roberts Court held that school systems could not use race as a factor in assigning students to schools to achieve desegregation.[6]

Outside of the area of race, the Warren Court's emphasis on advancing equality has had significant continuing impact. Prior to the Warren Court, the Equal Protection Clause of the Fourteenth Amendment was rarely used. But in the years immediately following and ever since, the Supreme Court has built on the Warren Court's equal protection vision and jurisprudence. In the early 1970s, the Supreme Court for the first time declared unconstitutional laws that discriminated based on sex and against noncitizens and nonmarital children.[7] Subsequently, the court found discrimination based on sexual orientation unconstitutional, culminating in laws prohibiting same-sex marriage being invalidated in 2015.[8]

The Warren Court's legacy in expanding liberty also is complicated. Its recognition of privacy rights in *Griswold v. Connecticut* led,[9] just a short time later in 1973, to *Roe v. Wade*,[10] which protected a constitutional right to abortion until it was overruled in 2022.[11] The court's protection of privacy also led to *Lawrence v. Texas*,[12] which held that states cannot prohibit consenting adults from engaging in private same-sex sexual activity. Yet, there also is reason for skepticism that the current court would have decided these cases the same way, pessimism that privacy rights will be extended, and worry that more precedents in this area will be overruled.

The Warren Court's protection of democracy has had lasting impact. The court's decisions allowing judicial challenges to malapportionment and requiring one person, one vote remain the law and significantly changed the political landscape. But the court subsequently refused to extend this to allow challenges to partisan gerrymandering, and the Roberts Court has significantly weakened the protections of the Voting Rights Act.[13]

The legacy of the Warren Court as to the First Amendment is itself complicated. As Professor Horwitz shows, the Warren Court changed the direction of constitutional law with regard to freedom of speech. Rarely before the tenure of Earl Warren as chief justice had the Supreme Court ever ruled in favor of claims of free expression. The Warren Court did so in striking down loyalty oaths,[14] making it much more difficult to prove incitement of illegal activity,[15] and in the landmark ruling of *New York Times v. Sullivan*.[16] Yet, the Warren Court's record on freedom of speech was decidedly mixed. As Horwitz describes, the Warren Court also upheld the ability of a state bar to exclude those who refuse to answer questions about being affiliated with the communist party (*Konigsberg v. California*),[17] allowed civil rights protestors to be punished for violating clearly unconstitutional court orders (*Walker v. City of Birmingham*),[18] ruled that obscenity is not protected by the First Amendment (*Roth v. United States*),[19] and upheld a federal law allowing those burning their draft cards to be punished (*United States v. O'Brien*).[20] There is a strong sense that since 1969, the court has become even more committed to protecting freedom of speech, even deeply offensive expression.[21]

As to religion, though, the Warren Court's legacy is in great jeopardy. The Warren Court saw the Establishment Clause of the First Amendment as embodying Thomas Jefferson's admonition that there should be a wall separating church and state. This position is reflected in its decisions limiting prayer in public schools and restricting government aid to religious schools. But the current Supreme Court rejects the idea of a wall separating church and state. It is far more likely to see limits on religion as violating free exercise of religion as reflected in *Kennedy v. Bremerton School District* (2022), where the court held that it infringed the free speech and free exercise rights of a high school football coach to prevent him from silently praying on the field after games along with his players.[22]

Another complicated legacy is the area of the rights of criminal suspects and defendants. It is clear in reading this book how much the Warren Court dramatically changed the law of criminal procedure. It is easy to forget that only a handful of Bill of Rights provisions were incorporated and applied to the states when the Warren Court began in 1953, but almost all applied to state and local governments by the time it concluded in 1969. It is hard for today's students of constitutional law to realize, as Professor Horwitz describes, that there was an intense fight over incorporation in the 1950s and 1960s. This advance in the law has not been rescinded. There have been no reversals of the Warren Court's rulings finding provisions of the Bill of Rights to be incorporated; in fact, other rights have been deemed incorporated over the last fifteen years.[23]

Yet, there has been a substantial cutback in the rights of criminal suspects and defendants, beginning almost immediately with the end of the Warren Court. Richard Nixon ran for president in 1968, in part against the Warren Court on a pledge to appoint "law and order" justices. A crucial aspect of the Burger Court's agenda was to roll back Warren Court decisions in the area of criminal procedure. Most dramatically, the Burger Court rollback was furthered by Congress, which drastically changed the law of habeas corpus and made it far harder for a person convicted in state court to be heard in federal court on a claim that a conviction was unconstitutional.

Federalism—the relationship between the federal government and the states—is an area where the Supreme Court abandoned the Warren Court's jurisprudence. As Professor Horwitz explains in chapter 10, the Warren Court continued the post-1937 approach to federalism: it broadly construed congressional powers and rejected the view that the Tenth Amendment limits a zone of activities to the states. For example, in *Heart of Atlanta Motel v. United States*[24] and *Katzenbach v. McClung,*[25] the court expansively interpreted Congress's commerce power to uphold Title II of the 1964 Civil Rights Act, which prohibits hotels and restaurants from discriminating based on race. In *Katzenbach v. Morgan*, the court held that Congress has the authority under Section 5 of the Fourteenth Amendment to enact legislation expanding the scope of rights.[26] During the sixteen years of the Warren Court, not once did it declare a federal law unconstitutional as exceeding the scope of congressional power or infringing states' rights.

But the law in this area changed dramatically, especially during the Rehnquist Court era (1986–2005). In a series of 5–4 decisions, with the justices divided along ideological lines, the court limited Congress's power under the commerce clause,[27] constrained Congress's authority under Section 5 of the Fourteenth Amendment,[28] and struck down federal laws as violating the Tenth Amendment.[29] Strikingly, the Rehnquist Court did this in invalidating laws of unquestionable social desirability: federal statutes that banned guns near schools, allowed victims of gender-motivated violence to sue in federal court, expanded protections of religious freedom, and required states to clean up their nuclear waste and do background checks before issuing permits for firearms.

The ideological difference between the Warren Court and its successors over federalism reflects a disagreement between progressives and conservatives that traces back to the earliest days of the country. Historically, liberals have sought broad federal power to deal with problems plaguing society, while conservatives have championed states' rights. That divide goes a long way toward explaining why the Warren Court's approach to federalism was abandoned by its more conservative successor Supreme Courts.

There also has been a profound shift in the method the justices use in interpreting the Constitution. As Professor Horwitz shows, *Brown v. Board of Education* reflected and advanced the idea that the Constitution should be regarded as a living document. The importance of *Brown*—for the Warren Court and ever since—cannot be overstated. Simply put, *Brown* could not be justified under an originalist approach to the Constitution. The same Congress that ratified the Fourteenth Amendment also voted to segregate the District of Columbia public schools, and there is no indication that Congress meant to outlaw racial segregation.

Conservatives such as Robert Bork developed originalism as a way of criticizing Warren Court decisions, and this school of interpretation gained currency as a way of attacking *Roe v. Wade*. But originalism was initially widely seen as a dangerous approach to constitutional law. In 1987 Bork—despite impeccable qualifications—was decisively rejected by the Senate for a seat on the Supreme Court because of his originalist views.

Over time, especially thanks to the Federalist Society, originalism has gained adherents. Three of the current justices—Clarence Thomas, Neil Gorsuch, and Amy Coney Barrett—are self-avowed originalists. The other conservative justices often write in originalist terms and join originalist opinions.

Originalism is a terrible approach to interpreting the Constitution.[30] Even if it were possible to divine the original meaning of constitutional provisions, which it usually not the case, it makes no sense to be governed by what people meant in the late eighteenth century, as they wrote for a small country where only white men could vote and many people were enslaved. Although Professor Horwitz's book is not specifically about originalism, it is clear that the Warren Court's jurisprudence was its antithesis. None of its accomplishments—*Brown* and ending segregation, incorporating the Bill of Rights, ending malapportionment, protecting the rights of criminal suspects and defendants in cases like *Gideon v. Wainwright* and *Miranda v. Arizona*, safeguarding freedom of speech in rulings such as *New York Times v. Sullivan*, and establishing the right to privacy—would have been possible under originalism.

Most of all, this wonderful book shows that the Supreme Court is about the human beings who wear the robes and hand down the decisions. That was true during the Warren era, it has been true ever since, and it always will be true. My favorite parts of the book were the stories throughout its chapters of the interpersonal dynamics among the justices in their conferences and memos and interactions. Unquestionably, the most important figure in this book and this constitutional era was the chief justice, Earl Warren. It was not the Warren Court in name only. His political skills are evident throughout, as is his basic decency and humanity. There is a strong sense that he was the right person for the right time: a wise and skilled leader committed to advancing equality and justice who guided the court through a difficult time in American history. Perhaps what has been missing most since 1969 is a chief justice with these values and a commitment to advancing freedom and equality. No one would say that has been the agenda for Earl Warren's successors—Warren Burger, William Rehnquist, and John Roberts.

What, then, has been the legacy of the Warren Court? In terms of constitutional doctrine, the answer is at best mixed. In some areas, the Warren Court's decisions have remained unscathed. But in many areas they have been eroded or even discarded. In few areas has the Supreme Court, especially in recent years, followed the Warren Court's lead in expanding freedom and equality. Perhaps the Warren Court's greatest legacy is in reminding us what the Supreme Court can accomplish for society. It can protect minorities and enhance liberty in ways that legislatures can't and won't. It can lead society to be better and to do more to fulfill its best vision of itself.

Now, more than a half century after the Warren Court ended in 1969, it is possible to look back at the Warren Court with admiration for what it accomplished and sadness for what might have been if only it had lasted longer. Professor Horwitz tells us the story of the Warren Court—and does so brilliantly.

APPENDIX 1

Earl Warren's Appointment

The claim that Earl Warren's appointment to the chief justiceship by President Dwight Eisenhower was not the result of an earlier deal between them has always seemed scarcely credible. "Few doubt," Phillip Kurland wrote in 1982, "that Warren exchanged the California delegation, whose vote cost him as well as Robert Taft the possibility of the Presidency, for the promise of the judicial chair that he came to occupy."[1] American political historians have agreed that without Warren's help at the 1952 Republican Convention, Eisenhower's come-from-behind victory over Robert A. Taft could not have succeeded.[2]

Warren aided Eisenhower in two separate votes. Early in the convention, Warren cast the votes he controlled in favor of an Eisenhower-sponsored delegate challenge that enhanced Eisenhower's vote count. Later during the first ballot, Warren supported Eisenhower's strategy by refusing to release pledged delegates who might otherwise vote for Taft. Without Warren's tacit support, Eisenhower could not have won the nomination and the presidency.[3]

Far behind in the delegate count, Warren's hopes for success at the Republican Convention hinged on the convention turning to him after a stalemate between Eisenhower and Taft.[4] In assisting Eisenhower to win, Warren was abandoning his own ambitions for the presidency.

Despite the circumstantial evidence that there had been a deal, historians, until recently, have been reluctant to go beyond Eisenhower's and Warren's own versions of events.[5] Though in their respective memoirs each presented a somewhat different narrative of the circumstances of Warren's appointment as chief justice, both versions supported their mutual interest in squashing any suspicion that Warren's appointment to the Supreme Court was the product of a political deal, that Warren's judicial quid was in exchange for Eisenhower's presidential quo.[6]

In his memoirs, published ten years after the event, Eisenhower denied that he had ever promised Warren a seat on the Supreme Court. "I owed Governor Warren nothing," Eisenhower declared in Olympian tones that could only have led knowledgeable readers to wonder whether the president was not protesting too much.[7] The peremptory tone of Eisenhower's denial also shows that suspicions of a deal had not yet died. That Eisenhower buttressed his narrative by misleadingly claiming that he really did not need Warren's help in winning the nomination also suggests that Eisenhower needed to indulge in historical fiction in order not to be seen as having taken the low road in gaining the presidency and then appointing Warren.[8]

In his memoirs, Warren's account of Eisenhower's offer of a seat on the court hews to the line that the offer was first made in a phone conversation with Eisenhower in December 1952.[9] And like Eisenhower's narrative, Warren's version also ignores the credentials vote and highlights the fact that Eisenhower won on the first ballot without Warren's help. But Warren is otherwise very critical of Eisenhower's version. The president-elect, Warren remembered, first called to say that he did not have a cabinet position to offer, and Warren responded that he never wanted to serve in the cabinet and was perfectly content to remain governor of California. Then, according to Warren, Eisenhower continued: "But I want you to know that I intend to offer you the first vacancy on the Supreme Court." "That is very generous of you," Warren responded. "That is my personal commitment to you," Eisenhower concluded (according to Warren).[10]

Warren adds that he had put the offer out of his mind "because I had often heard of newly elected officials who promised positions in the indefinite future, only to forget when the jobs actually became open for appointment. I was not wrong in this instance. . . . The general's recollection and mine do not fully agree, but my part in the selection of a replacement for Vinson was so simple that there would be little room for faulty memory."[11]

The problem for Warren was that Eisenhower's account had explicitly admitted that after the death of Chief Justice Fred Vinson, "the President shopped around for a successor," including an offer to Secretary of State John Foster Dulles, which was refused, "and [then] seriously considered others, who were eliminated for one reason or another. Only then did he decide on me."[12] Warren's account suggested that even though Eisenhower eventually delivered on his promise, his declaration that he "owed Governor Warren nothing" was inaccurate overkill that ignored even the December promise for the sake of denying that any deal had occurred. Without ever mentioning Eisenhower's declaration, an appalled Warren offered enough detail to contradict the major premise of Eisenhower's narrative, which sought to deny that Eisenhower ever had made a commitment to Warren.

Warren was clear that Eisenhower was under no obligation to appoint him chief justice if the president decided to elevate a sitting justice. Warren then would have contented himself with filling the resulting vacancy of an associate justice. But that Eisenhower, perhaps to further emphasize that he had never made a deal with Warren, chose to reveal that he had first turned to Secretary of

State Dulles and then to others before making an offer to Warren was incompatible with Warren's "simple . . . recollection" of Eisenhower's promise. In further
support of Warren's recollection was his decision to resign from the California governorship and accept appointment as solicitor general. Is it plausible
to suppose that Warren would have agreed to retire from the governorship of
California to become solicitor general without any assurance that he was in
training to join the Supreme Court?

Despite the undertone of resentment in Warren's discussion of Eisenhower's
account, they both sought to throw cold water on any suspicion that there had
been a deal at the convention five months earlier. But one insider has seemed
to contradict the Eisenhower/Warren accounts and suggested there had been
a quid pro quo. General Lucius Clay had long been one of Eisenhower's closest military aides, serving at his side even before General Eisenhower assumed
command of the Allied forces in Europe during World War II.[13] During the
maneuvering at the 1952 Republican nominating convention, Clay stood shoulder to shoulder with future attorney general Herbert Brownell in speaking for
General Eisenhower.[14]

Clay told a pro-Eisenhower biographer that a promise to Warren of a future
Supreme Court appointment was "the only deal we ever made" at the Republican Convention.[15] While reporting Clay's statement, the biographer sought to
shield Eisenhower from the suggestion of a deal by asserting that Clay had only
reported the appointment offer to Eisenhower "days later" and that therefore
the "commitment was Clay's alone, not Eisenhower's. No deal was struck, no
quid pro quo."[16]

This interpretation, however, seems strained, as it is inconsistent with the
point Clay emphasized to the author: that Warren was given "the only commitment *we* ever made" at the Republican Convention.[17] Moreover, Clay punctured
the misleading assertions of both Eisenhower and Warren that Eisenhower had
prevailed at the Republican Convention without Warren's help. "All we wanted
was for Governor Warren to stay in and not release his votes on the first ballot.
We were more concerned about denying the California vote to Taft than getting
it ourselves," Clay told his biographer.[18]

In his memoirs, written four decades after the events, Herbert Brownell
continued to adhere to the Eisenhower/Warren account, denying "the rumors
that Eisenhower and Warren had made a deal for Warren's appointment to the
Court" at the Republican Convention. "Eisenhower first considered a Warren
nomination to the Court well after the election," Brownell declared. "The votes
of Warren's delegates to the convention certainly did not play any part in Ike's
convention victory."[19]

But Brownell was not entirely consistent. He reiterated the official position in
a memorandum he wrote in advance of a 1974 interview. Reports of a deal, he

noted, "at various times embarrassed both General Eisenhower and Governor Warren for the obvious reason that any such 'deal' was entirely contrary to the demonstrated standards of conduct of both men. I am confident that none of the reports was well-founded."[20]

In the interview, however, Brownell seemed to cast doubt on that version, acknowledging that before the 1952 election Lucius Clay had "undoubtedly talked to [Warren] about coming into the Eisenhower administration, and I would imagine he mentioned the Supreme Court as a possibility." When the interviewer cited evidence of Clay's convention offer, Brownell replied that he could "well imagine Clay talking to Warren" about a Supreme Court appointment. But he quickly added that "in the first place, he wasn't authorized. *Nobody* was authorized to offer any position by Eisenhower before the election." The interviewer pressed: "If he *did* offer it, it was unauthorized?" "Right," Brownell replied.[21]

In an interview only months before he died in 1996, Brownell seemed to have dropped all pretense. Asked about Warren's appointment, he told an interviewer that "Eisenhower understood who had helped him at a crucial moment in the convention . . . *he knew what the score was.*"[22] Finally, forty-four years after the Republican Convention, the evidence seemed sufficient for the historian to conclude that there had been a "deal" between Warren and Eisenhower over a Supreme Court appointment.

APPENDIX 2

Robert Jackson's Concurring Opinion
in *Brown v. Board of Education*

I wrote this Appendix after I discovered the existence of Justice Robert Jackson's unpublished opinion in the archives. Only later did I come to realize that David M. O'Brien had already published this opinion, with elaborate commentary, as *The Unpublished Opinion of Supreme Court Justice Robert H. Jackson in Brown v. Education* (2017). Because I differ with O'Brien on several points of interpretation and emphasis, I decided to print my commentary and leave it to the reader to compare the two. But there is one major difference that I need to emphasize here. As will become clear, Jackson wrote six versions of the draft over a four-month period. In the third version, after writing fourteen pages, he finally announces that he was prepared to overrule *Plessy v. Ferguson*. O'Brien treats the first three versions as a single draft that culminates in Jackson's announcement in the third version of his willingness to overrule *Plessy*. I see each of the versions as meant to be a stand-alone (if incomplete) opinion. Thus, I have concluded that the first two versions were probably meant to justify refusal to overrule *Plessy*, while the third version represents the beginnings of Jackson's change of mind. In addition, I feel that O'Brien does not adequately capture the profound pessimism that even Jackson's final version expresses.

Robert Jackson's unpublished concurring opinion in *Brown v. Board of Education* represents a bold, blunt, and brilliant effort to express his deep reservations about overruling *Plessy v. Ferguson*. As the only written opinion in *Brown* besides Chief Justice Earl Warren's, it both underlines the vulnerability of Warren's approach and suggests that Jackson may have had more of an influence in shaping that approach than has been previously thought.

Jackson's draft has never been published in full. It went through six versions, one in December 1953 and then in 1954 two in January, one in February, and two in March. Jackson's heart attack and hospitalization on March 30 brought further possible revisions to an end, culminating in Warren's hospital room visit and Jackson's agreement to sign on to Warren's opinion and not publish a separate concurrence.[1] The drafts permit us to trace the evolution of Jackson's thinking and to pinpoint the period in which he reached the conclusion that

Plessy should be overruled. His December 7 and January 6, 1954, drafts seem to have been written to justify refusing to overrule *Plessy*. Likewise, the January 11 revision offers no clue that Jackson has changed direction, until the last paragraph of a fourteen-page draft announced: "I favor at the moment going no further than to enter a decree that a state statute holding segregation necessary is unconstitutional."[2] It is clear from his February 15 additions that Jackson had found a way to overcome his doubts about overruling *Plessy*. The March 1 revisions of the previous draft make clear that, despite continuing doubts, he had begun to justify overruling *Plessy*.

Even Jackson's final draft of March 15 cannot be read as a ringing endorsement of Warren's *Brown* opinion. Twenty-three pages long, the draft keeps the reader in suspense until page 21 before revealing that Jackson is prepared to strike down *Plessy*. The seriously unbalanced structure of Jackson's last draft was succinctly captured by his law clerk, E. Barrett Prettyman Jr., who pointedly told Jackson that his declaration of willingness to overrule *Plessy* was presented in the opinion as "almost an afterthought."[3]

Most of Jackson's final draft continued to express quite open sympathy with the southern constitutional position. If it had been published, the opinion would certainty have supplied additional ammunition to southern white resistance to *Brown*.

From the earliest of his drafts, Jackson refused to draw any conclusion about the original meaning of the Fourteenth Amendment.[4] In this respect, in his second draft he agreed with Chief Justice Warren's eventual conclusion that the legislative history was "inconclusive."[5] "All that I can fairly get from the legislative debates in searching for the original will and purpose expressed in the Amendment, is that it was a passionate, confused and deplorable era," Jackson wrote.

> As often is characteristic of legislative history, the sponsors played down the consequences of the legislation they were proposing in order to ease its passage, while the opponents exaggerated the consequences in order to frighten away support. . . . [M]ost of the leaders and spokesmen for the movement that put the Civil War Amendment through appear never to have reached a point in their thinking where either negro education or negro segregation was a serious or foreseeable problem, let alone reaching any conclusion as to a solution. The legislative debates, as I read them, result in either a blank or a match [tie]."[6]

The greatest contrast between Warren's opinion and Jackson's was expressed in the latter's next point. "But, if deeds, rather than words, count as evidence of understanding, there is little to show that these Amendments condemn the practice here in question." Jackson piled on legal history to show that even northern jurists after the Civil War assumed the constitutionality of racial segregation. "The layman must wonder how it comes that the best informed judges who had risked their lives for these Amendments did not understand their meaning, while we at this remote time do understand them."[7]

Warren's opinion, by contrast, chose simply to remain silent concerning the mass of judicial and legislative precedents supporting segregation that had accumulated during the eighty-six years since the Fourteenth Amendment became law. Jackson pointedly inquired, "Can we honestly say that the states which have maintained segregated schools have not, until today, been justified in understanding their practice to be constitutional?"[8] "Convenient as it would be to reach an opposite conclusion, I simply cannot find in the conventional material of constitutional interpretation any justification for saying that in maintaining segregated schools any state or the District of Columbia . . . violated the Fourteenth Amendment."[9] By highlighting Warren's resounding silence on the constitutional legitimacy of state-imposed segregation before *Brown*, Jackson's opinion would surely have fed southern white resistance if it had been published.

Jackson's second draft—elaborating on a point introduced in his first draft—ended with the conclusion that only Congress, not the Supreme Court, had the power to ban school segregation. "It is said, however, that the South has enough representation to prevent such a step. But that is to say that the Court should intervene to promulgate as a law that which our Constitutional representative system will not enact. . . . It means nothing less than that we must act because our representative system has failed."[10] "The premise is not a sound basis for judicial action."[11]

Jackson's second draft introduced a theme that, in later versions, became the entering wedge for his willingness to overrule *Plessy*. "No informed person can be insensitive to the fact that the past few years have witnessed a profound change in the responsible and rational public opinion towards segregation and all related problems," Jackson declared. Alluding to his own service as chief U.S. prosecutor at Nuremberg, Jackson pointed to a growing "revulsion" against racism in reaction to "the awful consequence of racial prejudice revealed by the post mortem upon the Nazi Regime." But in a characteristic midparagraph surprise, he began to question the role public opinion should play in decisions of the court. He went on to dismiss this evidence of a shift in public opinion as an inadequate basis for changing constitutional interpretation: "if construed in the light of public opinion, [it] would mean that it was being construed by those who have not had the advantage of studying an argument instead of by those who had."[12]

By the fourth draft (February 15) only five weeks later, changing perceptions of African Americans over time became the key to Jackson's shift. "I think the change which warrants our decision [to overrule *Plessy*] is not a change in the Constitution but in the Negro population," he wrote.[13] "Certainly in the 1860's and throughout the nineteenth century the Negro population, as whole, was a different people than today." In the aftermath of slavery, African Americans had not yet demonstrated a "capacity for education or assimilation or even . . . that they could be self-supporting or in our public life anything more than a pawn for white exploiters." Nor was segregated education "wholly to the Negro's disadvantage," given their "spectacular . . . progress" under these conditions.[14]

But important changes had occurred, as described in three observations: "Whatever may have been true at an earlier period, the mere fact that one is in some degree colored no longer creates a presumption that he is inferior, illiterate, retarded or indigent."[15] "Tested by the pace of history, the rise of the Negro in the South, as well as the North, is one of the swiftest and most dramatic advances in the annals of man."[16] "Moreover, we cannot ignore the fact that assimilation today has proceeded much beyond . . . earlier periods. . . . More and more a large population with as much claim to white as to colored blood baffles any justice in classification for segregation."[17]

Finally, in a paragraph that anticipated a similar statement in Warren's *Brown* opinion, Jackson observed that since the nineteenth century "the place of public education has [also] markedly changed."[18] "Once a privilege conferred on those fortunate enough to take advantage of it, it is now regarded as a right of a citizen and a duty enforced by compulsory education laws. Any thought of public education as a privilege which may be given or withheld as a matter of grace has long since passed out of American thinking."[19]

Jackson had navigated his way to reversal through a convergence of two premises. The first was his belief that the "spectacular . . . progress" of African Americans since slavery required eliminating the presumption of inferiority on which segregated institutions had been built. Indeed, it was very important to Jackson that he could narrowly characterize the point as a change in "not a legal, so much as a factual assumption," a change in the "state of facts" that every common lawyer would recognize as involving the familiar problem of applying a common-law rule to changed circumstances.[20] But Jackson's broad-brush conclusion that a "spectacular" advance of Black people under segregation justified eliminating racial classifications was surely subject to debate, to precisely the sort of debate on historical, sociological, or extralegal grounds that Jackson in all of his drafts did his best to mock as too subjective or legally irrelevant.

The second premise that permitted Jackson to reverse *Plessy* was his all-too-brief discussion of the effect of "changing conditions," which, as he knew, had a long and rich Progressive history dating back to the Brandeis Brief.[21] Jackson's emphasis on the changing social situation of Black people and the recent development of public education were invoked in the service of the "changing circumstances" doctrine, which as solicitor general he had often deployed before the court to justify New Deal constitutional innovations. "Of course," he reasoned, "the Constitution must be construed as a living instrument and cannot be read as if written in a dead language." "It is neither novel nor radical doctrine that statutes once held constitutional may become invalid by reason of changing conditions," Jackson continued, "and those [statutes] held to be good in one state of facts may be bad in another."[22] "In recent times, the practical result of several of our decisions has been to nullify the racial classification for many of the purposes as to which it was originally held valid. I am convinced that present-day conditions require us to strike from our books the doctrine of separate-but-equal facilities and to hold invalid provisions of state [laws] which classify persons for separate treatment in matters of education based solely on possession of colored blood."[23]

But there remained in Jackson's last draft a chilling pessimism about the likely success of social reform initiated by the judiciary. "In embarking upon a widespread reform of social customs and habits of countless communities we must face the limitations on the nature and effectiveness of the judicial process," Jackson observed. "The futility of effective reform of our society by judicial decree is demonstrated by the history of this very matter"—by the fact that the requirement of equality in *Plessy*'s "separate but equal" doctrine had

> remained a dead letter in a large part of this country. . . . I see no reason to expect a pronouncement that segregation is unconstitutional will be any more self-executing or any more efficiently executed than our pronouncement that unequal facilities are unconstitutional. . . . With no machinery except that of the courts to put the power of the Government behind it, it seems likely to result in a failure that will bring the court into contempt and the judicial process into discredit."[24]

Court decisions striking down segregation, Jackson believed, will not produce a social transformation, nor is the judiciary the agency to which the people should look for that result.

> Our decision may end segregation in Delaware and Kansas, because there it lingers by a tenuous lease of life. But where the practice really is entrenched, it exists independently of any statute or decision as a local usage and deep-seated custom sustained by the prevailing sentiment of the community. School districts, from habit and conviction, will carry it along without aid of state statutes. To eradicate segregation by judicial action means two generations of litigation. It is apparent that our decision does not end but begins the struggle over segregation.[25]

It is difficult to believe that Jackson wrote these paragraphs after he had per-suaded himself to overrule *Plessy*, for they seem to be a carryover from the first draft's conclusion that only Congress has power under the Fourteenth Amendment to eradicate segregation.[26] The contradictory coexistence of these sentiments with Jackson's support for overruling *Plessy* was the source of his law clerk's pointed observation that Jackson's willingness to overrule came as "almost an afterthought" in the opinion.[27] It demonstrated that Jackson had never managed to entirely overcome his greatest fear: that the unenforceability of a desegregation order would "bring the court into contempt and the judicial process into discredit."[28]

Jackson's final draft remained contrarian in one other important respect. Though he remained a leader of the gradualist camp, he differed dramatically on how to achieve that result. While the justices in mid-January appeared to arrive at a consensus on the wisdom of a gradualist decree by informally endorsing Warren's and Frankfurter's proposal that federal district judges should fashion their decrees taking "local conditions" into account, Jackson, who said nothing on that occasion, made a point of disapproving of this arrangement in his final draft written two months later.

Jackson blamed the problem on the government brief, which also had pro-posed remanding the cases to district courts with few standards to guide them. "Nothing has raised more doubt in my mind as to the wisdom of our decision than the character of the decree which the Government conceives to be nec-essary to its success."[29]

> New facilities are necessarily to be provided, and that involves taxation, the sale of bonds, and the votes of taxpayers and affirmative actions by public bodies. . . . While our decision may invalidate existing laws and regulations governing the school, the Court cannot substitute constructive laws and regulations for their governance. Local or state or federal action will have to build the integrated school systems if they are to exist. A gigantic admin-istrative job has to be undertaken.[30]

But the justices and the government together had arrived at the conclusion that the only available judicial institutions that could undertake the daunting task of desegregating southern public education were the federal district courts. Jackson disagreed. "I will not be a party to thus casting upon the lower courts a burden of continued litigation under circumstances which subject district judges to local pressures and provide them with no standards to justify their decisions to their neighbors, whose opinions they must resist."[31]

Jackson ignored the fact that under the system of "senatorial courtesy," many lower federal court judges from the South owed their positions to a U.S. senator and shared these southern senators' segregationist sentiments. But there were also many conscientious southern federal judges who, as Jackson predicted, were "subject to local pressures," including threats of violence.[32]

There seems to be little doubt that as of March 15, 1954, Jackson was preparing a concurring opinion that would not only have substantially challenged the grounds of Warren's eventual opinion but also would have bluntly predicted that the judiciary would fail in any broad effort to implement the *Brown* decision.

Jackson was prescient about a political truth that only slowly began to emerge after *Brown*.

During the first decade after the landmark decision, the Supreme Court stood institutionally alone and almost helpless in attempting to desegregate southern schools. As Gerald Rosenberg highlighted, there was virtually no desegregation in the Deep South a decade after *Brown*. Until the Civil Rights Act of 1964 brought Congress into the fray, the congressional leadership on desegregation that Justice Jackson had hoped for had not materialized. Nor was there any serious support from the executive until President Lyndon Johnson approved cutting off federal funding to any noncomplying school district.[33]

Jackson's pessimism about the Supreme Court's capacity to achieve social change arguably was justified by not only subsequent events. His concurrence was also filled with New Deal legal learning about the inferior institutional competence of the judiciary—as compared to legislative or administrative bodies—in achieving broad social change through law.[34]

POSTSCRIPT

It should be noted that seventeen years after Jackson drafted his opinion, its orientation became a controversial item in William Rehnquist's 1971 confirmation hearings as associate justice.[35] Rehnquist had served as Jackson's law clerk during the Vinson Court's initial deliberations over *Brown*. After it was revealed that Rehnquist had written a memo to Justice Jackson stating that "*Plessy v. Ferguson* was right and should be re-affirmed," the nominee defended the memo as written to support Justice Jackson's own views.[36] Rehnquist's claim has been subject to much scholarly scorn; "most scholars have concluded that Rehnquist's account that the *Plessy* memo represented Justice Jackson's views, but not his own, cannot be totally accurate."[37]

University of Chicago law professor Phillip Kurland, the custodian of Justice Jackson's papers, pointedly contradicted Rehnquist at the time, labeling the future chief justice's contention that he was merely expressing Justice Jackson's views "implausible."[38] Kurland revealed at the time the existence of an unpublished Jackson draft that, if submitted, could have served as a concurring opinion to Warren's opinion for the court, that is, an opinion that supported overruling *Plessy*. Presumably, Kurland was referring to the final March 15 Jackson draft. The professor, however, failed to mention Jackson's first two drafts, written two and three months earlier, which seemed to point in the direction of affirming *Plessy*. Rehnquist's memo to Jackson, written two years earlier, might well have corresponded to Jackson's probable inclination at that time to uphold the infamous 1896 decision. Although Jackson's first two drafts seemed to point in the direction of exercising judicial restraint and affirming *Plessy*, this does not mean the memo at issue reflected Jackson's views and not those of his law clerk. The tenor and rationale of the memo, not simply the result, would need to be examined. Moreover, it is important to note that Professor Kurland's reasons for asserting the implausibility of Rehnquist's claims were not primarily based on the March 15 Jackson draft.[39]

The most comprehensive and damning analysis of Rehnquist's account, legal scholar Brad Snyder asserts, was set forth by Richard Kluger in *Simple Justice*.[40] As Snyder explains, Kluger concluded "that Jackson never asserted that *Plessy* was 'right and should be re-affirmed,' as Rehnquist's memo suggested. Rather, Jackson [initially] could not find a legal reason for overruling segregation."[41] The arguments of Kluger and other legal scholars and the evidence introduced to buttress their assertions persuasively show that the clear language of Rehnquist's memo, in conjunction with much other evidence, supports the conclusion that he personally advocated affirming *Plessy*.

NOTES

CHAPTER 1

1. David L. Halberstam, "Professors Blast Recess Choice of Gov. Warren," *The Harvard Crimson*, October 2, 1953.
2. JOHN GUNTHER, INSIDE U.S.A. (Harper & Bros., 1947) [hereinafter cited as INSIDE USA].
3. *Id.*, at 18.
4. *Id.*
5. INSIDE USA, at 18 & 20–21.
6. INSIDE USA (50th Anniversary edition) (Book-of-the-Month Club, 1997), Foreword, Arthur Schlesinger Jr., at xxi.
7. INSIDE USA, at 20 & 18.
8. DAVID M. KENNEDY, FREEDOM FROM FEAR (Oxford University Press, 1999), at 754.
9. In 1988, Congress "acknowledge[d] the fundamental injustice of the evacuation, relocation, and internment of United States citizens and permanent resident aliens of Japanese ancestry during World War II; [and] apologize[d] on behalf of the people of the United States for the evacuation, relocation, and internment of such citizens and permanent resident aliens." Title 50, Appendix United States Code, Section 1989 (Pub. L. 100-383, Section 1, Aug 10, 1988, 102 Stat 903). In Section 1989a the act stated, "The Congress recognizes that . . . a grave injustice was done to both citizens and permanent resident aliens of Japanese ancestry by the evacuation, relocation, and internment of civilians during World War II. . . . [T]hese actions were carried out without adequate security reasons and without any acts of espionage or sabotage documented . . . and were motivated largely by the racial prejudice, wartime hysteria, and failure of political leadership. . . . For these fundamental violations of the basic civil liberties and constitutional rights of these individuals of Japanese ancestry, the Congress apologizes on behalf of the Nation." Title 50, Appendix U.S.C. § 1898a (Pub. L. 100-383, Section 2, Aug. 10, 1988, 102 Stat. 903).
10. ED CRAY, CHIEF JUSTICE (Simon & Schuster, 1997), at 123.
11. G. EDWARD WHITE, EARL WARREN: A PUBLIC LIFE (Oxford University Press, 1982), at 71 & 75. "Warren was one of the individuals most responsible for bringing the relocation program into being. He was in a position, as the official ostensibly in charge of California civilian defense, to influence all other policy makers, including the military and the federal authorities. He was . . . a persistent advocate of some form of evacuation, and his skillful marshaling of arguments, some of

them spurious and others based primarily on racial prejudice, significantly contributed to the decision to intern and evacuate the Japanese." WHITE, at 74.

12. "'[Who], I ask you, could tell the difference between a loyal Japanese on our coast line and a saboteur?' The Japanese, 'wherever born,' were indoctrinated" in the imperial ambitions of Japan. "[W]e could not expect the *average* Japanese born in this country to give his loyalty to America in this war of survival." CRAY at 158 quoting Earl Warren. More than twenty years later, Warren asked a biographer not to quote this letter. CRAY, at 158, unnumbered fn.

13. CRAY, at 157, quoting Earl Warren.

14. FREEDOM FROM FEAR at 757–58; PETER IRONS, JUSTICE AT WAR (Oxford University Press, 1983), at 280–84.

15. WHITE, at 75.

16. INSIDE USA, at 18.

17. Even as he was advocating internment, in a letter to FBI director J. Edgar Hoover, Warren questioned the exemption of German and Italian Americans from the removal order. CRAY, at 121.

18. CRAY, at 271.

19. CRAY, at 370.

20. WHITE, at 76.

21. CRAY, at 520.

22. *Id.*, quoting a former Warren law clerk.

23. *Id.*, quoting a former Warren law clerk.

24. CRAY, at 520.

25. *Id.*, quoting a former Warren law clerk.

26. *Id.*, quoting Warren's son, Earl Jr. At the urging of Earl Jr., the retired chief justice did break his self-imposed silence about governmental legislation and endorsed repeal of the McCarran Act's provision for internment camps for suspected subversives in time of war. "It took a lot of persuading on my part," Earl Warren Jr. remembered. CRAY, at 520.

27. THE MEMOIRS OF EARL WARREN (Doubleday, 1977). In his memoirs Warren stated, "I have since deeply regretted the removal order and my own testimony advocating it, because it was not in keeping with our American concept of freedom and the rights of citizens. Whenever I thought of the innocent little children who were torn from home, school friends, and congenial surroundings, I was conscience-stricken. It was wrong to react so impulsively, without positive evidence of disloyalty, even though we felt we had a good motive in the security of our state. It demonstrates the cruelty of war when fear, get-tough military psychology, propaganda, and racial antagonism combine with one's responsibility for public security to produce such acts. I have always believed that I had no prejudice against the Japanese as such except that directly spawned by Pearl Harbor and its aftermath." *Id.*, at 149.

28. INSIDE USA, at 21 & 18.

29. California's population was 7,735,000 in 1942 and 8,506,000 in 1943. By 1953, it had risen dramatically to 12,101,000. California Department of Finance, Demographic Research Unit, California Statistical Abstract, 2001, Table 13-1.

30. DEL DICKSON, THE SUPREME COURT IN CONFERENCE (Oxford University Press, 2001) [hereinafter cited as SUPREME COURT IN CONFERENCE].

31. SUPREME COURT IN CONFERENCE, concerning Chief Justice Stone, at 90–93, 95. "Most of Stone's contemporaries, even his closest allies, judged him a failure as Chief Justice. . . . [T]he other Justices often found his conferences inefficient, frustrating, and unsatisfying. . . . There was little discipline or focus to discussions" (id., at 91). With regard to Chief Justice Vinson, "In his brief tenure as Chief Justice, Fred Vinson proved even less able to lead the conference than Stone. Vinson lacked the intellect, legal reputation, administrative competence, political skills, or personality necessary to hold the Court together. He came to the job amid whispers that he was a legal lightweight and a hack politician whose primary qualification to become Chief Justice was that he was a crony of Harry Truman's. Vinson did little to change anyone's mind" (id. at 100). Concerning Chief Justice Burger, id. at 111–13, 117: "Behind his back the other Justices mocked his modest education, mediocre legal abilities, poor grasp of federal law, and pompous manner. . . . He was a vain, arrogant, self-aggrandizing, and insecure man" (id., at 112). See also MELVIN I. UROFSKY, DIVISION AND DISCORD: THE SUPREME COURT UNDER STONE AND VINSON, 1941–1953 (University of South Carolina Press, 1997), at 30–32 (regarding Chief Justice Stone) and at 148–51, 213 (concerning Chief Justice Vinson).
32. SUPREME COURT IN CONFERENCE, at 100: "The other Justices agreed that Vinson was shallow and disorganized. He stressed the obvious points of a case in his conference summaries, while avoiding the subtle issues and complex problems. Everyone liked him . . . but they did not respect him."
33. SUPREME COURT IN CONFERENCE, at 91: Chief Justice Stone "often talked in conference at great length, and he constantly interrupted the other Justices to argue. . . . Instead of trying to mediate disagreements in conference, [he] usually jumped into the fray."
34. SUPREME COURT IN CONFERENCE, at 112 & 117. "Burger was not particularly skilled at leading conference discussions. . . . [He] was rarely focused or concise in his case summaries. . . . Justices criticized his lack of conference preparation, his poor organizational skills, and his tendency to editorialize, whether or not his comments were relevant to the case" (id., at 112). "There was considerable dissatisfaction inside the conference room. Several Justices complained about a decline in conference discipline, saying that Burger tolerated too many interruptions and too much cross-talk. Most of the Justices—including some of Burger's closest allies—found Burger's conference behavior frustrating" (id., at 117).
35. Roger K. Newman, "The Warren Court and American Politics: An Impressionistic Appreciation. Book Review: The Warren Court and American Politics, by Lucas A. (Scot) Powe Jr.," Constitutional Commentary, 2001, at 688 (citing his interview of former Brennan law clerk Richard Arnold).
36. SUPREME COURT IN CONFERENCE, at 107.
37. SUPREME COURT IN CONFERENCE, at 113; TINSLEY E. YARBROUGH, JOHN MARSHALL HARLAN: GREAT DISSENTER OF THE WARREN COURT (Oxford University Press, 1992), at 321.
38. INSIDE USA, at 18.
39. Warren's biographer Ed Cray also saw Warren as a man of gravitas; indeed, Cray titled one of his chapters "The Man of Gravitas." CRAY, chap. 40, at 511. Lucas Powe also associated Warren with gravitas. See LUCAS POWE, THE WARREN COURT AND AMERICAN POLITICS (Harvard University Press, 2002), at 500.

40. WHITE, at 6, 171, 264.
41. KAZUO ISHIGURO, THE REMAINS OF THE DAY (Vintage Books, 1993).
42. ISHIGURO, at 42.
43. ISHIGURO, at 201.
44. WHITE, at 21; CRAY, at 31.
45. WHITE, at 18.
46. CRAY, at 31.
47. CRAY, at 31; WHITE, at 18.
48. *See* WHITE, at 11.
49. *Id.*
50. WHITE, at 10–11.
51. WHITE, at 11–12.
52. *See* WHITE, at 11.
53. *Id.*
54. See WHITE, at 28–31; CRAY, at 54–58.
55. CRAY, at 75, quoting Warren.
56. CRAY, at 75.
57. CRAY, at 75, quoting Warren.
58. CRAY, at 75.
59. CRAY, at 87. A fifth man, it seems, although indicted escaped custody before trial. *See* WHITE, at 39.
60. CRAY, at 82.
61. CRAY, at 85.
62. CRAY, at 89.
63. CRAY, at 88.
64. CRAY, at 110.
65. CRAY, at 111, 108.
66. *See* CRAY, at 176, WHITE, at 109–10.

CHAPTER 2

1. *Brown v. Board of Education*, 347 U.S. 483 (1954).
2. THURGOOD MARSHALL, *Law and the Quest for Equality*, 1967 WASHINGTON U. L.Q., *reprinted in* THURGOOD MARSHALL: HIS SPEECHES, WRITINGS, ARGUMENTS, OPINIONS, AND REMINISCENCES (Mark V. Tushnet ed., Lawrence Hill Books, 2001) at 223.
3. For the classic work assessing historians' reliance on notions of inevitable steps and progress—engaging in Whig history—see H. BUTTERFIELD, THE WHIG INTERPRETATION OF HISTORY (G. Bell and Sons, 1931, reprinted AMS Press, 1978).
4. *Plessy v. Ferguson*, 163 U.S. 537 (1896).
5. GUNNAR MYRDAL, AN AMERICAN DILEMMA: THE NEGRO PROBLEM AND MODERN DEMOCRACY (Transaction Publishers, 1996) (originally published by Harper & Row, 1944) [hereinafter AMERICAN DILEMMA], vol. I at 183. In 1910, African Americans constituted less than 2 percent of the total population of the North and West. *Id.*
6. AMERICAN DILEMMA, vol. I, at 183. In 1940, less than 4 percent of the total northern population was African American. As Myrdal acknowledges, "There are no data available to determine the exact size of the net migration of Negroes from

South to North between 1910 and 1940. The figure presented in the text is simply the difference between the Northern Negro population for 1940 and that for 1910 [derived from U.S. Bureau of Census data]." *Id.* at 1229 n.3.

7. *See* Philip M. Hauser, *Demographic Factors in the Integration of the Negro,* in THE NEGRO AMERICAN (T. Parsons & K. B. Clark eds. [Beacon Press, 1966]) at 74. As Gunnar Myrdal correctly notes, the census data for migration of Black people from the South is to some extent "unreliable." AMERICAN DILEMMA, vol. I, at 1229. Thus, I have used "estimated" and "about" when citing census data concerning migration.

8. ISABEL WILKERSON, THE WARMTH OF OTHER SUNS (Random House, 2010) at 9.

9. AMERICAN DILEMMA, vol. II at 1002.

10. AMERICAN DILEMMA, vol. I at 233. *See also* NEIL R. MCMILLEN, DARK JOURNEY: BLACK MISSISSIPPIANS IN THE AGE OF JIM CROW (University of Illinois Press, 1989), at 111–54.

11. *Id.* at 237.

12. *Id.* at 237. In absolute numbers, the peak of 220,000 Negro farmer-owners was reached in 1910 and declined by more than 20 percent over the next thirty years. *Id. See also* Manning Marable, *The Politics of Black Land Tenure 1877–1915,* 53 AGRIC. HIST. 142 (1979).

13. *Id.* at 251. *See also* SVEN BECKERT, EMPIRE OF COTTON: A GLOBAL HISTORY (Knopf, 2014), at 274–311, 393–96.

14. *Id.* at 232.

15. *Id.* at 234–35. *See also* Robert Higgs, *The Boll Weevil, the Cotton Economy, and Black Migration 1910–1930,* 50 AGRIC. HIST. 335 (1976).

16. *Id.* at 251.

17. *Id.* at 251. During the 1920s, the Black rural farm population in the South fell 8.6 percent. During the 1930s, it shrank by another 4.5 percent. *Id.* at 1245 n.13 (fns. to ch. 12).

18. *Id.* at lxix.

19. *Id.* at xxxiii (author's preface to the twentieth anniversary edition, 1962).

20. *Id.*

21. AMERICAN DILEMMA, vol. II at 668.

22. *Id.*

23. *Smith v. Allwright,* 321 U.S. 649 (1944), overruling *Grovey v. Townsend,* 295 U.S. 45 (1935).

24. *Steele v. Louisville and Nashville Railroad,* 323 U.S. 192 (1944).

25. *Morgan v. Virginia,* 328 U.S. 373 (1946).

26. *Sipuel v. Oklahoma State Bd of Regents,* 332 U.S. 631 (1948). In *Sipuel,* the U.S. Supreme Court unanimously overturned a ruling by the Oklahoma Supreme Court that, on procedural grounds, had upheld a lower state court's rejection, also on procedural grounds, of a Black woman's claim that she had been denied equal protection of the law when she was denied admission to the state's law school because of her race. The U.S. Supreme Court, in a short per curiam decision issued only four days after oral argument, interceded to prevent the state courts from using technicalities and procedural niceties to deny an equal protection claim brought pursuant to the Fourteenth Amendment. *Sipuel, supra.* (For some detail on the state court's rejection of Sipuel's claims on procedural niceties and technicalities, see Mark V. TUSHNET, THE NAACP's LEGAL STRATEGY AGAINST SEGREGATED EDUCATION, 1925–1950 (University of North Carolina Press, 1987) [hereinafter

NAACP LEGAL STRATEGY], at 121.) The U.S. Supreme Court made this clear in *Fisher v. Hurst*, 333 U.S. 147 (1948) (per curiam) at 150: "The Oklahoma Supreme Court upheld the refusal to admit petitioner [Ida Sipuel, now, after marrying, Ida Fisher] on the ground that she had failed to demand establishment of a separate school and admission to it. On remand, the district court correctly understood our decision to hold that the Equal Protection Clause permits no such defense." It is hard to see how this could correctly be characterized, as Kluger asserts, as a "setback." RICHARD KLUGER, SIMPLE JUSTICE (Random House, 2004) (originally published in 1975) [hereinafter SIMPLE JUSTICE] at 259. Indeed, "*The Chicago Defender*, a black newspaper, welcomed the decision in *Sipuel* as showing that 'the props of Jim-Crow are buckling.'" NAACP LEGAL STRATEGY at 123. Moreover, in practical terms it was a success, as Sipuel was admitted to the all-white law school, albeit more than a year later, and graduated in 1951. THE SUPREME COURT IN CONFERENCE (Del Dickson, ed., Oxford University Press, 2001) [hereinafter SUPREME COURT IN CONFERENCE], at 637.

    The court emphasized that the issue of "separate but equal" was not before it, but rather than being a setback, this helped the NAACP in its carefully constructed drive to achieve racial justice in education. Thurgood Marshall had been concerned that the minimal trial record in the Oklahoma litigation might lead the court to reaffirm the "separate but equal" standard. NAACP LEGAL STRATEGY at 121. For this reason, Marshall wanted the Texas case, *Sweatt v. Painter*, to come before the court first. MARK V. TUSHNET, MAKING CIVIL RIGHTS LAW: THURGOOD MARSHALL AND THE SUPREME COURT, 1936–1961 (Oxford University Press, 1994) [hereinafter MAKING CIVIL RIGHTS LAW], at 129.

27. *Shelley v. Kraemer*, 334 U.S. 1 (1948). The opinion in *Shelley* was unanimous; three justices, however, did not participate in the case.
28. Louis Henkin, Shelley v. Kraemer: *Notes for a Revised Opinion*, 110 U. PENN. L. REV. 473 (1962).
29. *Sweatt v. Painter*, 339 U.S. 629 (1950).
30. SIMPLE JUSTICE at 281.
31. *Sweatt v. Painter*, 339 U.S. at 633.
32. *Sweatt*, 339 U.S. at 634.
33. *Id.*
34. *Id.*
35. *McLaurin v. Oklahoma State Regents for Higher Education*, 339 U.S. 637, 639 (1950). Although during trial conditions were improved—plaintiff was assigned a seat in the classroom, in a row solely for Black students, and to a table on the main floor of the library, one set aside for Black students—the court ruled that the school's actions were still unconstitutional. 339 U.S. at 640.
36. *Henderson v. United States*, 339 U.S. 816 (1950).
37. NAACP LEGAL STRATEGY at 111–13.
38. AMERICAN DILEMMA, vol. I at 319.
39. Thurgood Marshall, *The Supreme Court as Protector of Civil Rights: Equal Protection of the Laws*, 275 ANNALS OF THE AM. ACAD. OF POL. & SOC. SCI. (May 1951), *reprinted in* THURGOOD MARSHALL, Mark V. Tushnet ed., at 124.
40. SIMPLE JUSTICE at 290–94; NAACP LEGAL STRATEGY at 135–37.
41. Marshall, *Supreme Court as Protector*, at 123.
42. Marshall, *Supreme Court as Protector*, at 124.

43. Missouri *ex rel.* Gaines v. Canada, 305 U.S. 337 (1938).

44. SUPREME COURT IN CONFERENCE at 647.

45. *Id.* at 640.

46. *Id.* at 640.

47. Reed declared, "In the Deep South separate but equal schools must be allowed. I uphold segregation as constitutional." *Id.* at 649.

48. *Id.* at 649.

49. *Id.* at 653.

50. *Id.* at 653.

51. *Id.* at 659.

52. *Id.* at 659.

53. *Id.* at 659.

54. *Id.* at 648.

55. *Id.* at 653.

56. *Brown v. Board of Education of Topeka*, 347 U.S. 483 (1954).

57. *Briggs v. Elliot*, 342 U.S. 350 (1952).

58. *Davis v. County School Board of Prince Edward County*, 142 F. Supp. 616 (1956).

59. *Gebhart v. Bolton*, 33 Del. Ch. 144, 87 A.2d 862, *aff'd*, 91 A.2d 137 (1952).

60. *Bolling v. Sharpe*, 347 U.S. 497 (1954).

61. *Brown v. Board of Education*, 347 U.S. 483 (1954) (*Brown I*).

62. *Brown v. Board of Education*, 349 U.S. 294 (1955) (*Brown II*) at 301.

63. *Bolling v. Sharpe*, 347 U.S. 497 (1954).

64. SUPREME COURT IN CONFERENCE at 646.

65. *Id.*

66. *Id.* at 646–47. Vinson stated that he thought that "Congress has the power to act for the District of Columbia and for the states." Kluger misinterprets Burton's parenthetical addition in his conference notes: "May act for DC—probably *not* for the states" is a "more telling" concession from Vinson than it is, reading it as essentially contradicting the statement in the text. SIMPLE JUSTICE (2004 ed.) at 593. But the editor of the conference notes translates Burton's entry to read "Congress may act for the District of Columbia, but probably will *not* act for the states." SUPREME COURT IN CONFERENCE at 647. For him, Vinson was making only a forecast of political reality, not a statement of Congress's limited constitutional power.

67. SUPREME COURT IN CONFERENCE at 647.

68. *Id.*

69. *Id.*

70. *Id.* at 647 n.41.

71. Dennis J. Hutchinson, *Unanimity and Desegregation*, 68 GEO. L.J. 1 (1979) at 22–25.

72. 345 U.S. 461 (1953).

73. Only Justice Murphy had indicated an earlier willingness to overrule *Plessy*. He did so in 1948 at conference in *Sipuel*. SUPREME COURT IN CONFERENCE at 636.

74. SUPREME COURT IN CONFERENCE at 638.

75. *Id.*

76. *Id.* at 639.

77. *Id.* at 648.

78. *Id.* at 648.

79. *Id.* at 653. A longer rendition is contained in a letter to Felix Frankfurter in SIMPLE JUSTICE at 612–13. "Dear Felix," wrote Burton, "I have been increasingly impressed with the idea that under the conditions of 50 or more years ago it probably could be said that a state's treatment of negroes, within its borders, on the basis of 'separate but equal' facilities might come within the constitutional guaranty of an 'equal' protection of the laws, because the lives of negroes and whites were then and there in fact *separately* cast and lived. Today, however, I doubt that it can be said in any state (and certainly not generally) that compulsory 'separation' of the races, even with equal facilities, *can* amount to an 'equal' protection of the laws in a society that is lived and shared so '*jointly*' by all races as ours is now."

80. *Id.* at 653.

81. Mary L. Dudziak, *Desegregation as a Cold War Imperative*, 41 STAN. L. REV. 61 (1988).

82. Brief for the United States as amicus curiae in *Brown* at 6–8, reprinted in LANDMARK BRIEFS AND ARGUMENTS OF THE SUPREME COURT OF THE UNITED STATES (Philip Kurland and Gerhard Casper, eds., University Publications of America, 1975) [hereinafter LANDMARK BRIEFS AND ARGUMENTS] vol. 49 at 121–23. Much of the Soviet propaganda was aimed at the emerging postcolonial states in Africa. Dudziak, *supra* note 80, at 62, 100, 114–15.

83. SUPREME COURT IN CONFERENCE at 650.

84. *Id.* at 651.

85. *Id.* at 650.

86. *Id.* at 651.

87. *Id.* at 651.

88. William O. Douglas, May 17, 1954, Memorandum for the File, reprinted in SUPREME COURT IN CONFERENCE at 660–61.

89. Frankfurter letter to Stanley Reed, May 20, 1954, FELIX FRANKFURTER PAPERS, HARVARD LAW SCHOOL, box 72, file 14, Proquest, Law and Society since the Civil War: American Legal Manuscripts from the Harvard Law School Library, Felix Frankfurter Papers, Folder: 001756-004-0001, p. 404.

90. SUPREME COURT IN CONFERENCE at 654.

91. *Id.* at 654–55.

92. For a discussion setting forth the close connection between sociological jurisprudence and legal realism, see MORTON J. HORWITZ, THE TRANSFORMATION OF AMERICAN LAW, 1870–1960 (New York: Oxford University Press, 1992) [hereinafter TRANSFORMATION II], at 169–71.

93. Roscoe Pound, *Mechanical Jurisprudence*, 8 COLUM. L. REV. 605 (1908).

94. Roscoe Pound, *Law in Books and Law in Action*, 44 AM. L. REV. 12 (1910).

95. For a discussion of the Brandeis brief, see PHILIPPA STRUM, LOUIS D. BRANDEIS: JUSTICE FOR THE PEOPLE (Harvard University Press, 1984) at 114–31.

96. *Id.* at 121. In addition to 2 pages of legal argument and 95 pages of economic and sociological data, the Brandeis brief contained 15 pages of "excerpts from state and foreign laws limiting women's hours," for a total of 112 pages. *Id.* Thus, less than 2 percent of the brief consisted of traditional legal argumentation.

97. *See generally* Kenneth W. Mack, *Rethinking Civil Rights Lawyering and Politics in the Era before* Brown, 115 YALE L.J. (2005). For the view that Charles Hamilton Houston was a legal realist—indeed, "the most substantial contributor to Legal Realist thought . . . in the area of race relations"—see *Legal Realism and the Race*

Question: Some Realism about Realism on Race Relations, 108 HARV. L. REV. 1607 (1995) [hereinafter *Legal Realism and the Race Question*] at 1621–24. This note also elaborates on the largely ignored writings concerning race relations of important legal realist thinkers Felix Cohen, Robert Hale, and Karl Llewellyn. *Id.* at 1611–19.

98. *Plessy v. Ferguson,* 163 U.S. 537 (1896) at 551.

99. *See* Sanjay Mody, Brown *Footnote Eleven in Historical Context: Social Science and the Supreme Court's Quest for Legitimacy,* 54 STAN. L. REV. 793 (2002) [hereinafter Brown *Footnote Eleven in Historical Context*] at 826. The quintessential example of such scholarship was the magisterial ENCYCLOPEDIA OF THE SOCIAL SCIENCES (Edwin R.A. Seligman ed.; Macmillan, 1930–1935). *See* TRANSFORMATION II at 182–83 and 316 fn.99. Interestingly and not fortuitously, the advisory editors for the encyclopedia were in law Roscoe Pound, in philosophy John Dewey, and in political science Charles Beard.

100. *See Legal Realism and the Race Question, supra* note 96, at 1623. *See generally* Mack, *Rethinking Civil Rights Lawyering.*

101. SUPREME COURT IN CONFERENCE at 639 (conference of April 8, 1950).

102. *Id.* at 648 (conference of December 13, 1952).

103. *See, e.g.,* AMERICAN DILEMMA, vol. I at 221–24; vol. II, chapter 31, at 667–88. Myrdal did not invent the concept of caste, nor was he the first social scientist to apply the concept to the American race problem. Myrdal himself acknowledges this. *See* AMERICAN DILEMMA, vol. 2, at 1377 fn.5.

104. SUPREME COURT IN CONFERENCE at 648. He also stated, "The caste system . . . is the negation of the idea of the Fourteenth Amendment." *Id.* at 639.

105. *Durham,* 214 F.2d 862 (D.C. Cir. 1954); *Gideon,* 372 U.S. 335 (1963). *See* LAURA KALMAN, ABE FORTAS (Yale University Press, 1990) at 178–83.

106. Felix Cohen, *Transcendental Nonsense and the Functional Approach,* 35 COLUM. L. REV. 809 (1935).

107. AMERICAN DILEMMA, vol. 1, at 19–21. Myrdal stated in vol. 2 at 1031–32: "We must voice our grave skepticism toward the simple explanatory scheme concerning the role of valuations in social life typified by William Graham Sumner's concepts, 'folkways' and 'mores.' . . . The concept of mores actually implies a whole social theory and an entire *laissez-faire* ('do-nothing') metaphysics and is so utilized. . . . The theory is . . . crude and misleading when applied to a modern Western society." For a discussion of fn.11 in *Brown v. Board of Education,* in which, famously and not without controversy, Myrdal's magisterial work was cited along with other social science studies, see *Brown Footnote Eleven in Historical Context.*

108. For the history of the notion of a changing constitution, see Morton J. Horwitz, *The Supreme Court, 1992 Term—Foreword: The Constitution of Change: Legal Fundamentality without Fundamentalism,* 107 HARV. L. REV. 30, 41–70 (1993).

109. Writing in dissent in 1966 in *Harper v. Virginia Board of Elections,* Justice Black insisted that he "did not join the opinion of the Court in Brown on any theory that segregation where practiced in the public schools denied equal protection in 1954 but did not similarly deny it in 1868 when the Fourteenth Amendment was adopted. . . . In *Brown* . . . , the Court today purports to find precedent for using the Equal Protection Clause to keep the Constitution up to date. I did not vote to hold segregation in public schools unconstitutional on any such theory. I thought

when *Brown* was written, and I think now, that Mr. Justice Harlan was correct in 1896 when he dissented from *Plessy v. Ferguson.*" 383 U.S. 663 (1966) at 677–78 n.7.

110. Jackson draft of March 1, 1954, at 11. See Appendix 2 for an extended discussion of Jackson's draft opinions.

111. Jackson draft of March 1, 1954, at 11 (also in Jackson draft of March 15, 1954, at 22).

112. Oral Argument in *Brown*, 347 U.S. at 24 (December 9, 1952), reprinted in LANDMARK BRIEFS AND ARGUMENTS, supra, vol. 49 at 301.

113. *See, e.g.,* Felix Frankfurter, *Hours of Labor and Realism in Constitutional Law*, 29 HARV. L. REV. 353 (1916); Felix Frankfurter and Nathan Greene, *Labor Injunctions and Federal Legislation*, 42 HARV. L. REV. 766 (1929); Felix Frankfurter, *Mr. Justice Brandeis and the Constitution*, 45 HARV. L. REV. 33 (1931).

114. FELIX FRANKFURTER PAPERS, HARVARD LAW SCHOOL, box 72, file 14 (undated memo), folder: 001756-004-0001, p. 439, quoted in SIMPLE JUSTICE at 688.

115. FELIX FRANKFURTER PAPERS, HARVARD LAW SCHOOL, box 72, file 7, folder: 001756-004-0001, p. 1–58. Bickel's memo was eventually published in the *Harvard Law Review*. Alexander M. Bickel, *The Original Understanding and the Segregation Decision*, 69 HARV. L. REV. 1 (1955).

116. FELIX FRANKFURTER PAPERS, HARVARD LAW SCHOOL, box 72, file 7, folder: 001756-004-0001, p. 59. Frankfurter's covering letter was titled "Memorandum for the Conference" and dated December 3, 1953.

117. FELIX FRANKFURTER PAPERS, HARVARD LAW SCHOOL, box 72, file 14, folder: 001756-004-0001, p. 217. In his unpublished drafts, Justice Jackson, remarkably, was developing ideas similar to Bickel's about the original meaning of the Fourteenth Amendment. "The Fourteenth Amendment," wrote Jackson, "does not attempt to say the last word on the concrete application of its pregnant generalities." He continued: "It thus makes provision for giving effect from time to time to the changes of conditions and public opinion always to be anticipated in a developing society." Jackson draft Brown concurrence of March 15, 1954, at 11. Jackson added that "exhaustive research to uncover the original will and purpose expressed in the Fourteenth Amendment yields for me only one sure conclusion: it was a passionate, confused . . . era." *Id.* at 6.

118. Dennis J. Hutchinson, *Unanimity and Desegregation: Decision Making in the Supreme Court, 1948–1958*, 68 GEO. L.J. 1 (1979) at 38.

119. *Id.* at 40.

120. *Brown*, 347 U.S. 483 (1954) at 489.

121. *Id.* at 492.

122. *Id.* at 492–93.

123. SUPREME COURT IN CONFERENCE at 649.

124. *Id.* at 655.

125. FELIX FRANKFURTER PAPERS, HARVARD LAW SCHOOL, box 72, file 14, folder: 001756-004-0001, p. 407–8. For Frankfurter's letter dated May 20, 1954, expressing "deep gratitude," to which Reed was responding, see box 72, file 14, folder: 001756-004-0001, p. 404.

126. SUPREME COURT IN CONFERENCE at 652.

127. *Id.* at 653.

128. *Id.*

129. *Id.* at 652.

130. *Id.* at 654.
131. SIMPLE JUSTICE at 689.
132. SIMPLE JUSTICE at 689; BERNARD SCHWARTZ, SUPER CHIEF: EARL WARREN AND HIS SUPREME COURT, A JUDICIAL BIOGRAPHY (New York University Press, 1983) [hereinafter cited as SUPER CHIEF] at 90–91.
133. SIMPLE JUSTICE at 604.
134. FELIX FRANKFURTER PAPERS, HARVARD LAW SCHOOL, box 72, file 14, folder: 001756-004-0001, p. 430.
135. Frankfurter's handwritten notes regarding the conference were dated "Saturday 16." FELIX FRANKFURTER PAPERS, HARVARD LAW SCHOOL, box 72, file 14, folder: 001756-004-0001, p. 448–53.
136. Jackson wrote, "I will not be a party to thus casting upon the lower courts a burden of continued litigation under circumstances which subject district judges to local pressures and provide them with no standards to justify their decisions to their neighbors, whose opinions they must resist." Jackson draft *Brown* concurrence of March 15, 1954, at 17.
137. SUPER CHIEF at 92–93. Black's prescience about the South's reaction to *Brown* extended to his own son's career. After graduating from Yale Law School, Hugo Jr. returned to Alabama to practice law, awaiting the opportunity to enter politics. Shortly before *Brown* was handed down, his chance came to run for a vacant congressional seat in Birmingham. When he called the justice for advice, he "was surprised and a little alarmed" when his father asked him to fly up to Washington. When he arrived, the justice told him "something in the strictest of confidence that has a lot to do with your decision." Black informed Hugo Jr. that *Brown* would soon be decided and that afterward it would be impossible to engage in southern electoral politics "unless, of course, you are willing to abuse the Supreme Court." "You understand, Son. I've got to do it even though it's going to mess up your plans." HUGO BLACK, JR., MY FATHER: A REMEMBRANCE (Random House, 1975) at 207–8. Hugo Jr. decided not to run. *Id.* at 208. He also was eventually forced to abandon his labor law practice and move out of state. *Id.* at 212–15.
138. 358 U.S. 1 (1958). Discussed in more detail in *infra* ch. 4.
139. *Southern Manifesto on Integration* (1956) in DOCUMENTS OF AMERICAN CONSTITUTIONAL AND LEGAL HISTORY (Urofsky and Finkelman, eds., Oxford University Press, 2002) at 735–37.
140. For a later consideration of antimiscegenation laws, see *Loving v. Virginia*, 388 U.S. 1 (1967), discussed *infra* at 33.
141. Dwight D. Eisenhower's Radio and Television Address to the American People on the Situation in Little Rock in STEVEN F. LAWSON AND CHARLES PAYNE, DEBATING THE CIVIL RIGHTS MOVEMENT, 1945–1968 (Rowan & Littlefield, 1998), at 60–64.
142. *Aaron v. Cooper*, 257 F.2d 33 (8th Cir., 1958) (en banc) reversing *Aaron v. Cooper*, 163 F. Supp. 13 (E. D. Ark. 1958).
143. SUPER CHIEF at 290.
144. 358 U.S. at 18.
145. In a long and sometimes confusing account of the holding in *Cooper v. Aaron*, Professor Tribe acknowledges that the court "asserted what is probably its broadest definition of its power," which, under certain not entirely clear circumstances, Tribe finds "troubling." LAURENCE H. TRIBE, AMERICAN CONSTITUTIONAL LAW (3d ed., Foundation Press, 2000), § 3-4.

146. *See, e.g.,* LARRY D. KRAMER, THE PEOPLE THEMSELVES: POPULAR CONSTITU-
TIONALISM AND JUDICIAL REVIEW (Oxford University Press, 2004) at 221 & 331
fn. 64 and 65. Brennan's broad claim of judicial supremacy met the resistance of
Justice John Marshall Harlan in the drafting stage, and Harlan sought to persuade
Brennan to eliminate the section on judicial power in Brennan's draft. SUPER
CHIEF at 299. That Harlan's resistance on this point eventually melted away in the
face of Brennan's refusal to change is further evidence of the high value the justices
placed on unanimity.

   Justice Brennan, writing for the court in *Baker v. Carr*, once again asserted what
scholars would define as "judicial supremacy": "Deciding whether a matter has in
any measure been committed by the Constitution to another branch of government,
or whether the action of that branch exceeds whatever authority has been committed, is itself a delicate exercise in constitutional interpretation, and is a responsibility
of this Court as ultimate interpreter of the Constitution." 369 U.S. at 211.

147. J. HARVIE WILKINSON III, FROM *BROWN* TO *BAKKE*: THE SUPREME COURT AND
SCHOOL INTEGRATION, 1954–1978 (Oxford University Press, 1979) [hereinafter
WILKINSON] at 94; MARK WHITMAN, THE IRONY OF DESEGREGATION LAW
(Markus Wiener Publishers, 1998) [hereinafter WHITMAN] at 36.

148. Governor Almond closed public schools in Norfolk, Charlottesville, and Warren
County in September 1958. JAMES W. ELY JR., THE CRISIS OF CONSERVATIVE VIR-
GINIA: THE BYRD ORGANIZATION AND THE POLITICS OF MASSIVE RESISTANCE
(University of Tennessee Press, 1976) at 74; BENJAMIN MUSE, VIRGINIA'S MAS-
SIVE RESISTANCE (Indiana University Press, 1961) at 74–75; WHITMAN at 36.

149. WHITMAN at 36, 37; *The Federal Courts and Integration of Southern Schools:
Troubled Status of the Pupil Placement Acts*, 62 COLUM. L. REV. 1448, 1452 n.23
(1962); Patrick E. McCauley, *"Be It Enacted," in* WITH ALL DELIBERATE SPEED
(Don Shoemaker ed., Harper & Brothers, 1957) at 136–39.

150. LUCAS A. POWE JR., THE WARREN COURT AND AMERICAN POLITICS (Harvard
University Press, 2002) at 165.

151. WILKINSON at 84.

152. WILKINSON at 84.

153. *The Federal Courts and Integration of Southern Schools: Troubled Status of the
Pupil Placement Acts*, 62 COLUM. L. REV. 1448, 1453 (1962).

154. WHITMAN at 38, quoting BENJAMIN MUSE, TEN YEARS OF PRELUDE (Viking,
1964) at 68–69.

155. *Shuttlesworth v. Birmingham Board of Education*, 358 U.S. 101 (1958).

156. *Shuttlesworth v. Birmingham Board of Education*, 162 F. Supp. 372 (N.D. Ala.,
1958).

157. 162 F. Supp. at 380 & at fn. 9.

158. 162 F. Supp. at 381.

159. *Bush v. Orleans Parish School Board*, 308 F.2d 491 (5th Cir. 1962) at 499;
WHITMAN at 45.

160. WILKINSON at 93.

161. Frank T. Read, *Judicial Evolution of the Law of School Integration since* Brown
v. Board of Education, 39 LAW & CONTEMP. PROBS. 7, 19 (1975). *See, e.g., Bush
v. Orleans Parish School Board*, 308 F.2d 491 (5th Cir. 1962) (Judge John Minor
Wisdom writing for the three-judge panel) at 499–500: "This Court . . . condemns
the Pupil Placement Act when, with a fanfare of trumpets, it is hailed as the

instrument for carrying out a desegregation plan while all the time the entire public knows that in fact it is being used to maintain segregation by allowing a little token desegregation. . . . [The Act] is not a plan for desegregation at all."

162. WILKINSON at 109–10.

163. WILKINSON at 111–12; *Singleton v. Jackson Municipal Separate School District,* 348 F.2d 729 (5th Cir. 1965) (*Singleton I*); *Singleton v. Jackson Municipal Separate School District,* 355 F.2d 865 (5th Cir. 1966) (*Singleton II*); *U.S. v. Jefferson County Board of Education,* 372 F.2d 836 (5th Cir.1966) (*Jefferson*). Judge Wisdom, in *Jefferson County, supra,* stated, "As we see it, the law imposes an absolute duty to desegregate, that is, disestablish segregation. *And an absolute duty to integrate,* in the sense that a disproportionate concentration of Negroes in certain schools cannot be ignored." *Jefferson,* n.5 (emphasis added). Later in his lengthy and important opinion, Judge Wisdom said of freedom of choice plans that "school authorities in this circuit, with few exceptions, have turned to the 'freedom of choice' method for desegregating public schools. The method has serious shortcomings. Indeed, the 'slow pace of integration . . . is in large measure attributable to the manner in which free choice plans have operated.' When such plans leave school officials with a broad area of uncontrolled discretion, this method of desegregation is better suited than any other to preserve the essentials of the dual school system while giving paper compliance with the duty to desegregate." 372 U.S. at 888. The detailed and demanding remedial portion of Judge Wisdom's *Jefferson* opinion significantly limited school board discretion that had impeded integration and required school authorities "to take affirmative action to bring about a unitary, non-racial system." 372 F.2d at 894. Judge Wisdom's opinion of December 29, 1966, also declared that delay would not be tolerated: "[A]fter twelve years of snail's pace progress toward school desegregation . . . [t]he clock has ticked the last tick for tokenism and delay in the name of 'deliberate speed.'" 372 F.2d at 896.

164. 391 U.S. 430 (1968). Although inactive for the most part, in school desegregation cases after *Cooper v. Aaron* and before *Green,* the court did assert itself a few times in the mid-1960s. *See, e.g., Rogers v. Paul,* 382 U.S. 198 (1965); *Griffin v. City School Board of Prince Edward County,* 377 U.S. 218 (1964). Indeed, Judge Wisdom noted "the Supreme Court's increasing emphasis on more speed and less deliberation in school desegregation." *Jefferson, supra,* at 861. In doing so, he quoted from the Warren Court's 1964 *Griffin* opinion, *supra,* 377 U.S. at 229: "There has been entirely too much deliberation and not enough speed in enforcing the constitutional rights which we held in *Brown* . . . had been denied Prince Edward County Negro children." *Jefferson, supra,* fn.55.

Moreover, it should not be forgotten that after *Cooper* and prior to *Green,* the Supreme Court issued several landmark opinions protecting the NAACP, which was essential to school desegregation efforts. *See, e.g., Bates v. Little Rock,* 361 U.S. 516 (1960); *Shelton v. Tucker,* 364 U.S. 479 (1960); *NAACP v. Button,* 371 U.S. 415 (1963); *Gibson v. Florida Legislative Investigating Committee,* 372 U.S. 539 (1963). Much of the school desegregation litigation, including *Green,* was spearheaded by the NAACP Legal Defense Fund.

165. WILKINSON at 115.

166. 391 U.S. at 438–39. The court reinforced *Green* in two companion cases, both also unanimous opinions authored by Justice Brennan, and litigated for African American students by the NAACP Legal Defense Fund. *Monroe v. Board of*

Commissioners, 391 U.S. 450 (1968); *Raney v. Board of Education*, 391 U.S. 443 (1968). *See* POWE at 296–97. For a discussion of what he labels "the *Green* trilogy" and also Judge Wisdom's opinion in *Jefferson*, see WHITMAN at 89–103.

167. In his well-known book *Hollow Hope*, Gerald Rosenberg has offered a misleading account of desegregation between 1964 and 1971 in support of his claim that "*Brown* and its progeny stand for the proposition that courts are impotent to produce significant social reform." GERALD N. ROSENBERG, THE HOLLOW HOPE: CAN COURTS BRING ABOUT SOCIAL CHANGE? (University of Chicago Press, 1991) at 71. Adopting an arbitrary distinction between "direct" and "indirect" causes of desegregation in the Deep South, he asserts that *Brown* was not a direct cause of desegregation. Instead, he maintains that while *Brown* directly caused the southern backlash against the decision, it had little influence on the growth of the civil rights movement or, indeed, on the passage of the historic Civil Rights Act of 1964. He concludes that the clear increase in desegregation between 1964 and 1971 can be attributed not to *Brown* but rather the belated support of Congress and the executive branch to desegregating southern public schools.

There are a number of difficulties with Rosenberg's thesis. In a situation of multiple causation, he forces his account into a linear narrative rather than seeing the process as the result of the convergence of multiple influences. For example, he marginalizes the important work of the courts of appeal in producing early and widespread desegregation in the border states. He also fails to give credit to Judge John Minor Wisdom and the Fifth Circuit for independently striking down pupil placement and freedom of choice laws, which had slowed desegregation to a snail's pace in the Deep South during the previous decade. Yet, it must be acknowledged that any attribution of sole causation to these Fifth Circuit opinions, which spanned the years 1964–1966, will be debatable since it is not possible to separate out the clearly acknowledged deference to Supreme Court opinions from other causes such as the civil rights movement, the election of President Kennedy, the Civil Rights Act, and executive enforcement by the Department of Health, Education, and Welfare.

Despite Rosenberg's claim, there does seems to be a close "direct" link between *Brown* and the civil rights movement in the person of Martin Luther King Jr., who launched the Montgomery bus boycott in December 1955 after acknowledging that *Brown* provided legitimacy and inspiration to the movement. In his first sermon as the newly appointed minister of Ebenezer Baptist Church, King declared that unlike white people, there "will be nobody among us who will stand up and defy the Constitution of this nation. . . . And we are not wrong. We are not wrong in what we are doing. If we are wrong—the Supreme Court of this nation is wrong." TAYLOR BRANCH, PARTING THE WATERS (Simon and Schuster, 1989) at 140.

Finally, the significant number of cases brought by the NAACP casts doubt on Rosenberg's effort to portray the newly active Department of Health, Education, and Welfare as the primary cause of the lawsuits that ended segregation.

Despite Rosenberg's efforts to portray school desegregation as dramatically increasing after 1964 (ROSENBERG at 52), it is clear from his own statistics that in 1965–1966 little had changed. In 1966, Black children were in school with whites at the rate of 0.43 percent in Alabama, 2.7 percent in Georgia, 0.85 percent in Louisiana, 0.59 percent in Mississippi, and 1.7 percent in South Carolina. By 1970–1971, the figures for Alabama had skyrocketed to 80 percent, for Georgia

83.1 percent, for Louisiana 75.9 percent, for Mississippi 89.1 percent, and for South Carolina 92.9 percent. *See* ROSENBERG, Appendix I, at 345–46.

As we can see, the remarkable change that did occur took place only between 1966 and 1971, during the last three years of which newly elected President Nixon reversed the aggressive stance of the Department of Health, Education, and Welfare. Ironically, it may have been the Supreme Court's unanimous 1968 decision in *Green* that provided the needed spark of inspiration and expression of support to the judges of the Fifth Circuit Court of Appeals.

The six- or seven-year interval between the passage of the Civil Rights Act and any substantial desegregation in the South is similar to the decade between *Brown* and the passage of the Civil Rights Act. Rosenberg uses the later interval to attribute direct causation to the Civil Rights Act and treats the earlier interval as illustrating that *Brown* had little causal influence.

The post–Warren Court 1969 *Alexander* case, *Alexander v. Holmes County Board of Education*, 396 U.S. 19 (1969) (per curiam) as well as the 1970 *Carter* case, *Carter v. West Feliciana Parish School Board*, 396 U.S. 290 (1970) (per curiam), also undeniably played a role in reinforcing the court's position in *Green*. (The justices sitting for both of these cases were all Warren Court justices, with the exception of Chief Justice Burger having replaced Earl Warren.) And the NAACP Legal Defense Fund's efforts were essential, especially since the U.S. Department of Justice (as well as the U.S. Department of Health, Education, and Welfare) opposed the position argued by the NAACP in *Alexander* and adopted by the court to brook no further delay. WILKINSON at 119–20. "The Court that once badly needed executive support now moved in the face of executive opposition." WILKINSON at 121. For a discussion of the importance of *Green*, *Alexander*, and *Carter*—one that implicitly but effectively counters Rosenberg's thesis—see Read, *supra* note 160, at 28–32.

168. WILKINSON at 121. These figures cited by Wilkinson are estimates from the U.S. Department of Health, Education, and Welfare. *Id.* at 121. "A half century [after *Brown*], racial segregation is still the norm in northern public schools. The five states with the highest rates of school segregation . . . are all outside the South." THOMAS J. SUGRUE, SWEET LAND OF LIBERTY: THE FORGOTTEN STRUGGLE FOR CIVIL RIGHTS IN THE NORTH (Random House, 2008) at xix.

169. 388 U.S. 1 (1967).

170. The court went to great lengths, even when provoked by the Virginia Supreme Court, to avoid addressing the issue of miscegenation. *Naim v. Naim*, 350 U.S. 985 (1956) (in response to appeal in *Naim v. Naim*, 197 Va. 734 [1956]; *Naim v. Naim*, 350 U.S. 891 (1955) (in response to appeal from *Naim v. Naim*, 197 Va. 80 [1955]. Around the same time, Justice Frankfurter also succeeded in blocking review of an Iowa cemetery's refusal to bury Native Americans. *Rice v. Sioux City Memorial Cemetery*, 349 U.S. 70 (1955).

171. The court, in brief per curiam rulings and without articulating its rationale, held segregation to be unconstitutional. *See, e.g., Gayle v. Browder*, 352 U.S. 903 (1956) (public buses); *Mayor of Baltimore v. Dawson*, 350 U.S. 877 (1955) (public beaches). Because of these and similar cases, it soon came to be clearly understood that the Equal Protection Clause extended beyond public school racial segregation.

172. Frank Newport, "In U.S., 87% Approve of Black-White Marriage, vs. 4% in 1958," GALLUP, July 25, 2013, https://news.gallup.com/poll/163697/approve-marriage -blacks-whites.aspx.

173. Cited in WALTER MURPHY, ELEMENTS OF JUDICIAL STRATEGY, 178.

174. Richard Delgado, *Naim v. Naim*, 12 NEV. L.J. 525, at 528.

175. *See* GREGORY MICHAEL DORR, SEGREGATION'S SCIENCE: EUGENICS AND SOCI-ETY IN VIRGINIA (University of Virginia Press, 2008); PETER WALLENSTEIN, RACE, SEX, AND THE FREEDOM TO MARRY: *LOVING V. VIRGINIA* (University Press of Kansas, 2014).

176. Newport, *supra* note 172.

177. *Id.*

178. Gretchen Livingston and Anna Brown, "Intermarriage in the U.S. 50 Years after Loving v. Virginia: 2. Public Views on Intermarriage," PEW RESEARCH CENTER, May 18, 2017, https://www.pewsocialtrends.org/2017/05/18/2-public-views-on -intermarriage/.

179. *Id.*

180. Especially the passage of the Civil Rights Act of 1964 and the Voting Rights Act of 1965.

181. ROSENBERG, HOLLOW HOPE.

182. "Roper Fortune #9: Roosevelt Balance Sheet; Tariffs; Negroes; Sex; General" (survey, The Roper Organization and *Fortune* magazine, September 1939), retrieved from the iPOLL Databank, The Roper Center for Public Opinion Research (henceforth, RCPOR) (USRFOR1939-009). The poll results illustrate why one must not draw too rigorous conclusions from data assembled during the early days of polling, when organizations were experimenting with different ways of asking questions. The Roper question on Black and white intelligence cited in the text was followed up with a second question asked only of the 71 percent who originally replied that Black people were less intelligent. The second question inquired about the causes of lower intelligence among Negroes. Thirty-two percent replied that Black people "lacked opportunities," 43 percent answered that they were "less intelligent," and 21 percent replied "both." While both questions seemed designed to elicit beliefs about inherent or biological inferiority, the second set of answers makes clear that at least 40 percent of the respondents did not understand "intelligence" that way. Those who designed the survey probably understood intelligence as a measure of "capacity to achieve or perform" but not of "inherent" ability or "native intelligence." As we shall see, later questions sought to cure this ambiguity.

183. "OPOR Poll: Roosevelt Survey #52" (survey, Office of Public Opinion Research, July 19, 1945), RCPOR (USOPOR1945-052).

184. "Attitudes toward Negroes" (National Opinion Research Center, University of Chicago, May 1944), RCPOR (USNORC1944-0225).

185. SUGRUE, SWEET LAND OF LIBERTY, at 64.

186. *Id.*

187. "Gallup Poll #419" (survey, Gallup Organization, May 28–June 2, 1948), RCPOR (USAIPO1948-0419).

188. "Roper Fortune #69: Anti-Minority Sentiment in the U.S. Today" (Surgery, The Roper Organization and *Fortune* magazine, September 1948), RCPOR (USRFORR 1948-069).

189. "Roper Fortune #9."

190. Gallup Organization, "Gallup Poll #1963-0673: Kennedy/Cuba/Race Relations/ Presidential Election" (survey, Gallup Organization, May 23–28, 1963), RCPOR (USAIPO1963-0673).

191. Sugrue, Sweet Land of Liberty, 247–48.

192. "NORC Survey #1944-0225: Attitudes Toward Negroes." RCPOR (USNORC1944-2025). Here one encounters the fascinating process of seeing the early pioneers of polling test run different versions of a question. Two questions on desegregating restaurants, with a slight difference in wording, yielded a significant shift in answers. To the question "Do you think that some restaurants in this town should serve both Negro and White people?" respondents answered in the negative by a margin of 47 percent to 46 percent. When the question was rephrased as "Do you think you would eat in a restaurant that served both Negro and White people?" the answer became 51 percent to 42 percent in favor. Due to the apparently more personalized wording, the proponents gained by 5 percent, while the opponents shrank by 5 percent.

193. "Gallup Poll #1948-0414: Foreign Policy/States/Civil Rights/Presidential Election" (survey, Gallup Organization, March 5–10, 1948), RCPOR (USAIPO1948-0414); "Gallup Poll #450" (survey, Gallup Organization, November 27–December 2, 1949), RCPOR (USAIPO1949-0450).

194. "NORC Survey #1944-0225: Attitudes Toward Negroes."

195. "Gallup Poll #349" (survey, Gallup Organization, June 14–19, 1945), RCPOR (USAIPO1945-0349).

196. "Roper Commercial #1952-059: NBC Political Study" (survey, The Roper Organization and National Broadcasting Company, May 1952), RCPOR (USRCOM1952-059).

197. "Gallup Poll #1949-0439: Pyramid Clubs/Lobbyists/Taxes/Japan/Truman" (survey, Gallup Organization, March 20–25, 1949), RCPOR (USAIPO1949-0439).

198. "Gallup Poll #531" (survey, Gallup Organization, May 21–26, 1954), RCPOR (USAIPO1954-0531); "Gallup Poll #614" (survey, Gallup Organization, May 29–June 3, 1959), RCPOR (USAIPO1959-0614). The polled question in both surveys was "The U.S. Supreme Court has ruled that racial segregation in all public schools is illegal. This means that all children, no matter what their race, must be allowed to go to the same schools. Do you approve or disapprove of this decision?"

199. A less favorable to *Brown* "more time should be given to work out problems" was substituted for "reasonable time" in the last two surveys.

200. "Roper Commercial #64" (survey, The Roper Organization, late August–September 8, 1956), RCPOR (USRCOM1956-064); "Roper Commercial #1958-106: Party Line IV—The Public Pulse" (survey, The Roper Organization, June 7, 1958), RCPOR (USRCOM1958-106); and "Roper Commercial #107" (survey, The Roper Organization, October 4, 1958), RCPOR (USRCOM1958-107).

201. Michael Powell, *Witnesses to Dream Speech See a New Hope*, N.Y. Times, Aug. 28, 2008, A1.

202. Philip Roth, The Plot against America 114 (2004).

203. Quoted in David Brooks, *Fragile at the Core*, N.Y. Times, June 19, 2009, A27.

204. "Gallup Poll #1961-0649: Presidential Election/Electoral College" (survey, Gallup Organization, August 24–29, 1961), RCPOR (USAIPO1961-0649).

205. "Gallup Poll #604" (survey, Gallup Organization, September 10–15, 1958), RCPOR (USAIPO1958-0604).

206. "Gallup Poll #622" (survey, Gallup Organization, December 10–15, 1959), RCPOR (USAIPO1959-0622).

207. "Gallup Poll #1107G" (survey, Gallup Organization, July 21–24, 1978), RCPOR (USAIPO1978-1107G).
208. William Julius Wilson, The Declining Significance of Race (3rd ed, University of Chicago Press, 2012).
209. Wilson at 18.
210. Wilson at 18.
211. Wilson at 19.
212. Mikyung Ryu, Minorities in Higher Education Twenty-Third Status Report, 2009 Supplement (American Council on Education, 2009), 5.
213. Needless to say, one can begin the story of cultural crossover much earlier with, say, gospel music or, as is well understood by cultural historians, jazz. Likewise, sports figures such as Joe Louis and opera singers Marian Anderson and Leontine Price were much admired by some whites. But these earlier crossover successes cannot be compared to the King Cole–Poitier–Cosby–Oprah phenomenon that produced not simply white acceptance but also identification. The rise of mass media, especially radio, television, and movies, was a necessary precondition for the growing influence of African Americans celebrities on the shape of white popular consciousness.
214. Hastie had previously been appointed as a district court judge in the Virgin Islands, a non–Article III jurisdiction. Two other African Americans followed him in this position. He was appointed to the Third Circuit Court of Appeals by President Truman in 1949.
215. Marshall was nominated in 1961 but took his seat in 1962.

CHAPTER 3

1. Indeed, one scholar contends that McCarthy's importance has been "ludicrously exaggerated." M. J. Heale, American Anticommunism: Combatting the Enemy Within, 1830–1970 (Johns Hopkins University Press, 1990) [hereinafter Heale] at 150.
2. Richard M. Fried, Nightmare in Red: The McCarthy Era in Perspective (Oxford University Press, 1990) [hereinafter Fried] at vii, 9, 36.
3. Heale at 152, 156, 157, 161, 177.
4. Heale at 180–81; Ellen Schrecker, Many Are the Crimes: McCarthyism in America (Princeton University Press, 1998) [hereinafter Many Are the Crimes] at 240–41, 255, 259–64.
5. As Richard Fried explains, "With deep roots in American culture, anti-communism flourished long before the Senator from Wisconsin adopted the issue in 1950. . . . Similarly, . . . anti-communism does not end with McCarthy's censure by the Senate in 1954. . . . [A]nti-communism's . . . death scene was a lingering one." Fried at vii–viii.
6. For an insightful analysis of the notion and history of fellow travelers, see David Caute, The Fellow-Travellers: Intellectual Friends of Communism (Yale University Press, rev. ed., 1988 [1973]). For McCarthyism's impact on Hollywood, see Victor S. Navasky, Naming Names (Viking, 1980).
7. Randy Shilts, Conduct Unbecoming: Gays and Lesbians in the U.S. Military (St. Martin's, 1993) at 105–9; David K. Johnson, The Lavender Scare: The Cold War Persecution of Gays and Lesbians in the Federal Government (University of Chicago Press, 2004).

8. DAVID CAUTE, THE GREAT FEAR: THE ANTI-COMMUNIST PURGE UNDER TRUMAN AND EISENHOWER (Simon and Schuster, 1978) [hereinafter THE GREAT FEAR] at 456–84.

9. Ellen Schrecker has examined McCarthyism in the academy. ELLEN W. SCHRECKER, NO IVORY TOWER: MCCARTHYISM AND THE UNIVERSITIES (Oxford University Press, 1986). For illuminating discussions of loyalty oaths in a broader context, see SANFORD LEVINSON, CONSTITUTIONAL FAITH (Princeton University Press, 1988) at 90–121; GEORGE P. FLETCHER, LOYALTY: AN ESSAY ON THE MORALITY OF RELATIONSHIPS (Oxford University Press, 1993) at 65–68.

10. THE GREAT FEAR at 224–60.

11. Contributing to the anxiety, in 1948 Czechoslovakia, "under . . . pressure . . . became a Soviet satellite," and the Soviet Union also blockaded Berlin. HEALE at 142.

12. FRIED at 89–90.

13. FRIED at 8.

14. FRIED at 88, 113, 116.

15. For a brief discussion of the creation of HUAC in 1938 and the anti-Nazi and anti-communist sentiment of the time, see FRIED at 46–50.

16. For the antecedents and background of the passage of the Smith Act in 1940, see MICHAL R. BELKNAP, COLD WAR POLITICAL JUSTICE: THE SMITH ACT, THE COMMUNIST PARTY, AND AMERICAN CIVIL LIBERTIES (Greenwood, 1977) [hereinafter cited as BELKNAP] at 19–27.

17. BELKNAP at 35.

18. For a detailed discussion of the District Court trial of American Communist Party leaders, see BELKNAP at 77–116. The Communist Party leaders were indicted in 1948; the lengthy and politically fraught trial in U.S. district court took place in New York City in 1949.

19. ATHAN G. THEOHARIS AND JOHN STUART COX, THE BOSS: J. EDGAR HOOVER AND THE GREAT AMERICAN INQUISITION (Temple University Press, 1988) at 3–14 [hereinafter THEOHARIS AND COX]. The authors ask, "What facilitated this remarkable transformation of the FBI's role and of Hoover's power?" Their answer: "quite simply, . . . [his] successful promulgation of the belief that a strong FBI was needed to safeguard the nation's security from the threat of subversion at home." *Id.* at 6. "Hoover had acted to expand the FBI's investigative role, and in the process to obtain . . . authority to monitor dissident political movements and activists, even prior to U.S. involvement in World War II." *Id.* at 179. "By the end of World War II, . . . [Hoover] had established the [FBI's] dominance in the domestic intelligence field, in part by demonstrating his usefulness to [Roosevelt]." *Id.* at 199; *see* FRIED at 51. "Having also forged a covert alliance with conservatives in the media and Congress, he had . . . assured himself a degree of autonomy with which to pursue . . . [perceived threats] in the postwar era." THEOHARIS AND COX at 199.

20. Information in government files in Moscow and also Budapest, only available to Western scholars after the collapse of the Soviet Union, seem to indicate that Hiss was a spy for the Soviet Union. Sam Tanenhaus, *The Red Scare*, N.Y. REV. BOOKS, January 14, 1999. Tanenhaus wrote, "Hiss's close friend, . . . Noel Field, . . . identified Hiss as his accomplice in a statement long held in Budapest files and made public in 1993." "More recently," Tanenhaus added, "Soviet intelligence files have also identified Hiss as a Soviet agent." *Id.*

21. *See* THE GREAT FEAR at 62–69; RICHARD GID POWERS, SECRECY AND POWER: THE LIFE OF J. EDGAR HOOVER (Free Press, 1987) at 301–5.

22. 341 U.S. 494.
23. Justice Clark, who had served as attorney general when the *Dennis* prosecutions were initiated, did not participate in the decision. Only Justices Black and Douglas dissented. Justices Frankfurter and Jackson each wrote separate opinions concurring with the decision of the court.
24. 249 U.S. 47.
25. 249 U.S. at 52.
26. *Abrams v. United States*, 250 U.S. 616 (1919); *Schaefer v. United States*, 251 U.S. 466 (1920); *Pierce v. United States*, 252 U.S. 239 (1920); *Gitlow v. New York*, 268 U.S. 652 (1925); *Whitney v. California*, 274 U.S. 357 (1927) (technically a concurrence but dissenting on the issue of free speech).
27. Justice Holmes, in his *Abrams* dissent, in which Justice Brandeis concurred, famously stated that "when men have realized that time has upset many fighting faiths, they may come to believe even more than they believe the very foundations of their own conduct that the ultimate good desired is better reached by free trade in ideas—that the best test of truth is the power of the thought to get itself accepted in the competition of the market, and that truth is the only ground upon which their wishes safely can be carried out. That at any rate is the theory of our Constitution. . . . I think that we should be eternally vigilant against attempts to check the expression of opinions that we loathe and believe to be fraught with death, unless they so imminently threaten immediate interference with the lawful and pressing purposes of the law that an immediate check is required to save the country." 250 U.S. at 630.
    Justice Brandeis, as famously, in his *Whitney* concurrence eloquently defended free speech, with more of a focus on democratic citizenship: "Those who won our independence . . . believed that freedom to think as you will and to speak as you think are means indispensable to the discovery and spread of political truth; that without free speech and assembly discussion would be futile; that with them, discussion affords . . . adequate protection against the dissemination of noxious doctrine; that the greatest menace to freedom is an inert people; that public discussion is a political duty. . . . Believing in the power of reason as applied through public discussion, they eschewed silence coerced by law. . . . Recognizing the occasional tyrannies of governing majorities, they amended the Constitution so that free speech and assembly . . . functions essential to effective democracy . . . should be guaranteed. . . . Fear of serious injury cannot alone justify suppression of free speech and assembly. Men feared witches and burnt women. It is the function of speech to free men from the bondage of irrational fears. To justify suppression of free speech, there must be reasonable ground to fear that serious evil will result . . . [and that] the danger . . . is imminent. . . . If there be time to expose through discussion the falsehood and fallacies, to avert the evil by the processes of education, the remedy to be applied is more speech, not enforced silence." 274 U.S. at 375–77. Justice Holmes joined Brandeis's *Whitney* concurrence.
28. PAUL L. MURPHY, THE CONSTITUTION IN CRISIS TIMES, 1918–1969 (Harper & Row, 1972) [hereinafter MURPHY] at 180–83, 191–93, 197–201, 264, 266.
29. Chief Justice Vinson, writing for himself and three other justices (Reed, Burton, and Minton) in *Dennis*, indicated approval for the clear and present danger test advocated by Holmes and Brandeis, noting that "there is little doubt that" cases after *Gitlow* and *Whitney*, although not expressly overruling those decisions, "have

inclined toward the Holmes-Brandeis rationale." He continued: "In this case we are squarely presented with the application of the 'clear and present danger' test." Vinson then began to backtrack famously: "Obviously, the words cannot mean that before the government may act, it must wait until the *putsch* is about to be executed." He then set forth the balancing test enunciated by Judge Learned Hand in deciding the *Dennis* case in the court of appeals below: "'in each case [courts] must ask whether the gravity of the "evil," discounted by its improbability, justifies such invasion of free speech as is necessary to avoid the danger.'" Vinson then declared, "We adopt this statement of the rule." 341 U.S. at 506–10.

30. 341 U.S. at 526–27.
31. 341 U.S. at 524–25, 542–43.
32. 341 U.S. at 539–40.
33. 341 U.S. at 525–26.
34. 354 U.S. 298 (1957).
35. Other significant cases handed down by the court on Red Monday, June 17, 1957, were *Watkins v. United States*, 354 U.S. 178, and *Sweezy v. New Hampshire*, 354 U.S. 234.
36. Harlan stated, "We are thus faced with the question whether the Smith Act prohibits advocacy and teaching of forcible overthrow as an abstract principle, divorced from any effort to instigate action to that end, so long as the advocacy or teaching is engaged in with evil intent. We hold that it does not." He continued, insisting that there was a "distinction between advocacy of abstract doctrine and advocacy directed at promoting unlawful action." 354 U.S. at 318. Later in his opinion for the court, he did admit that "distinctions between advocacy or teaching of abstract doctrines . . . and that which is directed to stirring people to action, are often subtle and difficult to grasp." *Id.* at 326. Justice Clark, in dissent, correctly pointed out that Harlan's reasoning in *Yates* was inconsistent with *Dennis*. 354 U.S. at 349–50. Harlan sought, it would seem, to eviscerate *Dennis* without formally overruling it.
37. 354 U.S. 178 (1957).
38. 354 U.S. 234 (1957).
39. Murphy at 294.
40. Playwright Lillian Hellman's 1952 letter to the chairman of HUAC is instructive. "I am most willing to answer all questions about myself," began Hellman, "But I am advised by counsel that if I answer the committee's questions about myself, I must also answer questions about other people and that if I refuse to do so, I can be cited for contempt. My counsel tells me that if I answer questions about myself, I will have waived my rights under the Fifth Amendment and could be forced legally to answer questions about others. This is very difficult for a layman to understand. But there is one principle that I do understand: I am not willing . . . to bring bad trouble to people who, in my past association with them, were completely innocent of any talk or any action that was disloyal or subversive. . . . [T]o hurt innocent people . . . to save myself is, to me, inhuman and indecent and dishonorable. I cannot and will not cut my conscience to fit this year's fashions." Lillian Hellman to Representative John Stephens Wood, chairman of HUAC, May 19, 1952, in Ellen Schrecker, The Age of McCarthyism: A Brief History with Documents (St. Martin's, 1994) at 201–2.
41. Ronald L. Goldfarb, The Contempt Power (Columbia University Press, 1963) at 196–97. For more detail and statistics, see Carl Beck, Contempt of

CONGRESS: A STUDY OF THE PROSECUTIONS INITIATED BY THE COMMITTEE ON UN-AMERICAN ACTIVITIES, 1945–1957 (Hauser, 1959).

42. For a lengthy and enlightening excerpt of the HUAC testimony of the author of *The Crucible* and *Death of a Salesman*, see THIRTY YEARS OF TREASON: EXCERPTS FROM HEARINGS BEFORE THE HOUSE COMMITTEE ON UN-AMERICAN ACTIVITIES, 1938–1968 (Eric Bentley ed.; Thunder's Mouth, 2002) (1971) at 791–825. Miller testified that "my conscience will not permit me to use the name of another person" and that "my counsel advises me that there is no relevance" to this question. *Id.* at 822. "I am not protecting . . . Communists. . . . I am trying to . . . protect my sense of myself. I could not use the name of another person and bring trouble on him. . . . I will tell you anything about myself." *Id.* at 820. Contrast Miller's refusal to name names with the testimony of the director of *On the Waterfront* and other well-known films and Broadway successes, Elia Kazan. *Id.* at 484–96.

43. 354 U.S. at 201–6.

44. 354 U.S. at 200.

45. 354 U.S. at 187–88, 195–98.

46. 354 U.S. at 198, 200–202.

47. 354 U.S. at 206–8.

48. 354 U.S. at 214–15.

49. 354 U.S. at 216.

50. DEL DICKSON, SUPREME COURT IN CONFERENCE (1940–1985): THE PRIVATE DISCUSSIONS BEHIND NEARLY 300 SUPREME COURT DECISIONS (Oxford University Press, 2001) at 299.

51. BERNARD SCHWARTZ, SUPER CHIEF: EARL WARREN AND HIS SUPREME COURT, A JUDICIAL BIOGRAPHY (New York University Press, 1983) [hereinafter cited as SUPER CHIEF] at 239 (quoting from Frankfurter's April 23, 1958, letter to Harlan).

52. 354 U.S. at 258–59.

53. 354 U.S. at 261–67.

54. 353 U.S. 252.

55. 366 U.S. 36.

56. 350 U.S. 551, 565 (Harlan, J., dissenting). Reed's separate dissent was joined by Burton and Minton.

57. 350 U.S. at 557.

58. 350 U.S. at 566.

59. 350 U.S. at 566.

60. 357 U.S. 468 at 476.

61. *Beilan v. Board of Public Education*, 357 U.S. 399, 405–6 (1958).

62. *Scales v. United States*, 367 U.S. 203, 209 (1961).

63. 367 U.S. 290 (1961).

64. 367 U.S. at 296–300.

65. 367 U.S. 203 (1961).

66. 367 US at 250.

67. 367 U.S. at 209.

68. TINSLEY E. YARBROUGH, JOHN MARSHALL HARLAN: GREAT DISSENTER OF THE WARREN COURT (Oxford University Press, 1992) at 196–97.

69. 367 U.S. 1 (1961).

70. 367 U.S. at 81.

71. 360 U.S. 109.

72. 360 U.S. at 116–17.
73. 360 U.S. at 123–24.
74. Harlan conceded "that the memorandum which [Barenblatt] brought ... to the Subcommittee hearing contained the statement ... 'I might wish to challenge the pertinency'" and that Barenblatt also quoted from an earlier Supreme Court opinion "language relating to a witness' right to be informed of the pertinency of questions asked." But Harlan unhesitatingly brushed this aside: "These statements cannot ... be accepted as the equivalent of a pertinency objection." 360 U.S. at 123–24.
75. *Watkins*, 354 U.S. at 206–9.
76. 360 U.S. at 126–34, 138.
77. 360 U.S. at 144. Black correctly added that "the obloquy which results from investigations such as this not only stifles 'mistakes' but prevents all but the most courageous from hazarding any views which might at some later time become disfavored." *Id.*
78. 360 U.S. at 144.
79. 360 U.S. at 139.
80. 360 U.S. at 128.
81. *See* 360 U.S. at 125.
82. 360 U.S. 72 (1959).
83. 360 U.S. at 81.
84. 360 U.S. at 77.
85. 360 U.S. at 82. Brennan wrote that "it is quite clear that exposure was the very core, and deliberately and purposefully so, of [this] legislative investigation." *Id.* at 98–99.
86. 360 U.S. at 90–92.
87. GERALD GUNTHER, LEARNED HAND: THE MAN AND THE JUDGE (2nd ed., Oxford University Press, 2011) (1994) at 568–70.
88. ROBERT A. CARO, THE YEARS OF LYNDON JOHNSON: MASTER OF THE SENATE (Knopf, 2002) at 1030–33.
89. GUNTHER at 570.
90. 367 U.S. 1 (1961).
91. *Albertson v. Subversive Activities Control Board*, 382 U.S. 70 (1965).
92. *Aptheker v. Secretary of State*, 378 U.S. 500 (1964).
93. 389 U.S. at 258.
94. 389 U.S. at 262.
95. 372 U.S. at 539.
96. 371 U.S. at 415.
97. SUPER CHIEF at 452–53.
98. SUPER CHIEF at 448 (quoting Frankfurter letter to Alexander Bickel); SUPREME COURT IN CONFERENCE at 317–20.
99. 395 U.S. at 444.
100. 395 U.S. at 444–45.
101. 274 U.S. at 357.
102. *Brandenburg* at 447 (quoting *Whitney*).
103. Nevertheless, on procedural grounds they concurred in the judgment.
104. 395 U.S. at 447, 449.
105. 395 U.S. at 447.

CHAPTER 4

1. *See* BERNARD SCHWARTZ, SUPER CHIEF: EARL WARREN AND HIS SUPREME COURT, A JUDICIAL BIOGRAPHY (New York University Press, 1983) [hereinafter cited as SUPER CHIEF] at 302–3; THE DOUGLAS LETTERS: SELECTIONS FROM THE PRIVATE PAPERS OF JUSTICE WILLIAM O. DOUGLAS (Melvin Urofsky ed., Adler & Adler, 1987) at 168. For examples of the long-standing hostility between Frankfurter and Douglas, see UROFSKY, THE DOUGLAS LETTERS, at 85, 90.
2. *See* SUPER CHIEF at 332–33.
3. On June 17, 1957, Red Monday, the court handed down three important decisions restricting governmental anticommunist witch hunts: *Watkins v. United States*, 354 U.S. 178 (1957); *Sweezy v. New Hampshire*, 354 U.S. 234 (1957); and *Yates v. United States*, 354 U.S. 298 (1957).
4. American Bar Association Special Committee to Study Communist Tactics, Strategy and Objectives, Report submitted by the Committee and its chairman Herbert R. O'Conor at the annual meeting of the American Bar Association in London during July of 1957, reprinted as *The Impact of the 1957 Supreme Court Decisions on Communism*, *in* A GUIDE TO ANTI-COMMUNIST ACTION 129 (Anthony Trawick Bouscaren ed., Literary Licensing, LLC, 1958). *See* Norbert C. Brockman, *The History of the American Bar Association: A Bibliographic Essay*, 6 AM. J. OF LEGAL HIST. 269, 282–84 (1962).
5. American Bar Association Special Committee on Communism report, reprinted in A GUIDE TO ANTI-COMMUNIST ACTION, *supra*, at 126. The report also noted: "In the last 15 months the United States Supreme Court has decided 15 cases which directly affect the right of the United States of America to protect itself from Communist subversion." *Id.* at 115.
6. On July 8, 1957, Senator William E. Jenner introduced his court-curbing bill "to limit the appellate jurisdiction of the Supreme Court in certain cases." *See* Sheldon D. Elliott, *Court-Curbing Proposals in Congress*, 33 NOTRE DAME L. REV. 597, 600 (1958). For a general discussion of Congress's power to carve out exceptions to the Supreme Court's appellate jurisdiction, see Gerald Gunther, *Congressional Power to Curtail Federal Court Jurisdiction: An Opinionated Guide to the Ongoing Debate*, 36 STAN. L. REV. 895 (1984).
7. ROBERT A. CARO, MASTER OF THE SENATE: THE YEARS OF LYNDON JOHNSON (Vintage, 2003) at 1030–33.
8. In 1868 the Reconstruction Congress, still in a rage over *Dred Scott* and "clearly worried that the Court would invalidate the post–Civil War Reconstruction Acts," restricted the jurisdiction of the Supreme Court. Gunther, *Congressional Power to Curtail Federal Court Jurisdiction*, *supra* at 904–5. And the court itself upheld Congress's 1868 curbing of its jurisdiction in *Ex parte McCardle*, 74 U.S. 506 (1869).
9. Felix Frankfurter, September 30, 1957, Memorandum for the Conference, FELIX FRANKFURTER PAPERS, Harvard Law School (microfilm, Part II, reel 36), folder: 001756-035-0836, at 38–45.
10. Felix Frankfurter, October 7, 1957, Memorandum for the Conference, FELIX FRANKFURTER PAPERS, Harvard Law School (microfilm, Part II, reel 36), folder: 001756-035-0836, at 57. *See* SUPER CHIEF at 262.
11. *See* note 23 *infra*.
12. *Cooper v. Aaron*, 358 U.S. 1 (1958).

13. SUPER CHIEF at 300; TINSLEY E. YARBROUGH, JOHN MARSHALL HARLAN: GREAT DISSENTER OF THE WARREN COURT (Oxford University Press, 1992) at 171.

14. SUPER CHIEF at 299.

15. SUPER CHIEF at 295.

16. William O. Douglas, Memorandum for the Files, October 8, 1958, reprinted in THE DOUGLAS LETTERS at 167–68. See SUPER CHIEF at 302.

17. SUPER CHIEF at 302.

18. SUPER CHIEF at 302 (quoting Burton's diary).

19. SUPER CHIEF at 302 (quoting from WARREN, MEMOIRS).

20. SUPER CHIEF at 302.

21. The DOUGLAS LETTERS at 168.

22. SUPER CHIEF at 302.

23. Bernard Schwartz offers a catalog of public exchanges between Warren and Frankfurter from 1957 to 1961 that show unmistakably that bad feelings had grown between them. SUPER CHIEF at 252–79. One justice is quoted pointing to an incident on June 30, 1958, that constituted "the final break" between them. SUPER CHIEF at 254. Three months later amid efforts to persuade Frankfurter not to publish a separate opinion in *Cooper v. Aaron*, Schwartz notes that Warren's "relations with Frankfurter had become too touchy for Warren personally to influence the Justice not to issue the opinion. But the Chief did ask others to talk to Frankfurter." *Id.* at 302. The "final break" may have occurred in September when Warren felt betrayed by Frankfurter's decision to write a separate opinion in *Cooper v. Aaron*. While the tipping point in Frankfurter's deteriorating relationship with the chief justice can be more or less placed between June and October 1958, the starting point is more difficult to identify. We do know that Frankfurter's opinion in *Rice v. Sioux City Memorial Cemetery*, 349 U.S. 70 (1955), deeply offended the chief justice. In that opinion, Frankfurter dismissed on a technicality a lawsuit that challenged the cemetery's policy of refusing to bury Native Americans. One can observe a radical change in Warren's votes between the year and half before and the year and a half after *Rice v. Sioux City* was decided. "Before the 1954 Christmas break, Warren agreed with Frankfurter in two thirds of the cases in which Frankfurter and Black disagreed as to result. However, after the justice returned from vacation, Warren would only vote with Frankfurter over Black in one case for the remainder of the 1954 term.... In the next nine cases in which the two justices disagreed, Warren preferred the same result as Black." Moreover, the pro-Black trend continued into the 1955 term in which Warren agreed with Black 86 percent of the time and with Frankfurter in only 56 percent of the cases despite an unusually high level of agreement among the justices. Finally, during the next eight terms—until Justice Black himself shifted—Warren voted with Frankfurter only twice when Frankfurter and Black disagreed. "In the other thirty-two cases involving disagreement between Frankfurter and Black, or 94 percent of the time, Warren voted with Black." Tim Smith, "The Jurisprudential Transformation of Earl Warren" 11–12 (2006) (unpublished L.L.M. thesis, Harvard Law School).

24. Frankfurter, September 12, 1958, letter to Harlan, HARLAN PAPERS, box 486.

25. Felix Frankfurter, August 27, 1958, Memorandum, FELIX FRANKFURTER PAPERS, HARVARD LAW SCHOOL (part II, reel 36), folder: 001756-036-0001, pp. 505–8. See SUPER CHIEF at 294–95.

26. SUPER CHIEF at 291 (quoting Justice Frankfurter).

27. Felix Frankfurter, August 27, 1958, cover letter with enclosed memorandum, FELIX FRANKFURTER PAPERS, HARVARD LAW SCHOOL (microfilm, part II, reel 36), folder: 001756-0036-0001, p. 500.

28. SUPER CHIEF at 289–92.

29. Frankfurter, September 12, 1958, letter to Harlan, HARLAN PAPERS, box 486.

30. Quoted in JAMES F. SIMON, THE ANTAGONISTS: HUGO BLACK, FELIX FRANKFURTER AND CIVIL LIBERTIES IN MODERN AMERICA (Schuster, 1989) at 238.

31. *Bartkus v. Illinois*, 359 U.S. 121 (1959).

32. Chief Justice John Marshall, writing for a unanimous Court in *Barron v. Baltimore*, 32 U.S. 243 (1833), confirmed this view.

33. *Slaughterhouse Cases*, 83 U.S. 36 (1873).

34. *Chambers v. Florida*, 309 U.S. 227 (1940).

35. *Id.* at n.8.

36. *Adamson v. California*, 332 U.S. 46 (1947).

37. Justice Reed wrote the opinion for the court, which was joined by three justices. Frankfurter, making the fifth vote, wrote a lengthy concurrence, which became the intellectual undergirding for the anti-incorporation position.

38. *See* Felix Frankfurter, *Memorandum On "Incorporation" of the Bill of Rights into the Due Process Clause of the Fourteenth Amendment*, 78 HARV. L. REV. 746, 752 (1965), quoting *Louisville & Nashville R. Co. v. Schmidt*, 177 U.S. 230 (1900) at 236; *Hooker v. Los Angeles*, 188 U.S. 314, 318 (1903) at 318; *Rogers v. Peck*, 199 U.S. 425 (1905) at 435.

39. Frankfurter, *Memorandum*, at 751–53, quoting *Holden v. Hardy*, 169 U.S. 366 (1898) at 389; *Snyder v. Massachusetts*, 291 U.S. 97 (1934) at 105.

40. *E.g.*, *Hurtado v. California*, 110 U.S. 516 (1884); *Maxwell v. Dow*, 176 U.S. 581 (1900).

41. *E.g.*, *Betts v. Brady*, 316 U.S. 455 (1942) (right to counsel); *Twining v. New Jersey*, 211 U.S. 78 (1908) (self- incrimination); *Palko v. Connecticut*, 302 U.S. 319 (1937) (double jeopardy); *Weeks v. United States*, 232 U.S. 383 (1914) [and *Wolf v. Colorado*, 338 U.S. 25 (1949)] (search and seizure); *In re* Kemmler, 136 U.S. 436 (1890) (cruel and unusual punishments).

42. 302 U.S. 319 (1937).

43. *Chicago, Burlington & Quincy R'wy Co. v. Chicago*, 166 U.S. 226 (1897).

44. *Gitlow v. New York*, 268 U.S. 652 (1925).

45. *Id.* at 666 ("For present purposes we may and do assume that freedom of speech and of the press—which are protected by the First Amendment from abridgment by Congress—are among the fundamental personal rights and 'liberties' protected by the Due Process Clause of the Fourteenth Amendment from impairment by the States.").

46. *Id.* at 71. *Powell* as well as *Norris v. Alabama*, 294 U.S. 587 (1935), in which the court overturned convictions due to racially discriminatory jury selection, concerned the death sentences of the Scottsboro defendants. In 1936 in *Brown v. Mississippi*, 297 U.S. 278 (1936), the court, on due process grounds, overturned convictions for murder and death sentences when confessions were obtained through brutal whippings. For an excellent discussion of these three cases as well as *Moore v. Dempsey*, see Michael J. Klarman, *The Racial Origins of Modern Criminal Procedure*, 99 MICH. L. REV. 48 (2000). For an insightful Rashomon-like book on the Scottsboro defendants, see JAMES GOODMAN, STORIES OF SCOTTSBORO (Vintage Books 1995).

47. Indeed, language of the court in *Powell*, albeit not the holding, recognized the importance of counsel in criminal cases: "Even the intelligent and educated layman has small and sometimes no skill in the science of law. . . . He is unfamiliar with the rules of evidence. . . . He lacks both the skill and knowledge adequately to prepare his defense, even though he has a perfect one. He requires the guiding hand of counsel at every step in the proceedings against him. Without it, though he be not guilty, he faces the danger of conviction." *Powell* at 69.

48. 316 U.S. 455 (1942).

49. Black, Douglas, and Murphy dissented. The court, in an opinion delivered by Justice Roberts, expressly rejected Black's incorporation argument: "The Due Process Clause of the Fourteenth Amendment does not incorporate, as such, the specific guarantees found in the Sixth Amendment." *Id.* at 461–62. Roberts's opinion is one of many supporting the Frankfurter side that misreads Black's position. Frankfurter (and Roberts) thought that the only relevant question about incorporation was whether the Bill of Rights was incorporated into the Due Process Clause. In fact, Black based his argument for incorporation on the "whole" of the Fourteenth Amendment, including the long-ignored privileges and immunities clause. Black's broader claim seems more historically supportable than the due process argument standing alone.

50. 338 U.S. 25 (1949).

51. Justice Black concurred but in a manner that was consistent with his incorporation theory. Douglas, Murphy, and Rutledge dissented.

52. *Wolf* at 2

53. 359 U.S. 121 (1959).

54. *Bartkus* was reargued on October 21–22, 1958.

55. *Bartkus v. Illinois*, 355 U.S. 281 (1958) (January 6, 1958); SUPER CHIEF at 322.

56. *Bartkus v. Illinois*, 356 U.S. 969 (1958) (May 26, 1958).

57. *See* SUPER CHIEF at 322–23.

58. See footnote 73.

59. *Id.*

60. SUPER CHIEF at 324.

61. Roger K. Newman, *The Warren Court and American Politics: An Impressionistic Appreciation* 18 CONST. COMMENT. 661 (2001) at 665–66.

62. Clark had circulated a draft concurring opinion. See Memorandum by Justice Frankfurter in reply to the draft Concurring Opinion circulated by Justice Clark, FELIX FRANKFURTER PAPERS, HARVARD LAW SCHOOL (microfilm, part II, reel 36), folder: 001756-036-0509, pp. 44–47.

63. Tom Clark, February 4, 1959, letter to Frankfurter. FELIX FRANKFURTER PAPERS, HARVARD LAW SCHOOL (microfilm, part II, reel 36), folder: 001756-036-0509, pp. 286–90. In concluding this five-page letter to Frankfurter, Justice Clark reiterated his viewpoint: "in short, I would like to see the opinion leave out the incorporation discussion." *Id.*

64. Felix Frankfurter, February 24, 1959, letter to Tom Clark, FELIX FRANKFURTER PAPERS, HARVARD LAW SCHOOL (microfilm, part II, reel 36), folder: 001756-036-0509, pp. 177–78.

65. *Id.*

66. *Id.*

67. Tom Clark, February 24 letter to Felix Frankfurter, FELIX FRANKFURTER PAPERS, HARVARD LAW SCHOOL (microfilm, reel 36), folder: 001756-036-0509, pp. 175–76.

68. *Elkins v. United States*, 364 U.S. 206.
69. 364 U.S. at 217.
70. *Mapp v. Ohio*, 367 U.S. 643 (1961).
71. Frankfurter's *Bartkus* Appendix is set forth in 359 U.S. at 140–49.
72. Roger K. Newman, *The Warren Court and American Politics: An Impressionistic Appreciation* 18 CONST. COMMENT. 661 (2001) at 665–66.
73. Unprepared to endorse Black's incorporation of the double jeopardy clause, Brennan found enough evidence to conclude that after the first federal trial at which Bartkus was acquitted, the federal prosecutors actually assisted the state authorities in retrying Bartkus, thus effectively violating the existing Fifth Amendment bar on double jeopardy in the federal system. FELIX FRANKFURTER PAPERS, HARVARD LAW SCHOOL (microfilm, reel 36), folder: 001756-036-0509, pp. 341–42
74. SUPER CHIEF at 323.
75. YARBROUGH at 128 quoting Frankfurter's January 12, 1960, letter to Justice Harlan.
76. Felix Frankfurter, *Memorandum on "Incorporation" of the Bill of Rights Into the Due Process Clause of the Fourteenth Amendment*, 78 HARV. L. REV. 746 (1965).
77. Frankfurter, *Memorandum on "Incorporation,"* at 746.
78. *Staub v. City of Baxley*, 355 U.S. 313 (1958).
79. *E.g., Murdock v. Pennsylvania*, 319 U.S. 105 (1943); *Schneider v. State*, 308 U.S. 147 (1939); *Lovell v. City of Griffin*, 303 U.S. 444 (1938). *See also Douglas v. City of Jeannette*, 319 U.S. 157 (1943), a companion case of *Murdock* in which Chief Justice Stone, writing for the court in an opinion concerning Jehovah's Witnesses, stated, "We have repeatedly held that the Fourteenth Amendment has made applicable to the states the guaranties of the First. . . . Allegations of fact sufficient to show deprivation of the right of free speech under the First Amendment are sufficient to establish deprivation of a constitutional right guaranteed by the Fourteenth." *Id.* at 162.
80. *See* Charles Whittaker, December 12, 1957, letter to William Brennan, JOHN HARLAN PAPERS, Princeton University, box 486.
81. Felix Frankfurter, December 9, 1957, letter to Charles Whittaker, JOHN HARLAN PAPERS, Princeton University, box 610.
82. Charles Whittaker, December 12, 1957, letter to William Brennan, JOHN HARLAN PAPERS, Princeton University, box 486.
83. Felix Frankfurter, January 6, 1958, letter to Charles Whittaker, JOHN HARLAN PAPERS, Princeton University, box 610.
84. *Id.*
85. An exception may be *Beauharnais v. Illinois*, 343 U.S. 250 (1952) in which Frankfurter voted to uphold a state statute punishing hate crimes while implying he would not uphold an identical federal statute.
86. Felix Frankfurter, *Mr. Justice Brandeis and the Constitution*, 45 HARV. L. REV. 33 (1931) at 87–92; Felix Frankfurter, *Mr. Justice Holmes and the Constitution*, 41 HARV. L. REV. 121 (1927) at 138–40.
87. 302 U.S. 319 at 324–25.
88. *Palko* at 326–27. Cardozo's important role in securing freedom of expression against state infringement has not been appreciated, especially when after *Adamson* the *Palko* precedent became identified with Frankfurter's efforts to buttress his anti-incorporation position.
89. 355 U.S. 313 (1958). Frankfurter was joined in dissent only by Justice Clark.

90. *NAACP v. Alabama*, 357 U.S. 449 (1958) (decided June 30, 1958). *Staub* was decided, with Frankfurter and Clark dissenting, on January 13, 1958.
91. See, *infra*, chapter 6.
92. The modern reader might be surprised by the length and repetitiveness of Harlan's discussion of "direct" versus "indirect" restraints on freedom of speech. This distinction, once a central doctrinal category for analyzing speech cases, has become much less prominent in constitutional discourse. See HARRY KALVEN JR., A WORTHY TRADITION (Jamie Kalven, ed., Harper & Row, 1988) at 188–89, 197 (discussing Chief Justice Vinson's opinions for the court in *American Communications Assn. v. Douds*, 339 U.S. 382 (1950) and *Dennis v. United States*, 341 U.S. 494 (1951).
93. Justice Harlan's draft opinion of April 22, 1958, which was circulated with his Memorandum for the Conference of the same date. JOHN HARLAN PAPERS, box 46.
94. *Roth v. United States*, 354 U.S. 476 (1957).
95. See Harlan's later opinion for the court in *Cohen v. California*, 403 U.S. 15 (1971), in which he makes no distinction as to the reach of the First Amendment except in cases of obscenity and "fighting words," which overlapped with the states' police powers. See *Cohen* at 18, 19, 20, 23, and 26. Harlan's opinions in two obscenity cases, *Jacobellis v. Ohio* and *Smith v. California*, are also consistent with this analysis. See *Jacobellis v. Ohio*, 378 U.S. 184, 203–4 (1964) (Harlan dissenting) and *Smith v. California*, 361 U.S. 147, 169–70 (1959) (concurring in part, dissenting in part). But see *Memoirs*, another obscenity case, in which Harlan's dissent is only arguably consistent. *A Book Named "John Cleland's Memoirs of a Woman of Pleasure" v. Attorney General of Massachusetts*, 383 U.S. 413, 455–60 (1966) (Harlan dissenting).
96. Felix Frankfurter April 23, 1958, letter to John Harlan. JOHN HARLAN PAPERS, box 46. As Harlan's biographer observed, "Frankfurter was alert to even the slightest deviation from the anti-incorporationist faith." YARBROUGH at 125.
97. Frankfurter April 23, 1958, letter to John Harlan. JOHN HARLAN PAPERS, box 46.
98. Frankfurter, April 24, 1958, letter to John Harlan, JOHN HARLAN PAPERS, box 46.
99. YARBROUGH at 125–26 quoting Frankfurter, April 24, 1958, letter to John Harlan.
100. *See* Harlan, May 2, 1958, draft *NAACP v. Alabama* opinion, JOHN HARLAN PAPERS, box 46.
101. Hugo Black, May 2, 1958, letter to John Harlan, JOHN HARLAN PAPERS, box 46.
102. *Id.*
103. *Id.*
104. 357 U.S. at 460.
105. The exception was the American Civil Liberties Union amicus curiae brief that included a boilerplate request but no argumentation for reconsideration of *Wolf.*
106. SUPER CHIEF at 393.
107. SUPER CHIEF at 398.
108. SUPER CHIEF at 396.
109. SUPER CHIEF at 397.
110. SUPER CHIEF at 398.
111. SUPER CHIEF at 398.
112. *Duncan v. Louisiana*, 391 U.S. 145 (1968).
113. 391 U.S. 145 at 148.
114. 391 U.S. 145 at 148.
115. 391 U.S. 145 at 148.

116. *Robinson v. California*, 370 U.S. 660 (1962).
117. *Gideon v. Wainwright*, 372 U.S. 335 (1963).
118. *Ker v. California*, 374 U.S. 23 (1963).
119. 374 U.S. 23 at 30.
120. Ker at 44–45.
121. Ohio *ex rel.* Eaton v. Price, 364 U.S. 263 (1960).
122. *Adamson*, 332 U.S. 46, 66 (1947).
123. 302 U.S. 319 at 325.
124. Louisiana *ex rel.* Francis v. Resweber, 329 U.S. 459, 468. In the conference on this case, Frankfurter could only have heightened Black's concern expressed in his *Adamson* dissent that Frankfurter's approach to due process was entirely subjective when he declared that he found no due process violation because "it is not so offensive as to make me puke." DEL DICKSON, SUPREME COURT IN CONFERENCE (1940–1985): THE PRIVATE DISCUSSIONS BEHIND NEARLY 300 SUPREME COURT DECISIONS (Oxford University Press, 2001) at 604.
125. *Oliver v. U.S.*, 333 U.S. 257, 280 (1948).
126. *Malloy v. Hogan*, 378 U.S. 1 (1964).
127. Ohio *ex rel.* Eaton, 364 U.S. at 275 (1960). In this case, a 4–4 vote resulted in affirming the lower court decision from which Brennan dissented.
128. 391 U.S. 149 n.14.
129. As the Warren Court ended, "the provisions that were never incorporated are: the Eighth Amendment protection from excessive fines and bail; the Fifth Amendment grand jury requirement and the Seventh Amendment guarantee of a jury trial in many civil cases, . . . the Second Amendment right to bear arms; and Third Amendment [barring quartering of troops]." Stephen J. Wermiel, *Rights in the Modern Era: Applying the Bill of Rights to the States*, 1 WM. & MARY BILL OF RTS. J. 121, 129 (1992). *But see McDonald v. Chicago*, 561 U.S. 3225 (2010) (incorporating the Second Amendment's right to bear arms); *Timbs v. Indiana*, 586 U.S. __ (2019 [barring excessive bail]).
130. *Apodaca v. Oregon*, 406 U.S. 404 (1972).
131. In *Williams v. Florida* 399 U.S. 78 (1970), the court held that a six-person criminal jury was constitutional. In *Ballew v. Georgia* 435 U.S. 223 (1978), it held a five-person jury unconstitutional.
132. *Ramos v. Louisiana*, 590 U.S. ___, 140 S.Ct. 1390 (2020).
133. 391 U.S. 145 at 171.

CHAPTER 5

1. 369 U.S. 186 (1962).
2. *Id.* at 191.
3. "40% of the voters elect 63 of the 99 members of the House." 369 U.S. at 253 (Clark, J., concurring).
4. ROBERT B. McKAY, REAPPORTIONMENT: THE LAW AND POLITICS OF EQUAL REPRESENTATION (Twentieth Century Fund 1965) [hereinafter McKAY] at 46–47. In the California State Senate, as of 1962, Los Angeles's population of over 6 million was represented by one state senator, as were the fewer than 15,000 inhabitants of the smallest district in the state. Gordon E. Baker, *The California Senate*, in THE POLITICS OF REAPPORTIONMENT (Malcolm E. Jewell, ed., Atherton, 1962)

at 51. The vote of one citizen in the smallest district thus counted more than the votes of 400 residents of Los Angeles.

5. *See Baker v. Carr*, Brief of the United States as Amicus Curiae, 54–55, in LANDMARK BRIEFS AND ARGUMENTS OF THE SUPREME COURT OF THE UNITED STATES (Philip B. Kurland and Gerhard Casper eds., University Publications of America, 1975), vol. 56 at 332–33; GORDON E. BAKER, RURAL VERSUS URBAN POLITICAL POWER: THE NATURE AND CONSEQUENCES OF UNBALANCED REPRESENTATION (Random House, 1955) at 27–39.

6. 367 U.S. 643 (1961).

7. 338 U.S. 25 (1949).

8. DEL DICKSON, THE SUPREME COURT IN CONFERENCE (Oxford University Press, 2001) at 851.

9. 328 U.S. 549 (1946) at 552.

10. *Id.* at 556.

11. *Learned Hand, Chief Justice Stone's Concept of the Judicial Function* (1946) in THE SPIRIT OF LIBERTY: PAPERS AND ADDRESSES OF LEARNED HAND (Irving Dillard, ed., 3rd ed., Knopf, 1960) at 206. For a discussion of Judge Hand's 1946 eulogy of Chief Justice Stone, see MORTON J. HORWITZ, TRANSFORMATION OF AMERICAN LAW II (Oxford University Press, 1992) at 261–64.

12. VICTOR S. NAVASKY, KENNEDY JUSTICE (Atheneum, 1971) at 301.

13. *Id.* at 302–3.

14. KEN GORMLEY, ARCHIBALD COX: CONSCIENCE OF A NATION (Addison-Wesley, 1997) at 169.

15. Roy Schotland wrote the account of *Baker v. Carr* in *Opinions of William J. Brennan, Jr., October Term, 1961 (law clerks, Roy A. Schotland and Frank I. Michelman) NOTES* [hereinafter cited as THE HISTORIES].

16. *Id.* at 1.

17. *Hartsfield v. Sloan*, 357 U.S. 916 (1958). In Schotland's words, in *Hartsfield* "the Chief Justice and Justices Black, Douglas, and Brennan noted their votes for Mayor Hartsfield's suit attacking the Georgia county unit system, a system seemingly upheld shortly after *Colegrove* had been decided." THE HISTORIES at 1. Schotland added, "There is no certainty that those four Justices would have voted to hear the first apportionment case that came along, because when *Baker v. Carr* did find its way to the Court in the 1960 Term, *Gomillion v. Lightfoot* . . . was already pending decision. . . . [T]he Conference voted . . . to hold *Baker* for the decision in *Gomillion.*" THE HISTORIES at 1.

18. THE HISTORIES at 1–2.

19. For a description of the pressure applied to Cox from within Robert Kennedy's Justice Department, See NAVASKY at 300–303.

20. SUPREME COURT IN CONFERENCE at 845, 846.

21. GORMLEY at 166.

22. NAVASKY at 299; GORMLEY at 497, n.21. Archibald Cox himself confirmed this: "In fact, the decision to authorize filing an *amicus* brief in *Baker v. Carr* had been made under Lee Rankin in the previous administration." ORAL INTERVIEW OF ARCHIBALD COX, interviewer Thomas Hilbink for the Supreme Court Historical Society project on the Office of the Solicitor General, Session #2, June 20, 2000, at 161. Rankin "had already signed off on the certiorari petition in *Baker* on behalf of the United States, although this piece of paper got lost in the shuffle

of the transition." GORMLEY at 497, n.21. Cox agreed with Gormley's account: "Somehow that bit of paper got forgotten with the passage of a couple of years and changes in personnel." COX, *id*. From the above, it seems highly unlikely that Navasky's statement that "Solicitor Rankin had notified the court of the Justice Department's intention to come in as *amicus*" (NAVASKY at 301) is accurate, although it seems clear that Rankin did sign off, authorizing filing an amicus brief in *Baker v. Carr*.

23. *See* NAVASKY at 299.

24. THE HISTORIES at 2, 3.

25. One might alternatively consider *Roth v. United States*, 354 U.S. 476 (1957), or *Cooper v. Aaron*, 358 U.S. 1 (1958), as Brennan's first major assignment.

26. Handwritten note from Justice Brennan to Justice Douglas, with Justice Douglas's handwritten response at the bottom of Justice Brennan's note, undated, Brennan Papers, Library of Congress.

27. THE HISTORIES at 4.

28. *Id.*

29. *Id.*, at 5.

30. *Id.*

31. *Id.*, at 5, 6.

32. *Id.*, at 7.

33. *Id.*, at 7.

34. Anthony Lewis, *In Memoriam: William J. Brennan, Jr.*, 111 HARV. L. REV. 29 (1997) at 34.

35. THE HISTORIES at 7.

36. *Id.*, at 6, 7, 8. Roy Schotland emphasized the importance of Warren's continuing support: "this is stated briefly," said Schotland, "but its importance was great." *Id.*, at 6. Warren had originally written as a Notre Dame football fan might have: "It is a great day for the Irish," but he crossed out "Irish" and substituted "country." BRENNAN PAPERS, handwritten undated note from Chief Justice Warren.

37. GORMLEY at 170 (quoting Archibald Cox).

38. SUPREME COURT IN CONFERENCE at 850.

39. GORMLEY at 169 (quoting Cox).

40. GORMLEY at 169.

41. *Colegrove v. Green*, 328 U.S. 549 (1946). Justice Frankfurter famously stated in *Colegrove* that "courts ought not to enter this political thicket." 328 U.S. at 556.

42. SUPREME COURT IN CONFERENCE at 847 (conference of October 13, 1961).

43. Chief Justice Stone died before a decision could be announced, and Justice Jackson was abroad serving as the chief American prosecutor at the Nuremberg trials.

44. The political prudence approach of Frankfurter, perhaps best articulated by his former law clerk and disciple Alexander Bickel, was critiqued in Gerald Gunther's book review of Bickel's *The Least Dangerous Branch*. Gerald Gunther, *The Subtle Vices of the "Passive Virtues": A Comment on Principle and Expediency in Judicial Review*, 64 COLUM. L. REV. 1 (1964) (reviewing ALEXANDER BICKEL, THE LEAST DANGEROUS BRANCH: THE SUPREME COURT AT THE BAR OF POLITICS [1962]).

45. 369 U.S. at 210, 211.

46. *Id.* at 217.

47. *Id.* at 226.

48. *Rucho v. Common Cause*, 588 U.S.__, 139 S. Ct. 2484 (2019); *Nixon v. United States*, 506 U.S. 224 (1993); *Gilligan v. Morgan*, 413 U.S. 1 (1973).

49. 531 U.S. 98 (2000).

50. *But see, e.g.*, Erwin Chemerinsky, *Bush v. Gore Was Not Justiciable*, 76 NOTRE DAME L. REV. 1093 (2001).

51. 369 U.S. at 211.

52. GORMLEY at 164, 165.

53. NAVASKY at 298, 306.

54. NAVASKY at 318–19.

55. 369 U.S. at 265–66 (Stewart, J., concurring); 369 U.S. at 254, 261 (Clark, J., concurring).

56. 372 U.S. 368.

57. *Id.* at 379; *id.* at 376.

58. *Id.* at 381.

59. *Id.* at 386.

60. 376 U.S. 1.

61. *Id.* at 3.

62. *Id.* at 25–26.

63. *Id.* at 7–8.

64. *Id.* at 47.

65. NAVASKY at 298, 318.

66. 377 U.S. 533 (1964).

67. In response to *Baker v. Carr*, there was a flood of litigation in state courts and lower federal courts concerning reapportionment. *See* Robert G. McCloskey, *The Supreme Court 1961 Term, Foreword: The Reapportionment Case*, 76 HARV. L. REV. 54 (1962) at 56–58.

68. "During the over 60 years since the last substantial reapportionment in Alabama, the state's population increased from 1,828,697 to 3,244,286. Virtually all of the population gain occurred in urban counties, and many of the rural counties incurred sizable losses in population." 377 U.S. at 542–43, n.7.

69. 377 U.S. at 545–46.

70. *Id.*

71. *Id.* at 562, 566 (citations omitted).

72. *Id.* at 573–74.

73. GORDON S. WOOD, THE CREATION OF THE AMERICAN REPUBLIC (University of North Carolina Press, 1969), chap. 6, *Mixed Government and Bicameralism*. Justice Harlan, in dissent, mentioned "theories of bicameralism." 377 U.S. at 623.

74. ROBERT A. CARO, THE YEARS OF LYNDON JOHNSON: MASTER OF THE SENATE (Knopf, 2002) at 33.

75. *Id.* at 9 (quoting James Madison).

76. CARO at 9–10.

77. 372 U.S. at 381.

78. GARRY WILLS, LINCOLN AT GETTYSBURG: THE WORDS THAT REMADE AMERICA (Simon and Schuster, 1992) at 145; Morton J. Horwitz, Foreword, *The Constitution of Change: Legal Fundamentality without Fundamentalism*, 107 HARV. L. REV. 30 (1993).

79. 377 U.S. 713 (1964).

80. *Id.* at 717–18, 731.
81. *Id.* at 719.
82. *Id.* at 720–21, n.6 (quoting the opinion of the district court below).
83. "One of the most undesirable features of the existing apportionment scheme," Warren noted, "was the requirement that . . . all legislators must be elected at large from the county as a whole. . . . Ballots were long and cumbersome, and an intelligent choice among candidates . . . was made quite difficult." The rejected plan "would have perpetuated . . . this debatable feature of the existing scheme. . . . Thus, neither of the proposed plans was, in all probability, wholly acceptable to the voters in the populous counties, and the assumption of the court below that the Colorado voters made a definitive choice between two contrasting alternatives . . . does not appear to be factually justifiable." *Id.* at 731–32.
84. 377 U.S. at 737 n.30 (quoting Judge Doyle dissenting below).
85. *Id.* at 736.
86. EARL WARREN, THE MEMOIRS OF EARL WARREN (Doubleday, 1977) at 306, 308.
87. WILLS, LINCOLN AT GETTYSBURG, at 145.
88. In *Vieth v. Jubelirer*, 541 U.S. 267 (2004), four justices ruled that claims asserting partisan non–racially based gerrymandering were not justiciable; in concurrence, Justice Kennedy did not in theory preclude the possibility of such a claim being justiciable, but he seemed to indicate that he would be unlikely in practice to deem such a claim justiciable.
89. SAMUEL ISSACHAROFF, PAMELA S. KARLAN & RICHARD H. PILDES, THE LAW OF DEMOCRACY: LEGAL STRUCTURE OF THE POLITICAL PROCESS (4th ed., Foundation Press, 2012) at 158–63, 171–76, 315–18; Heather K. Gerken, *One Person, One Vote: A Theoretical and Practical Examination of the Costs and Causes of Minimalism in Voting Cases: Baker v. Carr and Its Progeny*, 80 N.C. L. REV. 1411 (2002); Samuel Issacharoff, *Judging Politics: The Elusive Quest for Judicial Review of Political Fairness*, 71 TEX. L. REV. 1643 (1993); Samuel Issacharoff and Richard H. Pildes, *Not By "Election" Alone*, 32 LOYOLA L.A. L. REV. 1173 (1999); Pamela S. Karlan, *The Right to Vote: Some Pessimism about Formalism*, 71 TEX. L. REV. 1705 (1993); Richard H. Pildes, Foreword, *The Constitutionalization of Democratic Politics*, 118 HARV. L. REV. 28 (2004).
90. *Baker v. Carr*, 369 U.S. 186 (1962) at 251.
91. SUPREME COURT IN CONFERENCE at 848–49.
92. 369 U.S. at 258–59.

CHAPTER 6

1. Francis B. Sayre, *Criminal Conspiracy*, 35 HARV. L. REV. 393, 401–9 (1922).
2. SHAWN FRANCIS PETERS, JUDGING JEHOVAH'S WITNESSES: RELIGIOUS PERSECUTION AND THE DAWN OF THE RIGHTS REVOLUTION (University Press of Kansas, 2000) at 31–33.
3. NAACP v. Alabama *ex rel.* Patterson, 357 U.S. 449 at 453–54, 462, 465.
4. HARRY KALVEN JR., A WORTHY TRADITION: FREEDOM OF SPEECH IN AMERICA (Harper & Row, 1989) at 316.
5. New York *ex rel.* Bryant v. Zimmerman, 278 U.S. 63, 75 (1928).
6. *Patterson*, 357 U.S. at 466 and 463 (citations omitted).

7. *Ex parte* NAACP, 268 Ala. 531, 532, 109 So.2d 138–39.
8. NAACP v. Alabama *ex rel.* Patterson, 360 U.S. 240 (1959).
9. DEL DICKSON, THE SUPREME COURT IN CONFERENCE (Oxford University Press, 2001) at 312.
10. *Id.*
11. *NAACP v. Gallion*, 368 U.S. 16 (1961).
12. NAACP v. Alabama *ex rel.* Flowers, 377 U.S. 288 (1964).
13. SUPREME COURT IN CONFERENCE at 312.
14. Memorandum from Chief Justice Earl Warren to Justice William Brennan (March 3, 1964), Library of Congress, Papers of William J. Brennan, box II: 6–8, "Part II: Case Histories, 1958–1989."
15. *Walker v. City of Birmingham*, 388 U.S. 307, 319 (1967).
16. 361 U.S. 516, 518 n.3.
17. *Bates v. Little Rock*, 361 U.S. 516, 523–24 (1960).
18. KALVEN, *supra*, at 262.
19. In the second edition of his treatise, Tribe uses the phrase "least restrictive alternative" twice (831–32, §§ 12-7 and 12-23) and the phrase "least restrictive means" once. (829 n.23).
20. *Shelton v. Tucker*, 364 U.S. 479, 488, 490 (1960).
21. *Id.* at 496–97, 498–99 (Harlan, J., dissenting).
22. *Shelton v. Tucker*, 364 U.S. 479, 496 (Frankfurter, J., dissenting) (emphasis added).
23. *See* NAACP v. Button, 371 U.S. 415, 445 (Douglas, J., concurring).
24. SUPREME COURT IN CONFERENCE, *supra*, at 314–15.
25. *Harrison v. NAACP*, 360 U.S. 167 (1959). One wonders whether five years later, after experiencing Alabama's use of procedure to achieve delay, Justice Harlan would have been as eager to invoke the abstention doctrine in civil rights cases.
26. SUPREME COURT IN CONFERENCE, *supra* at 316.
27. *Id.*
28. *Id.* at 315, 317.
29. *Id.* at 317.
30. *Id.* In *NAACP v. Patty*, 159 F. Supp. 503, 515 (E.D. Va. 1958), Judge Soper found that the package of Virginia laws were enacted "as parts of the general plan of massive resistance to the integration of schools of the state under the Supreme Court's decrees," citing a mountain of evidence.
31. SUPREME COURT IN CONFERENCE, *supra* note 1, at 317–18.
32. Frankfurter had made a similar point in criticizing Justice Harlan's first draft in *NAACP v. Alabama*. "An opinion in this case should be written as though the very same case pertaining to the NAACP had arisen in Minnesota or the very same demand for a membership list had arisen in Alabama but concerned the American Philosophical Society." Memorandum from Justice Felix Frankfurter to Justice John Marshall Harlan, April 23, 1958, *Harlan Papers*, Princeton University, box 46. Frankfurter's exchanges foreshadow Herbert Wechsler's criticisms of *Brown*: "The question posed by state-enforced segregation is not one of discrimination at all. Its human and its constitutional dimensions lie entirely elsewhere, in the denial by the state of freedom to associate, a denial that impinges in the same way on any groups or races that may be involved." Herbert Wechsler, *Toward Neutral Principles of Constitutional Law*, 73 HARV. L. REV. 1, 34 (1959).

33. SUPREME COURT IN CONFERENCE, at 318; *see NAACP v. Alabama*, 357 U.S. 449.

34. *Opinions of William J. Brennan, Jr., 1959 term* (hereinafter THE HISTORIES) at 11.

35. THE HISTORIES, 11–13.

36. *Id.* at 12.

37. *Id.*

38. Harlan's dissent reemphasizes the traditional norm of "prevent[ing] any interference with the uniquely personal relationship between lawyer and client" and of the "divided allegiance—to his employer and to his client" with which "[the NAACP] lawyer necessarily finds himself." *Button*, 371 U.S. at 460. *See* Derrick Bell, *Serving Two Masters: Integration Ideals and Client Interests in School Desegregation Litigation*, 85 YALE L.J. 470 (1976).

39. *Button*, 371 U.S. at 429–30, 431.

40. *Id.*, at 432–33, 435–36. After Brennan's original circulation of his opinion, Justice Harlan circulated a dissent whose opening paragraph caused Brennan to "protest . . . a strongly suggested accusation that the Court is giving special status to Negro litigants denied to others." Harlan replied that he would revise the paragraph, which he eventually did, but Brennan added a last paragraph to his own opinion denying the accusation, since he guessed that the revision "probably won't meet my objections." Memorandum from Justice William Brennan to Chief Justice Earl Warren, January 9, 1963, Library of Congress, *supra*. *See also* TINSLEY E. YARBROUGH, JOHN MARSHALL HARLAN: GREAT DISSENTER OF THE WARREN COURT (Oxford University Press, 1992) at 237.

41. *Speiser v. Randall*, 357 U.S. 513, 526 (1958).

42. *Button*, 371 U.S. at 433.

43. *New York Times Co. v. Sullivan*, 376 U.S. 254, 279, 300 (1964) (Goldberg, J., concurring). Before this case, the phrase "chilling effect" appeared twice in Supreme Court opinions: first in a dissenting opinion by Chief Justice Warren in *Times Films Corp. v. City of Chicago* 365 U.S. 43, 74 n.11 (1961), a film censorship case, and second in the majority opinion by Justice Goldberg in *Gibson v. Florida Investigating Committee* 372 U.S. 539, 557 (1963). *Times Film Corp. v. City of Chicago* cites its original usage by Professor Paul Freund in *The Supreme Court and Civil Liberties*, 4 VAND. L. REV. 533 (1951). The term's usage is discussed in Note, *The Void-for-Vagueness Doctrine in the Supreme Court*, 109 U. PA. L. REV. 67 (1960); Note, *The Chilling Effect in Constitutional Law*, 69 COLUM. L. REV. 808 (1969); Note, *First Amendment Overbreadth Doctrine*, 83 HARV. L. REV. 844 (1970).

44. *Button*, 371 U.S. at 432–33.

45. *Baggett v. Bullitt*, 377 U.S. 360, 372 (1964). It should be recalled that the year before in *NAACP v. Button*, White, in one of his earliest opinions, separately concurred by resting on Brennan's original grounds of overbreadth after Brennan had incorporated Black's more direct First Amendment grounds into his opinion for the court.

46. *Button*, 371 U.S. at 432–33.

47. *Dombrowski v. Pfister*, 380 U.S. 479 (1965).

48. *See id.* at 483.

49. THE HISTORIES, 1964 term, *supra* note 12 at 10. Brennan wrote: "The State must, if it is to invoke the statutes after injunctive relief has been sought, assume the burden of obtaining a permissible narrow construction in a noncriminal proceeding

before it may seek modification of the injunction to permit future prosecutions. On this view of the 'vagueness' doctrine, it is readily apparent that abstention [to await a state construction of the statute] serves no legitimate purpose where a statute regulating speech is properly attacked on its face, and where, as here, the conduct charged in the indictments is not within the reach of an acceptable limiting construction readily to be anticipated as the result of a single criminal prosecution and is not the sort of 'hard-core' conduct that would obviously be prohibited under any construction." *Dombrowski*, 380 U.S. at 491–92.

50. *Cameron v. Johnson*, 390 U.S. 611, 619 (1968).
51. Owen Fiss, *Dombrowski*, 86 YALE L.J. 1103 (1977).
52. *Younger v. Harris*, 401 U.S. 37 (1971).
53. *New York Times Co. v. Sullivan*, 376 U.S. 254 (1964).
54. There were two separate lawsuits against the *New York Times*. In addition to the advertisement (potential liability of $3 million), libel suits were also brought against the *New York Times* for a series of articles by reporter Harrison Salisbury (potential liability of $3.1 million).
55. *Opinions of William J. Brennan, Jr., 1963 term (law clerks, Stephen R. Barnett and Stephen J. Friedman)* at 1.
56. *Id.*
57. SUPREME COURT IN CONFERENCE at 379. The newspaper had a paid circulation in Birmingham of just 5 newspapers and statewide sales of 394 papers a day. "Of these, about 35 copies were distributed in Montgomery County." *New York Times v. Sullivan* 376 U.S. at 293 n.3.
58. SUPREME COURT IN CONFERENCE, at 380.
59. SUPREME COURT IN CONFERENCE, at 380–81.
60. Black to Brennan, February 26, 1964, THE HISTORIES, 1964, at 3.
61. The Histories 1964 at 3.
62. *NAACP v. Button*, 371 U.S. 415.
63. In another note to Brennan, Black added, "I do think, however, that in getting [Harlan] to agree to your opinion as it is, you have done a great service to the freedoms of the First Amendment. For your opinion I believe will inevitably lead to a later holding that people have complete immunity from having to pay damages for criticism of Government or its officials in the performance of their public duties." BRENNAN PAPERS, box 107, Justice Black to Justice Brennan.
64. THE HISTORIES, 1964 at 5.
65. THE HISTORIES, 1964 at 8.
66. THE HISTORIES, 1964 at 8–11.
67. THE HISTORIES, 1964 at 11–12.
68. *New York Times Co. v. Sullivan*, 376 U.S. 254 (1964).

CHAPTER 7

1. Walter V. Schaefer, *Federalism and State Criminal Procedure*, 70 HARV. L. REV. 1 (1956) at 2.
2. Henry P. Weihofen, *Supreme Court Review of State Criminal Procedure*, 10 AM. J. LEGAL HIST. 189 (1966) at 189, 191, 192. Weihofen notes that "until *Powell v. Alabama* in 1932, the federal Constitution hadn't shown much usefulness as a bulwark against abuses in state criminal procedure." *Id.* at 191.

3. Felix Frankfurter, *The Business of the Supreme Court of the United States: A Study in the Federal Judicial System, III; From the Circuit Courts of Appeals Act to the Judicial Code,* 39 HARV. L. REV. 325 (1926) at 341.

4. *Id.* at 341, n.73.

5. Michael J. Klarman, *The Racial Origins of Modern Criminal Procedure,* 99 MICH. L. REV. 48 (2000) at 53.

6. 261 U.S. 86.

7. *Id.* at 88–89.

8. *Id.* at 91. Holmes continued: "it appears to us unavoidable that the District Judge should find whether the facts alleged are true . . . if true as alleged they make the trial absolutely void." *Id.* at 92.

9. A second defendant's death sentence was eventually overturned on appeal because he was too young to be executed under state law. MICHAEL J. KLARMAN, FROM JIM CROW TO CIVIL RIGHTS (Oxford University Press, 2004) [hereinafter JIM CROW TO CIVIL RIGHTS] at 117.

10. *Powell v. Alabama,* 287 U.S. 45 (1932) at 51.

11. *Id.* at 71.

12. 294 U.S. 587 (1935) at 597.

13. 297 U.S. 278.

14. JIM CROW TO CIVIL RIGHTS at 117.

15. *Id.* at 117–18.

16. 309 U.S. 227.

17. *Id.* at 236.

18. JIM CROW TO CIVIL RIGHTS at 228.

19. ZECHARIAH CHAFEE JR., WALTER H. POLLAK & CARL S. STERN (CONSULTANTS), THE THIRD DEGREE: REPORT TO THE NATIONAL COMMISSION ON LAW OBSERVANCE AND ENFORCEMENT (1931) *reprinted in* (with new pagination) ZECHARIAH CHAFEE JR., WALTER H. POLLAK & CARL S. STERN, MASS VIOLENCE IN AMERICA: THE THIRD DEGREE (Robert M. Fogelson, Richard E. Rubenstein eds., Arno Press & The New York Times, 1969) [hereinafter WICKERSHAM COMMISSION]. *See also* KENNETH M. MURCHISON, FEDERAL CRIMINAL LAW DOCTRINES: THE FORGOTTEN INFLUENCE OF NATIONAL PROHIBITION (Duke University Press, 1994).

20. WICKERSHAM COMMISSION at 19, 153.

21. *Id.* at 153.

22. *Id.* at 90–91.

23. *Id.* at 103.

24. *Id.* at 126–27.

25. *Id.* at 110.

26. *Id.* at 111.

27. *Id.* at 104.

28. *Id.* at 113, 115.

29. *Id.* at 155.

30. FRED P. GRAHAM, THE SELF-INFLICTED WOUND (Macmillan, 1970) at 3–4.

31. GRAHAM at 4.

32. *The Law: The Nixon Radicals,* TIME, June 5, 1972.

33. 367 U.S. 643.

34. 372 U.S. 335.

35. 384 U.S. 436.

36. 367 U.S. 643 (1961).

37. 338 U.S. 25.

38. 389 U.S. 347.

39. 277 U.S. 438.

40. *People v. Defoe*, 242 N.Y. 13, 21; 150 N.E. 585, 587 (1926) (quoting Benjamin Cardozo during his tenure on the highest court of New York prior to his appointment to the Supreme Court).

41. 381 U.S. 618.

42. Justice Black, in dissent, made clear that this approach was unprecedented: "As the Court concedes, . . . this is the first instance on record where this Court, having jurisdiction, has ever refused to give a previously convicted defendant the benefit of a new and more expansive Bill of Rights interpretation." 381 U.S. at 646 (Black, J., dissenting).

43. 381 U.S. at 636–39.

44. 382 U.S. 406.

45. 384 U.S. 719.

46. The court in *Tehan v. Shott* held that *Griffin v. California*, 380 U.S. 609 (1965), did not apply retrospectively. In *Griffin v. California*, the court had ruled "that adverse comment by a prosecutor or trial judge upon a defendant's failure to testify in a state criminal trial violates the . . . privilege against compulsory self-incrimination." 382 U.S. at 407. In *Johnson*, the court, one week after handing down *Miranda*, held that neither *Miranda* nor *Escobedo* applied retroactively.

47. 381 U.S. at 644 (Black, J., dissenting).

48. 372 U.S. 335 (1963).

49. 316 U.S. 455.

50. Anthony Lewis, Gideon's Trumpet (Random House, 1964) [hereinafter Lewis] at 132–33.

51. Lewis at 202–3.

52. Lewis at 201.

53. Lewis at 199–200 (quoting Chief Judge Lumbard).

54. *See Justice Sequestered*, N.Y. Times, July 20, 2013 (Sunday Review/The Opinion Pages); *Public Defenders Are Tightening Belts Because of Steep Federal Budget Cuts*, N.Y. Times, August 23, 2013 (U.S. Section).

55. *See* Lincoln Caplan, *The Right to Counsel: Badly Battered at 50*, N.Y. Times, March 9, 2013 (Sunday Review/The Opinion Pages); Jesse Wegman, *The Right to an Attorney Who Actually Does His Job*, N.Y. Times: Taking Note, December 9, 2013, https://takingnote.blogs.nytimes.com/2013/12/09/the-right-to-an-attorney-who-actually-does-his-job [https://perma.cc/29WD-9HKT].

56. *Engel v. Vitale*, 370 U.S. 421 (1962); *Abington School District v. Schempp*, 374 U.S. 203 (1963).

57. 384 U.S. 436 (1966). The court's effort to tamp down some of the opposition to the *Miranda* opinion by ruling a week later in *Johnson v. New Jersey*, 384 U.S. 719 (1966), that it would not apply retrospectively did not quiet the virulent opposition to the decision. *See* Lucas A. Powe Jr., The Warren Court and American Politics (Harvard University Press, 2000) at 425–26. For a brief but excellent discussion of the reaction to the *Miranda* decision, see Powe at 394–99.

58. 297 U.S. 278.
59. *See* Yale Kamisar, *The Rise, Decline, and Fall (?) of* Miranda, 87 Wash. L. Rev. 965 (2012) [hereinafter Kamisar] at 969–70.
60. DEL DICKSON, THE SUPREME COURT IN CONFERENCE (Oxford University Press, 2001) at 515.
61. 378 U.S. 478 at 479, 491.
62. SUPREME COURT IN CONFERENCE at 515.
63. "He must be advised (1) of his right to remain silent; (2) that what he says may be used against him; (3) that in time the court may appoint a lawyer; (4) he must be given an opportunity to get a lawyer before he is interrogated, unless he waives that right; (5) the burden is on the government to show a waiver; and (6) no distinction should be made between one who has a lawyer and one who does not, or between one who can hire one and one who cannot." SUPREME COURT IN CONFERENCE at 515–16.
64. SUPREME COURT IN CONFERENCE at 515.
65. 378 U.S. 1.
66. THE HISTORIES (Stephen R. Barnett and Stephen J. Friedman, law clerks to Justice Brennan) (Manuscript Division, Library of Congress) [hereinafter cited as THE HISTORIES], 1975 term, at 41.
67. SUPREME COURT IN CONFERENCE at 515.
68. *Miranda*, 384 U.S at 457. Warren wrote, "It is obvious that such an interrogation environment is created for no purpose other than to subjugate the individual to the will of his examiner. . . . [Although] not physical intimidation, . . . [t]his atmosphere carries its own badge of intimidation . . . [and] is equally destructive of human dignity. The current practice of *incommunicado interrogation* is at odds with one of our Nation's most cherished principles—that the individual may not be compelled to incriminate himself. Unless adequate protective devices are employed to dispel the compulsion inherent in custodial surroundings, no statement from the defendant can truly be the product of free choice." *Id.* at 457–58 (emphasis added).
69. *See* Kamisar at 970.
70. Kamisar at 971.
71. Kamisar at 971 (quoting Judge Friendly).
72. THE HISTORIES, 1965 term, at 41.
73. *Miranda*, 384 U.S. at 467.
74. THE HISTORIES, 1965 term, at 41–42.
75. THE HISTORIES at 42.
76. THE HISTORIES at 42–43.
77. Kamisar at 978–80, 984–91, 995–97, and 1002–8. Ironically, Chief Justice Rehnquist, writing for the court in *Dickerson v. U.S.*, 530 U.S. 428 (2000), did uphold *Miranda*, rejecting the view of the U.S. Court of Appeals for the Fourth Circuit that the protections afforded in *Miranda* were not constitutionally based and that therefore a law of Congress that intended to overrule *Miranda* could do so. Rehnquist found that "*Miranda* is a constitutional decision. . . . *Miranda* announced a constitutional rule . . . [even though] we have created several exceptions . . . and . . . have repeatedly referred to the *Miranda* warnings as 'prophylactic.'" 530 U.S. at 437. In support of his contention "that *Miranda*

is constitutionally based," *Id.* at 440, Rehnquist argued that "the warnings have become part of our national culture." *Id.* at 443. *Dickerson* did not deter the court under Rehnquist and after from continuing to dilute *Miranda*. Kamisar at 1002–21.

78. SETH STERN & STEPHEN WERMIEL, JUSTICE BRENNAN: LIBERAL CHAMPION (Houghton Mifflin Harcourt, 2010) at 239.

79. Robert B. Semple Jr., *Nixon Links Crime to "Legal System,"* N.Y. TIMES, Sept. 27, 1967.

80. Ward Just, *Nixon, RFK, Aim at Crime, Urban Rioting,* WASH. POST, May 31, 1968; Robert B. Semple Jr., *Nixon Decries "Lawless Society" and Urges Limited Wiretapping,* N.Y. TIMES, May 9, 1968; Robert B. Semple Jr., *Nixon Withholds His Peace Ideas,* N.Y. TIMES, Mar. 11, 1968.

81. Fred P. Graham, *Congress Tackles the Court,* N.Y. TIMES, May 12, 1968; Fred P. Graham, *Congress Tries to Curb the Court,* N.Y. TIMES, Apr. 28, 1968.

82. MORTON J. HORWITZ, THE WARREN COURT AND THE PURSUIT OF JUSTICE (Hill and Wang, 1998) at 95.

83. Earl C. Dudley Jr., *Terry v. Ohio, the Warren Court, and the Fourth Amendment: A Law Clerk's Perspective,* 72 ST. JOHN'S L. REV. 891, 893 (1998).

84. *Terry v. Ohio,* 392 U.S. 1, 4–8 (1998).

85. BERNARD SCHWARTZ, SUPER CHIEF: EARL WARREN AND HIS COURT (New York University Press, 1983) [hereinafter cited as SUPER CHIEF] at 685–86; SUPREME COURT IN CONFERENCE at 453–55; John Q. Barrett, *Deciding the Stop and Frisk Cases: A Look Inside the Supreme Court's Conference,* 72 ST. JOHN'S L. REV. 749, 784–90 (1998).

86. SUPER CHIEF at 688.

87. THE HISTORIES, 1967 term, at 33, 37.

88. Earl C. Dudley Jr., *Terry v. Ohio, the Warren Court, and the Fourth Amendment: A Law Clerk's Perspective,* 72 ST. JOHN'S L. REV. 891, 893 (1998).

89. THE HISTORIES, 1967 term, at 36; although the history refers to Edwards as the former police commissioner of Chicago, the only Edwards who was an appellate judge at that time and a former police commissioner was George Edwards of Detroit.

90. Barrett, *Deciding the Stop and Frisk Cases,* at 771–72 (1998).

91. John Q. Barrett, *Deciding the Stop and Frisk Cases: A Look Inside the Supreme Court's Conference,* 72 ST. JOHN'S L. REV. 749, 771–72 (1998).

92. *Terry v. Ohio,* 392 U.S. 1 (1998). The race of neither the police officer nor the defendant is mentioned; the only reference to race is a generic reference to "the wholesale harassment by certain elements of the police community, of which minority groups, particularly Negroes, frequently complain." *Id.* at 14.

93. THE HISTORIES, 1967 term, at 42.

94. *Id.* at 32.

95. *Id.*

96. *Id.* at 37.

97. *Id.* at 38.

98. *Id.* at 40.

99. *Id.*

100. *Id.* at 41–42.

101. *Id.* at 42.

102. SUPER CHIEF at 690–91; Barrett, *Deciding the Stop and Frisk Cases*, at 821–27 (1998).

103. SUPER CHIEF at 691–92; Barrett, *Deciding the Stop and Frisk Cases*, at 749, 827–32.

104. *Terry v. Ohio*, 392 U.S. 1, 39 (1998) (Douglas, J., dissenting).

105. THE HISTORIES, 1967 term, at 43.

106. *Adams v. Williams*, 407 U.S. 143, 162 (Marshall, J., dissenting).

107. *Id.* at 153 (Brennan, J., dissenting) quoting *Williams v. Adams*, 436 F.2d 30, 39 (2d Cir. 1970) (Friendly, J., dissenting).

CHAPTER 8

1. *Maxwell v. Bishop*, 398 U.S. 262 (1970).

2. 408 U.S. 238 (1972).

3. *See Gregg v. Georgia*, 428 U.S. 153 (1976).

4. 391 U.S. 510 (1968).

5. 356 U.S. 86 (1958).

6. *Trop v. Dulles*, 356 U.S. 86 (1958), at 101, 103. Justices Black, Douglas, and Whittaker joined Warren's plurality opinion. Justice Brennan concurred, providing the fifth vote. His concurrence rested on narrower grounds unrelated to the Eighth Amendment: that there was not a sufficiently rational relationship between the statute authorizing expatriation for wartime desertion and Congress's war power. *Id.* at 114.

7. *Mackenzie v. Hare*, 239 U.S. 299 (1915).

8. *Savorgnan v. United States*, 338 U.S. 491 (1950).

9. *See* BERNARD SCHWARTZ, SUPER CHIEF: EARL WARREN AND HIS SUPREME COURT, A JUDICIAL BIOGRAPHY (New York University Press, 1983) [hereinafter cited as SUPER CHIEF] at 316 (discussing Justices Brennan, Harlan, and Whittaker).

10. *Perez v. Brownell*, 356 U.S. 44 (1958).

11. *Trop v. Dulles*, 356 U.S. 86 (1958).

12. *Id.* at 114 (Brennan, J., concurring).

13. *Perez v. Brownell*, 356 U.S. at 77–78 (Warren, C. J., dissenting).

14. *Trop v. Dulles*, 356 U.S. at 101.

15. *Id.*

16. *Kennedy v. Mendoza-Martinez*, 372 U.S. 144 (1963).

17. *Schneider v. Rusk*, 377 U.S. 163 (1964).

18. *Afroyim v. Rusk*, 387 U.S. 253 (1967).

19. The majority was made possible by Justice Brennan's abandoning his "swing" position in *Perez* and *Trop*. But a further question arises: Why didn't Warren take for himself the writing of the opinion in *Afroyim*? It was, after all, the culmination of ideas he had originally introduced. Justice Black's opinion in *Afroyim*, while faithful to Warren's political theory, ignores Warren's simultaneous argument that involuntary denaturalization is a "cruel and unusual punishment." It may be that Brennan's or Black's vote in *Afroyim* was predicated on eliminating the cruel and unusual punishments argument.

20. Peter J. Spiro, Afroyim: *Vaunting Citizenship, Presaging Transnationality*, in IMMIGRATION STORIES (David A. Martin and Peter H. Schuck eds., Foundation Press, 2005) at 147–68.

21. *Id.* at 163.

22. *Perez v. Brownell*, 356 U.S. at 64 (Warren, C. J., dissenting).

23. *Trop v. Dulles*, 356 U.S. at 92–93.

24. *Perez v. Brownell*, 356 U.S. at 78 (Warren, C. J., dissenting).

25. *Id.* at 64.

26. *Trop v. Dulles*, 356 U.S. at 101.

27. *Perez v. Brownell*, 356 U.S. at 64 (Warren, C. J., dissenting).

28. *Id.* (quoting DECLARATION OF INDDEPENDENCE) (internal quotation marks omitted).

29. *Id.*

30. *Id.* at 78.

31. *Afroyim v. Rusk*, 387 U.S. at 268.

32. *Afroyim v. Rusk*, 387 U.S. at 257.

33. *Id.* at 268.

34. SUPER CHIEF, at 313.

35. *Trop v. Dulles*, 356 U.S. at 119 (Frankfurter, J., dissenting).

36. *Id.* at 128.

37. *Id.* at 103 (majority opinion).

38. *Afroyim v. Rusk*, 387 U.S. at 268.

39. *O'Neil v. Vermont*, 144 U.S. 323 (1892) at 332.

40. *Weems v. United States*, 217 U.S. 349 (1910).

41. *See, e.g., In re* Kemmler, 136 U.S. 436 (1890), at 446–47; *Wilkerson v. Utah*, 99 U.S. 130 (1878), at 134–36.

42. *Weems v. United States*, 217 U.S. at 380–81. *Weems* was decided under the cruel and unusual punishment clause of the Philippine Bill of Rights; the U.S. Supreme Court found that it "was taken from the Constitution of the United States and must have the same meaning." 217 U.S. at 367.

43. *Weems v. United States*, 217 U.S. at 373.

44. Louisiana *ex rel.* Francis v. Resweber, 329 U.S. 459 (1947).

45. Justice Reed's opinion for the court was joined by three other Justices: Black, Jackson, and Vinson.

46. 329 U.S. at 464.

47. Justice Frankfurter wrote a separate concurrence expressly avoiding reliance on the Eighth Amendment or the notion of cruel and unusual punishment and relying instead on a due process analysis. *Id.* at 466–72.

48. *Trop v. Dulles*, 356 U.S. 86 (1958) at 100–101.

49. 356 U.S. at 103.

50. 370 U.S. 660 (1962).

51. *Robinson v. California*, 370 U.S. 660, 666.

52. *Id.* at 666–67.

53. 392 U.S. 514 (1968).

54. The chief justice, Justice Black, and Justice Harlan shifted from *Robinson* to *Powell*. Originally in the *Powell* conference a majority voted to apply *Robinson* and reverse the conviction. Justice Fortas circulated a draft majority opinion, which was

brilliantly attacked by Justice Black. As a result, Fortas lost his majority, and the court affirmed the conviction. *See* Bernard Schwartz, *More Unpublished Warren Court Opinions*, 1986 SUP. CT. REV. 317, 335–72.

55. *Rudolph v. Alabama*, 375 U.S. 889 (1963) at 889.

56. Arthur J. Goldberg, *Memorandum to the Conference Re: Capital Punishment October Term, 1963*, 27 S. TEX. L. REV. 493 (1986) [hereinafter cited as Goldberg Memorandum].

57. Goldberg Memorandum at 493.

58. William J. Brennan Jr., *Constitutional Adjudication and the Death Penalty: A View from the Court*, 100 HARV. L. REV. 313 (1986) (Holmes lecture, 1986) at 314–15.

59. *Id.* at 315.

60. Public *Opinion Polls, Gallup Polls*, The Clark County Prosecuting Attorney, The Death Penalty (www.clarkprosecutor.org/html/death/opinion.htm) [https://perma.cc/LW9V-5EH8].

61. *Id.*

62. STUART BANNER, THE DEATH PENALTY (Harvard University Press, 2003) at 240; Robert Ruby, *Capital Punishment's Constant Constituency: An American Majority*, PEW RESEARCH CENTER PUBLICATIONS (2007) (www.pewresearch.org) [https://perma.cc/3QFP-4R7Y]. These percentages were in response to Gallup's question asking whether the respondent approved of the death penalty for murder. Gallup began more or less regularly to ask this question in 1953, though it had once before been asked in 1937, when a substantial majority (60% to 33%) also supported capital punishment. *Public Opinion Polls, Gallup Polls, supra.* The polling organization later introduced another question asking whether the respondent favored the death penalty or life in prison without parole for murder, which produced a lower approval for capital punishment.

63. Goldberg Memorandum at 498.

64. *Id.* at 497–98.

65. *Rudolph v. Alabama* denial of *certiorari*, 375 U.S. 889 (1963), Goldberg dissenting at 890 quoting *Trop v. Dulles.*

66. Frankfurter had agreed in the conference discussion of Louisiana *ex rel.* Francis v. Resweber, 329 U.S. 459 (1947), that "cruel and unusual punishment is a progressive notion, shocking the feelings of the time." Nevertheless, he concluded that although the actions of the State of Louisiana in the case at hand were "hardly a defensible thing for a state to do, it is not so offensive as to make me puke—it does not shock my conscience." DEL DICKSON, THE SUPREME COURT IN CONFERENCE (Oxford University Press, 2001) [hereinafter cited as SUPREME COURT IN CONFERENCE] at 605. This was probably the moment at which Justice Black came to the realization that he would express in *Adamson v. California*, 332 U.S. 46 (1947), that Frankfurter's standard for deciding whether the protections of the Bill of Rights applied to the states would turn on subjective formulations such as whether the alleged violation "shocks the conscience" or made Frankfurter "puke."

67. ALAN M. DERSHOWITZ, THE BEST DEFENSE (Random House, 1982) at 308. *See* BANNER, THE DEATH PENALTY, at 250.

68. DERSHOWITZ at 308; BANNER, THE DEATH PENALTY, at 250.

69. When arguing against capital punishment for rape in the original memo, Goldberg stated, "This would also eliminate the well-recognized disparity in the imposition

of the death penalty for sexual crimes committed by whites and nonwhites." Goldberg Memorandum at 505, n.18.

70. MICHAEL MELTSNER, CRUEL AND UNUSUAL: THE SUPREME COURT AND CAPI- TAL PUNISHMENT (Random House, 1973) [hereinafter MELTSNER] at 77.

71. MELTSNER at 28, 30–31.

72. DERSHOWITZ at 308–10.

73. MELTSNER at 30.

74. 391 U.S. 510.

75. *Boulden v. Holman*, 394 U.S. 478 (1969) at 482 (quoting *Witherspoon*). The Supreme Court in *Boulden* added that potential jurors could not be dismissed for cause based on their statement that they "had 'a fixed opinion against' capital punishment." *Id.* at 483. The court also stated that "other [potential jurors] seem to have been excluded merely by virtue of their statement that they did not 'believe in' capital punishment. Yet it is entirely possible that a person who has 'a fixed opinion against' or who does not 'believe in' capital punishment might neverthe- less be perfectly able as a juror . . . to consider fairly the imposition of the death sentence in a particular case." *Id.* at 483–84.

76. MELTSNER at 125.

77. MELTSNER at 123–24.

78. MELTSNER at 125.

79. *Fryrear v. Com.* 471 S.W. 2d 321, 323 (Ky. 1971); *State v. Mercer*, 618 S.W. 2d. 1, 7 (Mo. 1981) (en banc); *State v. Pace*, 80 N.M. 364, 366 (1969); *Ex Parte Chambers*, 612 S.W. 2d. 572, 574 n.1 (Tex. Crim. App. 1981) (en banc); *Smith v. State*, 437 S.W. 2d. 835, 841; *vacated*, 408 U.S. 934 (1972).

80. *Maxwell v. Bishop*, 398 U.S. 262 (1970).

81. 393 U.S. 997 (1968); BANNER, THE DEATH PENALTY, at 255.

82. BANNER, THE DEATH PENALTY, at 255–56; BERNARD SCHWARTZ, THE UNPUB- LISHED OPINIONS OF THE WARREN COURT (Oxford University Press, 1985) [here- inafter UNPUBLISHED OPINIONS] at 396.

83. UNPUBLISHED OPINIONS at 396–400.

84. *Id.* at 396 (quoting Justice Harlan).

85. UNPUBLISHED OPINIONS at 399; SUPREME COURT IN CONFERENCE at 611–12.

86. UNPUBLISHED OPINIONS at 397–99.

87. For a discussion of Fortas's resignation, see LAURA KALMAN, ABE FORTAS (Yale University Press, 1990) at 370–78.

88. UNPUBLISHED OPINIONS at 399 (quoting Harlan).

89. SUPREME COURT IN CONFERENCE.

90. *Id.* at 397–98.

91. UNPUBLISHED OPINIONS at 415.

92. *Id.* at 397.

93. UNPUBLISHED OPINIONS at 418–19.

94. UNPUBLISHED OPINIONS at 399.

95. 398 F.2d 138 (8th Cir. 1968).

96. *Id.* at 147.

97. 481 U.S. 279.

98. BANNER, THE DEATH PENALTY, at 228.

99. *Id.* at 228.

100. *Id.* at 230.

101. *Id.* at 230.
102. *Id.* at 230.
103. In Justice Goldberg's memo, he did note "the well-recognized disparity in the imposition of the death penalty for sexual crimes committed by whites and non-whites." *Goldberg Memorandum, supra,* at 505 n.18. *See also* BANNER, THE DEATH PENALTY, at 230.

CHAPTER 9

1. *Garner v. Louisiana, Briscoe v. Louisiana,* and *Hoston v. Louisiana* were consolidated and decided together by the Supreme Court, 368 U.S. 157 (1961).
2. Six judges voted to reverse on the grounds that there was no evidence, citing *Thompson v. Louisville,* 362 U.S. 199. *Garner v. Louisiana,* 368 U.S. at 163. Frankfurter concurred on similar grounds, 368 U.S. at 175–76. Harlan, rejecting the court's rationale, concurred on the grounds that in two of the cases, *Garner* and *Hoston,* management had implied consent, and the conduct was protected "as a form of expression," and that in all three cases the statute as applied was unconstitutionally vague. 368 U.S. at 199, 205. Only Douglas reached the ultimate constitutional question, holding that because restaurants were public facilities, there was "state action" sufficient to bring it within the Equal Protection Clause. 368 U.S. at 184–85.
3. The first session, on March 17, 1961, was formally about whether to exercise discretion and grant certiorari. The second session, devoted to discussion of the merits, took place on October 20, 1961.
4. THE SUPREME COURT IN CONFERENCE 709 (Del Dickson ed., Oxford University Press, 2001) [hereinafter SUPREME COURT IN CONFERENCE].
5. SUPREME COURT IN CONFERENCE at 709–10.
6. SUPREME COURT IN CONFERENCE at 710.
7. 109 U.S. 3.
8. *Avent v. North Carolina,* 373 U.S. 375 (1963) (per curiam); *Gober v. City of Birmingham,* 373 U.S. 374 (1963) (per curiam); *Wright v. Georgia,* 373 U.S. 284 (1963); *Lombard v. Louisiana,* 373 U.S. 267 (1963); *Peterson v. City of Greenville,* 373 U.S. 244 (1963); *Shuttlesworth v. City of Birmingham,* 373 U.S. 262 (1963), related case. *Peterson* was the lead case. In all of the cases except the per curiam decisions, Chief Justice Warren delivered the opinion of the court.
9. SUPREME COURT IN CONFERENCE at 712.
10. SUPREME COURT IN CONFERENCE at 713–14.
11. Harlan did not dissent in the lead case, *Peterson v. City of Greenville,* as he found state action there, 373 U.S. at 253, although unlike all of the other justices who had signed on to the chief justice's opinion, he thought that "the *mere existence*" of a city ordinance requiring segregated facilities was insufficient in and of itself to be considered state action. 373 U.S. at 250. The position of all the other justices on this issue, he declared, was "alluring but . . . a fallacious proposition." *Id.* at 251. In *Lombard,* Harlan wanted the case remanded "for a new trial so that the issue of state action may be properly explored." 373 U.S. at 255. (Harlan's dissent in *Lombard* appears directly after his concurring opinion in *Peterson*). In *Gober,* Harlan also wanted a new trial "so that the bearing of the ordinance on the issue of state action may be fully explored." 373 U.S. at 257 (appearing directly after

Harlan's *Lombard* dissent). In *Avent*, Harlan characterized his opinion as a dissent, although only "to [an] extent," 373 U.S. at 258, as he agreed with the other justices "that the case should be returned to the State Supreme Court for further consideration." *Id.* In *Shuttlesworth*, Harlan agreed with the other justices that "these convictions cannot stand," 373 U.S. at 259, but he deemed it appropriate to remand the case to the Alabama courts for a new trial.

12. SUPREME COURT IN CONFERENCE at 714.

13. SUPREME COURT IN CONFERENCE at 714 (Douglas), 716 (Goldberg).

14. SUPREME COURT IN CONFERENCE at 714 (Clark and Harlan), 715 (Stewart). Stewart is perhaps misquoted as saying "There is state action, but there is not necessarily a denial of equal protection," which hardly makes sense if there is concededly racial discrimination. *Id.* at 715.

15. SUPREME COURT IN CONFERENCE at 715 (Brennan), 716 (White).

16. THE HISTORIES, OCTOBER TERM, 1963 (Stephen R. Barnett and Stephen J. Friedman, law clerks to Justice Brennan) (Manuscript Division, Library of Congress) [hereinafter cited as THE HISTORIES] at xii.

17. THE HISTORIES, OCTOBER TERM, 1963 at xii.

18. THE HISTORIES at xiii.

19. THE HISTORIES at xiii–xiv.

20. SUPREME COURT IN CONFERENCE at 718–19 (Conference of October 23, 1963).

21. THE HISTORIES at xiii.

22. SUPREME COURT IN CONFERENCE at 720 (Conference of October 23, 1963).

23. THE HISTORIES at xiv.

24. SUPREME COURT IN CONFERENCE at 721 (Conference of October 26, 1963). Several of Goldberg's reported comments presupposed that Justice Joseph Bradley's majority opinion in the *Civil Rights Cases*, 109 U.S. 3 (1883), conceded that the Equal Protection Clause, even without state action, reached public accommodations, which was incorrect. Goldberg's draft dissent in *Bell v. Maryland*, The Supreme Court Papers of Arthur J. Goldberg, Northwestern University, Pritzker Legal Research Center at 24–26; SUPREME COURT IN CONFERENCE at 721. None of the other members of the minority mentioned this point, suggesting either that Goldberg was misquoted or that they too believed Goldberg was incorrect.

25. SUPREME COURT IN CONFERENCE at 721–22.

26. SUPREME COURT IN CONFERENCE at 722.

27. THE HISTORIES at xv–xvi.

28. Arthur Goldberg's April 1964 lengthy draft dissent in *Bell v. Maryland*, in The Supreme Court Papers of Arthur J. Goldberg, Northwestern University, Pritzker Legal Research Center, at 3 (http://plrccollections.org/items/show/96) [https://perma.cc/X3ZA-MX4U].

29. Elizabeth Black, *From the Diaries of Elizabeth Black*, in MR. JUSTICE AND MRS. BLACK: THE MEMOIRS OF HUGO L. BLACK AND ELIZABETH BLACK (Paul R. Baier ed., Random House, 1986) [hereinafter *Diaries of Elizabeth Black*] at 87, 92.

30. *Diaries of Elizabeth Black* at 92.

31. *Cox v. Louisiana*, 379 U.S. 559 (1965). In this case, Reverend Cox had been convicted for picketing near a courthouse. "Upon the same set of facts," Reverend Cox, in a separately docketed case, 379 U.S. 536 (1965), also had been convicted of "disturbing the peace" and "obstructing a public passageway." 379 U.S. 560. Justice Goldberg wrote the majority opinion in both cases. Although the court

reversed the convictions on all three charges, the alignment of the justices in the courthouse picketing decision differed from that in the case addressing the other two issues. Justice Black's opinions on all three issues—he concurred with Justice Goldberg in the "disturbing the peace" and "obstruction" decisions but, importantly, dissented on the picketing issue—appear together after Goldberg's opinion for the court addressing the picketing near a courthouse issue. 379 U.S. at 575–84.

32. 379 U.S. at 539–44.

33. 379 U.S. at 560, 574.

34. BERNARD SCHWARTZ, SUPER CHIEF: EARL WARREN AND HIS COURT (N.Y. University Press, 1983), at 559.

35. 379 U.S. at 554, 558.

36. 379 U.S. at 584.

37. *Diaries of Elizabeth Black* at 112 (quoting Justice Black).

38. *Diaries of Elizabeth Black* at 114.

39. *Diaries of Elizabeth Black* at 121.

40. LAURA KALMAN, ABE FORTAS: A BIOGRAPHY 281 (Yale University Press, 1990) (quoting Justice Douglas).

41. *Id.* at 281 (quoting Justice Douglas).

42. 383 U.S. 131 (1966).

43. 383 U.S. at 162, 168.

44. ROGER K. NEWMAN, HUGO BLACK (Fordham University Press, 2d ed., 1997) [hereinafter NEWMAN] at 249–50; GERALD T. DUNNE, HUGO BLACK AND THE JUDICIAL REVOLUTION (Simon and Schuster, 1977) [hereinafter DUNNE] at 63–64.

45. NEWMAN at 94. "Dressed in full Klan regalia . . . he attended and addressed [Klan] meetings around the state. . . . A Klan hood and mask with his name written in it was found forty years later in a trunk with other Klan ornaments in an old Clay County Klan gathering place. . . . [T]he highlight of his Klankraft was initiating new members into the Invisible Empire. The job falls to the Kladd of each Klavern. The Lee Klan letterhead listed Hugo Black as an officer." *Id.*

46. NEWMAN at 115. Black finished first in the 1926 Democratic Party primary, which was tantamount to election, receiving 85,000 votes, or 30 percent of the vote, in a five-person contest, running best in Jefferson County and in the countryside, the areas where the Klan was strongest. . . . [T]he *Montgomery Advertiser* noted . . . [that] '. . . above all he is the darling of the Ku Klux Klan.' . . . The final tally showed that Black's total number of votes closely paralleled the total Klan membership in the state." *Id.*

47. DUNNE at 66.

48. SUPREME COURT IN CONFERENCE at 638–39 (Conference of April 8, 1950); 648 (Conference of December 13, 1952).

49. SUPREME COURT IN CONFERENCE at 648; NEWMAN at 428, 432, 438–39.

50. NEWMAN at 440–41; DUNNE at 325–26.

51. *See Adamson v. California*, 332 U.S. 46, 68–92 (1947) (Black, J., dissenting).

52. *See Diaries of Elizabeth Black* at 121. The reported numbers of killed and wounded vary somewhat. At the time of the event, the *Los Angeles Times* reported 32 deaths and 873 treated at hospitals, and the *New York Times* reported 33 deaths and 874 treated at hospitals. *Riot at a Glance*, L.A. TIMES, August 17, 1965, p. 1; Gladwin Hill, *Calm Returning to Los Angeles; Death Toll Is 33*, N.Y. TIMES, August 17, 1965, p. 1.

53. "By the fall of 1966," wrote Lucas Powe, well over 50 percent of those polled thought the national government "was moving 'too fast' on civil rights." Powe added: "Urban riots provide a sufficient explanation." POWE at 274.

54. *Adderley v. Florida*, 385 U.S. 39 (November 14, 1966); *Walker v. City of Birmingham*, 388 U.S. 307 (June 12, 1967). For a brief discussion of the riots, see LUCAS A. POWE JR., THE WARREN COURT AND AMERICAN POLITICS (Harvard University Press, 2000) at 275–76. For a detailed description and analysis of the 1967 riots, see REPORT OF THE NATIONAL ADVISORY COMMISSION ON CIVIL DISORDERS (E. P. Dutton, 1968) [hereinafter KERNER COMMISSION] at 40–108. (The National Advisory Commission is generally known as the Kerner Commission, after Illinois governor Otto Kerner, the commission's chairman.) Significant riots, not as large as the ones that would erupt in Newark and Detroit a month after the court handed down its decision in *Walker*, had taken place earlier in the summer in Tampa and Cincinnati as the court was handing down its decision.

55. 385 U.S. 39.

56. 385 U.S. 39, 40.

57. 385 U.S. 39, 49–51, 56.

58. 388 U.S. 307.

59. *See* 388 U.S. at 325–26, n.1.

60. *See* 388 U.S. at 309.

61. 388 U.S. at 310–11; 388 U.S. at 323–24 (Appendix B to the opinion of the court).

62. Martin Luther King Jr., *Letter from Birmingham Jail*, in WHY WE CAN'T WAIT (Harper & Row, 1964) [hereinafter WHY WE CAN'T WAIT] at 83–84.

63. As Justice Brennan explained, "The holding of the Alabama Supreme Court, and the affirmance of its decision by this Court, rest on the assumption that petitioners may be criminally punished although the parade ordinance and the injunction be unconstitutional on their faces as in violation of the First Amendment, and even if the ... ordinance was discriminatorily applied. It must therefore be assumed, for purposes of review of the Alabama Supreme Court's decision, and in assessing the Court's affirmance, that petitioners could successfully sustain the contentions ... that the ordinance and injunction are in fact facially unconstitutional ... and that the ordinance had been discriminatorily applied." 388 U.S. 307, 342–43 (Brennan, J., dissenting). Brennan added, "It should be noted ... that there is clearly sound basis in fact for this assumption." 388 U.S. at 343.

    Chief Justice Warren, also dissenting, stated that "the Court concedes that '[t]he generality of the language contained in the Birmingham parade ordinance ... would unquestionably raise substantial constitutional issues.... That concession is well-founded but minimal. I believe it is patently unconstitutional on its face." 388 U.S. at 328.

64. Justice Brennan, in his *Walker* dissent, which was joined by Chief Justice Warren, Justice Douglas, and Justice Fortas, characterized the ex parte injunction as "a devastatingly destructive weapon for suppression of cherished freedoms" 388 U.S. at 338.

65. 388 U.S. at 346 (Brennan, J., dissenting).

66. *See, e.g., NAACP v. Alabama*, 357 U.S. 449 (1958), and its aftermath. *See* chapter 6.

67. 388 U.S. at 319.

68. 388 U.S. at 330.

69. 388 U.S. at 327.
70. 388 U.S. at 349.
71. KERNER COMMISSION at 1. "The summer of 1967 again brought racial disorders to American cities. . . . This is our basic conclusion: Our nation is moving toward two societies, one black, one white. . . . Reaction to last summer's disorders has . . . deepened the division. Discrimination and segregation have long permeated much of American life; they now threaten the future of every American. . . . To pursue our present course will involve the continuing polarization of the American community." *Id* at 1.
72. WHY WE CAN'T WAIT at 83–84.
73. *See, e.g.*, WHY WE CAN'T WAIT at 37; DENNIS DALTON, MAHATMA GANDHI: NONVIOLENT POWER IN ACTION (Columbia University Press, 1993) at 182.
74. DALTON, MAHATMA GANDHI, at 106 (quoting Gandhi): "only 'nonviolence . . . expressed through civil disobedience' will achieve . . . the 'conversion' of the British people, making 'them see the wrong they have done to India.'" *Id.* at 115: "by the end of the year" in which Gandhi's famous Salt March took place, "more than 60,000 Indians" were imprisoned for, as a gesture of civil disobedience, picking up salt.
75. Morton J. Horwitz, *Natural Law and Natural Rights*, in LEGAL RIGHTS: HISTOR-ICAL AND PHILOSOPHICAL PERSPECTIVES (Austin Sarat & Thomas R. Kearns eds., University of Michigan Press, 1996) [hereinafter *Natural Law*] at 42. King himself in *Letter from Birmingham Jail* stated, "I would agree with St. Augustine that 'an unjust law is no law at all.'" *Letter from Birmingham Jail* at 82.
76. *Natural Law* at 42.
77. RUSSELL B. NYE, WILLIAM LLOYD GARRISON AND THE HUMANITARIAN REFORMERS (Little, Brown, 1955) at 141–42; JOHN L. THOMAS, THE LIBERATOR: WILLIAM LLOYD GARRISON (Little, Brown, 1963) at 375–77.
78. ABE FORTAS, CONCERNING DISSENT AND CIVIL DISOBEDIENCE (New American Library, 1968) at 68.

CHAPTER 10

1. This tendency was already apparent before the Civil War. LOUIS HARTZ, ECO-NOMIC POLICY AND DEMOCRATIC THOUGHT: PENNSYLVANIA, 1776–1860 (Harvard University Press, 1948) at 190, 202.
2. *The Slaughter-House Cases*, 83 U.S. 36 (1873); *The Collector v. Day*, 78 U.S. 113 (1871). Edward S. Corwin, *The Passing of Dual Federalism*, 36 U. VA. L. REV. 1, 15–16, 18–19 (1950); DAVID BRION DAVIS, INHUMAN BONDAGE: THE RISE AND FALL OF SLAVERY IN THE NEW WORLD (Oxford University Press, 2006) at 300, 327.
3. *Wickard v. Filburn*, 317 U.S. 111 (1942); *United States v. Darby Lumber Co.*, 312 U.S. 100 (1941); *Steward Machine Co. v. Davis*, 301 U.S. 548 (1937); *National Labor Relations Board v. Jones & Laughlin Steel Corp.*, 301 U.S. 1 (1937). The 1937 cases—*Steward* and *Jones & Laughlin*—were decided 5–4, whereas, by contrast, the cases decided in 1941 and 1942—*Darby* and *Wickard*—despite more far-reaching language and rejection of the significance of the Tenth Amendment, were unanimous.
4. Illustrative of the pre-1937 dual federalism approach is *Bailey v. Drexel Furniture Co.*, 259 U.S. 20 (1922) (the Child Labor Tax case), in which Chief Justice William Howard Taft, speaking for all of the justices except one, stated that "a court must

be blind not to see that the so-called tax is imposed to stop the employment of children. . . . It is the high duty and function of this Court . . . to decline to recognize or enforce seeming laws of Congress, dealing with subjects not entrusted to Congress but left or committed by the supreme law of the land to the control of the States. . . . The good sought in unconstitutional legislation is an insidious feature because it leads citizens and legislators of good purpose to promote it without thought of the serious breach it will make in the ark of our covenant. . . . In the maintenance of local self-government, on the one hand, and the national power, on the other, our country has been able to endure and prosper." 259 U.S. at 37. Chief Justice Taft continued: "Grant the validity of this law, and all that Congress would need to do . . . to take over . . . subjects of public interest, jurisdiction of which the States have never parted with, and which are reserved to them by the Tenth Amendment, would be to enact a detailed measure of complete regulation of the subject and enforce it by a so-called tax upon departures from it. To give such magic to the word 'tax' would be to break down all constitutional limitation of the powers of Congress and completely wipe out the sovereignty of the States." *Id.* at 38. In *Schechter Poultry Corp. v. United States*, 295 U.S. 495 (1935), the court, in an opinion delivered by Chief Justice Charles Evans Hughes that invalidated the centerpiece of Franklin Roosevelt's early New Deal legislation, the National Industrial Recovery Act, made clear that the Tenth Amendment still retained its vitality: "The Constitution established a national government with powers deemed to be adequate . . . but these powers of the national government are limited by the constitutional grants. Those who act under these grants are not at liberty to transcend the imposed limits because they believe that more or different power is necessary. Such assertions of extra-constitutional authority were anticipated and precluded by the explicit terms of the Tenth Amendment." 295 U.S. at 528–29. Another important piece of New Deal legislation, the Agricultural Adjustment Act, also failed to pass constitutional muster with a Supreme Court still wedded to the notion of dual federalism and the importance of the Tenth Amendment. Justice Owen Roberts, writing for the court in *Butler v. United States*, 297 U.S. 1 (1936), stated, "It hardly seems necessary to reiterate that ours is a dual form of government; that in every state there are two governments—the state and the United States. Each State has all governmental powers save such as the people, by their Constitution, have conferred upon the United States, denied to the States, or reserved to themselves. The federal union is a government of delegated powers. It has only such as are expressly conferred upon it and such as are reasonably to be implied from those granted." 297 U.S. at 63. The Agricultural Adjustment Act, concluded Roberts, "invades the reserved rights of the states. It is a statutory plan to regulate and control agricultural production, a matter beyond the powers delegated to the federal government. . . . From the accepted doctrine that the United States is a government of delegated powers, it follows that those not expressly granted, or reasonably to be implied from such as are conferred, are reserved to the states or to the people. To forestall any suggestion to the contrary, the Tenth Amendment was adopted. The same proposition, otherwise stated, is that powers not granted are prohibited. None to regulate agricultural production is given, and therefore legislation by Congress for that purpose is forbidden." *Id.* at 68.

In sharp contrast to *Butler*, the court in 1937 in *Steward Machine Co. v. Davis*, 301 U.S. 548 (1937), did not let the Tenth Amendment or notions of federalism prevent it from upholding the Social Security Act, albeit with the four horsemen dissenting, vehemently claiming, in the words of Justice Pierce Butler, that "the statutory scheme is repugnant to the Tenth Amendment." 301 U.S. at 616. For a discussion of the rise and fall of dual federalism, see Edward S. Corwin, *The Passing of Dual Federalism*, 36 U. Va. L. Rev. 1 (1950).

5. *United States v. Darby Lumber Co.*, 312 U.S. 100, 124 (1941); *National League of Cities v. Usery*, 426 U.S. 833 (1976), *overruled by Garcia v. San Antonio Metropolitan Transit Authority*, 469 U.S. 528 (1985).

6. Justice Black, at the Conference of October 5, 1964, in Del Dickson, The Supreme Court in Conference (Oxford University Press, 2001) at 727.

7. While joining Justice Tom Clark's opinion for the Court, Justices Black, Douglas, and Goldberg each filed separate concurrences in the companion cases *Heart of Atlanta Motel, Inc. v. United States*, 379 U.S. 241 (1964), and *Katzenbach v. McClung*, 379 U.S. 294 (1964), both handed down December 14, 1964. All three concurring opinions were set forth in *Heart of Atlanta Motel* but also expressly applied to *Katzenbach v. McClung* (Ollie's Barbecue) 379 U.S. at 268 (Black, J., concurring); 379 U.S. at 279 (Douglas, J., concurring); and 379 U.S. at 291 (Goldberg, J., concurring). Black, Douglas, and Goldberg, while clearly indicating their support for the view that the Civil Rights Act of 1964 was a legitimate exercise of congressional authority under the commerce clause in each of their concurrences, went on to discuss Congress's enforcement powers under Section 5 of the Fourteenth Amendment. Douglas "prefer[red] to rest on the assertion of legislative power contained in § 5 of the Fourteenth Amendment" (379 U.S. at 280); Goldberg concluded his concurring opinion by stating that "in my view, Congress clearly had authority under both § 5 of the Fourteenth Amendment and the Commerce Clause to enact the Civil Rights Act of 1964" (379 U.S. at 293); Black, like Clark in his opinion for the court, saw "no need to consider whether this Act is also constitutionally supportable under section 5 of the Fourteenth Amendment" (379 U.S. at 279). But Justice Black wanted to make sure that his dissenting opinion in *Bell v. Maryland*, 378 U.S. 226 (1964), a restaurant sit-in case decided early the same year, was not misconstrued: "my dissenting opinion in *Bell v. Maryland* . . . stated only that the Fourteenth Amendment in and of itself, without implementation by a law passed by Congress, does not bar racial discrimination in privately owned places of business in the absence of state action. [That] opinion did not discuss the power of Congress under the Commerce and Necessary and Proper Clauses or under section 5 of the Fourteenth Amendment to pass a law forbidding such discrimination." 379 U.S. at 278–79.

8. 379 U.S. 241 (1964).

9. 379 U.S. 294 (1964).

10. *Katzenbach v. McClung*, 379 U.S. at 303–5; *Heart of Atlanta Motel* at 258, 261–62.

11. *McClung* at 296, 298. The McClungs' family-owned restaurant, Ollie's Barbecue, which specialized in "barbecued meats and homemade pies," had bought its meat from a local vendor, and the total at issue was under $70,000. These facts and that "there is no claim that interstate travelers frequented the restaurant" carried no weight with the court. *Id.* at 296, 298.

12. 317 U.S. 111 (1942).

13. *McClung* at 300–301.

14. The other justices, including Black in his separate concurrence, thought that in light of the commerce clause, a ruling concerning Section 5 of the Fourteenth

Amendment was unnecessary and therefore in these companion cases declined to address the issue. 379 U.S. at 249–50 (Clark, J., for the Court) 379 U.S. at 279 (Black, J., concurring).

15. 384 U.S. 641 (1966).

16. "Our task is limited to determining whether such legislation is, as required by § 5, appropriate legislation to enforce the Equal Protection Clause. By including § 5 the draftsmen sought to grant to Congress, by a specific provision applicable to the Fourteenth Amendment, the same broad powers expressed in the Necessary and Proper Clause, Art. I, § 8, cl. 18." *Morgan*, 384 U.S. at 649–50. Brennan then cited Chief Justice John Marshall's oft-quoted opinion in *McCulloch v. Maryland* to buttress an extremely expansive definition of "appropriate legislation" under Congress's Section 5 power. *Id.* at 650–51. In applying this standard to the case at hand, Brennan applied what amounted to a minimalist rational basis test. He wrote, "It was for Congress . . . to assess and weigh the various conflicting considerations. . . . It is not for us to review the congressional resolution of these factors. It is enough that we be able to perceive a basis upon which the Congress might resolve the conflict as it did." *Id.* at 653.

17. *See* 384 U.S. at 668, citing *Lassiter v. Northampton County Bd. of Elections*, 360 U.S. 45 (1959) while discussing *Morgan*; and see 384 U.S. at 661–62, discussing *Lassiter* while writing concerning a companion case to *Morgan* that "present[ed] a straightforward Equal Protection problem," 384 U.S. at 659, such case being discussed in Part I of Harlan's dissent in *Katzenbach v. Morgan.* Harlan addressed *Morgan*, Section 4(e) of the Voting Rights Act, and Congress's enforcement powers pursuant to Section 5 of the Fourteenth Amendment in Part II of his *Katzenbach v. Morgan* dissent.

18. 384 U.S. at 668. Harlan wrote, "In effect the Court reads § 5 of the Fourteenth Amendment as giving Congress the power to define the *substantive* scope of the Amendment." He continued: "If that indeed be the true reach of § 5, then I do not see why Congress should not be able as well to exercise its § 5 'discretion' by enacting statutes so as in effect to dilute equal protection and due process decisions of this Court." "The final decision . . . as to whether or not a denial of equal protection or due process has occurred . . . is one of judgment. Until today this judgment has always been one for the judiciary." *Id.* at 668.

19. SUPREME COURT IN CONFERENCE at 828 (April 22, 1966).

20. *Morgan* at 651, n.10. In articulating what came to be known as his "one-way ratchet," Brennan stated in this footnote that "contrary to the suggestion of the dissent . . . Section 5 does not grant Congress power to exercise discretion in the other direction and to enact 'statutes so as in effect to dilute equal protection and due process decisions of this Court.' We emphasize that Congress's power under Section 5 is limited to adopting measures to enforce the guarantees of the Amendment; Section 5 grants Congress no power to restrict, abrogate, or dilute these guarantees." *Id.*

21. In footnote 10 itself, for justification of the one-way ratchet, Justice Brennan offered only that "for example, an enactment authorizing the States to establish racially segregated systems of education would not be—as required by Section 5—a measure 'to enforce' the Equal Protection Clause since that clause of its own force prohibits such state laws." *Id.* at 651–52 n.10.

22. 384 U.S. at 671.

23. *See also South Carolina v. Katzenbach*, 383 U.S. 301 (1966) (Fifteenth Amendment, Congress's Section 2 powers interpreted expansively); *Jones v. Alfred H.*

Mayer Co., 392 U.S. 409 (1968) (Thirteenth Amendment, Congress's Section 2 powers construed broadly).

24. *United States v. Lopez*, 514 U.S. 549 (1995); *City of Boerne v. Flores*, 521 U.S. 507 (1997); *United States v. Morrison*, 529 U.S. 598 (2000). The John Roberts Court has continued this trend. *See National Federation of Independent Business v. Sebelius*, 567 U.S. 519 (2012); *Shelby County v. Holder*, 570 U.S. 529 (2013).

25. Michael J. Klarman, *The Racial Origins of Modern Criminal Procedure*, 99 MICH. L. REV. 48 (2000) at 53.

26. *See* WILLIAM E. LEUCHTENBURG, FRANKLIN D. ROOSEVELT AND THE NEW DEAL (Harper & Row, 1963) at 187.

27. In NAACP v. Alabama *ex rel.* Flowers, 377 U.S. 288 (1964) (June 1, 1964), the court remanded the case to the Alabama Supreme Court, expressly stating that it should dissolve the state court injunction that had been issued ex parte in 1956. In late August 1964, the Alabama Supreme Court complied. *NAACP v. State*, 277 Ala. 89, 167 So. 2d 171 (1964) (August 27, 1964). Justice Harlan's original decision in this litigation, well known for its clear statement that the right of association was a First Amendment freedom, was issued in 1958. NAACP v. Alabama *ex rel.* Patterson, 357 U.S. 449 (1958) (June 30, 1958).

28. *New York Times Co. v. Sullivan*, 376 U.S. 254 (1964).

29. SUPREME COURT IN CONFERENCE at 380. In Harlan's words, "We must lay down new constitutional rules for state libel laws. We should finally dispose of this case. The rule must not permit retrial of this case, but should not leave loopholes for other cases." *Id. See also* BERNARD SCHWARTZ, SUPER CHIEF: EARL WARREN AND HIS SUPREME COURT, A JUDICIAL BIOGRAPHY (New York University Press, 1983) at 534–35; TINSLEY E. YARBROUGH, JOHN MARSHALL HARLAN: GREAT DISSENTER OF THE WARREN COURT (Oxford University Press, 1992) at 223.

30. "When it was discovered that the provision on which Harlan based his proposal had never before been applied to a state court, and after Brennan had shared . . . concerns about the statute's constitutionality 'as applied to deny a state the right to apply its law governing new trials,' Harlan withdrew his original suggestion." YARBROUGH at 223.

31. YARBROUGH at 223.

32. 376 U.S. at 288. "Applying these standards, we consider that the proof presented to show actual malice lacks the convincing clarity which the constitutional standard demands, and hence that it would not constitutionally sustain the judgment . . . under the proper rule of law." *Id.* at 285–86.

33. *Fay v. Noia*, 372 U.S. 391 (1963).

34. *Dombrowski v. Pfister*, 380 U.S. 479 (1965).

35. *Id.* at 402–15.

36. Although Noia was not African American, the issue of race and southern justice could not have been far from the justices' minds when deciding this case. Indeed, the two habeas petitioners in *Daniels v. Allen*, the decision the court effectively overruled in *Fay v. Noia*, which was expressly mentioned in Justice Brennan's opinion for the court, were "Negroes . . . convicted in the North Carolina courts on a charge of murder [and] . . . sentenced to death." 344 U.S. at 482 (companion case decided with *Brown v. Allen*, 344 U.S. 443 (1953)). They were "17 and 18 years old and illiterate." William J. Brennan, *Federal* Habeas Corpus *and State Prisoners: An Exercise in Federalism* 7 UTAH L. REV. 423, 430. They alleged racial discrimination in jury lists and coerced confessions but were denied review on habeas for failure

to satisfy a state procedural requirement, as their attorney filed their state appeal one day late. 344 U.S. at 482, 484–85. There were further extenuating circumstances relating to their attorney's failure to file a timely appeal. *See* 7 UTAH L. REV. at 430.

37. *See* Fiss, *Dombrowski*, 86 YALE L.J. 1103, 1104 (1977).
38. *Id.* at 1103.
39. *Id.* at 1116.

CHAPTER 11

1. *New York Times Co. v. Sullivan*, 376 U.S. 254, 270, 269 (1964).
2. 354 U.S. 476 (1957).
3. *Id.* at 484.
4. *Id.* at 487.
5. *Id.*
6. *Id.* at 489 (emphasis added).
7. *See* EDWARD DE GRAZIA, GIRLS LEAN BACK EVERYWHERE: THE LAW OF OBSCENITY AND THE ASSAULT ON GENIUS (Vintage, 1993).
8. ALEXANDER MEIKLEJOHN, FREE SPEECH AND ITS RELATION TO SELF-GOVERNMENT (Harper Brothers, 1948) at 38, 63–65, 94–95, 99, 104; Alexander Meiklejohn, *What Does the First Amendment Mean?*, 20 U. CHI. L. REV. 461, 464, 466–71, 473–74 (1953).
9. 378 U.S. 184, 197 (1964).
10. *See id.*
11. *Roth*, 354 U.S. at 484.
12. Obscenity Memorandum, n.d., Box 101, Brennan Papers, quoted in W. WAT HOPKINS, MR. JUSTICE BRENNAN AND FREEDOM OF EXPRESSION (Praeger, 1991) at 26.
13. *See* LAWRENCE W. LEVINE, HIGHBROW/LOWBROW: THE EMERGENCE OF CULTURAL HIERARCHY IN AMERICA (Harvard University Press, 1988).
14. *Paris Adult Theatre I v. Slaton*, 413 U.S. 49, 103 (1973) (Brennan, J., dissenting).
15. Jeffrey T. Leeds, *A Life on the Court*, N.Y. TIMES MAG., Oct. 5, 1986.
16. Nat Hentoff, *The Constitutionalist*, NEW YORKER, Mar. 12, 1990.
17. *See, e.g.*, ANDREA DWORKIN, PORNOGRAPHY: MEN POSSESSING WOMEN (Plume, 1991); Catharine A. MacKinnon, *Pornography, Civil Rights, and Speech*, 20 HARV. C.R.-C.L. L. REV. 1 (1985).
18. *See* Catharine A. MacKinnon, *Pornography as Sex Discrimination*, 4 LAW & INEQ. 38 (1986); CATHARINE A. MACKINNON, ONLY WORDS (Harvard University Press, 1996). *See also* CAROLYN BRONSTEIN, BATTLING PORNOGRAPHY: THE AMERICAN FEMINIST ANTI-PORNOGRAPHY MOVEMENT, 1976–1986 (Cambridge University Press, 2011).
19. *See, e.g.*, *Communist Party of U.S. v. Subversive Activities Control Bd.*, 367 U.S. 1, 164 (1961) (Black, J., dissenting) ("I see no possible way to escape the fateful consequences of a return to the era in which all governmental critics had to face the probability of being sent to jail except for this Court to abandon what I consider to be the dangerous constitutional doctrine of 'balancing' to which the Court is at present adhering."); *Bates v. City of Little Rock*, 361 U.S. 516, 528 (1960) (Black, J., and Douglas, J., concurring) ("First Amendment rights are beyond abridgment either by legislation that directly restrains their exercise or by suppression or impairment through harassment, humiliation, or exposure by government."). For a discussion of

Justice Black's views on balancing, see Harry Kalven Jr., *Upon Rereading Mr. Justice Black on the First Amendment*, 14 UCLA L. REV. 428, 441–44 (1967).

20. 391 U.S. 367 (1968).

21. *Id.* at 376.

22. 393 U.S. 503 (1969).

23. *Id.* at 518, 525.

24. 403 U.S. 15 (1971).

25. *Id.* at 27.

26. *See* Edward S. Corwin, *The Supreme Court as National School Board*, 14 LAW & CONTEMP. PROBS. 3 (1949).

27. SHAWN FRANCIS PETERS, JUDGING JEHOVAH'S WITNESSES: RELIGIOUS PERSECUTION AND THE DAWN OF THE RIGHTS REVOLUTION (University Press of Kansas, 2000) at 31–33.

28. *W. Va. State Bd. of Educ. v. Barnette*, 319 U.S. 624, 633 (1943).

29. 268 U.S. 510 (1925).

30. 330 U.S. 1 (1947).

31. ROBERT K. NEWMAN, HUGO BLACK: A BIOGRAPHY (Fordham University Press, 1994) at 12.

32. FRANCES FITZGERALD, THE EVANGELICALS: THE STRUGGLE TO SHAPE AMERICA (Simon & Schuster, 2017) at 240.

33. ALAN WOLFE, THE FUTURE OF LIBERALISM (Vintage Books, 2010) at 169.

34. FITZGERALD, *supra* note 32, at 240.

35. WOLFE, *supra* note 33, at 169.

36. 330 U.S. 1, 15–16 (1947) (citation omitted).

37. *Id.* at 18–73.

38. *Id.* at 28–29 (Rutledge, J., dissenting) (quoting Virginia's 1786 Statute for Religious Freedom, written by Thomas Jefferson, and commenting "I cannot believe that the great author of those words, or the men who made them law, could have joined in this decision. Neither so high nor so impregnable today as yesterday is the wall raised between church and state by Virginia's great statute of religious freedom and the First Amendment, now made applicable to all the states by the Fourteenth." To drive this point home, Rutledge also appended to the decision James Madison's 1985 "Memorial and Remonstrance against Religious Assessments."). *See also* Corwin, *supra* note 26, at 10–14.

39. 370 U.S. 421 (1962).

40. *Sch. Dist. of Abington Twp. v. Schempp*, 374 U.S. 203, 205 (1963).

41. 381 U.S. 479 (1965).

42. *See* NICOLA BEISEL, IMPERILED INNOCENTS: ANTHONY COMSTOCK AND FAMILY REPRODUCTION IN VICTORIAN AMERICA (Princeton University Press, 1997).

43. DAVID M. KENNEDY, BIRTH CONTROL IN AMERICA: THE CAREER OF MARGARET SANGER (Yale University Press, 1970) at 271.

44. *See* ELLEN CHESLER, WOMAN OF VALOR: MARGARET SANGER AND THE BIRTH CONTROL MOVEMENT IN AMERICA (Simon & Schuster, 1992) at 66–73, 149–61, 313–98; LINDA GORDON, THE MORAL PROPERTY OF WOMEN: A HISTORY OF BIRTH CONTROL POLITICS IN AMERICA (3rd ed., University of Illinois Press, 2002) at 242–91; CATHY MORAN HAJO, BIRTH CONTROL ON MAIN STREET: ORGANIZING CLINICS IN THE UNITED STATES, 1916–1939 (University of Illinois Press, 2010).

45. *Griswold*, 381 U.S. at 527.

46. *Id.* at 486.
47. *Id.* at 482.
48. *Id.* at 485.
49. *Id.*
50. *Id.* at 484.
51. *Id.*
52. *Id.* at 529 (citing *United States v. Darby*, 312 U.S. 100, 124 [1941]).
53. 410 U.S. 113.
54. JOHN HART ELY, DEMOCRACY AND DISTRUST: A THEORY OF JUDICIAL REVIEW (Harvard University Press, 1980) at 73, 221 n.4; John Hart Ely, *The Wages of Crying Wolf: A Comment on* Roe v. Wade, 82 YALE L. J. 920 (1973).
55. *Griswold*, 381 U.S. at 507, 510 (Black, J., dissenting).
56. *Id.* at 511.
57. 332 U.S. 46 (1947).
58. *Id.* at 70.
59. *See* Sanford Levinson, *"The Constitution" in American Civil Religion*, 1979 SUP. CT. REV. 123 (1979).
60. HUGO LAFAYETTE BLACK, A CONSTITUTIONAL FAITH (Knopf, 1968) at 66.
61. *Katz v. United States*, 389 U.S. 347, 364 (1967).
62. *Id.* at 365 (Black, J., dissenting).
63. 277 U.S. 438 (1922).
64. *Griswold*, 381 U.S. at 492. Without invoking the Ninth Amendment, Justices Rutledge and Murphy had arrived at the same conclusion as Goldberg in their dissents in *Adamson v. California*.

CONCLUSION

1. Chart in Morton J. Horwitz, Foreword, *The Constitution of Change: Legal Fundamentality without Fundamentalism*, 107 HARV. L. REV. 30, 57 (1993).

AFTERWORD

1. Larry Tye, *Social Racial Gaps Found Nationwide*, BOS. GLOBE, Jan. 9, 1992, at 3.
2. Gary Orfield, *Schools More Separate: Consequences of a Decade of Resegregation* 2 (Civil Rights Project, Harvard University, 2001), https://civilrightsproject.ucla.edu/research/k-12-education/integration-and-diversity/schools-more-separate-consequences-of-a-decade-of-resegregation/orfield-schools-more-separate-2001.pdf.
3. General Accounting Office, "K–12 Education: Student Population Has Significantly Diversified, but Many Schools Remain Divided along Racial, Ethnic, and Economic Lines" (2022).
4. 411 U.S. 1 (1973).
5. 418 U.S. 717 (1974).
6. 555 U.S. 701 (2007).
7. *See, e.g., Reed v. Reed*, 404 U.S. 71 (1971) (first case finding sex discrimination to violate equal protection); *Graham v. Richardson*, 403 U.S. 365 (1971) (finding discrimination against noncitizens unconstitutional); *Mathews v. Lucas*, 427 U.S. 495 (1976) (finding discrimination against nonmarital children unconstitutional).

8. *Obergefell v. Hodges*, 576 U.S. 644 (2015).

9. 381 U.S. 479 (1965).

10. 410 U.S. 113 (1973).

11. *Dobbs v. Jackson Women's Health Org.*, 142 S.Ct. 2228 (2022).

12. 539 U.S. 559 (2003).

13. *See Rucho v. Common Cause*, 139 S.Ct. 2484 (2019) (holding that challenges to partisan gerrymandering are nonjusticiable political questions); *Shelby County v. Holder*, 570 U.S. 529 (2013) (invalidating the preclearance requirement of the Voting Rights Act of 1965).

14. *See, e.g., Sweezy v. New Hampshire*, 354 U.S. 234 (1957).

15. *Brandenburg v. Ohio*, 395 U.S. 444 (1969).

16. 376 U.S. 254 (1964).

17. 366 U.S. 36 (1961).

18. 388 U.S. 307 (1967).

19. 354 U.S. 476 (1957).

20. 391 U.S. 367 (1969).

21. *See, e.g., Snyder v. Phelps*, 562 U.S. 443 (2011) (upholding First Amendment right to protest at military funerals).

22. 142 S.Ct. 2407 (2022).

23. *See, e.g.,* Timbs v. Indiana, 139 S.Ct. 682 (2019) (finding the excessive fines clause of the Eighth Amendment to be incorporated); *McDonald v. City of Chicago*, 561 U.S. 742 (2010) (finding the Second Amendment to be incorporated).

24. 379 U.S. 241 (1964).

25. 379 U.S. 294 (1964).

26. 384 U.S. 641 (1966).

27. *See, e.g., United States v. Morrison*, 529 U.S 598 (2000) (declaring unconstitutional the civil damages provision of the Violence Against Women Act); *United States v. Lopez*, 514 U.S. 549 (1995) (declaring unconstitutional the federal Gun Free School Zone Act).

28. *See, e.g., City of Boerne v. Flores*, 521 U.S. 507 (1997); *University of Alabama v. Garrett*, 531 U.S. 356 (2001).

29. *See, e.g., Printz v. United States*, 521 U.S. 898 (1997); *New York v. United States*, 505 U.S. 144 (1992).

30. *See* Erwin Chemerinsky, Worse than Nothing: The Dangerous Fallacy of Originalism (Yale University Press, 2022).

APPENDIX 1

1. Philip Kurland, *Earl Warren: Master of the Revels*, 96 Harv. L. Rev. 331, 334 (1982) (reviewing G. Edward White, Earl Warren: A Public Life [1982]).

2. Gayle B. Montgomery and James W. Johnson, One Step from the White House: The Rise and Fall of Senator William F. Knowland (University of California Press, 1998) at 117–19; Jean Edward Smith, Lucius D. Clay (Henry Holt, 1990) [hereinafter Smith] at 597; William Bragg Ewald Jr., Eisenhower the President: Crucial Days, 1951–1960 (Prentice-Hall, 1981) [hereinafter Ewald] at 78.

3. *Id.*

4. Earl Warren, The Memoirs of Earl Warren (Doubleday, 1977) at 249.

5. *See, e.g.*, G. EDWARD WHITE, EARL WARREN (Oxford University Press, 1982) at 138, 144, 148.

6. WARREN, MEMOIRS, *supra*, at 253, 260–61; DWIGHT D. EISENHOWER, THE WHITE HOUSE YEARS: MANDATE FOR CHANGE, 1953–1956 (Doubleday, 1963) at 228–29.

7. EISENHOWER, WHITE HOUSE YEARS, at 228.

8. Eisenhower focused on his first ballot convention victory over Taft, which was achieved without Warren's votes because the governor refused to release California delegates pledged to him until after the first ballot was completed. EISENHOWER, WHITE HOUSE YEARS, at 228–29. As Eisenhower aides made clear, however, Warren's move was welcomed by the Eisenhower forces as a means of limiting Taft's first ballot vote. Moreover, Eisenhower failed to acknowledge that his first ballot victory could only have succeeded because earlier in the convention Warren had already made the difference by taking Eisenhower's side in a credentials challenge of Taft delegates. In truth, as historians have made clear, Warren's support of Eisenhower's early successful challenge of some Taft delegates was critical to Eisenhower's come-from-behind victory at the convention.

9. Warren's account was confirmed by Attorney General Brownell in his memoirs. WARREN, MEMOIRS, *supra*, at 260–61; HERBERT BROWNELL, ADVISING IKE: THE MEMOIRS OF ATTORNEY GENERAL HERBERT BROWNELL (University Press of Kansas, 1993) at 164–65.

10. WARREN, MEMOIRS, *supra*, at 260.

11. WARREN, MEMOIRS, *supra*, at 261.

12. WARREN, MEMOIRS, *supra*, at 261.

13. *See, e.g.*, SMITH at 79. Indeed, Clay regarded Eisenhower as one of his closest friends: "I think General Eisenhower regarded me, and I certainly regarded him, as one of my closest friends." SMITH at 229 (quoting Clay). "General Eisenhower gave me a complete delegation of responsibility," stated Clay, "as long as I would keep him informed and we were seeing eye to eye on policy." SMITH at 229 (quoting Clay).

14. "Clay was so close to Eisenhower," stated future attorney general Herbert Brownell, "that people felt he could always get Eisenhower's concurrence to any program that he recommended. And it was an accurate appraisal. That was very helpful to me as campaign manager." SMITH at 596 (quoting Brownell).

15. EWALD at 13, 78. This acknowledgment of a deal seems consistent with Clay's earlier somewhat confusing account of Warren's appointment in a 1967 oral history interview. *The Eisenhower Administration Project, General Lucius D. Clay* (interview conducted by Ed Edwin in 1967), New York Times Oral History Program, Columbia University Oral History Collection (Glen Rock, NJ: Microfilming Corporation of America, 1976), Part III, No. 19, at 67.

16. EWALD at 78.

17. EWALD at 78 (emphasis added) (quoting Lucius Clay).

18. SMITH, *supra*, at 598. "The day before the balloting, an Associated Press poll showed Taft leading Eisenhower 533 to 427. The Eisenhower strategy—as devised by Brownell—was to hold enough state delegations behind 'favorite sons' to deny Taft the nomination on the first ballot. The strategy centered on . . . most important, California behind Earl Warren." SMITH at 597.

19. BROWNELL, ADVISING IKE, *supra*, at 165.

20. *Herbert Brownell, Earl Warren's Appointment to the Supreme Court: A Retrospective Memorandum with an Appended Interview Transcript, Conducted by Amelia R. Fry* (in October 1974), Earl Warren Oral History Project (The Bancroft Library, University of California, Berkeley, Regional Oral History Office, 1977) at 29.
21. *Id.* at 62–63. The assertions that Clay lacked authority are contradicted by Clay's 1967 Columbia University Oral History interview, *supra* note 15, which makes very clear that he believed that Eisenhower had both authorized and committed himself to offer Warren a seat on the court.
22. DAVID ALISTAIR YALOF, PURSUIT OF JUSTICES: PRESIDENTIAL POLITICS AND THE SELECTION OF SUPREME COURT NOMINEES (University of Chicago Press, 1999) at 45 (quoting Brownell from the author's interview with him on February 21, 1996).

APPENDIX 2

1. RICHARD KLUGER, SIMPLE JUSTICE (Random House, 2004) [hereinafter cited as SIMPLE JUSTICE] at 699.
2. Justice Jackson, *Brown* draft concurrence, January 11, 1954 (The Papers of Robert H. Jackson, box 184, Library of Congress, Manuscript Division) at 13–14.
3. SIMPLE JUSTICE at 694 (quoting Prettyman).
4. Jackson draft of December 7, 1953 at 5–6.
5. *Brown v. Board of Education*, 347 U.S. 483 (1954) at 489.
6. Jackson draft of January 6, 1954 at 6.
7. *Id.* at 6–8.
8. Jackson draft of March 15, 1954, at 5.
9. *Id.* at 10.
10. Jackson draft of January 6, 1954, at 13–14. See draft of December 7, 1953, at 13.
11. Jackson draft of March 15, 1954 at 17.
12. Jackson draft of January 6, 1954, at 11–12.
13. Jackson draft of February 15, 1954, at 13.
14. *Id.* at 8–9.
15. *Id.* at 12.
16. *Id.* at 9.
17. Jackson draft of March 15, 1954, at 21.
18. *Id.* at 21.
19. *Id.* at 21–22.
20. Jackson draft of March 15, 1954, at 19–22. In his memo to himself while trying to work out his position in *Brown*, Felix Frankfurter proposed a much more robust version of the "changing circumstances" doctrine. "Law must respond to transformation of views as well as to that of outward circumstances," he wrote. "The effect of changes in men's feelings for what is right and just is equally relevant in determining whether a discrimination denies the equal protection of the laws." FELIX FRANKFURTER PAPERS, HARVARD LAW SCHOOL, box 72, file 14 (undated memo), quoted in SIMPLE JUSTICE at 688.
21. *See* Morton J. Horwitz, *Foreword, The Constitution of Change: Legal Fundamentality without Fundamentalism*, 107 HARV. L. REV. 32 (1993).
22. Jackson draft of March 15, 1954, at 12.
23. Jackson draft of March 15, 1954, at 22.
24. Jackson draft of March 15, 1954, at 12–13.

25. *Id.* at 14.
26. *See* Jackson draft of December 7, 1953, at 12–14.
27. SIMPLE JUSTICE at 694 (quoting Jackson's law clerk, E. Barrett Prettyman Jr.).
28. Jackson draft of March 15, 1954, at 13.
29. Jackson draft of March 15, 1954, at 17.
30. *Id.* at 16.
31. *Id.* at 17.
32. J. W. PELTASON, FIFTY-EIGHT LONELY MEN: SOUTHERN FEDERAL JUDGES AND SCHOOL DESEGREGATION (Harcourt, 1961).
33. GERALD N. ROSENBERG, THE HOLLOW HOPE: CAN COURTS BRING ABOUT SOCIAL CHANGE? (University of Chicago Press, 1991) at 46, 52.
34. *See, e.g.,* Jackson draft of March 15, 1954, at 12–14. For an elaboration of Jackson's views in this regard, see ROBERT H. JACKSON, THE STRUGGLE FOR JUDICIAL SUPREMACY: A STUDY OF A CRISIS IN AMERICAN POWER POLITICS (Knopf, 1941). In this work, written while serving as Franklin Roosevelt's solicitor general, Jackson stated that courts were "inherently ill suited, and never can be suited, to devising or enacting rules of general social policy." *Id.* at 288.
35. *See* Brad Snyder, *How the Conservatives Canonized* Brown v. Board of Education, 52 RUTGERS L. REV. 383 (2000) [hereinafter cited as Snyder] at 439–36.
36. SIMPLE JUSTICE at 609 (quoting Rehnquist from his 1952 memo titled "A Random Thought on the Segregation Cases"). The quotation with analysis also appears in Snyder, *supra,* at 441. For the full text of Rehnquist's 1952 memo and also his 1971 letter claiming that the memo did not reflect his own views, see "Texts of Rehnquist Letter to Senator Eastland and Memo of 1952 on Rights Cases," *New York Times*, December 9, 1971, at 26.
37. Snyder at 451, *See* Brad Snyder and John Q. Barrett, "Rehnquist's Missing Letter: A Former Law Clerk's 1955 Thoughts on Justice Jackson and *Brown*," *Boston College Law Review* 53, no. 631, 2012.
38. Snyder at 451.
39. John P. MacKenzie, "Court Rules for Newspapers, 6–3: Decision Allows Printing of Stories on Vietnam Study," *Washington Post*, December 11, 1971, at A6.
40. SIMPLE JUSTICE, multipaged footnote beginning on page 609. *See* Snyder, *supra,* at 451–53. For a cogent critique of Rehnquist's assertions, see the statement of Senator Edward Brooke, Republican of Massachusetts and the first African American U.S. senator since Reconstruction, at Rehnquist's 1971 Senate confirmation hearings. CONG. REC., Vol. 117, Part 35 (December 9, 1971) at 45815.
41. *Snyder* at 452.

INDEX

ABOUT THE AUTHOR

Morton J. Horwitz is the Charles Warren Professor of American Legal History Emeritus at Harvard Law School. He is the author of numerous articles on American legal history, as well as the two-volume set *The Transformation of American Law, 1780–1860* (1979) and *1870–1960* (1994), the first volume of which won the Bancroft Prize in American History. He is also the author of *The Warren Court and the Pursuit of Justice* (1998) and a coeditor of *American Legal Realism* (1993).